# THE LANGUAGE OF METAPHORS

'Anyone genuinely interested in metaphor – whether literature or philosophy student, cognitive scientist, linguist, poet, dictionary addict, or advertising copywriter – will find their brains tickled and stretched by the multiplicity of ideas integrated in this absorbing and valuable contribution . . . This book is a gem.'
Michael Toolan, *School of English, University of Birmingham*

In this ambitious and wide-ranging textbook, Andrew Goatly looks at how we use metaphor to communicate meaning. Combining insights from functional linguistics and relevance theory, he provides a powerful model for understanding how metaphors work in real communicative situations.

*The Language of Metaphors*:

- Examines the boundary between metaphor and literal language and how words cross over.
- Explores the functions of metaphors in social context and in a variety of genres: conversation, advertisements, popular science, news reports, novels and poetry.
- Shows how abstract concepts are metaphorically structured in the English dictionary.
- Inventories the ways metaphors are signalled, expressed and interact in text.
- Contains numerous activities and suggestions for further research.

*The Language of Metaphors* presumes no prior knowledge of linguistics. By encompassing not only the cognitive, but also the social and linguistic aspects of metaphor, it provides a timely complement to recent psychological investigations. This book will be essential reading for all students and researchers interested in communication, language, literature and psychology.

**Andrew Goatly** lectures in English at the National Institute of Education, Nanyang Technological University, Singapore.

# THE LANGUAGE OF METAPHORS

*Andrew Goatly*

London and New York

First published 1997
by Routledge
11 New Fetter Lane, London EC4P 4EE

Simultaneously published in the USA and Canada
by Routledge
29 West 35th Street, New York, NY 10001

Reprinted 1998

Typeset in Times by
J&L Composition Ltd, Filey, North Yorkshire
Printed and bound in Great Britain by
Redwood Books, Trowbridge, Wiltshire

*British Library Cataloguing in Publication Data*
A catalogue record for this book is available from the British Library

*Library of Congress Cataloguing in Publication Data*
A catalogue record for this book has been requested

ISBN   0–415–12876–5 (hbk)
ISBN   0–415–12877–3 (pbk)

# CONTENTS

# ILLUSTRATIONS

## FIGURES

## PLATES

# TABLES

# ACKNOWLEDGEMENTS

I would like to acknowledge the considerate help of the following. Randolph Quirk and Deirdre Wilson, of University College London, who eighteen years ago started me and helped me along on the long road of metaphorical discovery. An anonymous reviewer who gave meticulous and penetrating comments and encouraging suggestions when I first submitted draft chapters of the book. Julia Hall, Alison Foyle and Miranda Filbee of Routledge, whose efficiency was behind its smooth and prompt publication, and on whom I inflicted an enormous amount of work in obtaining permissions. Marguerite Nesling, who worked long and hard and meticulously on a text which, given its demands on graphology, must have been maddening for a copy-editor. The National University of Singapore, who allowed me, in those pre-modular days, the leisure to do the bulk of my research and writing. In particular my colleagues at that institution, Desmond Allison, Graeme Cane, Anthea Fraser Gupta and Lionel Wee, as well as David Birch, who gave valuable comments on the penultimate drafts. My outstanding students Dorothy Koh and Ramona Tang and other students in the EL412 Honours Class, who provided essential feedback. My parents, Edgar and Eileen, who always encouraged and supported me in my academic pursuits. And my immediate family, Mathanee, Julia and Thomas, whose understanding and forbearance (all those late bedtimes, lost games of Monopoly and badminton!) made this book possible.

The author and publishers would like to thank the copyright holders for permission to reproduce extracts from the following:

'In a station of the Metro', from *Collected Shorter Poems* by Ezra Pound; 'An advancement of learning' and 'Death of a naturalist', from *Death of a Naturalist* by Seamus Heaney; 'The love song of J. Alfred Prufrock' and 'Burnt Norton', from *Collected Poems 1909–1962* by T.S. Eliot; 'The unknown citizen', from *Collected Poems* by W.H. Auden, edited by Edward Mendelson; 'Wind', from *The Hawk in the Rain* by Ted Hughes; *Darkness Visible*, *Free Fall*, *Lord of the Flies*, *Pincher Martin*, *The Inheritors* and *The Spire* all by William Golding: by permission of Faber and Faber Ltd;

'Only the moon' by Wong May, from *Seven Poets* edited by Edwin Thumboo: by permission of Singapore University Press (Pte) Ltd;

*Life on Earth* by David Attenborough: by permission of HarperCollins Publishers Limited;

*Bodily Harm* by Margaret Attwood: by permission of Jonathan Cape;

*Still Life* and *The Virgin in the Garden* by A.S. Byatt: by permission of Chatto & Windus;

*Waterflow in Plants* by J.A. Milburn: by permission of Longman;

*The Go-Between* by L.P. Hartley (Hamish Hamilton, 1953) p. 1, copyright © L.P. Hartley, 1953: by permission of Hamish Hamilton Ltd;

*Financial Times*, 16 December 1993: by permission of the *Financial Times*;

*Daily Mail*, 8 October 1993: by permission of Solo Syndication Limited;

Figure 3, 'Aspects of verbal communication', from *Relevance, Communication and Cognition* by D. Sperber and D. Wilson, p. 232: by permission of Blackwell Publishers;

Figures 6.1 and 6.2, from *Language and Power* (Language in Social Life Series) by N. Fairclough, p. 146: by permission of Addison Wesley Longman Limited;

*The Mask*, copyright 1994, New Line Productions, Inc. All rights reserved. Dialogue appears courtesy of New Line Productions, Inc.

Acknowledgement is also given to Volkswagen Group United Kingdom Limited for permission to reproduce text from an advertisement on p. 323.

The author wishes to thank HarperCollins Publishers Limited for permission to quote extensively from the COBUILD corpus data, and acknowledges the help of Professor J. Sinclair in facilitating access to COBUILD data, and Zoë James for preparing data on disk.

While the publishers have made every effort to contact copyright holders of material used in this volume, they would be grateful to hear from any they were unable to contact.

# TYPOGRAPHICAL CONVENTIONS

- In the body of the text:

  Italics are used for forms cited, or titles of works, for example, the word *metaphor*

  Single inverted commas are used to refer to meanings, e.g. *pupil* means 'a student'

  Double inverted commas are used for quotations from text and as "scare" quotes

  Words with an initial capital letter are being used in a technical sense explained previously in the text, e.g. these are Subjective metaphors

  Square brackets are used to enclose semantic features, e.g. [human]

- In quoted text (usually indented):

  Items in **bold** are Vehicle-terms

  Items <u>underlined</u> are Topic-terms

  Items in *italics* are Ground-terms, e.g. <u>the past</u> is **a foreign country**, *they do things differently there*

  Double marking by underlining and bolding indicates comparison rather than metaphor

  Items in small capitals are terms which are used literally but used as V-terms in the surrounding co-text, e.g. I established **a bridgehead** . . . I crossed THE BRIDGE

  → a transformation or reversal of a structure or metaphor

  * Asterisks follow markers of metaphor

  References to quoted text use initials corresponding to titles, followed by the page number, where relevant, e.g. LF10 refers to *Lord of the Flies*, page 10. The key to these abbreviations is found in the References section at the end of the book, and in the list of abbreviations.

  Square brackets are used to enclose supplied material

- In Analogies, where the lexical details of Root Analogies are given:

  (*x*) :  x = part of a phrase in which the metaphor typically participates

xiii

with this meaning, or an indication of the superordinate class such parts of phrases belong to, e.g. *launch* (*a newspaper*)

$(= x)$ :  $x$ = the T-term; e.g. *fire* (= dismiss from a post)

(cf. $x$) :  $x$  = the Vehicle, Vehicular domain, Vehicular colligate; e.g. (*emotions*) *run high* (cf. *tide, river*)

(B) = Buried, e.g. SUCCESS = MOVEMENT FORWARDS *progress* (B)

\> = reversing the analogy e.g. TIME = SPACE  *a short* (*time*), > an immediate (*neighbour*)

? = doubtful, e.g. MONEY = LIQUID ?*quid*

! = possible folk etymology, e.g. WORDS = FOOD *macaronic* (*verse*)!

(x = x) = other Root Analogy applicable to the lexical item, e.g. EMOTION = HEAT *boiling with rage* (EMOTION = LIQUID)

# ABBREVIATIONS

| | |
|---|---|
| ACE | D. Crystal and D. Davy, *Advanced Conversational English* |
| AL | Seamus Heaney, 'An advancement of learning' |
| BOC | Graham Greene, *A Burnt-Out Case* |
| CEC | J. Svartvik and R. Quirk, *A Corpus of English Conversation* |
| DB | Matthew Arnold, 'Dover Beach' |
| DM | *Daily Mirror*, 8 May 1987 |
| DN | Seamus Heaney, 'Death of a naturalist' |
| DT | *Daily Telegraph*, 5 May 1987 |
| DV | William Golding, *Darkness Visible* |
| EU | J. Lyly, *Euphues* |
| FAE | Jeffrey Archer, *First Among Equals* |
| FEER | *Far Eastern Economic Review*, 19 May 1988 |
| FF | William Golding, *Free Fall* |
| FQ | T.S. Eliot, *Four Quartets* |
| GB | L.P. Hartley, *The Go-Between* |
| GH | *Good Housekeeping*, May 1987 |
| GW | lines from the COBUILD corpus |
| HSG | N. Hawthorne, *The House of the Seven Gables* |
| HZ | Saul Bellow, *Herzog* |
| IE | *International Express*, 1–7 June 1995 |
| LF | William Golding, *Lord of the Flies* |
| LFG | Ezra Pound, 'Lament of the frontier guard' |
| LL | Extract from Lord Lyttleton, 'To the memory of a lady' (1747), in Sutherland, *A Preface to Eighteenth Century Poetry* |
| LM | J. Fenimore Cooper, *The Last of the Mohicans* |
| LSJAP | T.S. Eliot, 'The love song of J. Alfred Prufrock' |
| M | William Shakespeare, *Macbeth* |
| MA | Alfred, Lord Tennyson, 'Morte d'Arthur', in *The Poems of Tennyson* |
| MD | Herman Melville, *Moby Dick* |

| | |
|---|---|
| ML | J.A. Milburn, *Waterflow in Plants* |
| NG | Nominal Group |
| NSJL | J. Lovelock, 'Gaia: the world as living organism' |
| NSLG | L. Gamlin, 'The human immune system' |
| NSMM | M. MacQuitty, 'Sulphur on the menu: cuisine for the hairy snail' |
| OF | R.S. Thomas, 'On the farm' |
| OWE | A.E. Housman, 'On Wenlock Edge' |
| P | *Punch*, 6 May 1987 |
| PL | John Milton, *Paradise Lost*, Book 1 |
| PM | William Golding, *Pincher Martin* |
| PMD | W.B. Yeats, 'Prayer for my daughter' |
| PQ | J.M. Cohen and M.J. Cohen, *The Penguin Dictionary of Modern Quotations* |
| Prep.G | Prepositional Group |
| QA | Graham Greene, *The Quiet American* |
| R | D.H. Lawrence, *The Rainbow* |
| SL | A.S. Byatt, *Still Life* |
| SM | George Eliot, *Silas Marner* |
| TD | Thomas Hardy, *Tess of the D'Urbervilles* |
| TH | Ted Hughes, 'Wind' |
| THP | Ted Hughes, 'Pike' |
| TI | William Golding, *The Inheritors* |
| TS | William Golding, *The Spire* |
| UC | W.H. Auden, 'The unknown citizen' |
| V | Charlotte Brontë, *Villette* |
| VG | A.S. Byatt, *The Virgin in the Garden*; Verbal Group |
| W | *Woman*, 9 May 1987 |
| WS | Jung Chang, *Wild Swans* |
| ∧ | followed by |
| ⇒ | presupposes that |

# INTRODUCTION

## WHY IS METAPHOR IMPORTANT?

Common-sense traditional teaching often presents metaphor as an anomaly, an unusual or deviant way of using language, a minority interest, or something you *do* in literature class. Taking a similar view, philosophers have often wanted metaphor strictly confined to literature, rhetoric and art, because of its supposed dangers to clear thinking. Locke, for example, denounced figurative language as follows:

> But yet, if we would speak of things as they are, we must allow that . . . all the artificial and figurative application of words eloquence hath invented, are for nothing else but to insinuate wrong ideas, move the passions, and thereby mislead the judgment, and so indeed are perfect cheat.
>
> (*Essay concerning Human Understanding*, Book 3, ch. 10, p. 105)

He is explicit about the desirability of metaphorless language, and implicitly assumes the possibility of a philosophical language without metaphor.

Over the last thirty years, however, philosophers, psychologists and linguists have begun to agree that metaphor is not something that can be easily confined, but is an indispensable basis of language and thought. The quote from Locke paradoxically provides evidence for this. Arguably "move", "mislead" and "cheat" are being used metaphorically, "eloquence hath invented" is a case of personifying metaphor, "insinuate" depends upon a metaphor borrowed from Latin, where its literal meaning is 'work its way in, penetrate', and literally we "allow" actions rather than propositions.

If, as I believe, metaphor and the mental processes it entails, are basic to language and cognition, then a clearer understanding of its working is relevant, not just to literature students, but to any students. Flick through the index of any of your textbooks and you will find plenty of terms which are metaphorical when you stop to think about them. An economics text, taken at random off my shelves, provides in its index ***balance of trade***,

1

*capital* **mobility**, **central**ized *planning*, **division** *of labour*, **consumption**, **raw** *materials*, *fund-flow* model, **greenhouse** *effect*, *great* **depression**, **inflation**, **marginal** *utility*, **spin-offs**, **underground** *economy*, *international* **growth race**, and so on. A book of popular science on Chaos theory gives me **arrow** *of time*, **communication** *among molecules*, *critical* **threshold**, *Laplace's* **demon**, *the* **baker** *transformation*, *entropy as* **barrier**, **free** *particles*, **far**-*from* **equilibrium** *conditions*, **commuting** *operators*, **feedback loops**, **wave** *function*, and so on. A book of popular natural history lists **vampire** *bats*, **butterfly** *fish*, **hermit** *crab*, **crane**-*fly*, **crown of thorns starfish**, **hammerhead** *shark*, **horseshoe** *crab*, **mouse**-*deer*, **sea**-**cucumber**, **tailor** *bird*, **midwife** *toad*, and so on. Metaphor is everywhere in the language we use and there is no escape from it.

But more important than their ubiquity (Paprotte and Dirven 1985), the metaphors we use structure our thinking, hiding some features of the phenomena we apply them to, and highlighting others. If, for example, I use chess as a metaphor for a battle, it will highlight features of the battle like casualties, relative power and mobility of fighters, and positions of forces. But it will downplay or ignore other important aspects of real battles such as supplies of weapons and provisions, topography, and weather.

## ■ EXERCISE

*Think of a board game you are familiar with, which models some human activity. What crucial features of the real activity does it ignore or distort? For example, Monopoly is a model or metaphor for property development and speculation: what aspects of real property dealings and investment are hidden or changed in the board game?*

It is because metaphors suppress features that, for instance, physicists need two alternative metaphors for light, both wave and particle, to model those aspects of light ignored by the other.

This highlighting and suppression of aspects of experience is obvious in the case of metaphor. But the ignoring of differences and highlighting of selected similarities is, in fact, absolutely necessary in any act of classification and conceptualization. Let's schematize simply what goes on in an act of classification with the following simple exercise. Look at the six boxes in Figure 0.1, and separate them into two classes containing three boxes each.

There are several valid ways of classifying these. You could divide them into 1, 4, 6 and 2, 3, 5 on the criteria of containing one letter or two; or into 1, 2, 6 and 3, 4, 5, because 1, 2, 6 contain only *O*s and no *X*s; or into 1, 3, 5, which have an upper-case letter in the centre, and 2, 4, 6 with their lower-case letters; or any number of other alternatives. Adopting any one criter-

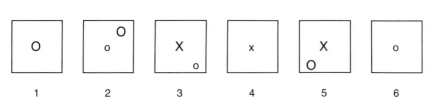

*Figure 0.1* Multiple possibilities for classification

ion for classification means excluding other possible criteria; or in other words classifying involves ignoring differences as well as selecting similarities.

So there is another important reason for studying metaphor: it demonstrates, in an exaggerated way, how all linguistic classification constructs a representation of experience on the basis of selective perception and selective ignoring of aspects of the world. The only difference between literal language and metaphorical language is that, in literal use, we adhere to conventional criteria for classification, whereas in metaphorical use, the similarities, the criteria for interpretation are relatively unconventional. For instance, if I literally refer to a Viking ship as "a ship", I am using conventional criteria. But if I metaphorically call it *the horse of the sea* I am drawing attention to unconventional criteria or resemblances shared by horses and ships, such as [up and down movement], [shape of neck and shape of prow], and so on, which a literal reference would have ignored or suppressed (Leech 1974: 44).

I have argued that the study of metaphor is important for two basic reasons. First, because, consciously or not, we are employing metaphors all the time. And also because the working of metaphor sheds light on the ways in which literal language operates. In fact, if literal language is simply conventional metaphor, then, far from being an anomaly, metaphor becomes basic.

## WHO IS THIS BOOK FOR?

Because metaphor is basic to language and thinking, any well-educated person should have some understanding of its processes. However, this book does assume a specific interest in language, linguistics and the analysis of texts. For the general linguistics student, it raises important questions about whether language can be conceived of as a code, and about how syntax affects interpretation. For the student whose special interest is in pragmatics and semantics, it can be exploited as a case study investigating two important questions: how to draw the borderline between semantics and pragmatics; and how pragmatic theory, in order to achieve explanatory adequacy, needs to be combined with a theory of social context and purpose. The student of text and discourse analysis will find a comprehensive account of the varieties of metaphor and metaphorical interpretation. And the book will enable the student of literary stylistics and literary theory to understand more fully, precisely and formally, the nature of literary metaphor and its interpretation, how it differs from metaphors in other genres, and the purposes and patterns of interplay between metaphors.

The early chapters of the book will also interest students of psychology, morphology and lexicology. Chapters 1 and 2 demonstrate the metaphorical basis of thought and classification, and illustrate Lakoff's experiential theory of meaning by applying it to the lexicon of English. Chapter 3 shows how morphological change and other derivational processes are devices for incorporating metaphorical meanings into the dictionary.

The book aims to be a comprehensive introduction to the linguistics of metaphor, its syntax, semantics and pragmatics, as manifest in different text-types. It should prove indispensable to any serious student of metaphor.

## BUT WHY ANOTHER BOOK ON METAPHOR?

Since the 1970s there has been an explosion of books and publications on metaphor, so why do we need yet another? The fact is that linguists of both the (transformational) generative tradition and the functional Hallidayan tradition have found metaphor difficult to integrate with their theories. In the first tradition, associated with North America, it is now recognized that metaphor and its interpretation belong with pragmatics, which is conceived of, not so much as a *branch* of linguistics, the scientific study of language, but some kind of *complement* to linguistics for those wishing to deal with the interpretation of utterances in specific contexts. In the Hallidayan tradition, associated more with Britain and Australia, writing on metaphor has concentrated on grammatical metaphors, processes like nominalization, because these destroy the neat correspondence between semantics and word-class. If we use nouns, instead of verbs and adjectives, to refer to processes and qualities this unfortunately complicates the elegance of the functional theory. The result of the tendency to marginalize metaphor within both these grammatical traditions has been that, though works on metaphor abound, they tend to be philosophical and psychological theories rather than linguistic ones.

I fill this gap in two ways. I devote three chapters to the syntax of metaphor (Chapters 6, 7, 8). And I develop a functionally oriented linguistic theory of metaphor which cross-fertilizes pragmatic theory with the Hallidayan analysis of register, to produce a more adequate model for metaphorical interpretation in particular, and communication in general (Chapters 5 and 10).

As part of this positive project the book also tries to avoid a number of pitfalls which are common in the philosophical and psychological literature:

- The choice of metaphors of only one degree of deadness or originality as examples, and the basing of description of the metaphorical process on these. Advocates of the substitution theory stated that in metaphor one meaning was substituting for another – for example 'monkey' was substituting for 'mischievous' in utterances like *Tom is a monkey*; and they chose to analyse relatively conventional metaphors. Advocates of the interaction view claimed that metaphorical meaning arose from interactions and tensions between the literal meaning of the lexical item and the concept it was metaphorically applied to – for instance *the beach is a bowstave* (resemblance in terms of shape) will mean something different from *his mind was a bowstave* (resemblance in terms of 'nervous tension'); and they analysed relatively original metaphors.

- The tendency to discuss examples of metaphors expressed in only one syntactic form, or by only one word-class, and to generalize theories from them: for example, theorists discussed metaphorical verbs as in *The stone **died***, which deviates from the grammatical semantic rule stipulating that only living things can die (Levin 1977). But in fact many metaphors are simply deviant in terms of reference, for example *the pig* used to refer to a driver who beats you to a parking space.

- The ignoring of the variety of purposes for which metaphor may be used and the range of effects it produces: most philosophical and linguistic analyses privilege the conceptual or ideational purposes of metaphors and underplay the interpersonal and foregrounding functions.

- The use of made-up or recycled examples which have no authentic co-text or context of use, rather than metaphors from a corpus of written/spoken material, within particular and identifiable genres: even a nodding acquaintance with the literature on metaphor will give you plenty of re-analyses of examples like *Man is a wolf, Sally is a block of ice, The girl is a lollipop, Encyclopaedias are goldmines* presented in isolation, and whose only context is the earlier different analysis of the same metaphor by other theorists.

## AN OUTLINE OF THE BOOK

The present book avoids these common pitfalls according to the following plan.

In Chapter 1, 'Metaphorical and Literal Language', I explore the overlap between metaphor, approximation and semantic subcategorization. What is the difference, for example, between the meaning of *a kind of* as used in *Margaret Thatcher was a kind of lapdog of Ronald Reagan, a wolf is a kind of dog* and *a collie is a kind of dog*? I discuss further the claim that language is fundamentally metaphorical, showing in detail that the strategies used for creating and processing metaphor are also used with "literal" language; and suggest that there are metaphorical clines from the most active original transfer metaphors at one end, to the most conventional, dead and approximative ones at the other.

Chapter 2, 'Metaphor and the Dictionary: Root Analogies', explores the ways in which conventional metaphorical analogies structure the cognition of speakers of English as this is reflected in the lexicon. Here I build on the theories of George Lakoff (1987) and Mark Johnson (1987), who claim that most of our cognitive processes depend upon metaphors derived from our preconceptual bodily experiences as infants.

For example, lexical evidence shows that we conceptualize successful activity or process by the metaphor of movement forward. We talk about processes and activities as though they were linear motion – *go* (of a watch/ machine), *put in motion*, *get things moving*; or more specifically walking or running – *make great strides*, *run an organization*. So causing an activity is causing movement – *propel/push* (= encourage someone to do something). To begin an activity is to start a journey/race – *get off to a good start*, *jump the gun*, *quick off the mark*. And to prevent/make difficult is to erect a barrier/impediment – *block*, *a hurdle*, *an obstacle*, *insurmountable* (*problems*). The salience and lexical significance of this metaphor derives from our first experiences of walking and crawling where we probably had a great deal of encouragement and praise for initial successes, so they became typical examples of successful "goal-directed" activity. Using the Birmingham University International Language Database and the *Cobuild English Language Dictionary* developed from it, I provide a detailed map of such metaphorical patterns in the English lexicon.

In Chapter 3, 'Metaphor and the Dictionary: Word-class and Word-formation', I discuss the important relationship between word-class and metaphorical interpretation, showing how word-formation processes affect metaphorical recognition and richness of interpretation. I ask why, for example, if the following clauses are applied to a human, *he was my dog* seems more strongly metaphorical than *he dogged me*. Considering the interpretative effects of word-class and derivation deliberately avoids the problem of generalizing theories based on only one word-class.

These first three chapters concentrate on the borderline between the literal and the metaphorical, and on those metaphors which have become incorporated in the lexicon. By doing so they recognize how metaphors vary in vitality or originality, and that theories adequate for conventional metaphors are not always adequate for more original ones.

Chapter 4, 'How Different Kinds of Metaphors Work', elaborates a definition of metaphor in terms of unconventional reference (e.g. as in *you rat*) and/or collocation (e.g. as in *he drank in praise*). Working through the definition, it demarcates seven kinds of metaphorical interpretation, and develops the distinction between analogy and similarity as part of the interpretative process. It covers other theoretical areas: different theories of metaphorical interpretation; the strategic social importance of subjective and asymmetrical metaphors, where there is no mutual recognition of metaphors between speaker and hearer; and the concept of phenomenalistic construal – that the unconventional reference of metaphor can be to an imaginary world. For instance *the lion spoke to the mouse* is literal within the fantastic metaphoric world of fables.

Chapter 5, 'Relevance Theory and the Functions of Metaphor', introduces the pragmatic theory known as Relevance, which can provide a framework for understanding the pragmatic processes involved in recognizing and understanding metaphor, providing we allow for the specific purposes for which metaphors might be used. With this proviso in mind it sketches out the most common metaphorical functions and purposes. It is an attempt to overcome the theoretical weaknesses which arise when we divorce the metaphorical process from the social process.

Chapters 6, 7 and 8 underline the importance of co-text and syntax as a factor in interpreting metaphor. They survey the textual resources which guide recognition and interpretation, and because they are relatively detailed and theoretical, especially Chapter 7, they may be more suitable to researchers than undergraduates, and readers may wish to use them as a handbook.

Unconventional metaphor is a relatively indirect use of language, and may cause problems of recognition. Chapter 6, 'The Signalling of Metaphor', details the main textual means by which metaphors are marked – downtoners, intensifiers, hedges, modals, and so on. It discusses the effect of the different markers on the vitality of metaphors and how they relate to point of view in narrative texts.

Chapters 7 and 8, 'The Specification of Topics' and 'The Specification of Grounds', assume that indirectness also necessitates guidance in interpretation. I detail and discuss the syntactic formulae most widely used for specifying the literal object/concept involved in the metaphor (i.e. the Topic) and the similarity or analogy underlying the metaphor (i.e. the Grounds). I show how the choice of syntactic formula affects interpretation and reflects the nature of the Topic and the Grounds. Both these chapters emphasize the syntactic contribution to metaphorical meaning, an area which has been badly neglected.

Chapter 9, 'The Interplay of Metaphors', analyses the relations between metaphors within literary texts (*The Rainbow*, *Macbeth*, Book 1 of *Paradise Lost* and six novels by William Golding), and develops a detailed taxonomy. It factors in three complicating phenomena: compounding, when one metaphor is embedded in another; literalization, where the same lexical item is used both literally and metaphorically in the same text; and overdescription, where obsessional repetition pushes the reader to a symbolic reading. And it outlines how these complicating factors are exploited for thematic purposes in literature.

Chapter 10, 'Metaphor in its Social Context', investigates how the varieties of metaphor established in the first five chapters, and their syntactic realizations catalogued in Chapters 6 to 9, correlate with different genres in English-speaking culture: conversation, written news reports, print advertising, popular science texts, prose fiction, and modern lyric poetry. As far as possible all metaphors cited in this volume are from authentic texts, in an effort to avoid the pitfalls inherent in using fabricated examples. Chapters 9 and 10, especially, by investigating a substantial number of texts of different styles, not only insists on authenticity, but provides a wider co-text and context for the testing of metaphorical theory.

The final chapter is the theoretical climax of the book. It develops the framework for text interpretation in Fairclough's *Language and Power* (1989) to show that a Hallidayan theory of contexts and socially determined purposes in combination with a pragmatic theory like Sperber and Wilson's Relevance, can give an adequate explanation of the phenomena I have been charting: the wide varieties of metaphorical interpretations and their syntactic realizations.

## TERMS AND A DEFINITION

It will be helpful to provide a general working definition of metaphor at the outset, though this will be refined in Chapter 4. For present purposes I define metaphor as follows:

> Metaphor occurs when a unit of discourse is used to refer[1] unconventionally to an object, process or concept, or colligates in an unconventional way. And when this unconventional act of reference or colligation is understood on the basis of similarity, matching or analogy involving the conventional referent or colligates of the unit and the actual unconventional referent or colligates.

The term "colligate", not very fashionable nowadays, applies to one kind of collocate. Collocation is any kind of co-occurrence of words in the text, but colligation is a syntactic relationship between the two words.

It will also be convenient to have terms corresponding to certain phrases in this definition. I adopt those of Richards (1965: 96–7) as adapted by Leech (1969: ch. 9), substituting the word *Topic* for their *Tenor*:

The conventional referent of the unit is the <u>Vehicle</u>.
The actual unconventional referent is the <u>Topic</u>.
The similarities and/or analogies involved are the <u>Grounds</u>.

If we work through an example, we can see how this terminology is applied.

(1)  The past is a foreign country; they do things differently there.

The concept 'foreign country' is the Vehicle, the concept 'the past' is the Topic and the similarity, the Grounds, is the fact that in both foreign countries and in the past 'things are done differently'.

We need to distinguish these objects/concepts from the language used to express them. We can label these units of discourse <u>Vehicle-term</u> (V-term), <u>Topic-term</u> (T-term) and <u>Ground-term</u> (G-term). In the example introduced above, the opening sentence of L.P. Hartley's *The Go-Between*, the V-term is a foreign country, the T-term is the past, the G-term is "they do things differently". (From now on these will be indicated in the quoted text by **bold** for Vehicle-term, <u>underlining</u> for Topic-term and *italics* for Ground-term.)

## ■ EXERCISE

*What are the Topic, Vehicle and Ground in the following sentences? Is there a T-term or G-term?*

(a)  *Director Matt Busby, the Godfather of the club. (DM31)*
(b)  *Life is a box of chocolates; you never know what you're going to get.*
(c)  *A committee is an animal with four back legs. (PQ199, Le Carré)*

The only sentence in which there is a T-term, V-term, and G-term is (b) – T-term <u>life</u>, V-term **a box of chocolates**, G-term *you never know what you're going to get*. In (a) the T-term is <u>Matt Busby</u>, the V-term is **the Godfather**. In (c) <u>a committee</u> is the T-term, and **an animal with four back legs** is the V-term.

While discussing terminology, please note that the word *metaphor* is used ambiguously in this book, but with an ambiguity which should not cause too many problems. As an uncountable noun *metaphor* refers to a particular way of using and processing language, as in our working definition. As a countable noun *metaphor(s)*, as in the title of the book, is used to refer to the metaphorical expression, as in the sentence *The dictionary is full of dead metaphors*.

## AN EXTENDED EXAMPLE:
## QUESTIONS ABOUT METAPHOR

As a taste of the rich variety of fascinating problems involved in the identification, categorization and analysis of metaphors, let's consider the

text of a whole poem by Seamus Heaney, a poem which is extremely dense
in its metaphorical patterning. As a preliminary exercise I invite you to
make a list of the expressions which you judge to be metaphorical. You
may then work through the paragraphs, (a)–(h), which follow the text. The
answers to these questions are not right or wrong, but may provide useful
evidence about how metaphors are perceived and interpreted. An indication
of the chapters in which the question receives discussion appears after each
question.

### An advancement of learning

I took the embankment path
(As always deferring
The bridge). The river nosed past,
Pliable, oil-skinned, wearing

A transfer of gables and sky.                                      5
Hunched over the railing,
Well away from the road now, I
Considered the dirty-keeled swans.

Something slobbered curtly, close,
Smudging the silence: a rat                                        10
Slimed out of the water and
My throat sickened so quickly that

I turned down the path in cold sweat
But God, another was nimbling
Up the far bank, tracing its wet                                   15
Arcs on the stones. Incredibly then

I established a dreaded
Bridgehead. I turned to stare
With deliberate, thrilled care
At my hitherto snubbed rodent.                                     20

He clockworked aimlessly a while,
Stopped, back bunched and glistening,
Ears plastered down on his knobbed skull,
Insidiously listening.

The tapered tail that followed him,                               25
The raindrop eye, the old snout:
One by one I took all in.
He trained on me. I stared him out

Forgetting how I used to panic
When his grey brothers scraped and fed                30
Behind the hen-coop in our yard,
On ceiling boards above my bed.

This terror, cold, wet-furred, small-clawed,
Retreated up a pipe for sewage.
I stared a minute after him.                          35
Then I walked on and crossed the bridge.
Seamus Heaney

(a) Are some metaphors more metaphorical than others? What effect does the word-class have on the detection and richness of metaphors? For example, were you or your fellow students more likely to identify "raindrop" (l. 26) than "in" (l. 13) as V-terms? Isn't it the case, generally, that V-terms derived from nouns such as "plastered" (l. 23), "clockworked" (l. 21) and "nosed" (l. 3) tend to be less rich in Grounds than deverbal nouns such as "transfer" (l. 5)? How would you rank these six metaphorical expressions on a scale of metaphoricity? (Chapters 1 and 3)

(b) If the parts of speech used do have such an effect, then this may result in certain syntactic configurations creating more metaphorical force than others. Which of the following did you feel created the strongest metaphorical effect? (Chapter 7)

the **raindrop** eye
a **transfer** of gables and sky
the river **nosed** past
**smudging** the silence

(c) In this particular poem there are many metaphors in which we are tempted to supply the "missing part" of the V-terms in order to make the Grounds more interesting (Leech 1969: 154ff.). These missing parts of V-terms, in parenthesis, range from the most specific colligates, e.g.

dirty-**keeled** [**ships**] swans;

through cases in which the V-term is slightly less specific and derived from a noun, e.g. "he clockworked" – with the rat compared to a clock or mechanical toy; to cases where the verb, adjective, or preposition V-terms suggest only a very general colligate:

| | | |
|---|---|---|
| **smudging** (l. 10) | suggests | some colouring or graphic medium |
| **pliable** (l. 4) | suggests | a flexible solid |
| **snubbed** (l. 20) | suggests | a person |

| | | |
|---|---|---|
| **sickened** (l. 12) | suggests | an animal/human |
| **deferring** (l. 2) | suggests | an action or event |
| **bunched** (l. 22) | suggests | plurality |

Did you include these more general analogies under the term *metaphor*? (Chapters 1 and 3)

(d) How important in detecting the metaphor behind the V-term "advancement" is the underlying analogy in English-speaking cultures which equates development and successful activity with movement forwards in space (see summary of Chapter 2 on p. 6 above). These dead and conventional analogies seem mostly to be used unconsciously, as perhaps is the case with "turned **down** the path" (l. 13) and "retreated **up** a pipe" (l. 34). (I am assuming the path was not literally downhill, and that the pipe did not slope upwards.) I doubt if you listed these two prepositions as metaphors. (Chapter 2)

(e) Metaphors in texts often interact with each other, sometimes successfully but in the case of "mixed metaphors" unsuccessfully. Did you find any examples of metaphors combining or mixing in what were for you unacceptable ways? Looking at lines 3–5 of the poem, do we feel that the transition between the five metaphorical expressions here is successful?

> The river **nosed** past,
> **Pliable, oil-skinned, wearing**
> A **transfer** of gables and sky.

Is the sharing of Grounds important here? (Chapters 8 and 9)

(f) Metaphors interrelate differently in different styles or registers of language. Did you identify "bridgehead", "trained on" and "retreated" as an extended military metaphor or mini-allegory? If you did, this was probably something to do with the fact that this is a poem, rather than, say, a newspaper report. (Chapters 9 and 10)

(g) How can one best characterize the relationship between symbolism and metaphor? The last sentence of the poem is a literal account of what happens in the world of the poem. But the action it describes is clearly symbolic of something like the facing and overcoming of a phobia. The two meanings of this sentence, the literal and the symbolic, seem to be related in a metaphorical fashion. An author can amplify these symbolic overtones, by, for example, using a similar lexical item both literally and metaphorically, e.g. "bridge" (l. 3, literal), "bridgehead" (l. 18, metaphorical), "bridge" (l. 36, symbolic). (Chapter 9)

(h) 'An advancement of learning' is an allusion to Francis Bacon's *The Advancement of Learning* (1605). Allusion, or quotation, is a means of creating large-scale metaphors, in which any aspects of the source and host works are made available for comparison. (Chapters 5 and 10)

So much for menus and trailers. I now offer starters and exposition.

# 1

# METAPHORICAL AND LITERAL LANGUAGE

## 1.1. INTRODUCTION

In this chapter we're going to look at the distinction between literal language use and metaphorical language use. Our general conclusion will be that the distinction is often a matter of degree, and that literal language processing depends on, and has built into it, the same kinds of mental processes that we associate with metaphor. Metaphoricity has a number of dimensions, such as contradictoriness, inexplicitness of comparison, conventionality and distance of transfer, and this chapter concentrates on the last two.

To understand the continuum between metaphorical and literal language, the approximative nature of communication and the general fuzziness of linguistic concepts we need to understand how communication works. So let's begin with a simple provisional model of linguistic communication in five stages (Figure 1.1).

Suppose a speaker wishes to describe something in the real world to a hearer. The discourse process has a starting point (A), a physically observable state of affairs which already exists in the actual world. By means of perception and cognition (1) we pass to (B), which is the speaker's thought, something which is mental and therefore not directly

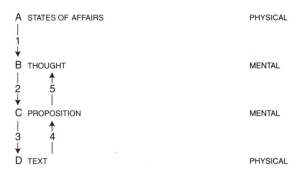

Figure 1.1 A simple model of linguistic communication

14

accessible to anyone except the speaker. The speaker proceeds (2) to form the proposition, (C), which is the most relevant for conveying her thoughts. In order to communicate this proposition, which is still mental, she has to make it accessible to her speakmate, and she can more or less achieve this by using the language code, (3). She uses conventional linguistic signs to pair her meanings with physical forms in a text, (D). The hearer can perceive the text, decode it and fill it out (4) to convey a full proposition, (C), and then interpret it (5) by guessing what thought of the speaker it is most likely to convey, (B). If this five-stage process is successful, then the hearer will be entertaining thoughts resembling those the speaker originally entertained, and thereby will have received a message about a state of affairs in the world which the speaker experienced but which the hearer did not.

In section 1.3 we will see that in most language uses, metaphorical or not, the thoughts the speaker intends to convey, (B), will approximate the propositions the speaker expresses, (C), to a greater or lesser extent. The larger the gap between the proposition expressed and the meaning intended, the more metaphorical the utterance will be. The smaller the gap, the more literal the language use. Sometimes the gap arises because the states of affairs in the real world, (A), do not neatly fit into concepts which we can economically put into propositional form, (C) and textualize in (D). Although some of these real-world phenomena are prototypical members of classes, others will be peripheral members, or lie on the boundary, so to speak, so we are uncertain how to classify them.

In section 1.4 we focus on the code, the system of linguistic signs which is important for the pathway between (B), (C) and (D). The words in the language code are by no means stable or agreed upon: in practice the boundaries between word-meanings are unclear or fuzzy and this creates uncertainties as to whether we are dealing with metaphor or approximation or subclassification.

Some of the fuzziness, and the blurring of the literal and metaphorical, is caused by diachronic change, the change of meanings over shorter or longer time spans: in the course of a text, where local systems of synonymy, hyponymy and so on can be set up (section 1.6); or during a speaker's life, as children, for example, acquire language and narrow "metaphorical" meanings down to the literal adult usage (section 1.7); and during the development of a language, so that what were once relatively original metaphors become part of the lexicon (section 1.8).

Underpinning all these perspectives on approximation, fuzziness and the diachronic processes of the conventionalization of metaphor lies the concept of similarity or analogy (section 1.2). Any classification of phenomena, as we saw in the Introduction with our alternative categorization of boxes (pp. 2–3), involves the selection of some features as critical, and the hiding or forgetting of other features which are not critical. The similarity and matching which goes on in literal language is, of course, achieved much more automatically, and relatively straightforwardly compared with the matching in original metaphors.

## 1.2. MATCHING AND SIMILARITY

The notion of matching or similarity (Tversky 1977: 327–52) is often used as a way of distinguishing metaphor from other figures of speech, and indeed similarity is important in our working definition. I restrict metaphor to cases where an "unconventional act of reference or colligation is understood on the basis of some **similarity, matching or analogy** involving the conventional referent or colligates of the unit and the actual unconventional referent or colligates". This excludes figures of speech like metonymy, e.g. *He drank six bottles* where the speaker's thought is 'he drank the contents of six bottles'. Although the noun phrase *six bottles* refers to some extent unconventionally here, we don't interpret this unconventional reference by similarity but by means of an association of container with contents.

But what do we mean by similarity? From a common-sense point of view we can regard "things" or entities (Lyons 1977: 442) as having certain characteristics or features which they may or may not share with other entities. So, for example, a chair shares with a stool the characteristic use of seating one person, but may differ in having a substantial support for the back. When we use language to classify our experience some of the features will be regarded as critical for that classification. So, in the previous example, possession of a back support is, at least for me, critical in distinguishing chairs from stools. Other features of the two objects will be non-critical or peripheral as far as classification is concerned: e.g. a particular chair, say an armchair, could be on casters, and without legs, and share this feature with a particular stool. However, because the English language does not recognize the possession of casters rather than legs as a critical feature, it does not set up a new class which would include those armchairs and stools.

If we provisionally accept that similarity is the sharing of certain features, then it is obvious that we depend on it in our literal use of language. When we refer literally to a newly encountered object, say a chair, we have previously matched certain characteristics of the object against that set of critical features which constitute our concept of 'chair'. If the object possesses these critical characteristics [artefact], [furniture], [for sitting], [for one person], [with support for back] we are justified in saying the use of the word *chair* is literal.

## ■ EXERCISE

*You are climbing a mountain with a friend, and, tired, you ask to stop for a rest. Your friend points to a boulder and says to you "Why don't you sit on that chair?" Would this be a literal use of the word* chair *or not? Why?*

I suppose that this would be a metaphorical use of the word, provided that some similarity or match could be perceived between this particular boulder and our concept of a chair, e.g. [used for sitting], [with support for back]. We could not call this use literal, however, because a boulder does not possess certain critical features of the concept, e.g. [object of furniture], [artefact]. Any entity referred to metaphorically, therefore, lacks at least one critical feature possessed by the conventional referents of the word. However, similarity or matching, and the sharing of characteristics, are important in both literal and metaphorical language use.

Were meanings as clear-cut, reference so straightforward, and critical features as unambiguous as the above account suggests, we could more easily define the boundary between the literal and the metaphorical. However, what count as non-critical or peripheral features, and what count as critical or central features vary from context to context, and sometimes from speaker to speaker. (For example, a reviewer of this book disagreed with me over the criterion [with support for back] as being critical for the concept 'chair'. While other informants agreed with me, there is clearly no unanimity.) In addition some of these critical features seem more central than others. And objects and thoughts are referred to with varying degrees of precision or approximation.

### 1.3. METAPHOR, APPROXIMATION AND PROTOTYPICALITY

This section is concerned, then, with the gaps, whether deliberate or inevitable, between (B) and (C) in Figure 1.1, between the speaker's thought and the propositional form. Sperber and Wilson in their book *Relevance* (1986) claim that the proposition expressed by a speaker will very often only approximate the thoughts of the speaker. As they point out, in the limiting, absolutely literal case the proposition expressed will share all the semantic properties of the speaker's thought. But it is easy to see that, in some circumstances, it may be a waste of time and effort to make the proposition expressed too accurate. For example, imagine the following scenario. We are about to travel from Birmingham to London in my car, I have to buy petrol at the next gas station, but we're short of money so we don't want to buy too much. We both know that my car does 10 miles to the litre, and the tank is nearly empty. If I ask you "How far is it from Birmingham to London?" and you know it's 103 miles, it will actually be more appropriate to reply "100 miles." Saying "103 miles" takes more effort to produce and process, and makes my calculations of how much fuel to buy more complex than the round figure. *100 miles* will be, in these circumstances, though not exactly truthful, more relevant as a reply.

Sperber and Wilson comment on examples like this one:

> We want to claim that there is no discontinuity between these loose uses and a variety of 'figurative' examples which include the most characteristic examples of literary metaphor. In both cases the propositional form of the utterance differs from that of the thought interpreted. In both cases the hearer can proceed on the assumption that these two propositional forms have some identifiable and logical contextual implications [Grounds of similarity] in common. In both cases the same interpretive abilities and procedures are involved.
>
> (Sperber and Wilson 1986: 235)

We can talk of metaphors as <u>Approximative</u> when the distance between the thought and proposition is small, and as <u>Transfer</u> metaphors when the gap is larger.

Sometimes the Approximative uses of language will be deliberate, as in the previous example. At other times the speaker may have no choice but to be approximate, because there is no single-term or sufficiently economical expression to refer more exactly. In Golding's *Free Fall* (p. 33), Sammy says

FF33    My mother was as near a whore as makes no matter.

Here there is not a complete match between the concept represented by the word "whore" and the woman in question, as is clear from the signal of approximation "as near as makes no matter". From the context we have plenty of evidence that his mother slept around, but none that she took monetary rewards for doing so, though she may have taken benefits in kind. Let's assume that we need both [sleeping around] and [for monetary gain] as semantic features of the term *whore* for it to refer precisely and literally. If so, Sammy's use will be a case where the concept available in the language only matches approximately the state of affairs being described. Presumably Sammy (or Golding) could have conveyed the thoughts describing his mother more accurately by being more long-winded and using a clause or two instead of a phrase. But there was no simple, ready-made concept conveniently packaged in a single noun phrase which would have conveyed this thought and feeling economically. So the expression he used was the most relevant and effective one to achieve the strikingly disrespectful effect of categorizing his mother as a whore. This is a particular example of the more general misalignment between the world and our concepts: we all know that phenomena, and thoughts, do not always fall neatly into the categories provided by language – whether a whale is to be categorized as a fish or a mammal, or a platypus as a reptile or mammal, can be open to question.

Such Approximative uses are related to, and may be one cause of, fuzziness in the semantic concepts themselves. Presumably if the insulting term *whore* is used approximatively on many occasions to mean 'a woman who sleeps around' without the approximation being marked, then speakers may begin to be unsure whether [for monetary gain] is a critical feature.

Another cause of fuzziness is the fact that some members of conceptual classes are felt to be more central than others, or that some referents of a noun phrase will be more typical than others. There is a tendency, when classifying, to use the metaphor of boxes, or circles, implying that there is a clear dividing line between what belongs inside and what does not, a so-called *typological* classification (Martin and Matthiessen 1991). There is an alternative metaphor, however, which sees distinctions as clines, and uses the metaphor of proximity for similarity, which is known as *topological* classification. If we consider the psychological evidence we will see that the semantics of nouns, while not being as topological as scalar adjectives, are still so to a considerable extent.

## ■ EXERCISE

*Which of the following would you regard as sports: fishing, chess, basket-ball, soccer, orienteering, swimming, boxing? Of those you selected in the sports category, which did you find easiest or most straightforward to select?*

Experiments by Rosch have shown that certain members of a class are perceived as more typical or central than others. For example balls and dolls are more centrally members of the category 'toy' than are swings and skates; basketball is more prototypically a sport than fishing (Rosch 1975; Lakoff 1972: 184). Fishing and swings would be closer to the boundaries of the concepts 'sport' and 'toy'.

This prototypical/marginal distinction suggests further reasons why the border between metaphor and approximation is blurred. If robins are more prototypical birds than ostriches and penguins (Rosch 1975) because the latter do not fly, then the statement *An ostrich is a kind of bird*, though not a metaphor, would be closer to metaphor than *A robin is a kind of bird*.

If conceptual distinctions depend on topological classification, clines of centrality, this also suggests that the borders between concepts will be bands or fuzzy areas rather than clear thin lines (Zadeh 1965). Were you and your fellow students in any disagreement about whether fishing and chess, for example, could be called sports? Whether a particular example like *chess is a sport* is literal or a metaphor, may be impossible to decide.

In 1972 George Lakoff published a list of what he considered the most common hedges, that is, those phrases or larger syntactic structures "whose meaning implicitly involves fuzziness" (Lakoff 1972: 195), in other words, whose meaning indicates non-central membership of a logical or referential category.

(1)  (He's) another (Caruso/Lincoln/Babe Ruth, etc.)
(2)  (America) is the (Roman Empire) of (the modern world)
(3)  sort of
(4)  kind of
(5)  as it were

(Lakoff 1972: 196)

It is interesting to note that many of these hedging forms are, in fact, used to signal metaphor rather than fuzziness or approximation ((1) and (2)), and that others are used ambiguously to indicate metaphor and/or approximation ((3), (4) and (5)). The ambiguous use of forms like these provides some evidence that metaphor and approximation overlap, or are not always distinguished.

## 1.4. THE FUZZINESS AND VAGUENESS OF SEMANTIC CONCEPTS

Our discussion of prototypicality seemed applicable to reference, that is referring to (A) in Figure 1.1, as well as semantic relations of, for example, subclassification or hyponymy. We shift now to a more deliberate concentration on semantic categories, the tools for coding thought and proposition into text, for mediating between (B), (C) and (D).

### ■ EXERCISE

*How would you define the meaning of the word* bottle? *What is it for? What is it made of? What kind of thing does it contain? What shape is it? How does it differ in meaning from the meanings of* jar, flask, phial, bowl, cup *and other containers?*

Many common words in a natural language are vague and uncertain in meaning, as was demonstrated by research into lexical fields carried out by Adrienne Lehrer. She wished to analyse the meanings of words for man-made containers, so first she suggested a number of components or features of the meanings of these words and asked her informants whether they regarded these components as obligatory or optional, in our terms, critical or non-critical. For example, for the word *bottle* a list of components might include [made of glass], [narrow at the top], [for containing liquid]. Analysing her results, she came up against the problem that if all optional components (those regarded as unnecessary by more than 90 per cent of the informants) were disregarded, there were not enough semantic features left with which to distinguish the different meanings from each other, e.g. for distinguishing the meaning 'bottle' from the meaning 'flask'. On the other hand, if all optional features, e.g. [made of glass] were made obligatory then a sentence such as *Some bottles are not made of glass* would be marked as contradictory (Lehrer 1974: 85–6).

Besides this overlapping or fuzziness of neighbouring concepts at the same degree of generality, horizontal fuzziness if you like, there might be fuzziness on a vertical dimension, a fuzziness about the relative specificity of concepts. This idea shows up a second point in Lakoff's list of hedges: (3) and (4), *kind/sort of*, are not only used to signal peripheral membership of a class but also subclassification. The evidence suggests that there may be a psychological "confusion" not only between metaphor and approximation but also between metaphor and subclassification or hyponymy, important though this latter distinction is from a logical point of view. Indeed, Lakoff and Johnson have claimed "subcategorization and metaphor are endpoints on a continuum" (Lakoff and Johnson 1980: 84–5).

## ■ EXERCISE

*What is the difference in meaning, if any, between* a kind of *as used in the following two sentences?*

   *(a)  A pike is a kind of fish.*
   *(b)  A sock is a kind of glove.*

When forms like *a kind of* are used in a clearly literal statement, like (a), they indicate that the first noun is the hyponym of the second, that is, refers to a member of the class referred to by the second. On the other hand these markers can equally well be used to signal a metaphor, as in (b). In (a) the pike possesses all the critical or central features necessary for the use of the term *fish*, plus extra features which distinguish it from the fishes mackerel, trout, minnow, etc. In (b), by contrast, a sock lacks some critical features necessary for the literal application of the word *glove*, namely [for the hand]["fingers"].

## ■ EXERCISE

*Would you say that* an escalator is a sort of staircase *is literal or metaphorical? Why?*

However, sometimes it is difficult to decide whether the use of *a sort of* is to mark metaphorical or subcategorizing statements. The problem is whether to regard *staircase* as the superordinate term for escalator or to decide that one of the critical features of staircases is that they are fixed and static, in which case we have a metaphor. The decision one way or another seems arbitrary and beside the point: we feel no urge to know whether subcategorization or metaphor is being signalled. In such examples the precise meanings of terms depend on the contrasts which they enter into with other terms at the same level in the system. And individual speakers and texts may vary their meanings by positioning them differently on the scale of specificity.

After all, such "confusion" about the level in a system at which a term operates has left its mark on the lexis of the language (Figure 1.2). Examples are rife, and some notorious, in which word-forms, e.g. *cow* and *man*, function as the signifier of two lexical items, one the super-ordinate of the other (Figure 1.2 (1) and (1b), (2) and (2b)). The suggestion that "this lexical complication could be avoided by claiming the words are univocal but allow a figurative extension" (Sadock 1979: 53) may seem rather curious, until we recognize the resemblance between subclassification and metaphor.

Distinguishing subclassification and metaphor is equally complex in cases where a word has no common hyponyms, because it is itself the most specific term available.

## ■ EXERCISE

*Consider the following examples of the use of the word* sigh.

(a)  A **sigh** *is a kind of noise.*
(b)  *A sort of **sigh** passed through those men crowded together as they looked with strange faces at the murderer.* (MS496)

*Are either or both of them examples of subclassification, that is, hyponymy?*

Example (a) is obviously a case of subclassification. But with (b), since there are no lexical items which are hyponyms of *sigh*, and consequently no readily accessible concept corresponding to the hyponym, the hyponym–metaphor distinction is made doubly difficult.

I suggest that the main function of phrases like (*a*) *sort of/kind of* is to direct attention to the lack of precision with which a certain lexical item is being used, and whether this is due to the lack of an appropriate hyponym or due to a deliberate metaphor is unimportant.

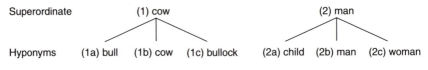

*Figure 1.2* Shared forms for superordinates and hyponyms

## 1.5. SUMMARY

We can draw several conclusions from sections 1.2 to 1.4:

- Similarity or matching, viewed as the sharing of characteristics, is a concept that is important not only for the definition of metaphor, but also for the classification of experience which underlies our literal use of the language.
- There will often be, deliberately or not, an approximation between (B) and (C), the thoughts of a speaker and the proposition she chooses to express; this is part of a wider problem, the lack of a completely snug fit between experience of the real world (A) and the concepts a language makes available (C)/(D).
- There is an overall vagueness or fuzziness in the meanings of common word-forms of the code, which are used for the transition from (B) to (C) to (D) in our model, with some members of classes more central than others, and with the horizontal and vertical boundaries between concepts unclear; as a result what counts as metaphorical and literal may be equally fuzzy.
- A symptom of lack of precision in language use, and fuzziness of concepts, is that signallers of approximation and hyponymy are ambiguous and sometimes function as signallers of metaphor.

The conclusions of sections 1.2 to 1.4 validate Sperber and Wilson's claim that the only difference between literal and metaphorical language is the degree of gap between a speaker's thought and the proposition expressed. However, they also give some explanations of why there may be more of a gap than the speaker intended: suitably concise expressions may not be available to represent the speaker's thoughts in propositional form; and even when they are available, most of these expressions will be somewhat unstable in their meanings, with their boundaries and positions in the semantic hierarchy variable according to context. In other words, what the terms in the expressed proposition mean will have to be negotiated in the social context and according to the co-text.

So far we have been talking about the metaphorical–literal distinction from the point of view of the language system, a relatively synchronic, non-temporal perspective. But to understand the causes and manifestations of the variations in usage of the system we need to consider diachronic, time-bound processes: the changes to meanings in the course of texts, section 1.6; the changes to an individual's system over time, section 1.7; and the changes to the language system over historical periods, section 1.8. Metaphor is located at the interface between the stability and unity of the language system and the mutability and diversity of its operational use in context.[1]

## 1.6. TEXT MEANINGS AND NEGOTIATION

In this section I show how the dictionary meanings of terms can be subtly changed in the course of texts. These changes might be giving words an emotional charge; or setting up unconventional relations of hyponymy, antonymy, or synonymy; or, alternatively, undermining synonymy.

My first example occurs in *Wild Swans* by Jung Chang (1992), the (auto)biography of three generations of Chinese women, and their struggle to survive during the Revolution and Cultural Revolution. Before reading this text I would have regarded the words *torment* and *torture* as roughly synonymous. But in this text they are clearly differentiated, so that *torment* refers to the mental and *torture* to the physical.

> WS378 Up to the beginning of the Cultural Revolution torture, as distinct from torment, had been forbidden.

An example of the opposite phenomenon, erasing differences, is taken from the transcribed text of a radio interview with the film director Ken Russell. This concerns the meanings of the words *fantasy* and *vision*. In their dictionary meanings they are by no means synonymous. 'Fantasy' stresses unreality, delusive imagination or hallucination, whereas 'vision' emphasizes the supernatural or mystical insight which makes possible the perception of what is real or possible but not present. But in the following extract from the interview they seem to be used synonymously, both as equal opposites to 'reality'.

> One has a vision of somebody and I suppose the vision often takes over the reality and er one shouldn't look at visions one should look at the reality and er keep looking at it. I suppose that was my my falling into my own fantasy trap I had a picture of my wife that wasn't the real picture and er so [inaudible] there's no reason why it it was in my my fault not her fault that the picture was a fantasy.
>
> (Transcript from 'Interview with Ken Russell',
> from the BBC Radio 4 series *In the Psychiatrist's Chair*)

On the basis of dictionary meanings 'fantasy' and 'reality' represent opposite extremes with 'vision' somewhere in the middle, while in this text 'vision' is shunted over to the same position as 'fantasy', a meaning simply the opposite of 'reality'.

### ■ EXERCISE

*In the following extract from an article 'The stress code' in the American teenage magazine* Seventeen, *what superordinate term is used to include and sum up the effects of glandular action on the skin and hair?*

*Your skin also responds to the extra glandular action by increasing oil production, which can lead to acne breakouts. You can fight back by using a gentle cleanser and an acne cream (or try Noxzema 2-in-1 Pads that do the job in one step). Also, check out our five-point make-up routine at night; it'll tell you how to brighten up when you're feeling especially pale and pasty. Since your scalp tends to go into the same oil overdrive as your skin, wash hair every day when stressed, using a specially formulated shampoo (we like Nexxus Exx/Oil shampoo).*

*But beyond dealing with these specific problems, try to get over stress in general.*

It is very common for texts to create somewhat spurious superordinates to group hyponyms together, and often this represents a clear ideological bias. 'The stress code' text uses the word *problem* to categorize oil on the skin and scalp, and acne. Constructed as problems they obviously need solutions, usually chemical ones of a cosmetic kind! This expresses an ideology of consumer capitalism in which problems are solved by purchasing products. (Advertisers have not yet constructed the loss of baby teeth as a problem – though in terms of maturation it is strictly comparable to adolescent pimples – because temporary false teeth for 6-year-olds are yet to be mass-produced.) Be that as it may, the meanings of *oil* and *acne* seem to have acquired a negative semantic feature by being lumped under this superordinate term, simply because a hyponym, logically speaking, has to possess all the semantic features of its superordinate. If 'dog' is the superordinate of 'poodle' then 'poodle' has to have, as part of its meaning, all the features of the meaning of 'dog' [living thing, animal, mammal, canine].

A more obvious case of attributing negative affective features to a previously neutral term can be cited from Carter's analysis of an article about Neil Kinnock in the *Daily Mail* (Carter 1987: 94ff.). Kinnock had been recently elected as leader of the Labour Party. In keeping with the anti-Labour stance of the newspaper the quite innocent lexical items *young* and *new* are made into smear words:

Neil Kinnock, just elected Labour's **youngest** leader at 41, saw an **old** party tide threaten to swamp his **new** beginning last night . . .

An angry session of the National Executive provided a curtain-raiser to a debate on Wednesday which may nail **young** Mr Kinnock more firmly than ever to getting rid of nuclear weapons.

It saw the **novice** leader frantically buttonholing colleagues in an attempt to avert what he sees as political suicide . . .

And there was a blunt message from **veteran** left-winger Joan Maynard at a fringe meeting . . .

But for a few moments the **trendy new** leader enjoyed the razzmatazz of an overwhelming victory.

*(Daily Mail*, 8 October 1983)

If you look at the meanings of the emboldened words in their context you will
see that equations are being suggested between the meanings of "young"
Kinnock and "new" policies for the Labour Party, as though the words are
synonymous, or entail each other. And an opposition is set up between
"young/new" and "old/veteran". But more important, we are invited to
construe the meanings 'young/new' as somehow synonymous with 'novice'
and 'trendy' which represent Kinnock as naive (and probably crucified as a
result), or as some fad or novelty associated with "razzmatazz".

Obviously the kinds of negotiation of meaning occurring in these last
two texts are attempts to create a reality rather than simply reflect a pre-
existing one. In this respect the way we have worked through Figure 1.1
starting from (A) and moving to (D) is misleading – the mental world of
thought and proposition is to some degree determined by the language code
of the speaker, and in turn determines how the states of affairs in the world
will be read. Language constructs these states of affairs, as well as representing them. If we use language categories to construct mental representations, thoughts, (B), or propositions, (C), our language thereby becomes a
distorting medium. It intervenes between our thoughts about the world, (B),
and the "reality out there", (A), so that we have no independent or direct
access to the truth.

These examples give ample evidence that the diachronics of text production and interpretation introduce an indeterminacy and fuzziness into word-
meanings, with the result that in co-text they may only approximate their
decontextualized dictionary meanings. This textual play or instability with
meanings both illustrates and suggests causes of the fuzziness of semantic
concepts.

## 1.7. ACQUISITION OF WORD-MEANINGS

We've seen how, in the course of their development, texts destabilize and
renegotiate the values of dictionary terms. Now we turn to the second
diachronic area with a wider time-span – an individual's acquisition of
word-meanings.

From the standpoint of developmental psychology the acquisition of
vocabulary is a process of narrowing meanings down until they are relatively literal, that is until they correspond more exactly to the conventional
adult usage. The first meanings a child attaches to words will be approximate to the extent of seeming metaphorical when compared with adults'
more literal usage. So children appear to use "metaphors" naturally from
infancy onwards (Rumelhart 1979: 80). For example my 3-year-old daugh-

ter Julia referred to a crust of bread as "shell". However, we must be careful about calling this kind of use "metaphorical", since, unlike typical metaphors, it may not be deliberate on the part of the speaker, even though an adult interprets it metaphorically. It may be one type of asymmetric metaphor, a metaphor which is not intended.

Children's apparent metaphors may occur for two reasons. First, because of lack of experience with the language, the child may not be aware of the conventional features of concepts; for example, although she has access to the two word-forms *door* and *gate* she might apply the word *door* to the kind of gate used to prevent children climbing the stairs, perhaps privileging the feature [inside a building] where the adult would privilege [solidity] or [height]. A second reason may be that the child is forced to refer unconventionally through lack of lexical resources, calling a crust of bread "shell" because *crust* is not yet in her vocabulary. From the adult viewpoint the first case results in an Approximative metaphor, because 'gates' and 'doors' are neighbouring concepts, and the second in a Transfer metaphor, because 'crust' and 'shell' are more distant concepts.

Is this second kind of overextension deliberately metaphorical on the child's part? It is difficult to decide. Winner's research has shown that, often, once the child has acquired the conventional term, e.g. *crust*, the lexical-gap filling overextension will drop out (Winner 1988: 91–2). However, this is not a reason for denying in general that deliberate overextension is a metaphorical process. In fact, I believe one of the major functions of metaphor is precisely the filling of lexical gaps, e.g. finding a word like *mouse* to refer to the attachment to a computer keyboard.

There is an opposite phenomenon when a child finds her original concept of the meaning of a word challenged by a literal adult usage. The child will probably react in much the same way an adult reacts to a metaphor, the reverse kind of asymmetry from that discussed above. For example, take a child who has previously thought the meaning of the word *mummy* was 'all female humans', and the meaning of the word *doggy* was 'all quadrupeds'. If the child hears the sentence *Your doggy is a mummy* she will treat it as an adult would a metaphor, though the sentence is relatively literal for the adult speaker. What were for the child critical features of the meaning of *mummy* are contradicted by its being predicated of *doggy*. She is forced to treat it as a more general, superordinate concept which will include both her mother and a dog. This concept of motherhood might well be worked out in conjunction with the context, for example the appearance of puppies (Leondar 1975: 278–9).[2]

And so we should recognize that the same interpretative processes or strategies are involved in a child's acquisition of conventional meanings as operate in the adult interpretation of a metaphorical use of language, including children's unintentionally metaphorical uses. This is a conclusion I can hardly endorse strongly enough and supports the claims made in sections 1.1–1.4.

### 1.7.1. Ostensive reference

One model of language acquisition which adequately accounts for these facts has been more fully formulated by Putnam in his theory of ostensive reference (Putnam 1975). He proposed that the range of reference of natural-kind terms like *water* and *gold* and of theoretical terms in science might be fixed ostensively rather than by definitional convention. That is to say, in order to learn what terms like *water*, *gold*, *electrical charge* or *game* mean, we are shown (ostension) a number of examples, or better still exemplars (prototypes), from which we form a concept applicable to other phenomena. For instance, if we have seen examples of tennis, football and chess and heard the term *game* used to refer to all of them, when we see people playing darts we will be able to recognize it as a game.

The boundaries of such concepts will be established as a function of two factors: first, the experience of the kinds of ostensive reference exemplified above; and second, competition with neighbouring concepts, e.g. the concept 'game' is defined in relation to 'fight', 'sport', and so on. It is by some such mechanism that what I have called the *critical features* of conceptual meanings are established, though, as we saw from Lehrer's research, these features will never be fully or finally established.

Putnam's theory emphasizes two points already made in this chapter. For one, concepts are constantly being adjusted by narrowing, widening or more wholesale modification. In the second place, these concepts are not acquired in isolation, but as part of a system involving neighbouring concepts.

### 1.7.2. Accommodation and assimilation

The theory of ostensive reference relies heavily on the idea that the semantic system is accommodated to experience. This leads us naturally into a brief discussion of the processes of accommodation and assimilation and how they relate to metaphors of different kinds.

Piaget distinguished two processes by which our mental world comes to terms with our experience, and he calls these *assimilation* and *accommodation*. Assimilation occurs when the environment is made cognitively accessible by incorporating some of its effects into relatively stable intellectual systems called *schemata*. Accommodation occurs when the schemata themselves change in response to changes in the environment (Piaget 1937: 272–7; Pylyshyn 1979: 544–7). Different kinds of metaphor seem to involve accommodation and assimilation in varying degrees, though it may be the case that all metaphors involve both processes to some extent.

Let's start by considering a case of ordinary literal language use. If I see a typical car, which I have not seen before, I may refer to it as "a car" thereby assimilating this experience to the existing concept or schema. By contrast, consider next the process of the acquisition of language meaning by children. The hypothetical but mistaken concept of 'mummy', in the example quoted above from Leondar, has to change when the parent says "Your doggy is a mummy." This would be an example of the accommodation of language concepts or meanings to a new experience.

Third, we can look at an example of a metaphor such as the word *wave* being used to conceptualize light. If this metaphor becomes accepted, so that users end up with some unitary concept of wave which includes the movements on the surface of the sea and rays of light, then both accommodation and assimilation have occurred: the original concept of 'wave' has been accommodated, expanded and modified, to include experience of light; and the concept of 'light' has been assimilated to the concept of a 'wave' – we will conceptualize light in a new way if we regard it as constituted of waves rather than rays.

Lastly we can consider metaphors of a more literary kind. If I refer to a dead man as holding "five **icicles** in his hand" (Causley, 'Death of a poet', in Larkin 1973: 495), using "icicles" to refer to fingers, the range of reference of the word *icicle* is being radically changed, for a moment, in a process of accommodation; but the concept of 'finger' is also assimilated to the concept of 'icicle' as we are, for the nonce, invited to explore the similarities between the two concepts or schemata. The most interesting active metaphors must have this mutual accommodation and assimilation if they are to be described as *interactive* (see section 4.3.2.). However, unlike our previous example, *wave*, this mutual effect is only transitory.

Of course, even with so-called literal language use, there is not always pure assimilation of experience to existing schemata or concepts. For the language speaker the concept or schema represented by a word carries in itself a history of all past uses, a history involving thousands of tiny adjustments or accommodations of that concept to an individual's experience of life and language. As we saw in our discussion of Lehrer's research, it is a mistake to believe there are exact conceptual meanings agreed on completely by the users of the language code; de-textualized conceptual meanings, in that sense, remain an idealized abstraction. So we can expect that, even in cases where the propositional form, (C), resembles exactly the thought of a speaker, (B), the thought it conveys to the hearer may not match the speaker's thoughts precisely: the terms of the proposition encoded in text will have slightly different meanings for speaker and hearer.

Having discussed some of the psychological factors involved in the individual's language acquisition, and their relation to metaphorical language, I will now broaden the temporal, diachronic perspective to discuss historical changes in the word-meanings of a language.

## 1.8. MEANING CHANGE IN THE LEXIS OF A LANGUAGE

If we take a sentence at random and analyse it etymologically we will find that several of the word-forms either co-represent a more "literal" meaning than the one in that sentence, or can be traced back to a time when they did. So we can assume that the new or actual meaning they represent was originally acquired through a figurative process, in many cases a metaphorical one.

## ■ EXERCISE

*Think carefully about the meanings of the words in the following sentence. Are there any which you would identify as once, if not still, metaphorical?*

*Throughout the centuries writers and thinkers have been critical of the shortcomings of language.*

*(Ullmann 1962: 116)*

To start with, the word "throughout" could represent two meanings: (a) through the whole of (a space, region); (b) during the whole of (a period of time or course of action). Although we seldom notice it, the meaning in this sentence is a transfer of the original use, based on metaphorical analogy, in which time is conceived in terms of space. In addition, "shortcomings", treated as derived from the literal verb *to come short*, might well have achieved its present meaning by a metaphorical process: perhaps *to come short* used of a missile aimed at a target, or of a material measured with a ruler, changed its use and came to mean 'to fail to reach a standard'. Either simultaneously with or after its change into a compound noun, its application was transferred from physical objects to abstractions and to human character.

The word-meanings of "throughout" and "shortcomings" are the ones most obviously based on metaphor. But even the word *write* has changed its meaning from the original High German, in which it meant 'to tear', through a meaning 'to score' or 'to outline' until it reached today's familiar meaning. At some stage in this process there was presumably a metaphorical change of meaning in which first the feature [to produce a shape] and, second, the narrower feature [to produce letters] were highlighted and became critical at the expense of the component [to produce a deep impression].

There are two distinct metaphorical diachronic processes by which word-forms acquire polysemy (i.e. two or more related meanings). The first is the narrowing or extending of the sense, perhaps as the concepts referred to changed or diverged. The history of the word *germ* is a case in point. Originally it had a single sense, because diseases were actually regarded as producing seeds. But as the medical concept changed, the meaning 'microbe' emerged from the earlier sense, by a process of narrowing (Waldron 1967: 173). (The former sense is now only encountered in compounds like *wheatgerm*.) The second process would be the deliberate metaphorical transfer of a word from a distant semantic field, as, for example, the use of *leg* to refer to part of a table, or *birdie* and *eagle* for 'one under par' and 'two under par' in golf.

The result of the two processes – widening and transfer – appears the same in many instances. So we may be surprised that, diachronically, the two senses of *current*, that is, 'flow of water' and 'movement of electrons', developed from one unitary meaning which included the two modern senses (Waldron 1967: 173). But synchronically, for users of the contemporary language system, the polysemic relation seems just as much an example of metaphorical transfer as *leg* or *eagle*. These facts lend extra weight to the arguments in sections 1–3, where we claimed that metaphor (a large distance between (B) and (C), or transfer) and approximation (a smaller distance between (B) and (C), widening) are not always easily distinguished.

The important point is that the metaphorical process has left its mark on the vocabulary of the language, by dint of the fact that various metaphorical extensions and transfers have been <u>Lexicalized</u>, that is to say have found their way into the dictionary with a second and separate conventional meaning. Dictionaries are certainly the cemeteries and the mortuaries, definitely the dormitories, and generally the resting place for the populations of metaphors.

### 1.8.1. Categories of inactive metaphors

■ **EXERCISE**

*Can you perceive any relation between the two meanings of* pupil – 'a young student' and 'circular opening in the iris', or between the two meanings of* vice – 'depravity' and 'a gripping tool'?

Chapter 3 will be partly devoted to a discussion of the connections between word-formation and metaphor. And Chapters 9 and 10 address the revitalization of Dead or Inactive metaphors. As a preliminary, and so as to provide a terminological framework, we can consider the lexical items in Figure 1.3.

The further one proceeds down the figure from Dead to Active, the more

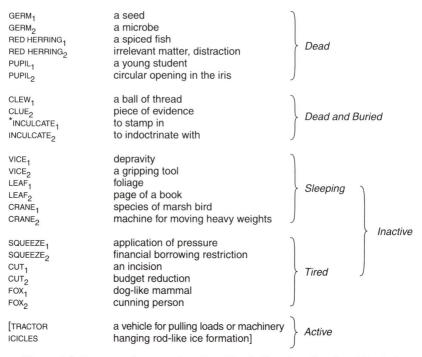

| | | |
|---|---|---|
| GERM₁ | a seed | |
| GERM₂ | a microbe | |
| RED HERRING₁ | a spiced fish | Dead |
| RED HERRING₂ | irrelevant matter, distraction | |
| PUPIL₁ | a young student | |
| PUPIL₂ | circular opening in the iris | |

*Figure 1.3* Degrees of conventionality: Tired, Sleeping, Dead and Buried
metaphors

likely that the expressions will be processed as metaphors, that is, that the item will be recognized as a V-term, and Grounds will be constructed. Towards the bottom of the table the Grounds will become less and less predictable.

RED HERRING and GERM, unlike our later examples, are lexical items which nowadays have no corresponding more literal meaning. (I am treating the idiom RED HERRING as a single lexical item.) In its original literal use *red herring* referred to a highly spiced fish that escaped convicts would scatter to put the chasing bloodhounds off the scent. When first used to mean 'distraction' one could have traced a metaphorical connection between the two meanings. However, nowadays the original Vehicle of the metaphor has passed out of our experience – we no longer encounter that kind of fish, and certainly do not see it being used as a decoy for hounds. In the case of GERM, the original Vehicle is now referred to by another term, *seed*. So a metaphorical connection can hardly be made. Similarly, unless one is an etymologist, it is difficult to make any metaphorical connection between the meanings of PUPIL₁ and PUPIL₂. Only a complicated reconstruction, involving remote associations of the original Latin meaning, would suggest the Grounds for such a transfer. These first three examples I shall label Dead metaphors, since their Topics and Grounds are so inaccessible.

CLEW$_1$, 'a ball of thread', is a slightly different case, as this lexical item is now rather rare compared with CLUE$_2$. The Grounds for the original metaphor might just be constructed if a schematic context could be provided, such as the story of Theseus and the Minotaur, in which Ariadne gave Theseus a ball of thread so that he could escape from the labyrinth. But what is interesting about CLEW and INCULCATE is that they demonstrate, weakly and strongly respectively, the tendency of a change of form to hide a metaphorical meaning relation. The Latin literal meaning INCULCATE$_1$ is not represented by the form *inculcate* in English, but by the form *stamp in*. So for most English speakers, unless they are Latin scholars, there is no opportunity for a metaphorical connection, and the meaning remains opaque. These two examples, because they are hidden by formal changes, I shall label Buried metaphors. More often than not they are Buried Dead.

VICE$_1$ and VICE$_2$ have no historical etymological connection. I put them in this list simply to demonstrate that language users are capable of making metaphorical connections, constructing folk etymologies, in spite of the historical facts. Presumably the personification of abstract vices (VICE$_1$) has led to phrases like *in the grip of a vice* meaning 'addicted to depravity', thereby creating possible Grounds for a metaphorical connection. LEAF and CRANE seem equally capable of metaphoric reawakening, as the Grounds of comparison involving shape are relatively salient. These might be dubbed Sleeping metaphors.

There is no clear line on the continuum of Inactive metaphors between Sleeping and Tired. Even so, SQUEEZE$_2$ appears more likely than any of the previous examples to involve or evoke reference to the original metaphor, with Grounds supplied by the MONEY = LIQUID metaphorical equation. The same is true for CUT$_2$. Even in popular journalism, not the most metaphorically sensitive stylistic register, it seems that CUT$_2$ can easily evoke CUT$_1$. At least it could for the writer of these phrases stemming from the original Vehicle: *Nigel Lawson's **axe**, **deep** financial **cuts***. *Axe* and *deep* improve the chances of CUT$_2$ evoking a double reference, and the perception of similarities or analogies involving these two referents.

Fox, my final example, may be the most likely to involve a sense of double reference. So it could be regarded as a clichéd metaphor, near the border of the lexicon, though still inside it. These last three examples I shall label Tired metaphors. (Note that *fox* also has a second metaphorical meaning, 'an attractive young woman'.)

To consider, in more detail, how Dead metaphors differ from Inactive (Tired and Sleeping) metaphors, and how they in turn differ from Active creative ones consult Table 1.1. Inactive metaphors, because their Topic and/or Grounds are relatively fixed by habit or convention, might be substituting for other more literal terms, e.g. *rat* substitutes for 'disloyal'.

33

*Table 1.1* Dead, Inactive and Active metaphors

|  | *Dead* | *Inactive* | *Active* |
|---|---|---|---|
| Topic | Is referred to through a fixed meaning of the former V-term | Is referred to directly through a second conventional and fixed meaning of the V-term | Is referred to indirectly via the Vehicle; has no fixed meaning or predictability |
| Vehicle | If still available wired in parallel with the Topic; difficult to evoke | Available, but will be wired in parallel under normal processing; capable of being evoked | More available and more strongly evoked than the Topic, because wired in series with the Topic |
| Grounds | Only in exceptional circumstances can they be recreated | May be perceived in the right circumstances; incorporated in the Topic concept, so predictable | Will be perceived or created, and highly unpredictable because context-dependent |
| Lexicon | Regarded as homonyms | Regarded as polysemes | No lexical relationship |
| Examples | *pupil* referring to a student | *crane* referring to lifting machine | "His *tractor* of blood stopped thumping. / He held five *icicles* in each hand" (Charles Causley, in Larkin 1973: 495) |

To put it another way, their word-forms represent two senses which are, as it were, wired "in parallel". It is possible to reach the conventionalized secondary meaning without going through the Vehicle concept, the primary meaning.[3] By contrast, Active metaphors for which no second meaning is listable in the dictionary, have to be interpreted via the Vehicle concept, or at least this concept has to be "switched on"; they can be thought of as being wired "in series". The difference between Dead and Inactive metaphors is that the Dead ones are perceived by language users as homonyms, as though there are no wires connecting them at all, no possible Grounds for a metaphor, e.g. PUPIL$_1$ and PUPIL$_2$. But with Inactive metaphors the metaphorical connections are in place and may be switched on, in which case the user perceives the word as polysemous.

Active metaphors are especially context-dependent for the Grounds they generate; above all they are dependent on the interaction of the Vehicle and the particular Topic being referred to, and their Grounds will consequently be variable according to this context.

## ■ EXERCISE

*How would you interpret these two metaphors?*

(a)   *The kidneys are the body's **sewers**.*

(b)   *a psychologist who threads the foul **sewers** of human despair*

I imagine the interpretations of these Active metaphors will be quite different, even though they share the V-term *sewers*. I guess (a) might be interpreted in terms of the function of the kidney in eliminating waste, whereas (b) is more likely to give a meaning to do with the evil and revolting aspects of the subconscious.

When interpreting Active metaphors, various associations of the Vehicle are selected on the basis of the Topic or surrounding co-text. This process could be called not only Active but <u>Interactive</u>: as the Topic differed in (a) and (b), so did the interpretations. With Sleeping/Tired metaphors, however, the Grounds are less variable, so much so that it is difficult to distinguish them from the Topic. If, for instance, the Tired metaphor *a fox* is used to refer to 'a cunning person' then this Topic incorporates the feature [cunning], the Ground for the original metaphor.

## 1.8.2. Degrees of conventionality: semantics or pragmatics

This is a convenient point to consider the word "conventional" in my working definition, which I have used quite liberally throughout this section. (Sadock (1979) highlighted the importance of conventionality, and much of the following discussion reflects his views.) Despite objections (see Kittay 1987: 88–90), I make an equation between the literal and the conventional. The bottom line is, of course, the fact that conventional classification involves the same process of feature-matching as takes place in metaphor. In addition, the previous paragraphs have shown that language items are used with different degrees of conventionality: entirely Dead metaphors and Sleeping metaphors have a second conventional meaning, whereas with Tired metaphors the convention linking form and meaning is slightly less well established. With Active metaphors the referent of the V-term is entirely unconventional.

It is interesting to place our discussion of conventionality in the framework of the distinction between semantics and pragmatics. One can explain this distinction as follows: what a sentence means (its decoded sense) is the domain of semantics, and what a speaker means by uttering it in context is the domain of pragmatics. Looking back to Figure 1.1, it's clear that what a sentence means, semantic meaning, will depend upon the conventional meanings of the coded items in the text, (D), and will more or less correspond to the propositional form, (C). But what a speaker means or intends by uttering a sentence, pragmatic meaning, will have more to do with the speaker's thought, (B).

Allow me an anecdote. A friend of mine in South-east Asia applied for a passport and bureaucratic procedures were causing a lengthy delay. When she visited the office to check the progress of her application an official offered to speed things up if she paid a bribe. Angry, she wrote to the official's superior accusing the official of corruption. A few days later the official visited her and asked her to write another letter withdrawing her accusation. Towards the end of the conversation he said, "You have two beautiful children. I see them every day on their way to school." In this example, working out the semantics of the two sentences by decoding only goes a small way towards telling us what the speaker wished to convey by their utterance. First of all there is the problem of establishing the referents of *you*, *I* and *them*, since until we do this the propositional form, (C), will be incomplete. But, more important, we have to account for the fact that in this context the utterance of these sentences is unlikely to be a compliment; even less likely to count simply as an assertion which conveys information; and almost certainly counts as a threat. Here, then, there is a clear case of a wide distinction between the coded sentence meaning, or even the full proposition, and the utterance meaning. There is no convention which says *You have two beautiful children. I see them every day on the way to school* means 'I will harm your children if you do not do as I say.' To reach the speaker's thought, (B), a great deal of pragmatic inferencing work is required. In the same way there is no convention which says that "icicles" refers to fingers, in the line from Charles Causley.

On the other hand, there are cases in which utterance meanings become predictable and relatively conventionalized. In many contexts the grammatical structure *Can you . . . ?* counts as a request for action rather than as a question about the hearer's ability. One could almost say that there are now two possible sentence meanings to be selected according to context, just as there are two possible lexical meanings to choose from with our pairs of metaphorically related items CRANE$_1$ and CRANE$_2$, etc. In such cases of polysemy in the code (Kittay 1987: 106–13) the role of pragmatics is reduced to simple disambiguation.

■ **EXERCISE**

*What is the most obvious meaning of the noun phrase* orange juice*? What else could it possibly mean? Compare it with a similar phrase* baby milk.

Conventionalization affects phrases as well. For example the semantics of the phrase *orange juice* only give us a vague meaning. In most contexts, with an appropriate stress pattern, however, the phrase has now become conventionalized as meaning 'juice made from oranges' rather than 'juice which is orange in colour' or 'juice used for feeding orange trees'. *Baby milk*, on the other hand, has a different conventionalized meaning!

At all levels from lexis to sentence grammar, there is no clear and watertight division between semantics and pragmatics (Leech 1983: 24–30). Grammatical structures and vocabulary have their meanings adapted to pragmatic constraints, and non-conventional uses of language, in our case metaphors, can achieve a kind of conventionality and literalness through Lexicalization. Frequent identical pragmatic interpretations cause a movement across the boundary from the domain of pragmatics into the code, the domain of semantics.

## ■ EXERCISE

*What do you think is the most likely response, (i), (ii) or (iii), to the following metaphorical statements?*

    *(a)    Virginity is a frozen asset.*
    *(b)    The past is a foreign country.*

*(i) Yes it is. (ii) No it isn't. (iii) I see what you mean.*

The degree to which metaphors have been conventionalized and Lexicalized into the semantics of the language can perhaps be measured, by considering whether the metaphorical statement can be agreed with/denied or questioned. Active metaphors are not open to agreement or rebuttal. "No it's not" and "Yes it is" appear to be inappropriate responses to metaphors (Sadock 1979: 54). Providing that the hearer recognizes that the statement is a metaphor, and not a lie, the appropriate response to a metaphor like (b) is more likely (iii) than (i) or (ii). Similarly, putting metaphors in question form seems pointless. "Is the past a foreign country?" is a nonsensical question, because the answer would, by definition, be "No."

However, even slightly Inactive or familiar metaphors often do give information which can provoke an affirmative or negative response. I would predict for instance that more readers would accept (i) and (ii) as possible answers to (a) because *asset* is a rather Tired metaphor, so it is obvious what the modification *frozen asset* means, quite apart from its suggestion of sexual frigidity. Inactive metaphors are open to agreement, negative questions and yes–no questions, as for example:

    (6)   The hours **dragged** by while we waited for the plane.
           Yes they certainly did.

(7)    Didn't the hours **drag** by as you waited for the plane?
(8)    Did the hours **drag** by as you waited for the plane?

This suggests that metaphors of this syntactic kind can be subjected to the following tests in the following order to determine their conventionality: the agreement test (cf. (6)); the negative-question test (cf. (7)); the yes–no question test (cf. (8)). The more tests they pass the more conventional they are.

### 1.8.3. Summary

Metaphors are constantly being coined to meet the demands of experience on language, either obviously, through the process of metaphorical transfer, or less clearly through the narrowing or extending of senses. Such metaphors, over time, become relatively Inactive and less original, and if used frequently may become part of the lexicon of the language. So there is a scale of metaphors stretching from the Dead and Buried at one extreme, through the Sleeping and merely Tired, to the novel and original. This scale suggests that what were once unconventional metaphorical language uses can acquire new, conventional and lexical status, in time becoming less reliant on pragmatics and more incorporated in semantics. These semantic changes are only possible because speakers frequently introduce a gap, deliberately or not, between their thoughts and the conventional meanings of the propositions which interpret them, or the texts which express them.

## 1.9. CLINES OF METAPHORICITY

We have seen in this chapter that some language uses are more metaphorical than others. In fact we can diagram metaphoricity according to five clines (Figure 1.4).

(1) Approximative Similarity —————————————— Distant Similarity/Analogy

(2) Conventionality ————————————————— Unconventionality

(3) Marking ——————————————————————— No Marking

(4) Non-contradictoriness ————————————— Contradictoriness

(5) Explicitness ——————————————————— Inexplicitness

*Figure 1.4* Five metaphorical clines

In this chapter we have been exploring the cline of metaphoricity in terms of (1) degrees of approximation between a speaker's thought and the proposition expressed, and (2), diachronically, between the degrees of conventionalization of metaphors into the lexicon.

We can draw a crude semantic diagram (Figure 1.5) to indicate the distance between Topic and Vehicle on cline (1).

## ■ EXERCISE

*Which of the following metaphors are most distant and which least distant?*

(a)  *Thatcher was Reagan's lapdog.*
(b)  *Women who remain housewives turn into vegetables.*
(c)  *Life is a box of chocolates.*
(d)  *My father was a kind of taxi-driver.*

Example (d) seems like a fairly Approximative metaphor, since both *father* and *taxi-driver* are in the same semantic field for 'humans'. Example (a) is a relatively close Transfer metaphor as we only have to travel up through one node from the Vehicle semantic field 'animal' before descending to the Topic field 'human'. Example (b) is a slightly more distant Transfer, ascending through two nodes from 'plant' before going down to human. Example (c) is the largest distance, because we have to cross through the topmost node from the concrete artefact to the abstract, crossing the thick line indicating that this is an analogical Transfer or <u>Concretizing</u> metaphor.

### 1.9.1. From explicit comparison to open-ended metaphor

There are, however, three more important clines of metaphoricity as in Figure 1.4: (3), the extent to which the metaphor is marked; which only partly overlaps with (4), the extent of tension and contradictoriness in the

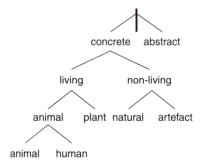

*Figure 1.5* A diagram of semantic distance

metaphorical expression; and (5), the degree to which its interpretation is made explicit by the co-text.

At one end of these third and fifth clines we have explicit comparisons:

> NSJL30   Could a planet, almost all of it rock and that mostly incandescent or molten, be alive? Before you dismiss this notion as absurd, think, as did the physicist Jerome Rothstein, about another large living object: **a giant redwood tree**. That is alive, yet 99 *per cent of it is dead* wood. Like[*] the earth it *has only a skin of living tissue spread thinly at the surface.*

This counts as a comparison because it uses the marker *like*, which turns it into a simile (from now on these markers are asterisked), and it is explicit because the T-term and G-term are provided.

At the other end of the third and fifth clines are the metaphors

(9)   Vancouver is a **cold** city.
(10)   He held five **icicles** in each hand.

Here it is not obvious that *cold* and *icicles* are operating metaphorically since they are not marked in any way as V-terms. Moreover, they do not provide any clues, in the immediate co-text, of what the Topic is, or what the Grounds of the implicit comparison might be. In (9) the lack of T-/ G-terms causes no problem as the metaphor is low on the scale of metaphorical unconventionality, having been Lexicalized with a second conventional meaning, 'unfriendly'. But (10) is high on the scales of both Inexplicitness and Unconventionality, which means its interpretation is much more open-ended.

Notice that the Marking and Contradiction clines are independent, since (9) and (10) are unmarked and non-contradictory, by contrast with the planet–redwood tree example (NSJL30) which is marked and non-contradictory. We can illustrate the contradictory end of the fourth cline by paradoxes such as *The child is father of the man.*

We have only considered briefly clines (3), (4) and (5). I reserve a fuller account until Chapters 6, 7 and 8, which deal in detail with the co-textual marking and specification of metaphors.

# 2

# METAPHOR AND THE
# DICTIONARY
## Root Analogies

## 2.1. INTRODUCTION

In Chapter 1 we established the important distinction between Active and
Inactive metaphors. We labelled the latter "Tired", "Sleeping" and
"Dead", and kept open the option that they might be "Buried". Inactive
metaphors become Lexicalized, that is acquire a second conventional
meaning and find their way into the dictionary. Chapters 2 and 3 are
concerned with these relatively Inactive and Lexicalized metaphors from
two aspects. Chapter 3 demonstrates how processes of word-formation
involve metaphor, and what effects the various kinds of word-class and
derivation have on metaphorical interpretation. Chapter 2 reports on
research into the ways in which certain basic analogies, first proposed by
Lakoff and Johnson (1980), can be seen as structuring the lexicon of
English. I give a guided tour of the metaphorical lexicon using a map
(Figure 2.1) of these analogies. I then comment on the importance of
metonymy as the basis for metaphor and on the interplay between the
various metaphorical lexical sets. In particular I illustrate the claim that
different Vehicles allow us to highlight different features of the same
Topic, using as a case study the diverse Vehicles for language found in
the English dictionary.

This chapter builds on the work of Lakoff and Johnson (1980), Lakoff
(1987), Johnson (1987), Lakoff and Turner (1989) and Sweetser (1990) and
gives evidence for their Experiential Hypothesis. This is based on the fact
that we have certain preconceptual experiences as infants, such as experiences of body movements, our ability to move objects, to perceive them as
wholes and retain images of them; and certain image-schemata which recur
in our everyday bodily experience, e.g. containers, paths, balance, up and
down, part and whole, front and back. The hypothesis claims that most
abstract concepts arise from these preconceptual physical experiences by
metaphorical projection (Lakoff and Johnson 1980: 267–8). So, for example, abstract concepts like amount are conceptualized by metaphorical
projection from the bodily experience of up and down, giving rise to a
number of Lexicalized metaphors:

(1)  a. The number of books printed each year keeps on going **up**.
   b. My income **rose/fell** last year.
   c. If you're hot, turn the heat **down**.
   d. He is **under**age.

(Lakoff and Johnson 1980: 14)

In the light of the lexical evidence for this hypothesis, Lakoff goes on in *Women, Fire and Dangerous Things* (1987) to develop an Experientialist philosophy, rejecting the Objectivist and Subjectivist paradigms. The problem with Objectivism is the independence assumption, namely:

> Existence and fact are independent of belief, knowledge, perception, modes of understanding, and every other aspect of human cognitive capacities. No true fact can depend on people believing it, on their knowledge of it, on their conceptualization of it, or on any other aspect of cognition.

(Lakoff 1987: 164)

The evidence for the powerful effect of metaphor on conceptualization leads us to abandon this naive Objectivism. It also allows us to avoid Subjectivism, because, after all, if our conceptual categories are based on universal infant experiences we share conceptual systems with our fellow humans.

Although Lakoff and his followers see metaphor as primarily a cognitive phenomenon, in this chapter (and book) I stress its linguistic and textual nature. Cognitive metaphors have to find expression in some medium, and when that medium is language the form of the expression will have important consequences for their recognition and interpretation. Lakoff and Turner (1989) have demonstrated convincingly that many poetic metaphors exploit conventional metaphors, but this exploitation generally depends upon rewording them in unconventional vocabulary.

For example there is a cognitive metaphor of the form HUMAN = PLANT (Analogy 2.1). However, when Shakespeare exploits this cognitive metaphor in Sonnet 73, he does so by using expressions which, unlike those listed in Analogy 2.1, are not conventionally used for instantiating it:

> That time of year thou may'st in me behold
> When yellow leaves, or none, or few do hang
> Upon those boughs which shake against the cold.

Similarly there exists a well developed cognitive metaphor DEVELOPMENT/ SUCCESS = MOVEMENT FORWARDS (Analogy 2.2), itself obviously related to ACTIVITY = MOVEMENT. So when Golding writes "The algebra was glue they were stuck in" (DV133) the word *stuck* is a perfectly conventional expression of this cognitive metaphor, but *glue* has no such secondary conventionality. It becomes quite mind-taxing to find any absolute Grounds of

---

### Analogy 2.1 **HUMAN = PLANT**

Kinds of humans are kinds of plants:

*cabbage, vegetable, couch potato, pansy, wallflower, weed, willowy* (B)

Parts of humans/humanity are parts of plants:

*flower (of youth), chaff, nutcase, root (of hair, nail, tooth), tendril (of hair), tuft (of hair cf. grass), (bone) marrow (cf. vegetable)*

Acting on humans is acting on plants:

*plant (an informer etc.), deflower, fell* (= knock down cf. *a tree), train (someone cf. a climbing rose), transplant (someone, organ cf. rice), crop/trim (hair cf. hedge, grass), uproot (oneself)*

The life cycle of humans is the life cycle of plants:

*put down roots, wilt, go to seed, crop (of school-leavers)*

especially, realizing human potential is flowering:

*blossom, bloom, budding, efflorescence* (B)

The qualities of (parts of) humans are the qualities of plants:

*barren, bushy, gnarled, green* (= immature, inexperienced), *luxuriant (hair cf. vegetation), seasoned (performer, campaigner cf. timber), dead wood*

in particular humans are fruits:

*gooseberry, peach, apple of my eye, lemon, ripe (old age), mellow, peeling (skin), peel off (clothes)*

---

Key

(x): x = part of a phrase in which the metaphor typically participates with this meaning, or an indication of the superordinate class such parts of phrases belong to, e.g. *launch (a newspaper)*

(= x): x = the T-term, e.g. *fire* (= dismiss from a post)

(cf. x): x = the Vehicle, Vehicular domain, Vehicular colligate, e.g. *(emotions) run high* (cf. *tide, river*)

(B) = Buried, e.g. SUCCESS = MOVEMENT FORWARDS *progress* (B)

similarity for such Concretizing metaphors: they depend on already established and accepted analogies. The Ground provided in the latter example – 'algebra' (Topic) resembles 'glue' (Vehicle) because both cause things to get 'stuck' (Grounds) – is in fact a *pseudo-ground*, simply restating the cognitive metaphor with a secondarily conventional expression.

My own metaphor for the cognitive metaphors which Lakoff, Turner and Johnson identify is the term <u>Root Analogy</u> (though Deleuze and Guatarri have also referred to these interlocking patterns as *rhizomes* (Lecercle 1990: 128–34)). Such cognitive metaphors resemble roots, which are

## Analogy 2.2 **DEVELOPMENT/SUCCESS = MOVEMENT FORWARDS**

If purposeful activity is movement in a direction, success is moving forwards:

*progress, advance, moving forward, make a go of, going concern, a lot going for him, make headway, a jump/leap (forward), move on, going places*

To develop or be more successful than others is to move ahead in a race:

*(rat) race, field (= the candidates cf. horses in a race), quick off the mark, head-start, run (in an election), a run for their money, get ahead, go-ahead, to leapfrog, outdistance, pull ahead, streets ahead, front runner, first past the post, keep up with, keep pace*

Contrast:

*get left behind, lag behind, backward (child)*

Distance moved is measure of success:

*to go far, to further (one's career), go a long way, he's come a long way, well on your way to*

Difficulty in succeeding is difficulty in moving forward:

*going is tough, mire, morass, quagmire, going through a sticky patch, stuck, uphill (task), (career developing) sideways, come full circle, circular argument, treadmill (i.e. no movement forwards)*

Preventing success is preventing movement forwards:

*brake, check (progress), thwarted at every turn, hamstrung*

or putting an obstacle ahead:

*up against (it etc.), come up against (e.g. a brick wall) obstacle, obstruct, stumbling block, pitfall*

To solve a problem/avoid failure is to pass over/through/round:

*get through/scrape through/pass (an exam), come/pull through (an illness), push through (legislation), skate/find a way round (a problem), sidestep/get around/skirt (a problem), lateral thinking, get over (an illness etc.), pushover (= easy)*

*Key*
(*x*): *x* = part of a phrase in which the metaphor typically participates with this meaning, or an indication of the superordinate class such parts of phrases belong to, e.g. *launch (a newspaper)*
(= *x*): *x* = the T-term, e.g. *fire* (= dismiss from a post)
(cf. *x*): *x* = the Vehicle, Vehicular domain, Vehicular colligate, e.g. *(emotions) run high* (cf. *tide, river*)

relatively unobtrusive, but which, in poetry, often develop shoots and flowers and become noticeable, not to say beautiful. Roots are alive and, for the most part, buried. This is true of Root Analogies as well. Burying, as I use the term, refers to a change of form which disguises the original morpheme expressing the analogy (see sections 1.8, 3.2.4). It includes processes like the use of forms from classical languages (*progress* in place of *advance*), archaisms (*brazen* rather than *brassy*), and changes of pronunciation (*raven* → *ravenous*), all of which bury the metaphor quite deeply; and changes of form by suffixation (*wooden, entangle, sheepish*), compounding (*frogman, bottleneck, honeymoon*), addition of prepositions/ adverbs to form phrasal verbs (*drone on, drink in, dredge up*), and incorporation into prefabricated phrases (*a hail of bullets, I haven't the foggiest idea, a binding agreement*), all of which work by attaching other morphemes to the metaphorical one. These latter are shallow kinds of burying, but nevertheless tend to undermine the morphemic status of the metaphorical expression, the V-term.

The vast majority of abstract vocabulary in the lexicon of English derives from conceptual metaphors, Root Analogies which are undetectable, extending deep underground because of classical borrowing/burying. Most parts of most roots are Buried. A thorough study of Root Analogies would have to take on the dimensions of an etymological dig, and would demand a book to itself, so in this chapter I shall concentrate on the kinds of Root Analogy which extend up to or near to the surface.

Most other Buried metaphors die because the original Vehicle no longer exists, but Root Analogies are still alive, and have the potential to grow vigorously. Their original Vehicles are, at least at the general level, so basic and universal to our experience, being concerned with objects, space, movement, orientation, and so on, that they have no chance of disappearing. And although in the majority of their uses, for example in spontaneous conversation, they are Tired or Sleeping, i.e. used unconsciously, they are constantly being reawakened both by poetry and even by carefully competent kitchen-garden prose.

There are various methodological problems involved in establishing the network of Root Analogies. It is all too tempting to operate on an *ad hoc* basis, positing Root Analogies according to the intuitions of the moment, without justifying them as important structural features of the lexicon (as seems to be the case with Lakoff and Turner's list (1989: 221–3)). The general principle which I adopt is to base my claims for the existence of a significant Root Analogy on the frequency of types of expression in the dictionary (Lakoff 1993: 205). The dictionary which I have used is the *Collins Cobuild English Language Dictionary*, whose list of headwords is, in itself, a reflection of the frequency of tokens of lexical items with a particular meaning, in a selected and balanced corpus. It goes without saying that I am highly indebted to the pioneering work of Lakoff and others in this field, and many of their intuitions are borne out by the lexicographical evidence.[1]

You may have noticed that the *bough* and *glue* examples cited above (pp. 42–3) represent two classes of metaphor from the point of view of abstraction of the Topic. The Shakespeare example is a Transfer metaphor, representing an analogy between one kind of first-order entity or thing, a human (Topic), and another kind of first-order entity or thing, a plant (Vehicle); whereas Golding's metaphor is Concretizing, conceiving a third-order abstract entity, achievement, in terms of a second-order entity or process, movement forwards. Although cognitively and epistemologically Concretizing metaphors are more important than those at the same level of abstractness, this chapter explores both.

## 2.2. METAPHORICAL PATTERNS IN THE ENGLISH LEXICON

To give an overview of these patterns let's take a look at Figure 2.1 (pp. 48–9), where each equation represents a significant number of lexical items in English (at least 6, sometimes up to 50). I do not have the space to give the lexical details for all these equations, but those spelt out in full elsewhere in this book are asterisked – exactly where is indicated in the index under Root Analogies.[2] The double horizontal line divides rows A, B, C and D, sets of Concretizing metaphors, from rows E and F, which are simply Transfer metaphors. As one moves down the table from rows A–C the Topics and Vehicles become more specific. Row D is to do with processes rather than things or states. We begin by considering row A.

### 2.2.1. General Reifying (Figure 2.1, row A)

The first and major step on which the metaphorical structuring of abstractions depends is reification. It is worth, at the outset, giving an indication of the kind of structuring which is achieved by this step, besides its paving the way for the more specific analogies which we list in rows B and C. The lexical items used to illustrate this structuring have been selected because they seem to apply very generally, that is to a large number of abstract entities.

Let's start at the top right-hand corner of Figure 2.1.

#### 2.2.1.1. Create, Destroy, Transform

Abstract entities are seen as concrete and integrated objects which can be created:

(2)   *create/shape/form (a plan, organization* etc.), *make (an offer, excuse, mistake, confession, mess,* etc., etc.), *construct (a theory, system,* etc.), *shape, structure, restructure*

However, they are subject to penetration, destruction and disintegration:

(3)   *infiltrate/penetrate (an organization* etc.), *(systems, institutions, theories) collapse, damage (economy, prospects), dash/shatter (hopes), devastate (economy), destroy, disintegrate, dissipate (time, money, energy), dissolve, erode, explode (a theory), fragmentation, melt away, break/shatter (the peace), smash (organization, system, career), go up in smoke, (put) strain on (the system)*

Even so, efforts can be made to prevent their destruction or decay:

(4)   *preserve, protect, renew (a relationship, contract,* etc.)

Their propensity to decay and disintegration will depend on their strength or weakness:

(5)   *brittle (character), delicate (problem), fragile/strong/feeble (argument, attempt,* etc.), *firm (evidence, decision), flaw/hole (in a theory, argument, plan), flimsy (excuse, evidence), hollow (promise, argument, threat), strong (beliefs, influence)*

## 2.2.1.2. Transfer, Handle, Possess, Impact

Like objects these abstract entities can be metaphorically handled, grasped, turned and manipulated:

(6)   *manipulate, handle (problem, situation, numbers), hold (opinions, feelings, qualifications, party, meeting, talks, interest, attention, your peace), invert (term, idea, snobbery), pick up (a habit, attitude, skill, illness, reputation), seize (opportunity), snatch/grab (sleep, opportunity, attention), take (offence, an interest, a bath,* etc., etc., etc.) . . .

They can then be possessed, or transferred/offered to others, or simply relinquished:

(7)   *possess (quality), keep (a promise, appointment, the peace), give (impression, life, right,* etc.), *present someone with (information, challenge, difficulty), proffer (advice, friendship, help), receive/d (reaction, attitude, impression,* etc.), *lend (support, quality), jettison (idea, chance), abandon (hope, activity,* etc.), *throw away (opportunity, chance)*

These abstract objects are, as it were, solid enough to have a physical impact on humans which they can protect themselves against:

(8)   *hard hit by, hit, impact on, leave its mark on, duck (responsibility), hedge against, protect, shield (against danger, from information)*

47

# ROOT ANALOGIES

*Figure 2.1* A map of Root Analogies in the lexicon of English

*Notes*: ⇔ indicates that the analogy is also reversed. * indicates that the lexical details of the Analogy are spelt out in full elsewhere in the book. Please see "Root Analogy" in the Index. The numbers in brackets refer to sources for these equations in the literature. See note 1 to Chapter 2.

| A | **GENERAL REIFYING** | | **PERCEPTION/SEEING** | **DIMENSION/SHAPE/PARTS** |
|---|---|---|---|---|
| B | **SPECIFIC REIFYING** | | **ABSTRACT QUALITY =** | FAILURE = DIVISION |
| | ORGANIZATION/SYSTEM = OBJECT | | **PHYSICAL** | MENTALLY DISTURBED = |
| | ORGANIZATION = MACHINE | | WORRY/RESPONSIBILITY = | DIVIDED/INCOMPLETE |
| | ORGANIZATION = SHIP* | | WEIGHT (2) | QUANTITY = DIMENSION |
| | SOCIETY = BUILDING | | SERIOUS/IMPORTANT = HEAVY | QUANTITY = WATER (FLOW) |
| | ORGANIZATION/SYSTEM = BUILDING | | CERTAIN/RELIABLE = SOLID | IMPORTANT = BIG (3) |
| | IDEA/WORDS = SUBSTANCE/OBJECT *(1) | | SANE/CALM = BALANCED (2) | IMPORTANT/POWERFUL = |
| | MIND = OBJECT/SUBSTANCE (1) | | SANE/NORMAL/CONVENTIONAL | CENTRAL (2) |
| | ARGUMENT/IDEA = BUILDING (1) | | = STRAIGHT | |
| | IDEA/WORDS/TEXT = CLOTH/CLOTHES* | | COMPREHENSIBLE = STRAIGHT | |
| | IDEA/INFORMATION/WORDS = LIQUID* | | TRUE/CORRECT = STRAIGHT | |
| | IDEA/INFORMATION/WORDS = FOOD/ | | JUSTICE/LAW = STRAIGHT (LINE) | |
| | DRINK* (1) | | GOOD (HONEST) = STRAIGHT | |
| | IDEA/EMOTION = OBJECT/SUBSTANCE* | | TRUE/HONEST = BARE/OPEN | |
| | EMOTION = LIQUID* | | BAD/WORTHLESS = WASTE | |
| | EXPERIENCE/ACTIVITY/EVENT | | BAD = DARK (3) | |
| | = LIQUID | | IMPRESSIVE/FAMOUS/REPUTED | |
| | QUALITY = MONEY/WEALTH | | = LIGHT | |
| | WORDS = MONEY* | | NERVOUS = TIGHT | |
| | RANK/VALUE/CHARACTER = METAL | | AFFECTIONATE = WARM (3) | |
| | AFFECTION ⇔ MONEY/WEALTH | | UNFEELING/HOSTILE = HARD | |
| | | | | |
| C | **PERSONIFYING ABSTRACT** | | | |
| | IDEA/EMOTION = HUMAN (ANIMAL) (1) | | MIND/EMOTION = BODY (2) | |
| | WORDS/LANGUAGE = HUMAN* | | EMOTION/IDEA = SENSE | |
| | ORGANIZATION/SOCIETY = BODY/ | | IMPRESSION (1) | |
| | HUMAN | | | |
| | | | | |
| D | **MATERIALIZING** | **COGNITION =** | **AFFECT = (OBJECT OF) PERCEPTION** | |
| | **ABSTRACT** | **PERCEPTION** | EXPERIENCE/EFFECT = FOOD | |
| | **PROCESS** | UNDERSTAND/ | RELATIONSHIP = MUSIC | |
| | | KNOW = SEE* (1) | EMOTION = TOUCH/FEELING | |
| | | OPINION = | EMOTION/EXCITED ACTIVITY = HEAT (3) | |
| | | PERSPECTIVE | EMOTION = BOMB | |
| | | UNDERSTAND = | EMOTION = LIGHT/COLOUR | |
| | | PENETRATE | EMOTION = WEATHER* | |
| | | | EMOTION/EXCITEMENT = ELECTRICITY | |
| | | | ANTAGONISM = FRICTION | |
| | | | | |
| E | **PROCESS =** | **SYNAESTHESIA** | **ACTIVITY = SPECIFIC** | |
| | **PROCESS** | SIGHT = TOUCH (3) | **ACTIVITY** | |
| | | SOUND = SIGHT | ACTIVITY = PLAYING (CARDS) | |
| | | SIGHT = SOUND | ACTIVITY = PERFORMANCE (3) | |
| | | | ACTIVITY/WORK = AGRICULTURE | |
| | | SOUND = LIQUID | ACTIVITY = SHOOTING | |
| | | LIGHT = LIQUID | ACTIVITY = FIGHT | |
| | | | WEATHER = HUMAN ACTIVITY | |
| | | | (/QUALITY) | |
| | | | | |
| F | **OBJECT = OBJECT** | | **OBJECT = HUMAN** | |
| | WORDS = MONEY | | OBJECT = ANIMAL     OBJECT/SUBSTANCE = HUMAN | |
| | TRAFFIC = BLOOD/LIQUID | | MACHINE = HUMAN     LANDSCAPE = HUMAN BODY* | |
| | MONEY = BLOOD/LIQUID | | STATE/COUNTRY = HUMAN/BODY | |
| | MONEY = FOOD | | BUILDING = BODY     BODY PART = HUMAN | |
| | COLOUR = PLANT | | | |

48

| PLACE/SPACE, PROXIMITY | ORIENTATION | TRANSFER, HANDLE, POSSESS, IMPACT | CREATE, DESTROY, TRANSFORM |
|---|---|---|---|
| IDEA/SUBJECT = PLACE | FUNCTIONING/ACTIVE = UP* | | |
| STATE/SITUATION = PLACE (3) | FUNCTIONING/HAPPENING = ON | | |
| ACTIVITY = PLACE* (1) | HEALTHY/LIVING = UP (1) | | |
| TIME = (MOVEMENT THROUGH) SPACE (3) | EXISTING/HAPPENING = UP/ DOWN* | | |
| SPACE = TIME | CAUSE = DOWN/UP | | |
| | PITCH = UP | | |
| CONSCIOUSNESS/INTEREST = PROXIMITY | LOUD = UP | | |
| | CONSCIOUS/EXPRESSED = UP (1) | | |
| AFFECTION = PROXIMITY | CONSCIOUS/EXPRESSED = OUT | | |
| MEMBERSHIP/UNITY = PROXIMITY | HAPPY = UP (1) | | |
| | MORE = UP (1) | | |
| CORRECTNESS/ACCURACY = PROXIMITY | GOOD (QUALITY/MORALITY) = UP (1) | | |
| | ACHIEVEMENT/SUCCESS = UP | | |
| SIMILARITY = PROXIMITY | BASIC/ELEMENTARY = DOWN | | |
| | CERTAIN/COMPREHENSIBLE = DOWN (1) | | |
| | CONTROL = UP (1) | | |
| | POWER = UP | | |
| | IMPORTANCE/STATUS = UP (1) | | |
| | IMPORTANT/GOOD = FIRST | | |

**ANIMIZING**             **RELATIONSHIP, CONTROL**      **LIFE, SURVIVAL**

ABSTRACT = ANIMAL
INFORMATION = QUARRY/PREY
IDEA/EMOTION/WORDS = LIVING THINGS
IDEA/EMOTION = PLANT (1)

**CHANGE = MOVEMENT**
CONTROL = HANDLE/OWN      CHANGE = MOVEMENT (3)
FREEDOM = SPACE TO MOVE/MOBILITY
CAUSE = LINE/LINK/CONNECTION (2)
INFLUENCE = PRESSURE/MARK

**PROCESS = MOVEMENT FORWARDS**
LIFE = PATH        PURPOSE = DIRECTION (3)
DEVELOPMENT/SUCCESS = FORWARD* (3)
THINKING/BELIEVING = WALKING/TRAVELLING

**SPECIFIC ACTIVITY = SPECIFIC ACTIVITY**     **ACTIVITY/PROCESS = MOVEMENT**
COMPETITION = WAR/VIOLENCE        ACTIVITY/PROCESS = MOVEMENT FORWARDS
SPEAKING/ARGUING = WAR/FIGHTING* (1)    ACTIVITY = PATH      ACTIVITY = VOYAGE*
SPEAKING/WRITING = (BALL) GAME*      COMMUNICATION = MOVEMENT/TRAVEL (1)
                             WRITING/SPEAKING = WALKING/RUNNING*

**HUMAN = LIVING THING**             **HUMAN = INANIMATE THING**
HUMAN = SUPERNATURAL/MYTHICAL BEING     HUMAN = FOOD*    HUMAN BODY = EARTH*
HUMAN = ARMY      HUMAN = PLANT* (3)      HUMAN = MACHINE/IMPLEMENT* (3)
HUMAN = ANIMAL      HUMAN = BIRD             HUMAN(S) = BUILDING
                                    CROWD/HUMANS = LIQUID
                                    HUMAN = CLOTH/MATERIAL
                                    HUMAN = VALUABLE OBJECT/COMMODITY

### 2.2.1.3. Place/Space, Proximity

If two abstract entities are concretized then they have positions in space relative to each other, can be separated/grouped, and can replace, interact or combine with each other in various ways:

(9) *pattern, group (of companies), interface, intersperse, gather (strength, courage, thoughts), sift (through the evidence, etc.), sort out (a problem), exclude (from calculation, etc.), in place of, replace, incorporate (group, system, area), intertwine, mesh, mix/mixture (feelings, etc.), amalgamate, forge (links, ties)*

### 2.2.1.4. Dimension/Shape/Parts

As objects these reified abstractions have centres and peripheries:

(10) *central, core (of a problem), frills, fringe, edge (of war)*

They can be divided into parts:

(11) *part of, piece (of luck), portion, sector (of the economy), shred (of evidence, proof, excuse, truth), chunk, layer (of ritual, meaning)*

possess dimensions:

(12) *big, colossal, enormity, immense, huge, little (chance, bit of luck), small (task, problem, business)*

and changeable shapes:

(13) *distort, contort, elastic (ideas, policies), (facts, punishment) fit (theory, description, crime), mould (industry, character, behaviour, etc.)*

### 2.2.1.5. Perception/Seeing

First-order entities are subject to visual perception:

(14) *aspect, appearance, (problems) loom, disappear, appear, mirror, obliterate (memories), display, demonstrate, exhibit*

And there is the possibility that they may be either present or absent in the visual field, be lost and found:

(15) *(the fact) emerges, find (time, money), lose, overlook (facts), seek (peace, revenge, answer, help, advice, etc.), recover/y (ability, health, state of mind, etc.)*

## 2.2.2. Specific Reifying (Figure 2.1, row B)

Turning to Row B on the left we can see the most frequent lexically represented specific categories of reified abstractions. Moving along the row, we notice the specific lexical set equations in which physical properties can figure as abstract qualities. Since physical qualities depend upon perception, these are below Perception/Seeing in row A. Similarly, the next group of analogical equations depends on Vehicles to do with dimensional properties of objects, and their capacity for division into parts. The next two sets of equations can be linked respectively to the notion of Place/Space and Proximity. Proximity and Orientation (Lakoff and Johnson 1980: 14–21) both provide a rich source of metaphorical lexis.

The fact that orientations like up and down are multivalent in the Topics to which they can be attached gives opportunities for metaphorical mixing and confusion.

## ■ EXERCISE

*A news article about the drunken behaviour of a cricket star, Ian Botham, contained the following verbatim eyewitness report:*

DM3   *"He collapsed and yelled 'get me a fucking whisky'.*
       *"The barman asked him to* **keep** *his language* **down***, as the bar was full of families . . .*
       *"Botham told Marcus Underwood to 'get me some fucking sandwiches'.*
       *"Again the barman asked him [Botham]* **to lower the tone of his language***."*

*What two metaphorical equations involving* UP *as Vehicle are being confused here?*

Two idiomatic expressions are mixed in this news report, *lower the tone* and *lower the volume*. They, of course, plug into the GOOD (MORALITY/QUALITY) = UP and the LOUD = UP equations.

### 2.2.3. Animizing and Personifying metaphors (Figure 2.1, row C)

So far we have been considering metaphorical sets which involve or depend on the Concretizing of abstract entities as substances/objects and their qualities. Row C catalogues the major sets of equations in which abstract entities are represented not simply as concrete, but as animate and human.

When considering reification we noted the general categories of metaphor which were made available to structure our cognition of abstracts. We can see how the animation and personification of abstracts is generally exploited in equivalent ways.

### 2.2.3.1. Life, Survival

Looking at the right-hand end of row C we can see the personifying category Life/Survival which is equivalent to, and so below, the reifying Creation/Destruction.

Abstract entities, conceived in terms of human life, both live and grow:

> (16)   *life (of a government,* etc.), *lifeblood, (an abstract thing or process) spawns (another), develop, feed, (economic) growth*

and need a shelter or house:

> (17)   *live (in memory), (abilities, qualities) reside in, protected, exposed, sheltered (existence, life)*

and can undergo attack, injury and death and its consequences/after-effects:

> (18)   *hurt (chances, government, country), emasculate, kick (a habit), (relationships) suffer, poison (a relationship, situation), (a) casualty (of), on its last legs, kill (an activity, process), exterminate, stillborn (action), stifle* (= smother, *an activity), suffocate (a company, business), death (of a custom, institution), deathblow/death-knell (of a plan, project, experiment), dying (tradition), fatal (to the enterprise), resurrect/revive (an activity, play), mourn for, post-mortem, graveyard, ghost of a (smile, chance), haunted (by worries)*

### 2.2.3.2. Relationships, Control

Moving along row C the next general category has to do with Relationship and Control (Sweetser 1990: 38), possibly equivalent to Transfer, Handle and Possess. Most noticeably, relationships between abstracts can be personified as human feelings/relationships:

> (19)   *relationship (between* x *and* y), *(a) rival (bid, plan,* etc.), *a stranger/no stranger to, subordinate to, subservient to, twin (ideas), support, help, meet (need, situation, death), welcome with open arms (situation, idea), court (disaster, punishment, death,* etc.), *marriage, married to (an activity), prostitute (talents, beliefs), kiss of life/death (to industry), devoted to, enamoured of, remorseless*

and interactions:

> (20)   *disturb, enrich, herald, lead to, ushers in* (state, activity), *(fate, luck) smiles, (an answer) stares you in the face, evade, avoid, give (an activity, subject) a rest*

Interactions between abstracts are seen as equivalent to speech acts and their perlocutionary effects:

(21)  *offer, invite (discussion, confidence, disbelief), (danger, trouble) threa-
tens/menaces, (events, facts) tell (you something), (a situation) demands
(action), undemanding (role, task), promise (to develop)*

More particularly the effect of or on an abstract entity is like the control or
government of humans:

(22)  *mistress (of a situation), reign (of terror), (a factor) dictates/governs
(another factor), muster/summon up (strength, energy, support)*

Moving further leftwards along row C are sets of equations representing the
Animizing and Personifying of abstracts. But towards the bottom of this
row are two equations identifying the Mind with the Body, an equation that
is central to the experiential hypothesis behind the theory of cognitive
metaphors. (Note that Johnson's (1987) book is called *The Body in the
Mind*.) They are located here in the figure under the Perception/Seeing
column, and in proximity to row D, which is concerned with relatively
Abstract Processes, those involving the mind, and their metaphorical representations as material or perceptual processes.

### 2.2.4. Materializing Abstract Process (Figure 2.1, row D)

In row D we begin, on the left, with consideration of how internal mental
processes, such as cognition and affection, thinking and emotion are metaphorically represented as perceptual processes.[3] These are central equations entailed by reification, since concrete objects are by definition
perceptible. The senser, perceptual process and phenomenon become an
analogy for thinker, cognitive process, and idea, or for feeling subject,
affective process, and emotion.

The first of these, COGNITION = PERCEPTION, is extremely prolific in terms
of lexis, especially the equation UNDERSTAND/KNOW = SEE (Analogy 2.3).

The individual equated sets in the next group, AFFECT = (OBJECT OF) PER-
CEPTION, obviously relate strongly to sets in row B, Specific Reifying and
ABSTRACT QUALITY = PHYSICAL, so that it is somewhat arbitrary where these
are placed. But since emotions are basically processes, any equations with
emotion as T-term have been placed here, and the nouns which are the V-
terms, like food and music, are salient in their perceptual qualities of taste
and hearing.

The next group, CHANGE = MOVEMENT, is purposely situated somewhere
below Handle, Transfer, Impact of row A, and Control, row C, since
movement is a common concept for all three sets of equations. The movement theme continues into row E, where the horizontal line disappears,
because the set of equations ACTIVITY/PROCESS = MOVEMENT often apply to
both material and non-material activities/processes.[4]

### Analogy 2.3 **UNDERSTAND/KNOW = SEE**

To understand or know is to see:

*(I) see (= understand), see (= experience), glimpse, see the light, see reason, see through, perceive/perception, get the picture*

Trying to understand/remember is looking (for):

*look at (= think about), examine, re-examine, regard, review (B), make out (what he's saying), survey, watch (a situation = beware), search (your mind for), searching (question), search me (= I don't know)*

Contrast:

*overlook (fault, bad behaviour)*

Something which is easy to understand is clear, i.e. transparent:

*clear, clarify, clarity, crystal clear, limpid (prose), transparent (situation, action, remark)*

Something difficult to understand is unclear, i.e. coloured/opaque:

*colours (judgement), opacity, opaque, unclear, diffuse*

Something easy to understand in detail is well defined, i.e. has a sharp narrow line or definite shape:

*definite, distinct, fine distinction, graphic (description), outline, profile, take shape, prominent (= well-known)*

Something difficult to understand or understood only partially is indistinct or shapeless:

*faint, blurred, indistinct, pale (into insignificance), shapeless, sketchy, can't make head or tail of something*

General and detailed understanding are broad and narrow respectively:

*sweeping, wide, wide-ranging, delicate/delicacy, narrow*

To give knowledge is to make a picture:

*paint a (gloomy) picture, portrait, portray, sketch*

To make knowledge available or direct attention to it you make it light:

*elucidate, enlighten, highlight, illuminate, cast/shed/throw light on (a subject), in the light of, spotlight (a problem etc.), reflect, reflection, newsflash*

Available knowledge is thus made visible:

*show forth, comes to light, dawns on (someone), dawn (of civilization), manifest, appear, screen (a candidate), show (= prove, i.e. cause to see*

= cause to know), *sketch/out* (*situation/argument*), *a picture of* (= idea, memory), *make a point of doing something* (= make it noticeable)

Knowledge/understanding that is unavailable/doubtful is obscured:

*hazy, murky, nebulous, obscure, obscurity, a shadow of a doubt, shadowy, pull the wool over someone's eyes, in a fog, cloud, the Dark Ages*

Cleverness in understanding/obtaining knowledge is brightness:

*bright, bright spark, brilliant, flash* (*of insight*), *sparkle* (*with wit* etc.)

Inability to understand is darkness:

*benighted, dim, dull, ?dense, ?thick* (= *light can't penetrate*)

Mental faculties are eyesight:

*blind, clear-sighted, focus attention, insight, in your mind's/the public eye, myopic, short-sighted, tunnel vision, blinkered*

---

*Key*
(*x*): *x* = part of a phrase in which the metaphor typically participates with this meaning, or an indication of the superordinate class such parts of phrases belong to, e.g. *launch* (*a newspaper*)
(= *x*): *x* = the T-term, e.g. *fire* (= dismiss from a post)
(cf. *x*): *x* = the Vehicle, Vehicular domain, Vehicular colligate, e.g. (*emotions*) *run high* (cf. *tide, river*)
(B) = Buried, e.g. SUCCESS = MOVEMENT FORWARDS *progress* (B)
? = doubtful, e.g. MONEY = BLOOD/LIQUID *?quid*

## 2.2.5. Process = Process (Figure 2.1, row E)

Unlike the previous sections in which Vehicles were generally less abstract than their Topics, rows E and F contain Transfer metaphors in which Vehicle and Topic belong to the same order of entity. Row E maps the metaphorical sets by which perceptual and material processes can be conceptualized as other kinds of processes. Besides the general Movement Vehicles on the right we notice to the left more Specific Activities as metaphors for Activity in general, which are substitutive symbols of the hyponymic kind. A move further to the left gives us sets where both Vehicles and Topics are specific. Following row E further to the left, beneath the perceptual sets of row D, is a group based on Synaesthesia, the mapping of one perceptual process on to another, of conceptualizing one sense in terms of another (Sweetser 1990: 36–7). The equations which represent sound and light as liquid are here since the Topics are perceptual processes and liquids are associated with touch.

## ■ EXERCISE

*White shirts are all too often splashed with loud colourful ties.*

*Can you explain how this sentence displays the various metaphorical equations under synaesthesia?*

The adjective *loud* depends upon the SIGHT = SOUND equation, and the verb *splashed* upon the LIGHT = LIQUID equation.

### 2.2.6. Object/Substance = Object/Substance (Figure 2.1, row F)

In row F we see metaphorically equated lexical sets whose Topics and Vehicles are both first-order entities. The most important are the categories with liquid (blood), food, human, animal, plant, machine/tool and building as Vehicle. In OBJECT = HUMAN we have Personification of objects, and in HUMAN = ANIMAL and HUMAN = OBJECT/SUBSTANCE we have less radical and more radical types of depersonification. In keeping with anthropocentric ideology, humans are the Topic in the majority of these metaphorical sets.

### 2.2.7. Categories of Root Analogy and preconceptual experience

Experientialist theory, remember, claims that metaphorical abstract concepts arise from our preconceptual physical experiences as infants. It is easy enough to relate this theory to the metaphorical Vehicles in our map (Figure 2.1). The notion of an 'object' itself (rows A, **Reifying**, and B, ABSTRACT = OBJECT/SUBSTANCE) and the notions of space and position (rows A and B, Space, **Place**, **Proximity**, **Orientation**) seem to depend for their development on the sense impressions (row C, MIND = BODY, row D, COGNITION = PERCEPTION) and the motor activities of infants (row D, PROCESS = MATERIAL PROCESS, CHANGE = MOVEMENT). A baby's interactions with objects presumably involve first sensing them (row D, COGNITION = PERCEPTION) and then dropping them, manipulating (CONTROL = HANDLE) and moving them (rows C and D, ACTIVITY/CHANGE = MOVEMENT). When the baby becomes mobile she will move towards objects (row D, ACTIVITY/CHANGE = MOVEMENT) and this movement forwards becomes a prototype of purposeful and successful action (row D, PURPOSE = DIRECTION, SUCCESS/DEVELOPMENT = MOVEMENT FORWARDS). And when capable of standing and turning around, she can change her orientation to them (row B, **Orientation**). The child's sense experiences or manipulation of objects/substances will give her a feeling for their parts (row A, **Parts**, **Dimensions**) and their physical properties (row B, ABSTRACT QUALITY = PHYSICAL QUALITY). Even before this, from the experience of bodily processes of ingestion develops the idea that the body is a discrete object with an inside and outside (row C, Mind = Body, Affect = Perception). Still more basically, the experience of the original confinement in the womb and the birth into a less constricting world is an important lesson in freedom (row D, FREEDOM = SPACE TO MOVE). Apparently these interactional physical experiences are sufficient to provide the basic Vehicular structure on which metaphorical cognition and the metaphorical lexicon are built.

## 2.3. COMMENTARY ON THE MAP

### 2.3.1. Metonymy and metaphor

Earlier we noted the distinction between metonymy and metaphor. However, one fact which emerges from my attempt at a schematic overview of metaphorical lexis is the metonymic basis of many metaphors. Metonymy provides foundations on which the metaphorical edifice is built. Among the most obvious Root Analogies with metonymic origins are the following:

- ACTIVITY = PLACE, based on the metonymy of place for activity, inherent in phrases like *I spent the afternoon watching Wimbledon* (see Analogy 2.4).

## ■ EXERCISE

*Explain the metaphoric/metonymic basis of the ambiguity in the phrase:* the office of the prime minister.

This metaphor depends upon the metonymy of occupations being associated with the building/office in which the employee works.

- IDEA/INFORMATION/WORDS are grouped together as one Topic because of the effect–cause metonymy – the physical form expressing the ideas/information comes to stand for the mental process which lies behind them, giving rise to *erase (thoughts, feelings), make a mental note.*
- MORE = UP and other orientational metaphors are based on the cause–effect metonymy: the more things one has in a pile the higher it becomes.
- TIME = (MOVEMENT THROUGH) SPACE: the measurement of time is often in spatial terms, so that phrases such as *twenty past the hour* can be interpreted as meaning literally 'when the minute hand of the clock has gone a distance equivalent to twenty minutes past the 12'.
- CONSCIOUSNESS/INTEREST = PROXIMITY is based on cause–effect metonymy – if something is close we are more likely to be conscious of it, and register its existence.
- MIND/EMOTION = BODY; EMOTION/IDEA = SENSE IMPRESSION: both these metaphors are influenced by effect–cause metonymies: emotions have corresponding physical effects on the experiencer, e.g. *flinch*, and this effect then comes to represent metaphorically the emotion which caused it.

---

### Analogy 2.4 **ACTIVITY = PLACE**

Activity is conceptualized as a place:

> *take place, take someone's place, resort to* (cf. *a resort*), *in the last resort, situation* (= *what is happening,* cf. *of a building*), *slot* (*in a timetable*), *sphere* (*of activity*), *spot* (*on TV*), *a post* (*job*)

This place has boundaries:

> *on the verge* (*of doing something*), *near to, on the threshold* (*of an activity*), (*within*) *the confines/framework* (*of*), *draw the line at*

It is possible to move into/around an activity:

> *enter/venture/rush* (*into an activity*), (*one process*) *leads to* (another process cf. another place), *precede* (someone *in a job/situation*), *shift* (*to do something else*), *know your way around/about* (*a job/situation*), *walk into* (*a job*)

cause others to move into an activity:

> *talk/frighten someone into/out of* (doing something)

occupy a role or job:

> *occupy, occupation, seat/sit* (*on a committee*), *unseat, stay* (*in a job*), *stick with* (*an activity*), *install* (*yourself in a position*), *tenure* (= living in a building/holding a job)

leave off or move/stay out of an activity:

> *abandon, leave* (something *till later*), *leave off, pull out of, quit* (*job,* doing something), *a quitter, keep out of, run/shy away* (*from something*), *withdraw from* (an activity), *wriggle out of, in recess, retire, retreat, shrink from* (doing something)

exclude or remove from or be outside an activity/function:

> *exclude* (*from an activity*), *remove* (*from a post*), *replace* x *with* y, *external to, out of order*

include or trap in an activity:

> *tied* (*to a job, way of life*), *trap* (*someone into doing something*), *get sucked into*

have someone fill a job or leave it empty:

> *fill a post, full up, stopgap* (= temporary staff), *vacant/vacancy/vacate* (*job, position*), (*power*) *vacuum, void*

---

*Key*

(*x*): *x* = part of a phrase in which the metaphor typically participates with this meaning, or an indication of the superordinate class such parts of phrases belong to, e.g. *launch* (*a newspaper*)

(= *x*): *x* = the T-term, e.g. *fire* (= dismiss from a post)
(cf. *x*): *x* = the Vehicle, Vehicular domain, Vehicular colligate, e.g. (*emotions*) *run high* (cf. *tide*, *river*)

As well as metonymy, colligation, invoked in our definition, is important for us in establishing membership of analogical sets. In fact these colligational relationships are often the syntactic equivalents of general metonymic relationships like CAUSE (Subject) = EFFECT (Verb), ACTIVITY (Verb) = PLACE (Location Adverbial), CONTENTS (Subject/Object) = CONTAINER (Location Adverbial), etc. The main colligational or syntactic relationships which we depend on in the network are Subject–Verb, Verb–Object, Premodifier–Noun Head. For example with the HUMAN = ANIMAL category Subject–Verb gives us *purr*, *bleat*; Verb–Object gives us *groom*, *muzzle*; Premodifier–Noun Head give us *rabid*, *wild*.

### 2.3.2. Interplay: multiple determination

It should be obvious by now that Root Analogies do not operate in isolation, but form an interacting web. Individual metaphorical lexical items will sometimes realize more than one analogy. The following examples show the extent of the over-determination.

*Short-sighted* simultaneously manifests several analogies: TIME = (MOVEMENT THROUGH) SPACE (future = forward), QUANTITY = DIMENSION, UNDERSTAND/KNOW = SEE. The item *yoke* as in the phrase *the yoke of tyranny*, could be determined by WORRY/RESPONSIBILITY = WEIGHT, CONTROL = UP, HAPPY = UP, ACTIVITY/PROCESS = MOVEMENT FORWARDS, FREEDOM = SPACE TO MOVE/MOBILITY, PURPOSE = DIRECTION, SIMILARITY = PROXIMITY, HUMAN = ANIMAL. A problem or responsibility is imposed on you from above by the tyrant/superior who is in control. It weighs you down and makes you unhappy, forces you to do certain things and adopt the same (proximate) purposes (direction) as the rest of society, the other ox, restricts your freedom (for lateral movement) and treats you like an animal.

If my own term *Root Analogy* is at all apt this is because of multiple participation of this kind: IDEA/EMOTION = PLANT, CONSCIOUSNESS = UP, UNDERSTAND/KNOW = SEE, CAUSE = LINE/LINK/CONNECTION.

### ■ EXERCISE

*How might you connect the phrases* boiling with rage, steamed up, *and* simmer down *to Root Analogies for emotion, and knowledge?*[5]

The more elements of a lexical item that are open to morphemic interpretation, the more chances there are for the lexical item to participate in several metaphorical analogies simultaneously (cf. Lakoff and Turner 1989: 70). In the case of multiple-word idioms, for example, single lexical items whose individual words function as separate morphemes in a non-idiomatic context, one can often detect the multiplicity of Root Analogies: e.g. *in the saddle* CONTROL/POWER = UP, ACTIVITY/PROCESS = MOVEMENT FORWARDS (to instruct/advise = to guide), HUMAN = ANIMAL. Perhaps judgements of the quality of a metaphorical expression depend upon the number of Root Analogies which it instantiates.

### ■ EXERCISE

*The following proverbs can be interpreted because they plug in to some of the Root Analogies which are common in the lexicon of English. Can you show how?*

(a)   *Pride comes before a fall.*
(b)   *Look before you leap.*
(c)   *Don't put all your eggs in one basket.*
(d)   *A rolling stone gathers no moss.*

*Conversely the following pseudo-proverb seems (to me) uninterpretable, because it cannot be connected to the metaphorical concepts we operate with.*

(e)   *No leg is too short to reach the ground.*

*Why is this difficult to interpret (anomalous, funny?) while the reworking below seems understandable?*

(f)   *No arm is too short to reach above your head.*

### 2.3.3. Interplay: extensions

Besides individual lexis realizing multiple analogies, one lexical item can interact with others or one set with another. The next four sections will illustrate Extension, Opposition, Reversal and Diversification, as apparent in the dictionary. These kinds of interplay when realized in text are more fully discussed in Chapter 9.

We cannot avoid mentioning Extensions of metaphors in some of the lexis of Root Analogies. Firstly, analogies often provide lexically extended allegories which operate internally, nicely illustrated in this sequence of metaphors based on the analogy IDEA/EMOTION = HUMAN. Initially one might *invite* ideas or suggestions, then *welcome* them *with open arms, entertain* them, *flirt with* them, *embrace* them, *find* them *seductive, espouse* them and end up *wedded to* them, before one finally *distances* and *divorces oneself from* them!

The Root Analogies ACTIVITY = VOYAGE (Analogy 2.5), ORGANIZATION =

---

### Analogy 2.5 **ACTIVITY = VOYAGE**

Activity in general is conceptualized as movement. More specifically it is a voyage.

Starting an activity is starting a voyage:

*embark on, to launch, (get) under way*

The activity is to sail/voyage:

*plain sailing, sail through*

To have difficulties with an activity/life is to have difficulties sailing (since difficulties are likely to cause emotions, EMOTION = WEATHER):

*ride out (a period of difficulty cf. a storm), make heavy weather (of something), weather a problem, takes the wind out of your sails, (change, try a different) tack, on the rocks, rough (time, on someone)*

To impede/prevent an activity is to impede/prevent a voyage:

*marooned, a snag, put someone off their stroke, torpedo (plans etc.)*

If an activity/person fails then it/they are shipwrecked (ORGANIZATION = SHIP):

*founder, to be sunk, wreckage (of plan, policy, career etc.), (throw a plan) overboard, in deep water, will have to sink or swim, washed up (on the shore), a wreck, wreck (someone's chances)*

To keep it/them going is rescue/protecting the boat:

*lifeline, keep your head above water, rescue package, salvage (the situation), clutch at straws, any port in a storm, sheet anchor (cf. of marriage)*

The place/pattern of an activity is the sea/water:

*stream (classes in school, i.e. the place in which they try activities), tidal (activity = periodic), rough/uncharted/deep waters, in the wake (of something)* (TIME = (MOVEMENT THROUGH) SPACE)

The actors are sailors and their actions those of sailors:

*pilot (scheme), pirate (an invention), know/learn/teach someone the ropes, ?stick your oar in*

A related metaphor is humans are a ship:

*hulk, nervous wreck, nerve-wracking (B), to harbour (somebody), (people) sail (past)*

*Key*
(x): x = part of a phrase in which the metaphor typically participates with this meaning, or an indication of the superordinate class such parts of phrases belong to, e.g. *launch (a newspaper)*

(= x): x = the T-term, e.g. *fire* (= dismiss from a post)

(cf. x): x = the Vehicle, Vehicular domain, Vehicular colligate, e.g. *(emotions) run high* (cf. *tide, river*)

(B) = Buried, e.g. SUCCESS = MOVEMENT FORWARDS *progress* (B)

(x = x) = other Root Analogy applicable to the lexical item, e.g. EMOTION = HEAT *boiling with rage* (EMOTION = LIQUID)

SHIP (Analogy 2.6), EMOTION = WEATHER (Analogy 2.7), and EMOTION = LIQUID (Analogy 2.8) potentially represent an allegory: ships make voyages through liquid and are at the mercy of the weather. Further networks and tangles in the rhizomes of Root Analogies can be traced by following up the capitalized equations given in parentheses.

## 2.3.4. Interplay: oppositions

Besides these kinds of Extension we also note the tendency of analogical sets to form in opposed homologies. I have provided below some details of the EMOTION = LIQUID analogy (Analogy 2.8). It is worth comparing this with the IDEA/WORDS = SUBSTANCE/OBJECT category (Analogy 2.9), as the pair then form a binary Opposition. The interesting implication of the EMOTION = LIQUID metaphor is that emotions are more changeable than facts, which depends on exploiting the other metaphor CHANGE = MOVEMENT. So facts are *solid* and can be *grasped* and *passed on*, whereas emotions are *fluid*, *flow* and *spread* like a liquid.

This binary opposition can turn into a ternary one, as strong emotions are conceptualized as gas, by combining allegorically with the EMOTION = HEAT analogy. Intense emotions, through heat (EMOTION/EXCITED ACTIVITY = HEAT)

---

### Analogy 2.6 ORGANIZATION = SHIP

*flagship, (newspaper) masthead*

Organizations are brought into existence and cease:

*launch, go under*

And have various people in degrees of power and activity on board:

*at the helm, figurehead, captain (of industry), run a tight ship, a passenger*

---

Key

(x): x = part of a phrase in which the metaphor typically participates with this meaning, or an indication of the superordinate class such parts of phrases belong to, e.g. *launch (a newspaper)*

### Analogy 2.7 **EMOTION = WEATHER**

Human affective processes are meteorological processes. The metaphor seems to work in two directions: either the emotion is itself weather; and/or the emotional effect is equivalent to the impression of weather on the senses, just as an emotional outburst in one person will have an emotional effect on others. In general it is conceived in terms of the air:

*atmosphere, emotional climate, barometer (of feeling)*

More especially emotions are kinds of wind, the greater the stronger:

*bluster, breezy* (contrast *stuffy*) (CHANGE = MOVEMENT), *gales (of laughter), gust (of anger* etc.), *temper is up* (cf. *wind*), *a rough (time* cf. *weather), calm, in the doldrums*

Violent emotions are storms:

*fulminate/thunder, storm (of laughter), stormy (relationship), storm in a teacup* (QUANTITY = DIMENSION), *tempestuous (relationship), black as thunder, weather a problem* (cf. *storm*), *(political) hurricane*

cloud and sun:

*bask, sunny (disposition), dark days, gloom, gloomy, blot, cloud*

temperature:

*sultry, raw* (EXPERIENCE/EFFECT = FOOD), *frosty*

The response to weather gives us an analogy for the emotional response to one's situation in life or fortune:

*fair-weather friends, storm, to weather, ill wind, it never rains but it pours, keep it for a rainy day, storm clouds, find out which way the wind is blowing, sunny prospects*

---

Key

(*x*): *x* = part of a phrase in which the metaphor typically participates with this meaning, or an indication of the superordinate class such parts of phrases belong to, e.g. *launch (a newspaper)*

(cf. *x*): *x* = the Vehicle, Vehicular domain, Vehicular colligate, e.g. *(emotions) run high* (cf. *tide, river*)

(*x* = *x*) = other Root Analogy applicable to the lexical item, e.g. EMOTION = HEAT *boiling with rage* (EMOTION = LIQUID)

or other means, produce a change of state, evaporation: *evaporate, seethe/ seething, boil/-ing, let off steam, steamed up, safety-valve, volatile, ferment*. Or the liquid may simply be agitated so much that it interacts with gas/air: *froth, in a lather, bubbly, effervescence*.

### Analogy 2.8 **EMOTION = LIQUID**

Feeling is represented metaphorically as the movement of water:

> *agitated, churn up, stir up (trouble* etc.), *(an event) causes a stir, (moods, feelings, ideas) stir, upset, ruffled* (cf. *lake), onrush/surge, tide, ripple, wave (of sympathy, alarm, panic,* etc.), *vortex* (= whirlpool)

To control emotion is to remain unmoved:

> *calm* (cf. *sea), unruffled* (cf. *surface of lake), pour oil on to troubled waters, still waters run deep*

The intensity of the emotion is represented by the volume/height of the liquid (QUANTITY = DIMENSION):

> *emotions are running high, (emotions) rise, (feelings) swell* (cf. *sea), (feelings) subside* (cf. *water), full*

The expression of emotion is a flow of feelings (CONSCIOUS/EXPRESSED = OUT):

> *exude, express* (cf. *milk from the breast), pour out (feelings, thoughts, your heart to someone), outpouring, brim over, effusion, flood (of emotion), flow, gush (of feeling), gushing, (feelings) overflow, outlet (for feelings)*

Contrast:

> *dam up*

Lack of emotion is absence of water:

> *arid, dry* (= emotionless), *drained, ebb away*

Too much emotion produces a change from solid to liquid:

> *sloppy* (= sentimental), *soppy* (B) (cf. *sopping), slushy (novel* etc.)

The effect of emotion on humans is analogous to the effect of liquid:

> *engulf, buoy up, overwhelm/-ing/-ed by (feelings), infuse (with hope), inject* (ORGANIZATION/SOCIETY = BODY/HUMAN), *drunk with (emotion, sensation, experience), test the waters* (= find out what people feel)

The strength or other qualities of emotions are those of liquids:

> *undiluted (feelings), water down, corrosive, corrode, deep/profound (feeling, concern), vitriol/-ic*

*Key*

(x): x = part of a phrase in which the metaphor typically participates with this meaning, or an indication of the superordinate class such parts of phrases belong to, e.g. *launch (a newspaper)*

(= x): x = the T-term, e.g. *fire* (= dismiss from a post)

(cf. x): x = the Vehicle, Vehicular domain, Vehicular colligate, e.g. *(emotions) run high* (cf. *tide, river*)

(B) = Buried, e.g. SUCCESS = MOVEMENT FORWARDS *progress* (B)

(x = x) = other Root Analogy applicable to the lexical item, e.g. EMOTION = HEAT *boiling with rage* (EMOTION = LIQUID)

---

### Analogy 2.9 **IDEA/WORDS = SUBSTANCE/OBJECT**

Ideas can be communicated or expressed in various ways like objects being moved or transferred:

*direct (a remark), drop (a hint, remark, brick, clanger), (name-) dropping, release (info), throw (a remark, question), fling out (an answer), pass (sentence, remark), lay out (ideas), share (joke, news), give (a promise, undertaking, etc., etc.), pass (the word), take back (what you said), second-hand (idea, joke), exchange/interchange (of ideas)*

So expression then becomes placing:

*put (it that way), lay down (the law, rules), lay (a proposal before), pose (a question), place (an advert), put (your case, point of view), put it (to someone), put down (on paper)*

Ideas/words can be actively sought after/received (CONTROL = HANDLE/OWN):

*catch (what someone says), pick up (point, topic), gather (information), cull, extract, find (an answer), prise (info out of someone) (TRUE/HONEST = BARE/OPEN), pry, retrieve/retrieval, accept, grasp, get hold of the wrong end of the stick, store away (facts)*

mentioned (touched), thought about or relied on (held):

*touch on (a subject), toy with (an idea), turn over in your mind, hang on to someone's words, hold (a belief)*

Whether they can be grasped or seen will depend on their degree of solidity, definition (cf. UNDERSTAND/KNOW = SEE) (CERTAIN/RELIABLE = SOLID):

*definite, (well) defined, definition, outline, distinct, hard/solid evidence, gel, tangible, palpable*

Contrast:

*fudge, intangible, morass, muddy, wishy-washy, woolly (ideas), woolly-minded*

---

*Key*

(x): x = part of a phrase in which the metaphor typically participates with this meaning, or an indication of the superordinate class such parts of phrases belong to, e.g. *launch (a newspaper)*

(x = x) = other Root Analogy applicable to the lexical item, e.g. EMOTION = HEAT *boiling with rage* (EMOTION = LIQUID)

### 2.3.5. Interplay: reversal

There is a tendency for metaphors to be reversed, so that the Topic and Vehicle roles are exchanged. This is not so surprising as far as row F is concerned. For example there is no reason why HUMAN BODY = EARTH cannot be reversed as LANDSCAPE = HUMAN BODY (Analogy 2.10), since, after all, these Vehicles and Topics belong to the same order of entity.

More surprising is the tendency for abstract Topics to be reversed so they become Vehicles. So under TRUE/CORRECT = STRAIGHT, we have *right, set the record straight, on the level*; but we also have *true* meaning 'straight', as in *the wall is true*, that is, perpendicular. And while JUSTICE = STRAIGHT as in *rights, square deal, even-handed* we also have margins which are *justified*. Other examples of reversal occur in TIME = (MOVEMENT THROUGH) SPACE: *an hour from, immediate (neighbour), light year*; SPACE TO MOVE = FREEDOM: *free-size*; COMMUNICATION = MOVEMENT: *communicating door*.

### 2.3.6. Metaphorical lexis and diverse structuring of concepts

The choice of metaphors in cases of Diversification has consequences for cognitive structuring and ideology, and also for syntactic relations. Given space one could provide a system diagram of the choices of Vehicle available for conceptualizing any particular entity, and try to explore the cognitive and grammatical consequences of the choice. However, one example will have to suffice.

If we assume that my taxonomy of Root Analogies above is complete we have, besides the more general IDEA/WORDS = SUBSTANCE/OBJECT, the following specific choices in conceptualizing language: WORDS = MONEY, IDEA/WORDS/TEXT = CLOTH/CLOTHES, IDEA/INFORMATION/WORDS = FOOD/DRINK, IDEA/INFORMATION/WORDS = LIQUID, WRITING/SPEAKING = WALKING/RUNNING, SPEAKING/WRITING = (BALL) GAME, SPEAKING/ARGUING = WAR/FIGHTING, WORDS/LANGUAGE = HUMAN.[6]

The first major choice in conceptualizing language is whether to emphasize that language is a discursive process or a static product. If the latter, we are more likely to conceptualize language/words according to IDEA/WORDS = SUBSTANCE/OBJECT, and in particular to choose WORDS = MONEY or IDEA/WORDS/TEXT = CLOTH/CLOTHES.

With WORDS = MONEY (Analogy 2.11) we are able to emphasize various characteristics of language: the token–type distinction; the value of words and its dependence on semantic relationships of difference/equivalence with other lexis in a system; the conventional nature of meaning – that the form/size of words is arbitrary and that they represent meanings by convention and agreement of society; that language is a social phenomenon and that (new) words can be created and achieve their value by circulating

## Analogy 2.10a **LANDSCAPE = HUMAN BODY**

Parts of the earth/landscape are parts of a human body:

arm (of land), backbone, bowels, brow, crown (of hill cf. head), face (of the earth), head (of a valley), foot (of a mountain), finger (of land), mouth (of cave, hole, river), neck (of land), shoulder (of a hill), heart (= centre), tongue (of land), ?fringe, ?leg of a journey

Parts or coverings of the earth are clothes:

belt, green belt, mantle (of snow, green), outskirts (of a town) (B)

The state/characteristic of a place is the state/characteristic or behaviour of a human:

bald, bare, denuded, gaunt, sterile, virgin (lands, forest), sleepy (place), dead (seaside resort), sprawling/straggling (village, town, etc.), placid, treacherous (ground), in/hospitable (soil), inimical, environment-friendly

Action on the countryside/landscape is like action on a human body:

comb (countryside), dominate, lie, gash, scar, rape (of the countryside), inject excitement into (a country, town, place)

## Analogy 2.10b **HUMAN BODY = EARTH**

Human bodies can be portrayed as earth/landscape.

Part of body is part of the landscape:

(alimentary) canal, region (of the body), (digestive) tract, furrow, stubble (= unshaven beard), to crop (hair cf. grass)

Quality/state of a human is quality/state of the earth:

clod, craggy, devastated, grit/-ty, rugged, sunken (face, cf. garden)

Action on/of a human is action on/of the earth:

bury face in hands, mould (person, character), plant (a kiss, blow, kick) on (someone), tremor, quake

Key
(x): x = part of a phrase in which the metaphor typically participates with this meaning, or an indication of the superordinate class such parts of phrases belong to, e.g. launch (a newspaper)
(= x): x = the T-term, e.g. fire (= dismiss from a post)
(cf. x): x = the Vehicle, Vehicular domain, Vehicular colligate, e.g. (emotions) run high (cf. tide, river)
(B) = Buried, e.g. SUCCESS = MOVEMENT FORWARDS progress (B)
? = doubtful, e.g. MONEY = BLOOD/LIQUID ?quid

---

### Analogy 2.11 **WORDS = MONEY**

Words are conceptualized as coins/money:

*currency (of a word), coin/mint (an expression), a coinage*

with a certain value:

*cheap remark, rich, enrich (description), beggar description* (i.e. no words are rich enough to describe it), *pay someone back* (*in their own words, coin*)

---

*Key*

(x): x = part of a phrase in which the metaphor typically participates with this meaning, or an indication of the superordinate class such parts of phrases belong to, e.g. *launch* (*a newspaper*)

in society. On the whole this is a very Saussurean or Derridean view of language (Derrida 1982).

By contrast, the metaphor IDEA/WORDS/TEXT = CLOTH/CLOTHES (Analogy 2.12) emphasizes the way words hang together in text, rather than viewing them atomistically as discrete units. The cloth, the texture of discourse can now be conceived in terms of the parts and their relationship to the whole, the patterns created by the discourse, with the strands of thread which are interwoven representing the strands of meaning or lexical *strings*. Language here is more syntactic than lexical. In keeping with Chomskyan notions of language creativity and productivity, clothes are more varied than coins, and their tactile and aesthetic qualities can be evaluated, and can be changed or improved. Whereas when words are coins there are no such possibilities. There is some emphasis on their function and use, at least to the extent that they can become worn out. Though this metaphor still gives a predominantly static view of language as text or product, it does allow us to talk about the processes which create or change the text.

Our next metaphor, IDEA/INFORMATION/WORDS = FOOD/DRINK (Analogy 2.13), gives us a very rich schema on which to hang our conceptions of language, and enables us to take the product view but to put especial emphasis on process. The processes of expression, the making of utterances, are analogous to the processes in the preparation and cooking of food. The addresser's teaching or communicating involves feeding the addressee. The addressee's understanding and gaining information from texts are analogous to eating/drinking. Language, according to this metaphor, is virtually a one-way process: we certainly do not expect examiners, for example, to digest, like nestlings, the regurgitated food provided by examinees! This metaphor also allows the exploration of aesthetic response to language use, in the same way as CLOTH/CLOTHES, but here, of course, instead of visual lexis, we will use the lexis for taste, smell and digestion/

---

### Analogy 2.12 **IDEA/WORDS/TEXT = CLOTH/CLOTHES**

Cloth/clothes, like text, have parts and texture:

*thread (of an argument), material (for my book), yarn, texture (of a piece of literature)*

Putting thoughts and words together is like making cloth/clothes:

*weave (a complicated story), weave in, interweave, tag on (a remark), tag (= quotation, question), make up (a joke, story, excuse), spin a yarn, tease (info out of . . . cf. wool), tailor (a plan, system), tailor-made (= planned specifically), fabricate (B)*

To improve your ideas/expression you:

*decorate, embroider, embellish, (add) frills*

You evaluate others' speech/ideas in terms of kind:

*woolly, flannel, padding*

quality:

*rag (= newspaper), ragbag*

sophistication:

*homespun*

efficiency:

*taut (writing)*

newness:

*well-worn remark, threadbare (joke, story, excuse)*

Old ideas you may no longer find useful or believable:

*grow out of, outgrow, outworn, divest (yourself of . . . )*

---

Key
(x): x = part of a phrase in which the metaphor typically participates with this meaning, or an indication of the superordinate class such parts of phrases belong to, e.g. *launch (a newspaper)*
(= x): x = the T-term, e.g. *fire (= dismiss from a post)*
(cf. x): x = the Vehicle, Vehicular domain, Vehicular colligate, e.g. *(emotions) run high (cf. tide, river)*
(B) = Buried, e.g. SUCCESS = MOVEMENT FORWARDS *progress* (B)

repletion, etc. Another lexical field available here is the rich fund of words for type of food, many of which are used to convey favourable/unfavourable evaluations (*cream, tripe, hogwash*), allowing us to see language as a product.

---

### Analogy 2.13 **IDEA/INFORMATION/WORDS = FOOD/DRINK**

Various kinds of food appear in this metaphorical equation:

> *food for thought, meat (of an argument), crumb, humbug, know your onions, nostrum, pap, titbit, tripe, waffle, a fudge, macaronic verse*!

The properties of information/expressions are analogous to the properties of food:

> *bland, half-baked, hot (news), pungent/pungency, raw (facts, data), redolent of, a staple (theme etc.), sugary (speech, phrase), tart (remark), crude*

Expression/thinking is equivalent to the cooking and provision of food:

> *concoct (excuse, account), dispense, lard/pepper (speech with expressions), scramble (a telephone message, cf. ?eggs), spice up (a speech), mince (your words), hash, rehash (old ideas), process (information cf. food), refine (substance), ?a scoop, traffic (drugs/info), dope (= restricted information), dose (of nationalism), spill the beans*

Teaching/imparting information = feeding:

> *spoon-feed, ram/force (something) down (someone's) throat*

Reception = eating:

> *browse, eat your words, devour, drink in, imbibe, chew on, chew the cud, ruminate, rumination, gobbet, swallow (a story, statement = believe; an insult = accept patiently), go down (well), digest, absorb, assimilate, hangover (from . . . ), regurgitate*

> *> repeat (= indigestion)*

A reader is an eater:

> *omnivorous (reader), voracious (reader), bookworm*

Other metonymical associations, objects/rooms:

> *(computer) menu, potted (biography), plate (= illustration)!, table (of contents)!!, galley (= printer's frame, cf. ?ship's kitchen)!*

---

*Key*
(x): x = part of a phrase in which the metaphor typically participates with this meaning, or an indication of the superordinate class such parts of phrases belong to, e.g. *launch (a newspaper)*
(= x): x = the T-term, e.g. *fire* (= dismiss from a post)
(cf. x): x = the Vehicle, Vehicular domain, Vehicular colligate, e.g. *(emotions) run high* (cf. *tide, river*)
> reversing the analogy, e.g. TIME = (MOVEMENT THROUGH) SPACE *a short (time) = an immediate (neighbour)*
? = doubtful, e.g. MONEY = BLOOD/LIQUID *?quid*
! = possible folk etymology, e.g. WORDS = FOOD *macaronic (verse)*!

With the IDEA/INFORMATION/WORDS = LIQUID metaphor the emphasis shifts further in the direction of language as a process (Analogy 2.14). Indeed one important aspect highlighted is the *expression* of information by the addresser, or the obtaining of information from a reluctant addresser. Language and text here is in dynamic motion but still unidirectional. There is not much emphasis on reactions to the text; WORDS = FOOD/DRINK is probably a preferable metaphor for Lexicalizing the addressee's reactions, though the qualities of language can be described by using the qualities of liquids. Minor aspects of this metaphor imply the existence of a text, but largely in terms of possible changes to the text like distillation/condensation, or in the lexis which sees the text as some kind of container or conduit for information (cf. Reddy 1993: 164–202). Most lexis is about the expression of emotions, in keeping with the opposition IDEA : EMOTION : : SOLID : LIQUID. The amount of language is conceptualized in terms of flow, governed by the analogy QUANTITY = WATER (FLOW).

Liquid is generally in motion, and the sense that language can be conceptualized as movement is given prominence by the next analogy, SPEAKING/WRITING = WALKING/RUNNING (Analogy 2.15). Again emphasis is on the addresser, and the qualities of the addresser's speech, whether it is fluent, irrelevant, long or short, or effective. Though it also allows us to conceptualize the cognitive effects of the speaking as the addressee is *led by* or *follows* the speaker. The other major emphasis is on the temporal rhythm or stages of the discourse – a path which has positions and points in/on it. This metaphor is influenced by the PURPOSE = DIRECTION, DEVELOPMENT/SUCCESS = FORWARD analogies, so that efficiency of language use is seen in terms of a straight path towards one's goal, with wandering being inefficient or irrelevant communication. The amount of speaking can be measured in terms of length, consistent with QUANTITY = DIMENSION.

So far language as process is basically unidirectional. The next two metaphors, SPEAKING/WRITING = (BALL) GAME, SPEAKING/ARGUING = WAR/FIGHTING, capture the intuition that language is dialogic, that utterances are co-operative events between two or more participants, and that one utterance depends upon the preceding utterance. Crucial here is the notion that language is not experienced as an abstract system, but that any use of language is dependent on the position on the court and the trajectory of the ball/shuttlecock. One's use of language, can, then, never be simply "putting ideas in your own words" but will be very much constrained by the intertextuality provided by other members of society and their previous uses. We might call this the Bakhtinian[7] view of language, or relate it to conversational analysis.

SPEAKING/WRITING = (BALL) GAME (Analogy 2.16) captures this sense of spontaneity constrained by intertextuality and reciprocity, of initiation (*getting the ball rolling*) and turn-taking, but it also suggests that discourse

71

### Analogy 2.14 **IDEA/INFORMATION/WORDS = LIQUID**

Expression is the production of liquid:

*spout, leak, pour (scorn on), spill out, spit (it) out, splash (a story), brim over, (information) dries up, ladle out (advice), meandering, in full spate, (stop talking) in midstream, fount/fountain/source (of information), torrent/stream (of questions), effusion (B), outpouring*

General beliefs and opinions are a current:

*current/tide (of opinion), against the stream/tide, mainstream, new wave*

An argument/text is a container of ideas:

*hold water, watertight argument, contains, contents*

Information becoming available is like the appearance of water:

*(news) filters through, (into an organization), seep out, leak, pours, percolate, permeate, osmosis*

Reception is experiencing a body of liquid:

*dip into, mull over, skim (a newspaper), wade through (a book, report), inundated (with)*

Extracting information is obtaining liquid:

*pump (someone), tap (your phone), wring (info out of . . . ), wire-tap*

Properties of texts/ideas are properties of liquids:

*flow, turgid (writing cf. water, mud), acid, caustic, gush/-ing, limpid (prose)*

Changes to texts/ideas are changes to liquids:

*condense, distillation, dilute (beliefs), recast*

Such changes are often seen in terms of change of state so undue prolixity = air:

*hot air, long-winded, windbag*

---

Key

(x): x = part of a phrase in which the metaphor typically participates with this meaning, or an indication of the superordinate class such parts of phrases belong to, e.g. *launch (a newspaper)*

(cf. x): x = the Vehicle, Vehicular domain, Vehicular colligate, e.g. *(emotions) run high (cf. tide, river)*

(B) = Buried, e.g. SUCCESS = MOVEMENT FORWARDS *progress (B)*

## Analogy 2.15 WRITING/SPEAKING = WALKING/RUNNING

The expression of thoughts is walking/running along a path which is a text:

> *running commentary, run over/through* (= rehearse), *he goes* (= he says), *as the saying goes, go on/about, run on, go over* (in your mind), *venture* (an opinion), *trot out* (info), *reach* (an agreement), *give way* (to the next speaker), *lilt* (in speech, cf. steps), *pedestrian, retrace our steps*

> < *(come to a) full stop*

To be irrelevant/communicate inefficiently is to move sideways:

> *ramble, wander, sidestep* (a question), *sidetrack, jump/lurch* (from one thing to another), *in passing, by the way* (= incidentally, i.e. slightly irrelevant), *put things in a roundabout way, direct/indirect* (speech act), *tortuous writing, ?elliptical, a plain* (statement)

Difficulty in speaking fluently is difficulty in walking smoothly:

> *falter, halting, stumble, trip* (someone) *up,* (speech) *impediment, lame* (excuse, proposal), *flounder, fumble, to wrongfoot, stop* (someone) *in their tracks*

Contrast:

> *smooth talker*

Amount of speaking is distance travelled:

> *further, long* (book etc.), *put things in a roundabout way, ranges over* (a topic), *a foot* (of verse)

To withdraw a remark is to move backwards:

> *go back on/retreat* (from a promise)

To understand/be influenced by text is to follow/be led:

> *follow* (a story, script, score), (newspaper) *lead, lead up to* (a subject), *lead* (someone *on/up the garden path*), *misleading, find your way, I don't follow, lost* (= can't understand cf. can't follow)

Text thus becomes a pathway and positions in a text are positions on the pathway:

> *passage* (in a book), *maze* (of ideas), (opinions) *converge/diverge, place* (in a book), *starting point* (of an argument, discussion), *make a point, take your point, end* (a conversation), *here, locus, past* (chapter 3), *point, go to* (p. 6)

Texts can also be conceptualized as vehicles:

> *carry, convey* (information), *omnibus edition, vehicle, ?overload* (of info), *??*(film) *trailer, stall, traffic* (in ideas), *streamlined*

*Key*

(*x*): *x* = part of a phrase in which the metaphor typically participates with this meaning, or an indication of the superordinate class such parts of phrases belong to, e.g. *launch* (a *newspaper*)

(= *x*): *x* = the T-term, e.g. *fire* (= dismiss from a post)

(cf. *x*): *x* = the Vehicle, Vehicular domain, Vehicular colligate, e.g. (*emotions*) *run high* (cf. *tide, river*)

< reversing the analogy, e.g. TIME = (MOVEMENT THROUGH) SPACE *a short* (*time*) = *an immediate* (*neighbour*)

? = doubtful, e.g. MONEY = BLOOD/LIQUID ?*quid*

types within an institutional context can be organized, scheduled and have various time limits, etc.

SPEAKING/ARGUING = WAR/FIGHTING (Analogy 2.17) is a more richly Lexicalized schema for representing language. While it shares with the (BALL) GAME the sense that languaging can be competitive, it also puts negative emphasis on its potentially damaging impact: the effect of language on the addressee, which may be to provoke a hostile response. Arguing can be represented as warfare, making available all the lexis to do with kinds of strategy, injury, weapons and especially ammunition. Here words are again objects, as with money, but missiles for which motion is an essential semantic component. Slight modification of the metaphor sees an argument as a building which is under attack rather than seeing the war directed against one's interlocutor, and therefore coalesces with metaphors like CERTAIN/RELIABLE = SOLID, BASIC/ELEMENTARY = DOWN.

The final analogy, WORDS/LANGUAGE = HUMAN (Analogy 2.18), accesses facets of language which have been ignored so far. First, there is the long-term diachronic aspect, that languages can be born or die, can evolve and are related, like animals, to other species. Second, the notion that language is action, that it is constituted by speech acts which are designed to have

---

**Analogy 2.16 SPEAKING/WRITING = (BALL) GAME**

Conversation/discussion/criticism is a game in which the missiles are balls:

*slanging match, bandy, volley (of words/questions), ball's in your court, start the ball rolling, kick off (discussion), kick around (ideas), opponent/opposition, opposing, score/points off someone*

---

*Key*

(*x*): *x* = part of a phrase in which the metaphor typically participates with this meaning, or an indication of the superordinate class such parts of phrases belong to, e.g. *launch* (a *newspaper*)

## Analogy 2.17 **SPEAKING/ARGUING = WAR/FIGHTING**

An argument is a battle:

*battle of wits, in-fighting, sally, skirmish, truce, tussle*

Disagreement is physical attack:

*assail, attack, lash out (at someone),* or to a lesser degree *poke fun at, pull your punches, biting (criticism), mordant (B), flay, hit back at, go for the jugular, close in for the kill, knock (someone), savage (someone), slam, spar/sparring partner/match, snipe, strike (industrial), strike at (= attack)*

Maintaining one's opinions/countering arguments is defence:

*defend/defence, deflect/disarm (criticism), fence, fend off, parry, resist, counter-attack*

To be likely to lose an argument is to be vulnerable, injured:

*cornered, in a tight corner, embattled (government), wound/-ed, indefensible, defeat, lose*

To be likely to succeed in argument is to win:

*(arguments) gain ground, invincible, stronghold (of beliefs), win*

Various weapons may be used:

*hatchet job, to needle, hammer and tongs, the knives are out*

Arguing/criticizing/speaking is throwing or firing:

*bombard, earshot, fire (away) (questions, suggestions, etc.), shoot their mouth off, shoot down (ideas), fusillade, barrage, volley (of questions), shoot, pitch (something at a level), stick to your guns, people in glass-houses shouldn't throw stones, hurl abuse, level (criticism at = aim), ?loaded, point.blank*

The arguments/criticisms expressed are ammunition/missiles:

*ammunition, bombshell, flak, shaft of humour, "sticks and stones may break my bones, but words will never hurt me"*

Their degree of hostility/effectiveness is sharpness:

*barbed comments, hard, cutting, harsh, pointed (remarks), blunt, ?double-edged, edge (to a voice), sharp, not to put too fine/delicate a point on it*

Miscellaneous:

*combative, partisan (war/argument), sides (in war/argument), "you win", notwithstanding!!*

perlocutionary effects and provoke action by humans. A related emphasis is that language use depends on the control of the user, so that vocabulary to do with government/employment can be accorded to words. Behind this conception of language is the idea that language has an autonomous life of its own, that it can influence us, or even more, possess us and think through

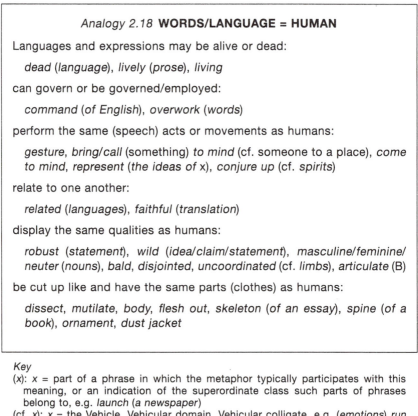

### Analogy 2.18 **WORDS/LANGUAGE = HUMAN**

Languages and expressions may be alive or dead:

*dead* (language), *lively* (prose), *living*

can govern or be governed/employed:

*command* (of English), *overwork* (words)

perform the same (speech) acts or movements as humans:

*gesture, bring/call* (something) *to mind* (cf. someone to a place), *come to mind, represent* (the ideas of x), *conjure up* (cf. *spirits*)

relate to one another:

*related* (languages), *faithful* (translation)

display the same qualities as humans:

*robust* (statement), *wild* (idea/claim/statement), *masculine/feminine/ neuter* (nouns), *bald, disjointed, uncoordinated* (cf. *limbs*), *articulate* (B)

be cut up like and have the same parts (clothes) as humans:

*dissect, mutilate, body, flesh out, skeleton* (of an essay), *spine* (of a book), *ornament, dust jacket* us. As a consequence language can have the same qualities as human beings. Investigation, violent or not, in the form of dissection, anatomy and so on, can be perpetrated on language or texts to reveal their parts or structure, a feature exploited here more than in the case of IDEA/WORDS/TEXT = CLOTH/CLOTHES.

Table 2.1 sums up what is highlighted by the diverse Vehicle schemata for language. The distinction between upper case and lower case reflects the relative prominence given to the aspects of the schemata by the lexis presented. The ways in which these diverse metaphors involve different Grounds of comparison and therefore highlight or create different features or ways of looking at a phenomenon is applicable to all the sets of diverse Vehicles displayed in the map (Figure 2.1). Clearly there is enormous scope for research in exploring the diversity of structuring in relation to other sets, explaining their ideological and ontological presuppositions, and validating the resulting hypotheses through experimentation, by, for example, testing whether a different metaphorical conception leads to different thought patterns or behaviour.

*Table 2.1* Diverse Vehicles for language in the English lexicon

| Vehicle | *Feature Emphasis* | | | | | |
|---|---|---|---|---|---|---|
| | Object/ Substance v. Process | Addresser v. Addressee | One-way v. Two-way | Message v. Code | Co-text and Intertext | Quality and Variety |
| Money | OBJECT Process | ADDRESSER | ONE-WAY | CODE | | QUALITY |
| Cloth | OBJECT Process | ADDRESSER | ONE-WAY | MESSAGE | CO-TEXT | QUALITY VARIETY |
| Human | OBJECT PROCESS | BOTH | ONE-WAY | MESSAGE Code | CO-TEXT | QUALITY VARIETY |
| Food | OBJECT SUBSTANCE PROCESS | BOTH | ONE-WAY | MESSAGE | | QUALITY VARIETY |
| Liquid | SUBSTANCE PROCESS | ADDRESSER Addressee | ONE-WAY | | | QUALITY |
| Walking | PROCESS Object | ADDRESSER Addressee | ONE-WAY | MESSAGE | CO-TEXT | QUALITY (Efficiency, Ability) |
| Game | PROCESS | BOTH | TWO-WAY | | INTERTEXT | Variety |
| War | PROCESS Object | ADDRESSEE | ONE-WAY Two-way | | Intertext | QUALITY (Effect) Variety (Munitions) |

### 2.3.7. Influence of phonology/submorphemery as part of *langue*

Anyone committed or mad enough to read in a linear fashion through the dictionary, encountering headwords in alphabetical order, quickly becomes aware of the submorphemic patterns in the vocabulary; the sense, for example, that certain consonant clusters are attempting to achieve morphemic status, e.g. *gl* to mean 'light', *gr* to mean 'friction' (Palmer 1981: 35; Rhodes and Lawler 1981). This tendency to motivate the phonemic properties of morphemes, to deny the arbitrariness of the sign, may be even more pronounced in the metaphorical lexicon, perhaps because metaphor is associated with poetry which deliberately exploits submorphemic correspondences through rhyme and alliteration. It has been suggested, for example, that one way of specifying or realizing metaphor is through the use of blends (see section 7.7 and Stockwell 1992b: 82)

The hypothesis that such submorphemic patterning has a particularly powerful effect on the metaphorical lexicon is suggested by word lists such as (23):

(23)   *stable, stack, stagnate, stagnant, stale, stall* (= wait cf. *a car*), *stance,*
       *stand* (= continue to be effective), *stand up* (*to use*), *standing*
       (*committee*), *standstill, staple* (= regular part of the diet), ?*starchy,*
       *static, stationary, stay, steady, stem* (*of word* = part remaining un-
       changed), *stick* (*to, at, with* something), *stiff-necked, stifle* (= stop it
       continuing), *still* (*doing* something = hasn't changed), *stonewall, stop,*
       *straitjacket, straitlaced, strangle* (= prevent development), ?*strapped,*
       *restrict, no strings attached, stuffy, sturdy*

Most of these lexical items can be related to the equations CHANGE = MOVEMENT, ACTIVITY = MOVEMENT/PROCESS, since their metaphorical meaning (and sometimes their literal meaning as well) includes the notion of lack of change/lack of activity. This semantic component is symbolized graphologically or phonologically by the Indo-European root *st-* and more particularly *sta-*.

Various theories have claimed that the origins of language are in some ways motivated, dependent on imitative onomatopoeia, or on sympathetic physical movement. This may be the case with a number of our items. IDEA/INFORMATION/WORDS = LIQUID gives us several items which have initial *sp*: *spit out, in full spate, spout, spill out*. The physical movements of the lips associated with speaking and spitting out liquid are mutually iconic here. And the tendency for lexical items representing speaking to begin with *sp* is one factor that attracts to the lexicon the following metaphorical items *spar, sparks fly* (= arguing) *sparkle* (*with wit*), *spin* (*a yarn* = story). From the mass of metaphorical possibilities a phonological magnet attracts, as it were, those forms which are to Lexicalize the conceptual metaphorical component in the dictionary.

An interesting recent publication by Lecercle (1990) draws attention to the non-logical side of the linguistic coin, the tendency of language to deconstruct itself or reconstruct itself. Obviously part of this tendency is what we have been describing above, the sort of popular malapropism or folk etymology which sees a playful counter-logic in theoretically arbitrary phonological patterns of the *langue*. This tendency to folk etymology extends to the recognition of metaphorical patterns in certain lexical items where, from a scientifically etymological perspective, none exist. If WORDS = FOOD then the printer's frame in which he sets type is a galley (= the kitchen of a ship or an aircraft). And who knows whether the equation MONEY = BLOOD/LIQUID had any influence on the coining of the slang *quid* meaning 'a pound'? A number of these punning items have been included in the lists above, though marked with an exclamation or question mark. For a sample:

(24)   WORDS = FOOD *macaronic* (*verse*)!
       MONEY = BLOOD/LIQUID ?*bank* (= *financial institution* cf. *of a river*)!
       MIND = OBJECT/SUBSTANCE and CHANGE = MOVEMENT *boring*!
       SPEAKING/ARGUING = WAR/FIGHTING *notwithstanding*!!

## 2.4. SUMMARY AND AFTERTHOUGHT

Undoubtedly our cognitive structure is determined by conventional metaphors, and evidence for this can be seen in the lexicon of English. The Inactive metaphors in the dictionary form patterns of intersections of lexical sets or semantic fields, and we have seen how these can be grouped in our map, though disentangling them is somewhat problematic. We also saw that the same abstract concept can be metaphorically structured in different ways, as we explored in the diverse metaphors for language. This suggests that the choice of metaphor can have far-reaching ideological as well as cognitive consequences, and that we need to raise awareness of these latent ideologies.

A question worth pursuing is whether literature exploits or undermines these metaphors, these Root Analogies. Literature often simply exploits or relexicalizes them and readability may depend upon this exploitation. For instance, notice how automatically, in this following passage, Charlotte Brontë[8] turns to conventional Root Analogies to represent emotion: EMOTION/IDEA = SENSE IMPRESSION, in particular EMOTION = LIGHT/COLOUR or TOUCH/FEELING or WEATHER or HEAT; as well as RELATIONSHIP = MUSIC:

V256   Dr John could think and think well, but he was rather a man of action
       than of thought. He <u>could</u> feel and feel **vividly**, in his way, but his heart
       had no **chord** for enthusiasm. To **bright, soft, sweet** influences his eyes
       gave **bright, soft** and **sweet** welcome, beautiful to see as **dyes of rose
       and silver, pearl and purple, embuing summer clouds**; for what

belonged to **storm**, what was wild and intense, dangerous, sudden and **flaming**, he had no sympathy and held with it no communion.

One almost feels cheated by this phenomenon of Root Analogy dependence. Literature and poetry claim to set themselves the task of defamiliarization (Tomashevsky 1965: 78–92), of being in some senses less than readable, of undoing our conventional ways of thinking and of categorizing experience, and transcending our latent ideologies. If this defamiliarization, this strangeness (Uspensky 1973), is actually only superficial, it means that we remain trapped in the prison-house of language, with the grid with which we map our conceptual categories as bars. If these Root Analogies are bequeathed us by the physical bodies and our preconceptual bodily experiences there is no transcendence, no escape, and our physical limitations guarantee our mental ones.

A versifier, rather than a poet, might often have recourse to a rhyming dictionary. This chapter is the semantic equivalent where a writer can find a guide to available metaphors. To use them with what passes for originality she only has to relexicalize them, expressing the same analogy by using synonyms of the lexical items which conventionally convey it; or exploit, through folk etymologies, the kinds of pun made transparently possible by the metaphorical sets in the map (Figure 2.1). The advertising industry too could make use of it, though graphically and visually as well as in copy; after all, cognitive metaphors are not confined to expression in language.

### ■ EXERCISE

(a) *The following text from the final paragraph of the Anglo-Irish Joint Declaration* (Financial Times, *16 December 1993, p. 10) uses a number of the Root Analogies mentioned in the map of Root Analogies (Figure 2.1). Analyse them and comment on their use.*

*The taoiseach and the prime minister are determined to build on the fervent wish of both their peoples to see old fears and animosities replaced by a climate of peace . . . They appeal to all concerned to grasp the opportunity for a new departure. That step would compromise no position or principle, nor prejudice the future for either community. On the contrary it would be an incomparable gain for all. It would break decisively the cycle of violence and the intolerable suffering it entails for the people of these islands, particularly for both communities in Northern Ireland.*

(b) *Take any short modern lyric poem, and show how it exploits some of the Root Analogies listed in the map (Figure 2.1.). If you need a model you might look at Lakoff and Turner's* More than Cool Reason *(1989), chapter 3, which analyses William Carlos Williams' 'The jasmine lightness of the moon'.*

*(c) Choose an academic non-linguistic textbook which you have been or are presently studying. Look at the index and find the most important metaphorical equations represented there. Analyse how the (diverse) metaphors structure the subject cognitively, as I did for language in section 2.3.6.*

*(d) Look at commercial magazine advertisements and find examples of visual metaphors based on Root Analogies/conceptual metaphors. Are these metaphors also exploited in the linguistic text of the ads?*

# 3

# METAPHOR AND THE DICTIONARY
## Word-class and word-formation

In the first chapter, I argued that there is a metaphorical cline from the least active Dead and Sleeping metaphors to the most Active ones. And I gave examples of how, over time, meanings which were extremely metaphorical and dependent on pragmatic inferencing become conventionalized and so more dependent on semantic decoding. In Chapter 2 I demonstrated that classes of these "Inactive" metaphors pervade the lexicon and form networks by which we conceptualize abstractions in concrete terms. In this chapter I explore how the choice of word-class has consequences for metaphorical interpretation, and how derivational processes of word-formation are used to bring about such Lexicalization or semanticizing of metaphor.

## 3.1. WORD-CLASS AND METAPHOR

The most obvious way of classifying metaphors is to categorize them according to the word-class to which the V-term belongs. Metaphors can readily be found which fall into all the major word-classes.

Nouns
DM31      Director Matt Busby, the **Godfather** of the club
AL      the **raindrop** eye
GB1      The past is a **foreign country**.

Verbs
CEC520      There are certain areas of the syllabus that students **queue up** for.
MD832      the lines that seem to **gnaw** upon all Faith
PQ172      She did not so much cook as **assassinate** food. (S. Jameson)

Adjectives
DT6      'I expect a treaty, a **full-fledged** treaty on medium-range missiles.'
DB      down the vast edges drear and **naked** shingles of the world
DN16      The air was **thick** with a bass chorus.

Adverbs
MD1291      Seat thyself **sultanically** among the moons of Saturn.

CEC534    a rather **heavily** qualified aggressive sort of applicant
MA        But as he walked King Arthur panted **hard**.

Prepositions
CEC519    Is there anyone **apart from** you that is strong **on** that?
DT3       A right extremist group is suspected of being **behind** the killing.
DM2       Saunders was arrested **within** hours of returning to Britain.

You have probably noticed that adverbial and prepositional V-terms are generally less recognizable as metaphors and less forceful than verbal and adjectival V-terms, and these in turn are less forceful than noun-based ones. We explore why nouns make such powerful metaphors in the next section.

### 3.1.1. Nouns

When language maps experience in the most straightforward or congruent way, nouns represent things, adjectives the properties of things, verbs realize states and processes, adverbs the properties of processes, and prepositions the relationships between things. Noun V-terms are either more recognizable as metaphors or yield richer interpretations than V-terms of other word-classes.

There are a number of reasons for this. To start with, recognition depends on unconventional reference and/or semantic contradiction. Because they are referring expressions, in the strictest sense, noun phrases reveal very strongly the clashes between conventional and unconventional reference, as in DM31 and AL (p. 10); and as V-terms they can be equated with Topics by the copula, *to be*, creating a strong sense of contradiction, as in GB1.

In addition, the things referred to by noun phrases are imaginable, because they have spatial dimensions. Indeed, it is impossible to imagine at all without picturing things. Through the vividness of their images, and their ability to enhance memory (Honeck *et al.* 1975), noun V-terms are more easily recognized, and their Vehicles less prone to oblivion than V-terms of other word-classes.

It will be helpful, at this point, to briefly sketch in the main differences between concepts and images. Let's assume that we have a continuum with two poles: actual experience, perceived through any of the senses, at one pole, and concepts at the other. Imagery is an intermediate category between actual experience and conceptualization. Images are more individually idiosyncratic and closer to the tokens of actual experience, while concepts will be socially conventionalized and relatively typed. Images are more contextualized and associated with episodic memory, the memory of events, while concepts are relatively decontextualized and dependent on semantic memory, the memory of word-meanings. While imagery can be used for communication between intimates who share the same experiences and memories, conceptual systems are vital for communication of new information beyond subcultures. Images are more concrete and sensual, concepts abstract and mental. The richness of images depends on their multiple and diverse associations, the clarity of concepts on their sparseness and the relative fixity of their boundaries. This freedom of association in imagery arises partly from emotional and perceptual processes, and the clarity of concepts from cognitive processes.[1]

Dan Sperber (1975: 115–17) gives a nice example of the way in which olfactory or smell "imagery" operates. (Remember – I am not limiting images to visual perception.) In the English language, at least, we have difficulty conceptualizing smells, because our language is poor in words to label them. This inadequacy of the conceptual system is the very reason that when we encounter them they evoke images, with all their associations. Trying to identify a familiar but uncategorized smell or taste, we explore our episodic memory for the events and places in which we previously encountered it, and with which we associate it. The train of associations it sets off can be incredibly rich and highly idiosyncratic, as, for example, the taste of madeleine biscuits which begins Proust's seven-volume novel *A la recherche du temps perdu.*

So, the multiple associations of metaphors with high image value create the potential for rich interpretation and multiplicity of Grounds, perhaps emotive, perhaps idiosyncratic, always evocative. And nouns, referring to things, can more directly evoke images than other parts of speech (Kosslyn, quoted in MacCormac 1990: 142–3). Besides, the meaning or sense of thing-referring nouns will often be conceptualized as bundles of semantic features, rather than as single semantic features, e.g. 'a cup': [artefact], [for drinking], [with handle], [cylindrical but base smaller than rim], etc. Taking these two aspects of noun-meaning together we can see why noun V-terms might lead to more open-ended or Interactive interpretations than V-terms in other parts of speech. There will be more candidates for Grounds, or the need to make choices among them will demand interactiveness – a careful consideration of the context and co-text to determine or narrow down the meaning.

A recent exchange on the internet Linguist discussion group is interesting on the question of the relation between nouns and metaphors.

DAN ALFORD:  Amethyst First Rider, Blackfoot, has insisted in a series of dialogues between physicists, Native Americans and linguists that when Native Americans are speaking their own languages, they don't use metaphors; that it only sounds like metaphor when translated into English.

MOONHAWK:  A native speaker of Blackfoot has confirmed to me that he can speak all day long without uttering a single noun – and that this is the rule rather than the exception . . . Since so many of our own metaphors are nouns, a significant lack of nouns in Blackfoot automatically means fewer metaphor candidates, and therefore mitigates [*sic*] toward Ms. First Rider's claim.

('Summary: non-metaphor and non-arbitrary claims', 10 October 1994)

The suggestion here too is that metaphorical force is associated with noun V-terms.

### 3.1.2. Nouns referring to processes

Of course the tendency sketched above by which nouns refer to things is only probabilistic. Nouns can be used to refer directly to processes, for example, as in *tennis,* or through nominalization as in *gurgling.* Despite this, I would suggest that a fair proportion of these process-referring nouns are habitually used to refer to a schema or script, and because they do so can be equally rich in the clusters of assumptions and images which they evoke. To make this claim clear it will first be necessary to explain exactly what is meant by a script or schema.

According to Schank and Abelson (1977) we communicate, for the most part, by making use of already formed ideas, stereotypes of human behaviour or schemata stored in our long-term memory. In one sense, understanding a text is finding a schema that will account for it. The fact that we can understand the utterance *I like apples* without any problems, suggests that we can easily access the eating schema.

### ■ EXERCISE

*Sometimes jokes depend upon misunderstandings due to the evocation of a deliberately idiosyncratic schema. Explain what schemata clash in the following child's joke.*

CHILD:   *Mummy, Mummy, I don't like Grandma.*
MOTHER:   *Well just leave it on the side of your plate, and eat up your potatoes.*

A schema or script can be defined as a predetermined stereotyped sequence of actions that defines a well-known situation. Schank and Abelson's most famous example is the Restaurant script which can be detailed as follows:

(1)   *Restaurant (setting)*
       props              tables, chairs, cutlery, food, plates, menu, etc.
       roles              customer, owner, cook, waiter, (cashier), (head
                          waiter)
       entry conditions   customer is hungry; customer has money

| results | customer has less money; customer is not hungry; owner has more money |
| --- | --- |
| Scene 1 *Entering* | going in, deciding where to sit, sitting |
| Scene 2 *Ordering* | (asking for menu, waiter bringing menu), choosing, signalling to waiter, giving order, waiter telling cook the order |
| Scene 3 *Eating* | cook giving waiter food, waiter bringing customer food, customer eating food |
| Scene 4 *Exiting* | customer asking for bill, waiter· writing bill, taking bill to customer (customer tipping waiter), customer going to cashier, paying cashier, leaving restaurant |

(adapted from Shank and Abelson 1977: 43)

If anyone mentions visiting a restaurant we assume, by default, that the stereotype of a restaurant script/schema applies, unless unexpected details of a visit have occurred, and are made explicit.

To return to the question of nouns which don't refer to things. Any such script or schema will involve "things" or first-order entities, which are relatively permanent and have spatial dimensions. These include the setting itself, which will sometimes be labelled directly, as with *restaurant* (though sometimes not, as with *tennis*); the props; and the roles. My main point is that though nouns can refer to events rather than things, when these events are stereotypical or scripted, they will be associated with things and therefore capable of evoking imagery and so contributing to metaphorical force. It may well be the props/setting that provide the richest potential for imagery. I also suspect that the very fact that the process has become scripted is what allows noun lexis to be conventionally employed to refer to it.

### 3.1.3. Verbs

The mention of processes brings us on to the second word-class, verbs. Metaphorically used verbs can indirectly evoke imagery but only by being hooked up to their conventional colligates – we cannot imagine kicking without imagining a foot. So that in the phrase from the Ted Hughes' poem 'Pike'

TH24   the gills **kneading** quietly

we are entitled to supply a subject colligate of "kneading", *hands*, and compare the slow movement and slatted structure of gills with the movement and structure of hands. This process is called Vehicle-construction. But precisely what particular verbs are capable of this kind of indirect image evocation?

### 3.1.3.1. Process types

Obviously enough the verbs most easily associated with imagery will be those referring to physical acts and events, or <u>Material processes</u>. This accounts for the phenomena discussed in this section: the frequency with which Material process verbs are used as metaphors of <u>Mental processes</u>, that is processes of perception, feeling and cognition; and the metaphorical use of Material processes for Verbal ones. But first, let's clarify these process types a little.

Halliday (1994: ch. 5) distinguishes four main processes within the transitivity function of the clause: Material, Mental (perception, affection, cognition), Verbal, Existential/Relational. Material processes are doings and happenings. Mental processes are those to do with thinking (cognition), emotion (affection) or sensing (perception). <u>Verbal</u> processes are those of saying, symbolic processes. <u>Existential/Relational</u> processes are to do with being and states of being.

### 3.1.3.2. Representing the Mental as Material

The general tendency is to use Material metaphors for Mental processes.

DM2a Only a third of crime is **cleared up**.
DM2b **basking** in the triumphant take-over of the Distillers' Group
DT3 Few Japanese could **bear** to be spotted poking through roadside rubbish.

In DM2a the Material process Vehicle is used for the Mental cognitive process of solving crime. In DM2b the Material process of basking in the sun does service for a Mental affective process. Example DT3, if we wake up the Sleeping metaphor, indicates a Mental process of affection, shame, by means of a Material process of carrying.

It is not surprising that Mental processes are regularly metaphorized as the more observable Material processes. Given the importance of imagery to metaphor, already demonstrated in relation to noun metaphors, and the dependence of imagery on the senses, this seems highly predictable.[2]

### 3.1.3.3. 'Please'/'like' and Mental processes

One aspect of Mental processes produces metaphor regularly. Mental processes can be represented either as *like* types or *please* types. This means that *I like x* is equivalent to *x pleases me*. When represented as *please* types metaphors are often employed:

(2)  *'like'*       *'please'*

    I forget      It **escapes** me.
    I notice      It **strikes** me.

| | |
|---|---|
| I mind it | It **upsets** me. |
| I admire it | It **impresses** me. |
| I enjoy it | It **sends** me. |
| I am confused | It **throws** me. |

(cf. Halliday 1994: 117)

### 3.1.3.4. Representing the Verbal as Material

So in order to describe our Mental activities we have to make raids on the verbs used for Material processes. Moreover, to communicate our ideas we indulge in a great variety of speech acts, and the following examples show how Material processes become Vehicles for Verbal ones:

CEC518   Isn't it an objection that Bunyans might **raise**?
CEC587   probably the best way of **putting** it
(3)       I don't think I'm **distorting** his argument.

### ■ EXERCISE

(a)   *The headlines of tabloid newspapers are particularly fond of drama-tizing and sensationalizing verbal acts by using Material process metaphors. Can you find examples?*

(b)   *Fowler (1991: 144–5) has claimed there are ideological contradic-tions inherent in this practice: newspapers which claim to condemn violence using the metaphors of violence. Do you agree?*

### 3.1.3.5. Specificity of the conventional colligate

The representing of Mental and Verbal processes by metaphorical Mate-rial process verbs may indirectly evoke imagery. But to do so Material process verbs have to be relatively specific: the more specific the conventional colligates of the verb the more easily an image can be evoked.

Consider examples (4) and (5):

(4)  *Physical*
     the **rising** antagonism (LF130)
     Darkness **thickened** under the trees. (LF62)
         *Inanimates*
         *Liquid*
         Their scent **spilled** out into the air. (LF62)
             *Blood*
             The sun mixed and **clotted** for a while among the thorns. (DV61)
         *Solid*
         His voice **struck** them into silence. (LF76)
             *Pliable solids*
             the walls of rock **folding** back (TI223)
             the **crumpled** woman (TI176)
             *Powdered solids*
             The trees **sifted** chilly sunlight over their naked bodies. (TI15)
             *Rigid solids*
                 *Sharp instruments*
                 Goody with her red hair˙would **stab** his mind and prick tears
                 out of his eyes. (TS112)
                 *Machine*
                 **overhauled** their clothes (DV129)
                     *Clock/watch*
                     Yet I was **wound up**. I **tick**. I exist. (FF10)

(5)  *Living objects*
     Small flames **stirred** at the bole of a tree. (LF48)
         *Plants*
         great bulging towers that **sprouted** away over the island (LF152)
         *Animals*
         Then the sea **breathed** again. (LF200)
         The European year of the environment **sees** the birth of a new
         scheme.
             *Birds*
             The flame **flapped**. (LF45)
             *Mammals*
             The new one **milked** her. (TI44)
                 *Cat*
                 He **mewed** before he sucked. (TI65)
                 *Horse*
                 Even that made his heart **trot**. (TS154)

The conventional colligate referents at the bottom of the respective
hyponymic chains, i.e. those under the headings *blood*, *clock/watch*, *pliable
solids*, *cat*, *horse*, etc., will in most cases be more imaginable than their
superordinates. It seems that we need something of at least medium specificity, a basic-level term (Hudson 1980: 92–4; Lakoff 1987: 31–40, 46–54),

to produce imagery, unless we have help from elsewhere in the text. For example, in TI15, in order to make the concept specific enough to be imagined we must hypothesize a specific member of the class powdered/ granular solid, perhaps flour. And we might well be guided in this interpretation by the fact that both sunlight and flour can be bright in colour.

### 3.1.4. Adjectives

Much of what we have said about verb-based metaphors is also true of adjective-based ones. Two main kinds of interpretation are possible: the referential kind, in which case the metaphor is likely to be Inactive, e.g. *a full-fledged treaty*, where *full-fledged* has a second dictionary meaning of 'fully developed'; or an analogical or Vehicle-construction interpretation as with ***naked** shingles of the world* (DB), which involves constructing the referent 'body', the conventional colligate of *naked*. In the latter case the specificity of the colligate will be important, as in the case of verbs. So that neither "refreshment for dry **thirsty** hair" nor "The air was **thick** with a bass chorus" (DN16) give us as specific an image as the Arnold metaphor (DB) with its evocation of a naked human body. The "air was **thick**" example (DN16) points us to a further similarity with verbs: because adjectives, prepositions and adverbs are syntactically dependent on nouns and verbs respectively, they are ways of expressing the kind of lexical gap-filling Root Analogy discussed in the previous chapter.

### 3.1.5. Adverbs and prepositions

As we shift from adjectives to adverbs and prepositions it is clear that we are more likely to be dealing with Inactive metaphors. There are several reasons for this.

- The *-ly* suffix can, as with most derivational markers, be interpreted as a signal that metaphorical meaning is involved, and therefore a softener of the incorporated metaphor. Thus, even if the metaphor is newly made up, e.g. "sultanically" (MD1291), it can be interpreted 'in a manner similar to that of a sultan'. Any sense of contradiction or anomaly will, therefore, be weak.

### ■ EXERCISE

*What is the difference in meaning between (a) and (b), and which is more precise ?*

(a)   *He clambered after her sheepishly. (TI27)*
(b)   *He clambered after her like a sheep.*

- Adverbs will often derive from denominal adjectives, e.g. *sheepishly* derives originally from *sheep* via *sheepish*. Because of the history of derivation and the Lexicalization at two stages in the derivational process, these adverbs have a considerably narrower range of meanings than, for example, their simile counterparts. Sentence (b) allows us to select from a whole range of expected features of sheep and the way they climb in order to arrive at an appropriate Ground. In (a) the Grounds have been narrowed down to a meaning like 'timidly'.

- A certain class of adverbs, those sharing forms with prepositions, e.g. *in*, *out*, *behind*, *over*, etc., form a closed finite class. As such they will have a tendency to promiscuous colligation with verbs, without putting up any resistance. Or, the corollary, because of their frequency they have an indeterminacy of meaning, which will be highly co-text dependent.

- Adverbs and prepositions contrast with adjectives and verbs in one crucial respect. It is not worth giving them a Colligational interpretation because their noun/verb colligates are too general to yield any imagery or to make manifest any specific schemata. So, for example, in understanding "I tick. I exist" (FF10) it may be worthwhile to evoke the schema of a clock, which is wound up and gradually winds down over a period of time, but it is pointless to attempt the same in cases of prepositions like *with*; for example, to suggest that "she hit her husband with a spanner" implies 'an instrument (in this case a spanner) is a companion' (though cf. Lakoff and Johnson 1980: 134–5).

- Adverbs and prepositions of this closed class have a tendency not simply to modify verbs but to combine with them to form one lexical unit, a phrasal verb with a determinate sense. Or they may combine with other adverbs/prepositions. This Burying smothers their metaphorical potential, and sometimes the ability to see them as contributing anything much to meaning.

No doubt, as we have seen in Chapter 2, adverbs and prepositions provide evidence of certain cultural or universal Root Analogies (Figure 2.1):

UC  He was **fully** sensible to the advantages of the instalment plan.
   (QUANTITY = DIMENSION, MIND = CONTAINER)

CEC540 Joan Jackson is **under** thirty.
   (MORE = UP)

Nevertheless, if we look carefully at the lexical details of the research reported in Chapter 2, we find further evidence of the metaphorical weakness of prepositions. Contradiction between the sets of metaphorical equations seems more prevalent in the case of orientational preposition metaphors than with other parts of speech, and with other analogical equations:

(6) EXISTENCE/HAPPENING = UP, exemplified by *arise, come up, crop up, emerge, surface, turn up, pop up, resurface, show up,* is contradicted by the expressions: something **befalls** you; one action **precipitates** another; an event **overtakes** you; a person/night **descends** on you.

(7) FUNCTIONING/ACTIVE = UP, exemplified by *get something off the ground, keep up/take up* (an activity), *spring into action, mount* (*a campaign/ exhibition*), *height of an* (activity), is contradicted when we talk about *a let-**up*** in activities.

Similarly *it's **up** to you* and *it's **down** to you* seem synonymous, and are a symptom of the larger-scale contradiction between Root Analogies CAUSE = UP and CAUSE = DOWN. In contrast with these prepositionally based metaphors, there were no contradictions noted in the category ABSTRACT QUALITY = PHYSICAL involving potentially contradictory adjectives in our Root Analogy map (Figure 2.1).

### 3.1.6. Summary

This section has argued that the reference to first-order entities associated with noun phrases increases the chances of metaphoric recognition and open-endedness of metaphoric interpretation. And that verbs/adjectives, adverbs and prepositions in that order are progressively less likely to be recognized as metaphorical, or give rise to rich interpretations. It is also worth recapping, here, on an overall three-way distinction: noun metaphors can undergo a referential interpretation and still be active; whereas verb/ adjective metaphors need to hook up to their conventional noun colligate, in order to preserve their metaphoric life; and adverbs and prepositions depend for any metaphoric force on their relationships to lexical gap-filling Root Analogies.

Given the fact that word-class will influence the interpretation of metaphors, it is worth considering the effects of word-formation involving changes in word-class, and this is the topic of the second half of this chapter.

### 3.2. WORD-FORMATION

We ought first to pause and consider the motivation behind word-formation and how it intermeshes with the functions of metaphor. One of the functions of metaphor is to plug lexical gaps, to give a label and a name to new concepts, new experiences, new objects (section 5.2.1). Presumably the same lexical gap-filling function is the motivation for word-formation by derivation. So, not surprisingly, metaphoric processes and derivational processes overlap, and, by combining, they produce metaphors which are Lexicalized and relatively Inactive simply because they are successful

(Low 1988: 127). Metaphor might be a more successful strategy for word-formation than, for example, borrowing, since the motivation/imagery it provides will have a positive mnemonic effect (Bauer 1983: 142).

### 3.2.1. Derivation and resemblance: resemblance incorporated in derivation

Of the whole set of derived lexical items in the dictionary there are important subsets which necessarily involve metaphor in their meaning. These include semantic classes of denominal verbs (verbs derived from nouns) such as:

> Verbs meaning 'to behave in the manner of, to act as, to resemble the person, animal or object denoted by the nouns' e.g. *dog, hog, parrot, shepherd, butcher* . . . Transitive verbs meaning 'to cause something to be, resemble the object denoted by the noun' or 'to treat something like the noun' . . . *sandwich, telescope, purse.*
>
> (Adams 1973: 44–5)

They also include a major set of noun compounds of the *resemblance* type which may be subdivided into

> 'B which is in the form of, has the physical features of A' . . . *apron stage, . . . box kite . . . sponge cake;* 'B which has some feature characteristic of A' . . . *mackerel sky, zebra crossing* . . . ; 'B which is like A's B' . . . *catcall . . . harelip . . . pug nose* . . . ; 'B which reminds one of A' . . . *frogman . . . hermit crab.*
>
> (ibid. 80–1)

*Table 3.1* Metaphorical meanings in word-formation

| Lexical item | Class | Meaning |
|---|---|---|
| CORNER$_1$ | Noun | angle enclosed by two walls |
| CORNER$_2$ | Verb | to put in, drive into an angle |
| CORNER$_3$ | Verb | to trap, put in a difficult position |
| | | |
| WHEEL OF A CART$_1$ | Noun | the wheel of a cart |
| CARTWHEEL$_2$ | Noun | the wheel of a cart |
| CARTWHEEL$_3$ | Noun | a sideways somersault |
| | | |
| WAGNER$_1$ | Noun | the composer Wagner |
| WAGNERIAN$_2$ | Adjective | belonging to the composer Wagner |
| WAGNERIAN$_3$ | Adjective | like that belonging to the composer Wagner |

A major set of adjective compounds of the comparative type can be subclassified as:

> Intensifying Comparatives . . . *crystal clear* . . . *razor sharp* . . . *dog tired*; and Particularizing Comparatives . . . *blood red* . . . *bottle green*.
> (Adams 1973: 97–8)

All such sets of derived lexical items are, according to my definition, capable of treatment as Inactive, Lexicalized metaphors.

### 3.2.2. Derivation and resemblance: resemblance associated with derivation

Even derived lexical items that are not intrinsically metaphorical, tend to extend their colligational range and to be used metaphorically. Consider the examples of a conversion (change of class without change of form), compound, and suffixed form in Table 3.1.

We start with the literal items, subscripted (1), which through derivation give us the still non-metaphorical meanings (2), and also a parallel metaphorical meaning (3).

Even though metaphor was not intrinsic to the derived items, as in meanings (2), the very act of derivation prepares the way for metaphorical transfer of meaning. In fact, we may have doubts whether CARTWHEEL$_2$ is commonly used any longer as a lexical item; as cartwheels go out of use so will the lexical item used to refer to them, and the metaphor will become deader (cf. *red herring*). CORNER$_3$ and CARTWHEEL$_3$ are more frequent meanings for these forms, closer to the core of the vocabulary. There is a touch of archaism, too, about the use of WAGNERIAN for meaning (2), the conversion, *Wagner*, being more likely for conveying this meaning, e.g. *Wagner operas*.

The suffix -(*i*)*an* is not unique in its tendency to produce derived forms which have both a literal and metaphorical meaning. Denominal adjectives, that is adjectives derived from nouns, with the suffixes -*ic*, -*ine*, -*ese*, -*ish* and -*al* regularly associate with such meanings:

| | | |
|---|---|---|
| (8) | *a musical language* | 'a language like music' |
| | *greenish colour* | 'colour like green' |
| | *meteoric rise* | 'rise like that of a meteor' |

Further evidence of the tendency to metaphorize derivatives comes from compounds – *molehill, antheap, crows'-feet, donkey-work, bull's-eye* – and denominal verb conversions (i.e. nouns turned into verbs without suffixation) – *cocoon, cloister, axe, catapult, hammer, plague, coin, pipe, flower, fish*. These verbs and compounds regularly occur as metaphorical clichés, in other words they tend to occur with a narrow range of colligates: e.g. *do the donkey-work, make a mountain out of a molehill, catapult to fame/*

Table 3.2 Word-formation processes in the HUMAN = ANIMAL analogy

| Conversions | | Suffixed adjectives | Compounds | Verb + preposition/ adverb | (Classical) burying of adjectives from species |
|---|---|---|---|---|---|
| Noun to verb | Noun to adjective/ premodifier | | | | |
| badger, dog, cow, crow (= boast), fox, hog, wolf (food down), fleece (victim = sheep) | cub (reporter), chicken, cuckoo, wildcat (strike), husky, ?kangaroo (court) | beefy, catty, horsey, kittenish, mousy, mulish, shrewish | catcall, copycat, crowsfeet, frogman, harelip, harebrained, horseplay, monkey-business, night owl, nitwit, outfox, pigheaded, pugnose, pussyfoot, rat-race, roadhog, scapegoat, black sheep | beaver away, clam up, chicken out, hare off, horse around | bovine, leonine, simian, reptilian |

*success, hammer home the point/argument, plagued with phone calls, coin a phrase, piped music, fish for compliments.*

The set of metaphors in the dictionary which conceptualize humans as animals shows how these processes of word-formation contribute to Lexicalization as in Table 3.2.

### 3.2.3. Conclusion on derivation and metaphor

The conclusion to be drawn from the lexical evidence is that the act of derivation is firmly associated with resemblance or metaphorical transfer of meaning.[3] In many cases the association is direct, because the derived form necessarily incorporates metaphor within its semantics. In other cases it is indirect: a history of derivation enhances the likelihood of lexical items being used metaphorically. For example, in a random sample of the words *dirt/dirty*, *angel/angelic* in the COBUILD corpus, the metaphorical meanings split as follows: *dirt* (12 per cent) vs *dirty* (26 per cent); *angel* (24 per cent) vs *angelic* (78 per cent): the suffixed forms always gave a higher proportion of metaphorical meanings than the noun from which they were derived.

One explanation for this phenomenon is that forms derived by suffixation and compounding are intermediate between one-word lexical items and multiple-word idioms. And, of course, they become even more like idioms in cases where they tend to form semi-fixed phrases or clichés. The point is that the individual morphemes are obscured or buried through the changes of form in compounding, suffixation, etc. However, this does not explain the ways in which denominal verb conversions (*cocoon, hammer*, etc.) achieve a semantic metaphorical meaning, as there is no change of form. We have to look back to our discussion of the image value of nouns for a fuller, psychological explanation.

### 3.2.4. The effects of derivation on metaphor: two hypotheses

With this in mind I would like to put forward and test against the textual evidence the following hypotheses about the effects of derivation on metaphor:

Given that

(1)    A sense of unconventional reference and/or semantic contradiction are essential for the recognition of a metaphor.

and

(2)    Noun phrases are more likely to produce a sense of unconventional reference or contradiction than other kinds of phrase.

it follows that

(Hypothesis A)    Derivation away from nouns will make the recognition of metaphors less likely.[4]

Given that

(3)    Congruently, straightforwardly, nouns refer to first-order entities.

and that

(4)    Reference to first-order entities is a condition for the richest kinds of image-based interpretation of Active metaphors.

it follows that

(Hypothesis B)    Derivation away from nouns will reduce the chances of an interpretation in which Topic and Vehicle concepts interact uniquely to generate Grounds.

In the following sections we survey the main kinds of denominal derivation which seem to have consequences for metaphorical interpretation. As we do so we will be illustrating the general points made in 3.2.1–3.2.3, and also be attempting to provide evidence for the above Hypotheses A and B.

### 3.2.4.1. Conversion: nouns and verbs

PM37    The seas **tented** up his oilskin till the skirt was crumpled above the waist.

PM63    He jerked the limpet away from him and the **tent** made a little flip of water in the sea.

This is an excellent example to begin our discussion since "tented", though a derived item, does not seem to be Lexicalized, i.e. is not to be found in the dictionary. If we can show that the metaphorical force is weakened and the interpretation less Interactive in such cases, then it is evidence for the effect of denominalization, quite separate from the effects of Lexicalization.

Indeed, multiplicity of Grounds, a richer Interactive interpretation, are more likely in PM63 than in PM37. Limpets resemble tents in several ways: certain tents are shaped remarkably like limpets, with slight ridges where the frame supports the canvas; tents, like limpet shells, are inhabited by living creatures; and a well-fixed tent is as solidly attached to the earth as limpets to a rock. If we try to subject the image of a tent to the same Interactive interpretation in PM37 then all we find are the rather vague Grounds of [shape] and [material] and perhaps [shelter]. PM37 loses little from a paraphrase *the seas pushed up his oilskin* etc.; pursuing a rich Interactive interpretation would not be worth the processing effort.

Other evidence for the hypotheses might be that Grounds are less likely to be contextually provided with the verb, than with the equivalent noun. Provision of Grounds is some guarantee that the metaphor is being used consciously (Hypothesis A), rather than as a cliché, and is also an attempt to narrow down the multiplicity of possible interpretations which interaction produces (Hypothesis B). This is clear with the following pair:

FF10     I am poised eighteen inches over the black **rivets** you are reading. I am in your place, shut in a bone box and trying *to fasten* myself on the white paper. The **rivets** *join* us *together*.

LM277    The eyes of most of the warriors **were riveted** on the earth.

The Grounds are supplied in FF10, to help us interpret the metaphor, but do not need to be in LM277, since it is both a denominal derivation and Lexicalized with a relatively narrow meaning.

Moreover, there is evidence that denominal verb metaphors do not intend us to evoke the image of the original Vehicle (Hypothesis A). We still talk about "dialling" on a push-button phone, even though there is no dial. In the following examples it makes nonsense to evoke an image of blots and clouds:

FF69    the broad figure **blotting out** the darkness

TI378   The light . . . **clouded** their night sight.

Blots are prototypically black, so to imagine blackness blotting out darkness causes confusion: *blot out* must be understood in its Lexicalized meaning 'to obscure'. Similarly confusion would be produced by trying to imagine a cloud covering the sun in TI378, since the light–dark relations would be reversed; *cloud* has to be interpreted as meaning 'to blur'.

We suggested in the previous section that denominal conversions often become Lexicalized with two meanings, a literal and a metaphorical one. FF62 supports the view that the metaphorical one is likely to be the most normal interpretation.

FF62    The verger had me cornered literally* in an angle.

The use of the word "literally" and the insistence on this literalness with the adverbial "in an angle" suggest that the normal interpretation is metaphorical.

*Table 3.3* Denominal adjective suffixes and their metaphorical semantics

| Suffix | Meanings | Productive | Examples of Lexicalized metaphors | Examples of unlexicalized metaphors |
|---|---|---|---|---|
| *-like* | metaphorical | extremely | **child**like | with **sloth**-like deliberation |
| *-y* | 'covered in' metaphorical | very | **mous**y (1) shy, (2) dull-brown | among the **fern**y weeds |
| *-ish* | 'of belonging to' metaphorical | moderately | **sheep**ish | the **clown**ish ill-made faces |
| *-oid* | 'of the shape/ substance' metaphorical Precision | moderately | **cub**oid | **fung**oid pallor |
| *-ous* | 'having plenty of' metaphorical | hardly | **monstr**ous (buried by clipping) | —— |
| *-ic/-iac/ -an/-ian* | 'of, belonging to' metaphorical (Precision) | hardly | **demon**iac (buried by stress shift) | —— |
| *-al/-ial/ -ine* | 'of belonging to' metaphorical (Precision) | hardly | **simi**an, **vestig**ial (classically buried) | —— |
| *-en* | 'of the substance' metaphorical | unproductive | **wood**en, **braz**en (formally buried; cf. brass) | —— |

*Note*: The following observations may be made about the individual suffixes in Table 3.3.

> *-like*: this can be tacked on any noun to form a hyphenated adjective. The more Lexicalized forms e.g. *childlike* are hyphenless.
>
> *-ish*: derivatives formed from the names of nationalities e.g. *Turkish, Polish* do not necessarily involve metaphor within their semantics. Novel uses are rarer than with *-y* and *-like*, and often include a sense of Approximation in their meaning; thus *Novemberish* might mean 'almost the same as that of November'.
>
> FF129 at that time, a **Novemberish** time of short days and cold and mud
>
> *-ic,-iac, -(i)an*: adjectives suffixed in *-(i)an* are grouped together with *-ic/-iac* forms since, at least when they are suffixed to proper names, they appear in a relation of morphological complementarity. Precision metaphorical interpretations are most common but not inevitable e.g. "the graph of his cyclic life" (his life is a cycle) (DV30).
>
> *-al/-ial/-ine*: these have a tendency to occur in combination with bases derived from classical roots.

### 3.2.4.2. Suffixation

#### Noun to adjective

Brooke-Rose (1958: 238) and Mooij (1976: 170ff.) suggested that the act of suffixation of nouns to form adjectives can be one way of marking and deadening metaphor (Hypothesis A). This section will demonstrate this suffocation by suffixation, as it were, and also consider how the degree of productivity of the most common suffixes affects the interpretation of the metaphor so signalled.

The suffixes under consideration in this section are *-like, -ish, -y, -ous, -ic/-iac/-ian/-an, -al/-ial/-ine, -oid* and *-en.* (See Table 3.3.) There are two general strategies of metaphorical interpretation which apply not only to these suffixes, but also to noun–noun compounds (see Section 2.3), similes (Chapters 6, 8) and noun premodifiers (Chapter 7). I shall call these Precision and Contradiction interpretations. To illustrate, "cavernous water" (TI126) and "elephantine woman" (FF15) require Contradiction interpretations: 'the water is (like) a cavern', 'the woman is (like) an elephant'. By contrast "fungoid pallor" (TI18) and "elephantine progress" (LF214) require Precision interpretations: 'pallor (like that) of fungus', 'progress (like that) of an elephant'. (Adams calls these *Intensifying* and *Particularizing* Comparatives (Adams 1973: 97–8)). With Precision interpretations the noun head provides the G-term for the metaphor, whereas with Contradiction interpretations the noun head provides the T-term.

#### Summary of Table 3.2

What then are the general conclusions from Table 3.2?

- Apart from *-like*, which necessarily involves resemblance, all the suffixes are ambiguous as to whether they include metaphor in their interpretations or not (column 2).

- *-oid* and *-ian/-ic/-an/-ian* when suffixed to proper nouns, usually receive Precision interpretations, but in all other cases both Contradiction and Precision interpretations are possible (column 2).

- The order in which I have placed these suffixes indicates decreasing productivity, and the more productive they are the more Active their interpretations are likely to be (column 3). The suffix *-like* has no restrictions on its productivity, *-y* is relatively productive, *-ish* less so. At the other end of the spectrum *-en* is not productive at all.[5] The remaining suffixes fall somewhere between *-ish* and *-en* in their levels of productivity and their potential for marking Active metaphor.

● The less productive suffixes have given rise to inactive Lexicalized metaphors (Hypothesis B), and this is often accompanied by a change of phonological and/or graphological form, a tendency to bury the Dead metaphor (column 4).

Incidentally we notice that the derived form may have a kind of "back-wash" effect on metaphorical uses of the original noun. It is difficult to use the original noun *mouse* as a V-term without its interpretation being skewed towards the Lexicalized meaning of *mousey*.

> SL162 There were three children . . . the girl with fine colourless curls so that Alexander thought of mouse fur and its shadowy paleness and only then remembered that that word, for hair, was rubbed clean of any lively associations.

## Nominalization

The basic theory of proper nominalization is that a nominalized form represents qualities and processes as abstracted from things and time respectively. We can talk of orders of entities in terms of existence in space, and existence in time. First-order entities/things have existence in space, second-order entities/processes have existence in time, and third-order entities/abstractions have existence in neither.

Nominalizations are Proper if they refer to third-order entities, e.g. *Cooking involves irreversible chemical changes*, in which *cooking* refers to the process as a generic type, abstracted from a particular token instance at a specific time.

Other kinds of nominalizations have been called Improper (Vendler 1968: 32–4, 40–3). These refer to first-order entities, entities with physical substance and dimensions in space, e.g. *I like John's cooking*, which refers to the food which results from the cooking.

It is clear that Improper nominalization, creating a noun which refers to a thing or substance, both enhances the likelihood of recognition and the image/activity level of the metaphor. However it is not always easy to decide whether nominalizations are Proper or Improper. One device for blurring the distinction is zeugma, where a concrete and abstract term are conjoined as objects of the same verb:

> FF67 The lady with the green leathery plant brought in a bucket of coal and some advice.

Proper nominalization, on the other hand, tends to weaken metaphorical effects. Often it makes possible the incorporation of the noun into a larger semi-fixed prefabricated phrase, which is processed as a unit, somewhat like an idiom, and this will have a debilitating effect on any underlying metaphor. Phrases like *give an impression, put pressure on*, etc. are examples.

*Table 3.4* Passivization, nominalization and metaphor

| Transitivity | Participants | Example |
|---|---|---|
| Active | Actor + Goal | MPs have pressed the prime minister for an enquiry |
| Passive | Goal [+ Actor] | the pressed face of the old man |
| Nominalization | [+ Actor/Goal] | there was a kind of interior pressure |

Similarly, a reduced metaphoric force is evident where nominalization operates on adjectives or other concrete nouns.

DV78    This experience removed any magnetism there was in London.

*London was less magnetic* or *London was less of a magnet*, hackneyed though they are, seem somewhat more vital than the metaphor in DV78.

Moreover, Proper nominalizations, and to a lesser extent passives/past participles, reduce the need to specify participants; as Table 3.4 shows, Actor (the person or thing that causes the action) can be omitted with passives, and with nominalizations both Actor and Goal (the thing affected by the action) are optional [in brackets]. This means we are less inclined to supply colligates which could enhance the metaphor's image value. In addition, selectional restriction violations signalling metaphors will not apply. So Proper nominalization and use of past participles tend to weaken metaphors.

## Deverbal participles/adjectives

DT1    the much **heralded** [a] and well **orchestrated** [b] public hearings

We can group our examples into two predictable sets. There are those which have undergone derivation before suffixation by *-ed/-ing*, though not necessarily incorporating metaphor into their semantics. Examples are "orchestrated" (DT1a) and

CEC703    a fairly **sheltered** residential secretarial college
PM174    a **flaming** needle
FF197    **shivering** laughter

And there are those for which metaphor is intrinsic to the semantics. For instance, "heralded" (DT1a) and

TI170    in **craning** glimpses
PM15    the **scalloped** and changing shape of the swell

DT1b and CEC703 show, once more, how a history of non-metaphoric derivation prepares the way for metaphorical uses. Though one can literally orchestrate music and shelter a person, *orchestrated* and *sheltered* have metaphorical proclivities.

What are the effects of this move away from verbs towards adjectival status? To the extent that they are Lexicalized as adjectives and/or form part of clichés, their new meanings obscure the original referents. Thus the more Lexicalized *orchestrated* is less likely to suggest music or an orchestra than "flaming" (PM174) is to evoke fire or flame.

There are plenty of examples of recursive derivation which can end up as participial adjectives.

## ■ EXERCISE

*Take the phrase* fortified wine. *What stages of derivation bring about the adjective* fortified, *and what effect does this derivation have on the metaphor?*

Such multiple derivations, starting from a noun, deriving a verb, and then resulting in a past participle used as an adjective, magnify the effects of denominal derivation and support our hypotheses. There is little chance of evoking the original image of a fort when processing this phrase.

### 3.2.4.3. Phrasal verbs

Phrasal verbs resemble compounds and suffixed forms, and perhaps idioms, because they all have the potential to obscure the morphemic structure of their constituent parts. So, for example, *carry out, public house, brazen* and *kick the bucket* each tend to be processed as one morpheme, rather than the two which they incorporate from a diachronic and derivational perspective. This dissolving of morpheme boundaries weakens the metaphoric potential of the original morphemes.

Let's first of all consider the relative metaphoric strength of denominal verb conversions compared with denominal verbs which have been phrasalized.

TI185    The fire **pulse**d out light with each addition.

PM143    Like his hands the sea **pulse**d.

(9)    The interview **whip**ped up half the British people into a frenzy of rage.

The attaching of a preposition/adverb in TI185 makes the interpretation more straightforward, probably because it could be conceived as helping to specify Grounds; the movement of the blood/light *outwards* as a result of pumping may well be intended. In PM143 by contrast, there is relatively little help in deciding on Grounds, and as a result the interpretation is more Interactive. "Whipped up" in (9) is much more Lexicalized as a phrasal verb than "pulsed out". In fact it does not necessarily suggest the image of a whip any more, being more likely to evoke wind or a food-mixer. This vagueness and extension of colligational range makes the metaphor less powerful.

Identification of phrasal verbs can be difficult. There may be problems in deciding whether an adverb/preposition is separate from the verb or a two-word verb. So there are two alternative analyses of (10a) and (11a):

| (10) | a. | The parachutist | dropped | out | at 7,000 feet. |
|------|----|-----------------|---------|-----|----------------|
|      | b. | Subject | IVerb | IAdverbial | IAdverbial |
|      | c. | Subject | IVerb | | IAdverbial |

| (11) | a. | We | put | the dog | down. |
|------|----|----|-----|---------|-------|
|      | b. | Subject | IVerb . . . | IObject | I . . . Verb |
|      | c. | Subject | IVerb | IObject | IAdverbial |

Metaphorical meaning is associated with the kind of parsing in (10c) and (11b) where the phrasal verb constitutes one lexical item (cf. Low 1988: 136). If the example (10a) above is literal, (10b) is a better analysis than (10c). If (11a) is metaphorical, meaning 'destroy humanely', then (11b) is a better parsing than (11c). To give another illustration, the literal (12), in the course of a driving lesson, is just possible:

(12)   Down we put the accelerator.

whereas if we try to front the adverb in the metaphorical phrasal verb we get something ungrammatical:

(13)   *Down we put the dog.

At the further extreme of metaphorical debilitation some phrasal verbs have become so entirely divorced from the meaning of the separate words that it is well-nigh impossible to perceive any metaphorical connection:

CEC689   She just passed out.
DM11     where he carried out assaults on the nine-year-old girl

### 3.2.4.4. Prefixes

Prefixation, too, gives much interesting evidence of the effects of Burying. Most prefixed forms are more likely to incorporate metaphorical resemblance in their semantics than their unprefixed equivalents. Notable examples are found with the prefixes *un-*, *dis-*, *re-*, *en-*.

We can see that the following lexical items fall into three groups.

(14)   a.   *rehash, disjointed, disclose,* where the unprefixed form represents only a literal meaning: *hash* = 'cut up small', *jointed* = 'connected by joints', *close* = 'shut'.

         b.   *unclean, unclear, unbridled, unburden, review, reproduce, reshuffle, restructure, disharmony, discover, discount* (verb), where the unprefixed form represents either a Lexicalized metaphorical or literal meaning, e.g. *clear, bridled*, but the prefixed form necessarily represents a metaphorical one.

c.   *recast, rekindle, replace, enmesh, enshroud,* where the probability of the prefixed form representing a metaphorical meaning is higher than with the unprefixed form.

The following *en-* prefixed verbs, unlike *enmesh* and *enshroud* (which have equivalent unprefixed verbs: *mesh, shroud*), show signs of a double and simultaneous Lexicalization strategy: the conversion of noun (or adjective) into a verb, and prefixation. In a sense, therefore, it is possible to suggest that they resemble category (14a) above.

(15)   *enfeeble, engulf, enlarge on, enlighten, enshrine, enthrall, entrance, entrench*

## ■ EXERCISE

*(LSJAP)   Time yet . . . for a hundred visions and revisions,*
    *Before the taking of a toast and tea.*

*Explain the wordplay in T.S. Eliot's lines, and say if and how metaphor might be involved.*

### 3.2.5. Word-formation and the delicate grammar of metaphorical lexis

We have seen, in sections 3.2.4.2–4, how morphological changes – suffixation, phrasalization of verbs, and prefixation – are used to Lexicalize metaphors and incorporate them into the semantic system. We can also note from Table 3.1, the lexis for HUMAN = ANIMAL, evidence of these and other kinds of Burying processes: compounding; and Latinate equivalents such as *leonine*, a deep burial. While all these changes are morphological, affixation often causes changes in the grammatical category of word-class too. And conversion (section 3.2.4.1) is not a change of form, but solely a change of word-class.

Besides these gross word-class changes, more delicate syntactic variations are equally significant in lexicalizing metaphors. As an example consider the verb *stick.* If used with a direct object and no adverbial it will invariably have a metaphorical use: *We stuck the full course, I don't know how I stuck it.* But if we use it with a direct object and an adverbial it is more than likely literal: *They went round sticking posters on walls and lamp-posts, Stick a numbered label on each case.* Similarly with *stick to.* If you use the verb + object + (*to*) adverbial then the use will probably be literal. If you use the verb *stick to* + adverbial then the meaning will be more metaphorical, e.g. *He insisted on sticking to his original idea, We'd better stick to the rules.*

Transitivity shift is often a marker of metaphorical uses (cf. Roper and

Siegel 1978: 202–3). Hence the shift from the intransitive and literal *I staggered to the nearest chair* to the transitive and metaphorical *An event that staggered the world* or *They staggered their church-going hours.*

If these delicate grammatical shifts in valency, like the grosser kinds of Burying, are means of Lexicalizing metaphors, then identity of form, word-class and valency can also be a guide to which analogy is valid. For example the many metaphoric possibilities with the verb *run* can be narrowed down if we insist on identical syntactic configurations for V-terms and T-terms. So the different syntactic configurations of *run* in the following examples suggests the pairs:

(16)  a.  run in a marathon
      b.  **run** in an election

(17)  a.  run a horse (in a race)
      b.  **run** a business

(18)  a.  The water is running clear.
      b.  Emotions are **running** high.

### 3.2.6. Summary

We have sufficient evidence to show that word-formation, especially of the denominal kind, involves or prepares the way for metaphorical extensions and transfers of meaning, while at the same time weakening those metaphors it makes possible.[6] They are weakened in the sense of being less noticeable (Hypothesis A), and less likely to give rise to Interactive interpretations (Hypothesis B). This inactivity will be most pronounced when the derived forms have been used so frequently that they are Lexicalized, all but one Ground of interpretation having been pruned away. In the area of denominal adjectives formed by suffixation, we showed that the productivity of the suffix can give some guide to the likely degree of Lexicalization undergone. These gross syntactic changes of word-class are also parallelled, at a more delicate level, by valency shifts for verbs, which also have a role in Lexicalizing metaphors.

We can conclude that since the main motive of word-formation is the plugging of lexical gaps, the metaphors facilitated by word-formation are doomed, from birth, to a life of inactivity and an early death, runts of the metaphorical litter, so to speak. In addition, any change of form, phonological or graphological, brought about or accompanied by affixation, compounding or phrasalization will further disguise or bury the metaphor.

Word-formation, and metaphor, working hand in hand, are devices for incorporating interpretations which were once highly dependent on pragmatics into coded meanings which are part of the semantic lexicon: coral polyps, as it were, incorporating the meanings in flux in the sea into the relatively solid structures of the reef of language.

# 4

# HOW DIFFERENT KINDS OF
# METAPHORS WORK

## 4.1. INTRODUCTION

This chapter elaborates and discusses a detailed definition/description of metaphor, showing seven different kinds of interpretation (section 4.2). It goes on to survey traditional theories of metaphorical interpretation, and concludes that metaphor is best conceived as an invitation to make comparisons (section 4.3). This being the case Similarity and Analogy are important factors and they are defined and exemplified (section 4.4). Finally it delineates less central kinds of metaphorical interpretation associated with literary and artistic representation (section 4.5), such as Subjective and Asymmetric metaphors, and discusses the concept of metaphorical worlds. These phenomena, which cannot be ignored when analysing metaphors in real texts, have a strong enough family resemblance to central kinds of metaphor to be subsumed under our definition.

### 4.1.1. Conventionality as a cline

In the first three chapters we demonstrated that the distinction between metaphorical and literal language is not clear-cut: the same processes of matching necessary for literal utterances come into play in the understanding of metaphorical utterances; and repeated metaphors provide us with cognitive furniture and become absorbed by word-formation and other Lexicalization processes into the dictionary.

How does this affect our working definition of metaphor? It means, of course, that we have to consider the adjective "conventional" as a scalar and relative one. It is possible for a use of a lexical item to be more or less conventional than another use. Thus with Tired metaphors such as *fox* interpreted as meaning 'cunning person', although this interpretation is conventional it can be regarded as less conventional than the interpretation 'dog-like mammal'. Unfortunately this distinction may prove to be too easy: conventions of language are not simply a matter of vocabulary use in some kind of decontextualized vacuum, but may be established by the genre. So that the conventions for the referent of *mouse* will be different in the genre of computer hardware catalogues and fairy stories. Conventions can also be stipulated by individual texts in much the same manner as algebra problems often start *Let* x *stand for* . . . . These are matters which we will explore further in Chapters 9 and 10.

Leaving aside the question of genre and specific text, we might be tempted to equate conventionality with frequency of occurrence in a general balanced corpus. But even this could raise problems with Inactive metaphors. Supposing we take the Sleeping metaphor *crane* interpreted as referring to the machine. The difficulty is that the 'machine' meaning might be more frequent in a corpus than the 'bird' meaning. To overcome this problem the language user may have to resort to other criteria or sources of knowledge besides frequency in order to decide on what was the original conventional referent.

Some of these criteria have been touched on in previous chapters, and include lack of derivation (section 3.2.4), concreteness (Figure 2.1, rows A, B, C and D), and historical awareness. The derivation criterion indicates that the original conventional referent is the uncompounded *wheel of a cart* rather than *cartwheel*. Being relatively concrete 'the opening in the eye' looks like the original conventional referent of *pupil* rather than 'student', which depends on second-order entities like teaching. As far as *crane* is concerned, our historical awareness tells us that cranes, the birds, predate cranes, the machines.

We can also interpret conventionality in the sense of arbitrariness and a tradition of agreement among members of a community. Though the members of the community have agreed that *crane* should refer to a hoisting machine, once they are aware of the metaphor, they know that this meaning is less traditional and more motivated, less arbitrary than when it refers to a bird.

Though this question of conventionality is a little tricky with Inactive metaphors, we resolved it by defining convention in terms of frequency, lack of derivation, first-order entity-hood, arbitrariness of tradition, and priority in history. Luckily, with Active metaphors unconventionality creates no particular problems and can therefore distinguish effectively language which is prototypically metaphorical in use.

## 4.2. AN IMPROVED DEFINITION

When we consider in detail and rigorously how different kinds of metaphor work we need to produce a more precise definition than our original working one.

(1)  A metaphor occurs when a unit of discourse$_{4.2.1}$ is used to refer$_{4.2.2}$ to an object, concept, process, quality, relationship or world$_{4.5.5}$ to which it does

not conventionally refer$_{4.2.3}$, or colligates with a unit(s) with which it does not conventionally colligate$_{4.2.4}$; and when this unconventional act of reference or colligation is understood$_{4.5.2}$ on the basis of similarity or analogy$_{4.4}$ involving at least two of the following: the unit's conventional referent; the unit's actual unconventional referent; the actual referent(s) of the unit's actual colligate(s); the conventional referent of the unit's conventional colligate(s)$_{4.2.5}$.

This is a difficult description to get one's mind round immediately, so most of this chapter will be devoted to explaining and exemplifying it. The subscripts refer to the sections of the chapter where each part of the definition is discussed.

### 4.2.1. Unit of discourse and the scope of the metaphor

The unit of discourse in the definition is what we have labelled the *Vehicle-term*. It would be wrong to assume that V-terms extend only over the single word, single lexical item, or simple noun phrase. To give a few examples, they may extend over verb phrases (in the generative grammar sense), i.e. predicates:

DM30    Although Atkinson **lost that fight** . . .

prepositional phrases:

GH38–9    You never know what's **around the corner**.

noun phrases postmodified by prepositional phrases or clauses:

PQ86    Sex is only **the liquid centre of the great Newberry Fruit** of friend-ship. (Jilly Cooper)

PQ72    Mankind is **a club to which we owe a subscription**. (G.K. Chesterton)

and verbs + adverbials:

DT16    until James Callaghan is **washed up onto the pebbles** of the Upper House

A particularly important variety of metaphor is one which extends over the clause or sentence. Here we find proverbs:

(2)    **Too many cooks spoil the broth**.

as well as other epigrammatic gnomic utterances:

SM42    **A man will tell you that he has worked in a mine for forty years unhurt by an accident, as a reason why he should apprehend no danger, though the roof is beginning to sink**; and it is often obser-vable that the older a man gets, the more difficult it is for him to retain a believing conception of his own death.

There is even a sense in which metaphors can extend over whole discourses or texts.

### 4.2.2. Reference and the pragmatic nature of metaphor

The words *occurs, is used, is understood, refer, referent* in the definition (p. 108) locate metaphor within pragmatics rather than semantics. This vocabulary suggests that metaphor is an event occurring at a particular time and that this occurrence depends on a language use and language interpretation on the part of the speaker and hearer. Although, as we have seen in Chapters 1 and 2, Inactive metaphors may become Lexicalized and acquire a new conventional semantic meaning, Active metaphor is highly dependent on inferential pragmatic principles to do with language use and users in contexts. One area of pragmatics – reference, the establishing of relations between language and the world – is central to my definition. And referential or connotative meaning, which may be defined as "what is communicated by virtue of what language refers to" (Leech 1974: 26), is crucially important for reaching the Grounds of interpretation.

I must point out, however, that the notion of reference employed in this definition is not the strictest kind used by philosophers of language, as for example in Searle (1969). According to the narrowest criteria, referring expressions have to be noun phrases. Some of the metaphorically used units of discourse will be noun phrases, e.g.:

NS4   The primary lymphatic organs are **the police training colleges**.

but others will not:

CEC520   The Restoration and the 18th Century is very well **catered for**.

We can explain the interpretation of CEC520 in terms of our definition, by saying that "catered for" is referring to a concept 'provided for' to which it does not conventionally refer.

### 4.2.3. The referent of the unit of discourse: Topic and Vehicle

There may be several kinds of Topic, i.e. unconventional referent of the V-term. These would include objects, qualities, processes, concepts, relationships. We could use the word *entity* to cover some of these referents: objects are first-order entities, imaginable because they have spatial dimensions; processes are second-order entities, which occur in time rather than having existence in space; and concepts are higher-order entities or abstractions.

One interesting idea is that the Topic may constitute a whole world. This accounts for our intuition that novels or plays, for example, are extended metaphors depicting a possible but non-literal world (Elam 1980: 99–113).

When we use language conventionally we tend to use it to refer to the real world rather than to imaginary worlds.

As for the Vehicle, the conventional referent of the referring term, this cannot be a token of an object or process but will be a more typical image or concept. So we have an asymmetry: Topics can be actual objects, part of the physical situation of discourse, but this is unlikely for Vehicles. For example, if a botanist were comparing two specimens of plants visible to both speakers, we would have deliberate literal comparison rather than a metaphorical expression.

### 4.2.4. Colligational and Referential interpretations

We already have, in this description, two major classes of metaphor which we may label the *Referential* and *Colligational*. In the Introduction I introduced the referential kind, but the trickier colligational variety needs exemplification. Look at this clause from Ted Hughes' poem 'Wind' describing a gale blowing:

TH24    Winds **stampeding** the fields

The V-term "stampeding" colligates unconventionally with "the fields", which is part of an extended T-term. Understanding involves supplying the conventional colligate for stampeding *cows/horses*, extending the V-term, and also supplying a term for the actual referent (the Topic), perhaps *blowing over*. The first stage of the interpretation might be diagrammed as follows:[1]

(3)    T-terms:    Wind        [blowing over]    the fields
          V-terms:                    stampeding        [cows/horses]

The Grounds can then be worked out by looking for similarities or analogies between the effect of the wind blowing on the fields, and the stampeding of cows/horses; perhaps the tossing of the corn resembles the bucking and rearing of horses or the rippling of their manes. As already noted metaphorical interpretation which depends upon supplying conventional colligates in this way has been called *Vehicle-construction* (Reinhart 1976).[2]

We will find that most metaphors both refer and colligate unconventionally. However, there are some whose Unconventionality is confined to their reference.

(4)    Singapore is **an island** of efficiency and cleanliness in South-east Asia.

Example (4) contains nothing in the way of unusual colligation since "island" may be interpreted literally or metaphorically. Similarly, when Pincher Martin refers to a rock as a suitcase:

111

PM61    He put his back against **the suitcase**.

the unconventionality lies primarily in its reference.

### 4.2.5. The pathways through the definition: seven kinds of metaphor

In this section I demonstrate the seven main combinations of options for metaphorical use which seem to be realized in practice. Table 4.1 details the kinds of Unconventionality (column 3), and which of the four elements are likely to be involved in interpretations (columns 4–7): the Vehicle (or conventional referent); the Topic (or conventional referent); the actual colligate referent (part of Topic); and the referent of the conventional colligate (Vehicle construct). Please note that this table is not concerned with whether the T-terms and conventional colligates are present in the text.

#### 4.2.5.1. Pathway 1

A unit of discourse is used to refer unconventionally and its understanding involves the unit's conventional referent (Vehicle) and the unit's unconventional referent (Topic), e.g. PM61 above where the conventional referent (Vehicle) is a suitcase and the actual unconventional referent (Topic) is the rock.

#### 4.2.5.2. Pathway 2

A unit of discourse is used to refer unconventionally and its understanding involves the unit's conventional referent (Vehicle) and the actual referent of the actual colligate (Topic):

TS    The building was **a barn**.

In this case "building" refers to a cathedral undergoing reconstruction work. The conventional referent (Vehicle) is a barn, and the actual referent of the actual colligate (Topic) is the cathedral.

#### 4.2.5.3. Pathway 3

The unit of discourse refers and colligates unconventionally and understanding involves the conventional referent (Vehicle) and the actual unconventional referent (Topic) which is referred to by the actual colligate (T-term):

TS8    The transepts were **his arms** outspread.
PQ36    (We roll back the lid of) **the sardine tin** of life. (Alan Bennett)

Table 4.1 Pathways of metaphorical interpretation

| Pathway | Example | Unconventional | Elements involved in interpretation | | | | |
|---|---|---|---|---|---|---|---|
| | | | Vehicle | Topic | Actual referent of actual colligate (Topic) | Conventional referent of conventional colligate (Vehicle construct) | Similarity Analogy |
| 1 | He put his back against **the suitcase** | Reference | √suitcase | √rock | | | Similarity |
| 2 | The building was **a barn** | Reference | √barn | √ = cathedral | √cathedral | | Similarity |
| 3 | **the sardine tin** of life | Reference Colligation | √sardine tin | √ = life | √life | | Similarity (Analogy) |
| 4 | John is **a pig** | Reference Colligation | √pig | √(G) greedy | √John | | Similarity |
| 5 | the **naked** shingles (of the world) | Reference Colligation | √naked | √uncovered | √shingles | √body | Analogy |
| 6 | the air was **thick** | Reference Colligation | √thick | (√)? | √air | √solid/liquid | Analogy |
| 7 | her son had been **damaged** in a crash | Colligation | | | √son | √object | Similarity |

In the case of TS8, which is comparing the parts of a cathedral with a prostrate human body, the unconventional referent and the unconventional colligate are identical because the copula is equative rather than ascriptive. PQ36 can similarly be regarded as the equivalent of an equative clause.

### 4.2.5.4. Pathway 4

A unit of discourse both refers and colligates unconventionally and its understanding involves the conventional referent (Vehicle) and unconventional referent (Topic/Ground) and the actual referent of the actual colligate(s) (Topic).

(5)     John is **a pig**.

DM7    A Tory MP's bid to rush through tough new obscenity laws **was blocked** yesterday by Labour and Alliance MPs.

In (5) the unconventional referent (Topic/Ground) would be the concept 'greedy' or 'dirty', the conventional referent (Vehicle) would be a pig, and the referent of the actual colligate would be the person, John (Topic). Superficially this looks like "The transepts were his arms outspread", but the difference is that (5) is Inactive, and much more ascriptive than equative, so that we have to locate the Topic in two places: the concept 'greedy' or 'dirty', where Topic is indistinguishable from Grounds; and the actual colligate referent 'John'. The same analysis can apply to DM7, where the unconventional referent of "was blocked" is the concept 'was prevented'. The role of the actual colligates in the case of Lexicalized Inactive metaphors such as these, is little more than that of disambiguation, a way of helping us choose between prepackaged meanings, one slightly less conventional than another.

### 4.2.5.5. Pathway 5

The unit of discourse refers and colligates unconventionally and understanding involves the conventional referent (Vehicle), the actual unconventional referent (Topic), the actual referent of the actual colligate (part of Topic), and the conventional referent of the conventional colligate (Vehicle construct).

DB    Down the vast edges dreàr and **naked** shingles of the world

In DB pathway 4 is a possibility; we need not incorporate the conventional colligate of "naked", i.e. *body*, in the interpretation. But in the context of the poem 'Dover Beach' by Matthew Arnold, where the sea has been previously described as "a bright girdle", it makes sense to do so. We then arrive at an interpretation which takes into account all four elements: . the actual unconventional referent (Topic) is the concept 'uncovered'; the

114

conventional referent (Vehicle) is the concept 'naked'; the actual referent of the actual colligate (part of Topic) is shingles; and the conventional referent of the conventional colligate (Vehicle construct) is the concept 'body'.

### 4.2.5.6. Pathway 6

The unit of discourse refers and colligates unconventionally and understanding involves the conventional referent (Vehicle), the referent of the actual colligate (part of Topic), and the conventional referent of the conventional colligate (Vehicle-construct). The point of the metaphor is to determine and/or label the actual referent of the unit (Topic).

DN   The air was **thick**

The interpretation depends on the conventional colligates, for example, of *thick* in order to recognize an analogy between solids (or liquids, e.g. *thick porridge*) and gases: the value of the referent of *thick* is X in the following formula:

thick : solid : : X : air

It is apparent that, although DN can be interpreted in terms of pathway 5, the unconventional referent of the unit of discourse (Topic) is elusive, and difficult to paraphrase. "Thick" refers to 'whatever, in relation to air, thick is in relation to solids (liquids)'.

### 4.2.5.7. Pathway 7

The unit of discourse refers conventionally but colligates unconventionally. Understanding involves the conventional referent of the conventional colligate (Vehicle construct) and the referent of the actual colligate (Topic).

VG16   a woman whose son had been **damaged** in a smash

There is no difference between the conceptual meanings of *injure* and *damage*. The difference lies in their typical colligations, *injure* with animates (and external body parts: *injure a foot*), *damage* with inanimates (and internal organs: *damage your liver*). The interpretation depends on similarity between the referent of the actual colligate and the referent of the conventional colligate: the boy referred to by "son" and an inanimate object.

You will have noticed that the labels Topic, Vehicle and Ground are not applied unproblematically in all these interpretative pathways. In the example in pathway 4, because it is an Inactive metaphor, there is an ascriptive merging of Topic and Ground and the Topic is a subset of the concepts associated with the Vehicle. But along pathways 2, 3 and 4 the referent of the actual colligate is also part of the Topic. In pathway 5, with its Vehicle-construction, the Topic and Vehicle are both extended beyond the metaphorical item itself. In pathway 6 the Topic seems unspecifiable unless such an extension takes place. Pathway 7 is an even more extreme version of pathway 6 since both Topic and Vehicle only seem to be hinted at by the metaphorical item itself, which I therefore hesitate to call the V-term. The conventional and actual unconventional colligates of this term are what refer to the Vehicle and Topic respectively. Rather than perceiving this difficulty in labelling as a problematic symptom, we could in fact use it as a diagnosis for recognizing different interpretive categories, the concern of the next section.

## 4.3.  INTERPRETATIVE THEORIES

Much of the early controversy in theories of metaphor arose from the failure to recognize the varieties of interpretative strategies which come into play. The three main theories which emerged were the Substitution Theory, the Interaction Theory, and the Comparison Theory. I will briefly describe each in turn.

### 4.3.1. Substitution Theory

The Substitution Theory stated that the V-term was substituting for a literal term, that the meaning of the metaphor can be discovered by replacing the literal term, and that metaphor was, therefore, a kind of decorative device (Black 1962: 224–5). Adherents of the substitution view tended to illustrate their ideas by the use of Tired metaphors, which could be interpreted out of context, e.g. *rat* (meaning 'disloyal person'). In the tradition of generative grammar, theorists in this framework would label some metaphors (i.e. the Tired ones) as "acceptable" and others like *quit donkeying with my car* as "unacceptable". And their decision would be based on the paraphraseability of the metaphor (Bickerton 1969: 39–41). This austere theory left no room for pluralism in metaphorical interpretation: it did not allow that any one token – particular instance – of a metaphorical expression might receive a number of different and partial interpretations, none of which amounted to an adequate paraphrase; and that different tokens of the same type of metaphorical expression might, in their differing co-texts and contexts, receive different interpretations; and, most important, it failed to recognize that Inactive metaphors and Active metaphors demand and receive different kinds of interpretation. In short, it overgeneralized a theory of metaphorical interpretation suitable only for Inactive metaphors.

Even with Inactive metaphors the Substitution Theory actually fails since, for example, it is impossible to paraphrase the meanings of place prepositions like *within* used to refer to time, without resorting to other place or space metaphors: **within** six months – **inside** six months – **before** six months have **passed** – etc. We should also note the convincing research of Gibbs (1992). He shows that many idioms, at least the non-opaque metaphorical kind, cannot be reduced to a literal paraphrase, because they carry with them a conceptual metaphorical schema; and that various features of the source domain, the Vehicle, are mapped on to the target domain. For example *blow your stack* does not mean the same as *get angry*, because the former implies pressure, lack of intention and force in a way that the paraphrase does not. The findings here support the idea that, although the meanings of such idioms are relatively predictable, the metaphor is not dead, that is to say the image schema behind it is still partially activated (Gibbs 1992: 504).

### 4.3.2. Interaction, Tension and Controversion Theories[3]

The more convincing Interaction Theory concentrated on Active metaphors. Adherents of this theory recognized that there are two distinct subjects, Topic and Vehicle; that the metaphorical utterance projects certain features of the Vehicle, i.e. Grounds, on to the Topic; and that the Vehicle and Topic interact in two ways: through a process of selection, suppression and emphasis of features which can be predicated of the Topic; and through the fact that not only is the Topic made to seem more like the Vehicle, but the Vehicle is made to seem more like the Topic. Black's example (1962: 231) makes this clearer:

(6)   A battle is a game of chess.

In Example (6) there are two distinct subjects, the battle (Topic) and the game of chess (Vehicle). The utterance of the metaphor projects features of the Vehicle on to the Topic. The selection of these features, suppression of some and emphasis of others, is determined by the interaction of Topic and Vehicle: in this case positions, relationships and status of combatants, casualties, speed of movement, will be presumably emphasized as Grounds, whereas other features of battles – topography, weapons, weather, supplies, etc. – will be suppressed. The theory suggests, finally, that not only is a battle made to seem more like a game of chess, but a game of chess is made to seem more like a battle (Black 1962: 230ff.).

The Interactive theory seems capable of dealing with Active metaphors following pathways 1, 2 and 3. Pathways 5, 6 and 7 are more of a problem, until we realize that the features which form the Grounds of the metaphor were originally formulated by Black as associated commonplaces (1962: 230). If these commonplaces may be verbal, then Interactive theory can include the conventional colligates. But the theory is weak in accounting for those aspects of interpretation in pathways 5 and 6 which involve analogy, and seems primarily oriented towards noun-based metaphors. We need a larger theory, a modified Comparison Theory, to encompass both the limited insights of Substitution Theory and the more fruitful Interaction Theory, while compensating for the latter's failure to recognize the importance of analogy and Vehicle-construction.

It is also worth questioning the claim in the Interaction Theory that Vehicles are necessarily made to seem more like the Topics, as well as vice versa. Certainly the lexical evidence in Chapter 2 gives some examples of reversal, e.g. JUSTICE/LAW = STRAIGHT (LINE) is reversed when, in printing, we talk of "*justifying* the margins". FREEDOM = SPACE TO MOVE/ MOBILITY can be turned round to give us *free-size*. And feminists object to the V-term *father* for referring to God partly because it makes fathers seem more like gods. But I doubt if this *inter*activity is very widespread. Black's choice of example was, anyway, somewhat disingenuous, since chess was originally modelled on war, so we can easily be reminded that chess is like a battle.

Building on the Interactive theory, Berggren (1962) and Beardsley (1967) developed the Tensional or Controversion Theory of metaphor, which stresses that metaphor's main effect is the emotional or logical tension brought about by semantic contradiction. Berggren claimed that metaphor is no longer vital when it is possible to reduce the metaphor's cognitive input to non-tensional statements (1962: 244). I think the impact of contradiction and tension is worth stressing as an aspect of the interaction between Vehicle and Topic. This is why one of the metaphorical clines introduced at the end of Chapter 1 is the cline of Contradictoriness. However, we can distinguish the initial impact of a metaphor from its interpretation, and for the latter the Comparison Theory seems to give the most satisfactory account.

### 4.3.3. Comparison Theory

The Comparison Theory states that metaphor is best viewed as an elliptical version of a simile or comparison. This is not a claim that a simile makes the same kind of apparent assertion or effect as its equivalent metaphor, but simply that interpretatively the simile and metaphor will be equivalent. Similes and overt comparisons are ways of specifying metaphorical interpretations, bringing to light the process of interpretation which is left implicit with metaphors proper. The Comparison Theory was dismissed by proponents of the Interaction Theory as being simply a modification of the Substitution Theory. However, following Mooij (1976: 171), I believe that the interaction view and the comparison view are quite compatible. After all, when the Interaction Theory mentions the selection of features of the Vehicle which are then mapped on to the Topic, it is talking about a process of comparison. And the advantage of the extended comparison view or the Similarity/Analogy view is that it accounts for all varieties of metaphor, not simply the Interactive or simply the Inactive types.

## 4.4. SIMILARITY AND/OR ANALOGY

Since I favour the Comparison Theory I devote sections 4.4.1–3 to elaborating the concepts of Similarity and Analogy. They can be used as a basis for distinguishing metaphor from other tropes such as irony etc. Moreover, they have already provoked a great deal of discussion in the literature (e.g. Searle 1993) and a considerable amount of work in psychological experiments on the processing of metaphor and simile (e.g. Verbrugge and McCarrell 1977; Ortony *et al.* 1978). Also, a detailed explanation of their workings will remedy some of the inexplicitness in our description by saying more about the psychological mechanisms of interpretation.

### 4.4.1. A definition of Similarity

Tversky (1977) defines <u>Similarity</u> according to what is known as the contrast model (7).

(7)   $S(a, b) = \theta f(A \cap B) - \alpha f(A - B) - \beta f(B - A)$

The similarity, S, between entities a and b is a function of the features shared by a and b $(A \cap B)$ and the weighting given to them $(\theta f)$, less the features possessed by a and not by b $(A - B)$ and the weighting given to them $(\alpha f)$, less the features possessed by b and not by a $(B - A)$ and the weighting given to them $(\beta f)$. Scale $f$ represents the weighting, the particular emphasis or salience given to similarity or contrast. For example, in approximative metaphors more weighting, a higher value for $\theta$, will be given to $A \cap B$, but in paradoxical metaphors such as *the child is the father of the man*, more weighting, higher values for $\alpha$ and $\beta$, will be given to $A - B$ and $B - A$. Weighting depends on psychological salience, and, as we shall see in Chapter 8, this may not correspond to logical contrasts and similarities.

Let's return to an example we used in Chapter 1 to see how this formula could apply to the "literal" use of items. If I used the word *chair* to refer conventionally to a newly encountered chair, an armchair for example, I would be matching certain critical features of the concept a, against the newly encountered object b.

Let's assume that the critical features of meaning in my concept of 'chair' are those found in the first column of Table 4.2. And that the armchair to which I am literally referring has a number of observable features, as listed in column 2. Applying Tversky's formula we arrive at the following equations:

*Table 4.2* Literal and metaphorical similarities

| 'chair' | Literal<br>(*armchair*) | Non-literal<br>(*boulder*) |
|---|---|---|
| [concrete] | concrete | concrete |
| [inanimate] | inanimate | inanimate |
| [artefact] | artefact | natural |
| [furniture] | furniture | stone |
| [sitting] | sitting | sitting |
| [for one person] | for one person | for one person |
| [support for back] | support for back<br>with arms<br>casters<br>upholstered<br>coffee-stained<br>etc. | support for back<br>covered in moss<br>etc. |

(8)  a.  A ∩ B = A
  b.  A − B = 0
  c.  B − A = (with arms/casters/upholstered/coffee-stained/etc.)

Suppose, on the other hand, that we are having a picnic during a mountain climb, and I use *chair* to refer to a boulder, b, you are sitting on. Assuming that the observed features of the boulder are those in column 3 the formula yields the following equations:

(9)  a.  A ∩ B = (concrete/inanimate/for sitting/for one person)
  b.  A − B = (artefact/furniture)
  c.  B − A = (natural/stone/covered in moss/etc.)

The fact that the reference is unconventional is captured by the output of the equation (9b), A − B. In literal uses this will be a null set, as conventional referents of the word contain the features [artefact] and [furniture]. The fact that the interpretation depends upon Similarity will be captured by the fact that there is some value for (9a) A ∩ B.

Applying the Similarity formula to Substitution interpretations of Inactive metaphors like *Thomas is a monkey* gives us a distinctively different output. Since the Topic/Ground, *b*, is one feature associated with monkeys, *a*, we find that A ∩ B is a subset of A, and that therefore B − A = 0. Notice that this differs from the literal application in which it is A − B which equals zero.

There remains the question of the value of the *f*-scale, the weighting or salience of the features. Not only must there be a value for A ∩ B, but this value must involve psychologically salient or relevant features. It does not seem that [concrete] and [animate] are sufficiently salient or relevant to make the metaphor work on their own. So, for example, if I say:

(10)   An elephant is a postbox.

positing the Grounds 'they are both concrete' will not be enough to yield a metaphorical interpretation. We will see how Relevance Theory comes to our rescue in this problem of Similarity in the next chapter. We can for the moment say that the features that are salient or relevant enough are likely to be near the bottom of the semantic-feature hierarchy of the vehicular concept, what Katz and Fodor (1963) liked to call *distinguishers* rather than *markers* (see also McCloskey 1964: 220–1).

At a further extreme would be those cases of irony in which one says the opposite of what one believes. This gives the following output from the formula:

(11)   a. $A \cap B = 0$
       b. $A - B = A$
       c. $B - A = B$

## 4.4.2. Antecedent and attributional Similarity

### ■ EXERCISE

*How would you interpret the metaphorical expression*: The human race is an amoeba?

Some metaphors, then, can be interpreted according to an antecedent Similarity. But there are others in which the Similarity is attributed in the very making of the metaphor. The Grounds are features of the Vehicle concept/schema which it is at least possible to attribute to the Topic but their antecedent associations with the Topic are only very weak. FF36 is a good example.

FF36   <u>We</u> are **an amoeba**, *perhaps waiting to evolve – and then perhaps not.*

It would be entirely pointless to attempt to enumerate all the possible features associated with the human race, salient or otherwise. Even if we attempted to, it would be difficult to say that the Grounds specified for this metaphor, the thoughts about the human race which they make manifest, had ever occurred before in the mind of the reader. The metaphor is indeed making an original observation about humankind. So this metaphor need not depend on the matching of antecedent features of mankind with assumptions associated with an amoeba. The fact that none of the more obvious existing assumptions about mankind helps us in interpreting the metaphor means that, unless the Grounds were specified, the metaphor would resist interpretation.

LF10   The <u>beach</u> was a *thin* **bowstave**.

LF10 is somewhat similar. Supposing one makes a list of the critical features and the features one associates with the prototypical schema for beaches:

> [concrete, inanimate, natural, mineral, area of the land, adjacent to the sea; covered by sea at full tide, made of rocks or pebbles or sand, used by holiday-makers for swimming, sunbathing etc.]

And then do the same for a prototypical bowstave:

> [concrete, inanimate, artefact, part of weapon (bow); attached by its ends to bowstring, long and curved, pliable, made of wood, metal or carbon fibre, held upright, bends and springs back to fire arrows etc.]

If we apply Tversky's formula to this collection of features we might find that there are none which are sufficiently salient and relevant within the set A ∩ B: [concrete, inanimate]. What we must do is to look through the salient features of the Vehicle schema, and see whether there are any which can be applied to a beach. Any of these which make previously ignored assumptions about beaches more salient might yield a satisfactory Ground. In this particular instance we have the help of the G-term *thin*, which guides us to consider the prototypical shape of beaches: they tend to be long and thin, and part of a bay which curves out to headlands. For me LF10 is different from FF36, in this way, as the Grounds do seem eventually to click into place, suggesting that though there were no highly accessible antecedent assumptions about beaches in general, there were some remotely accessible ones about particular kinds of beaches which could eventually be matched. In FF36, however, the assumptions which constitute the Ground were antecedently non-existent.

We now have two kinds of Similarity, antecedent and attributed, though as LF10 suggests, these might be endpoints on a continuum of accessibility rather than absolute divisions.

### 4.4.3. Analogy

Some metaphors demand Analogy as an interpretative device.[4]

> (12)  The hydrogen atom is a miniature solar system. (after Gentner 1982: 111–13)

In (12) there is no Similarity between hydrogen atoms and a solar system which does not first depend upon Analogy. The Grounds in the interpretation of this metaphor depend entirely on the relationships between the parts. When Rutherford used this metaphor he was not drawing attention to any Similarity between the sun and the nucleus of an atom, but, as the word "system" suggests, he was comparing the relationships: the sun is· "massier" than the planets, the nucleus is "massier" than the electrons; the planets are attracted to the sun in much the same way as the electrons are attracted to the nucleus; consequently the electrons revolve around the nucleus in the same way as the planets around the sun (Gentner 1982). We can probably assume that the relational equivalences are antecedent properties of the Topic, as we would with the Analogy:

(13)   Electricity is like water.

In other cases the Analogy may simply be one that is being suggested, hypothesized or imposed on the hearer in some way, e.g.

NSLJ25   The earth and the biosphere around it is like a giant redwood tree.

The relationship between the tree's living outer skin, with its leaves, and the dead wood which makes up 90 per cent of its bulk, is equivalent to the relationship between the biosphere and the minerals which make up the larger part of the earth's mass. This Analogy was suggested by James Lovelock in order to illustrate the revolutionary ecological theory known as *Gaia* which hypothesizes that the organic and inorganic matter on the earth interrelate as one superorganism. The equivalences in this analogy seem more attributive, suggestive and hypothetical than those in (12) and (13), where the theory is less in doubt.

Cases of analogical relations which are established by the metaphor itself occur when we cannot conceive of the Topic except in terms of the Vehicle.

(14)   Time passes slowly.

Here there can be no antecedent equivalence of relation since the elapsing of time is so abstract a process that we can hardly conceptualize it on its own terms, but only in terms used for movement in physical space. Such Concretizing Root Analogies, then, might be called attributive, rather than antecedent, creating new similarities (Lakoff and Johnson 1980: 147–55).

## ■ EXERCISE

*Try to interpret the following metaphor:*

*The yacht **ploughed** the waves.*

*Use the method I demonstrated in 4.2.4 with TH24. You should start by establishing T-terms and V-terms on different lines and supplying fillers for the gaps. Then go on to suggest Grounds, deciding which Grounds depend on Similarity and which on Analogy. Can you say whether these similarities and analogies are antecedent or not?*

We can, following Leech (1969: 154ff.), diagram the Topics and Vehicles thus:

(15)  a. T-term:   The yacht      [moved through]   the waves.
      b. V-term:   [The plough]   ploughed          [the field].

I suggest the following Grounds, the first two depending on Similarity and the last two on Analogy.

(16)   yacht/plough                    streamlined shape, shape of share and
                                          shape of keel

       waves/field                     wide, homogeneous expanse

       yacht moving/                   zig-zag movement of plough and
          plough ploughing                the tacking of a yacht?

       yacht moving through            continuous protracted movement,
       waves/plough                      creation of undulating shapes: waves,
       ploughing a field                 furrows

### 4.4.4. Colligations, analogies and schemas

It should be obvious from this analysis, which travels pathway 5, that Colligational interpretations in which all four terms figure, i.e. pathways 5 and 6, tend towards analogical interpretation. Column 8 in Table 4.2 gives an indication of where Analogy and Similarity tend to apply.

However, another factor will be the orders of entity to which the Topic and Vehicle belong. In theory there are at least four possible combinations of degrees of abstraction.

(17)          *Topic*         *Vehicle*
       1      image/thing     image        Similarity (Analogy)
       2      abstract        image        Analogy
       3      abstract        abstract     Analogy (Similarity)
       4      image/thing     abstract     Symbolic Similarity

It is generally thought that metaphor tends to have Concretizing tendencies rather than de-concretizing ones so that category (4) is very infrequent. In fact, especially in modern lyric poetry with its tendency to Symbolism, many examples of (4) can be found.

THP   **the dream darkness** . . . that rose slowly towards me watching
LFG   **a turmoil** spread over the middle kingdom, three hundred and sixty
      thousand
PMD   out of the **murderous innocence** of the sea

In Ted Hughes' 'Pike' (THP) the fish is referred to by the more abstract noun phrase "the dream darkness". In Pound's 'Lament of the frontier guard' (LFG) the three hundred and sixty thousand warriors are referred to by the V-term "a turmoil". In Yeats' 'Prayer for my daughter' (PMD) the genitive construction can be interpreted as though the literal sea becomes a symbol of murderous innocence. Remember too some of the reversals of

Root Analogies in Chapter 2: JUSTICE = STRAIGHT > *justified* text (section 2.3.5).

As we saw in Chapter 1, we can distinguish two ends of a metaphorical continuum with type 1 metaphors (sections 1.3, 1.9; Figure 1.4). At one end we have Approximation metaphors, at the other Transfer metaphors. Similarity is necessarily the interpretive force for Approximation, and is also likely to be involved with Transfer metaphors when one image or thing is compared with another. However, Similarity seldom works with (2), Concretizing metaphors, where, by definition, Topic and Vehicle belong to different orders of entity. So Analogy involving four terms is essential.

We should not be misled into thinking Concretizing metaphors can be interpreted using Similarity. Let me remind you of this example:

DV133    as if the <u>algebra</u> was **glue** *they were stuck in*

These Pseudo-grounds are really based on no more than an ambiguous clause stemming from the Root Analogy of movement forwards for solving problems.

## ■ EXERCISE

*How would you interpret the metaphor* Arrogance and hatred are the wares peddled in the thoroughfares*? (PMD) Does it belong to combination 1, 2 or 3? Does it depend on Analogy or Similarity?*

Analogy too seems important in the case of (3), which is what I take this example to be.

What makes Analogy possible with Transfer and Concretizing metaphors is the fact that a whole schema, not just isolated lexical items, is transferred. To quote Goodman:

> Shifts in range that occur in metaphor, then, usually amount to no mere distribution of family goods but an expedition abroad. A whole set of alternative labels, a whole apparatus of organization takes over new territory. What occurs is a transfer of a schema.
>
> (Goodman 1968: 73)

In fact, the "whole" set of alternative labels is not often transferred, which is precisely why in DV133 equation of glue with algebra appears at first to be giving us a novel metaphor. We can accept the idea that a general schema has been transferred, even if the set of lexical items normally used to realize this schema in its new territory is a subset of the set used in its home territory. But the main point is that as soon as more than one lexical item is transferred then analogy can start working, as with "wares" and "peddled" in PMD above. Consider the ways in which metaphors for under-par scores in golf form an analogical system:

(18)   1 under par : 2 under par : 3 under par : : birdie : eagle : albatross

The emphasis on the relationships between parts of schemata indicates that in analogical metaphors the Grounds of the metaphor are often dependent upon the extension of the V-term, whether lexically as in golf scores, or syntactically, as in DV133. In other words in DV133 it is difficult, indeed unnecessary, to decide whether *they were stuck in* is functioning as G-term or an extension of the V-term, because the Analogy depends precisely upon the equivalence of the relationship

(19)   algebra : failing to solve a problem : : glue : being stuck

In the previous sections, 4.4.1–5, we have discussed Similarity/Analogy in an attempt to show the validity of the Comparison (Interaction) Theory of metaphor. We noted that similarities and analogies may be pre-existing, or they may be constructed in the making of the metaphor. For the constructed kinds, the term *Comparison* may be a little misleading, though we can still talk about "making" comparisons.


## 4.5. LESS CENTRAL VARIETIES OF METAPHOR

Any serious attempt at textual analysis of metaphors throws up examples which may not be central, but which, nevertheless, can be fitted into our definition. Many of these are found in literary texts.


### 4.5.1. Symbolism: superordinate substitution, and analogical metonymy

There is one particular kind of substitution interpretation which we need to expound on here because it prepares us for later discussion of theme in literature (section 9.11). Perhaps the easiest way to illustrate what one might call this Symbolic Substitution interpretation is with proverbs. *Don't count your chickens before they are hatched* can be subject to a Substitution interpretation. Its conventional meaning is something like 'Don't anticipate a favourable event or success before it materializes.' Here we have a general abstract meaning which is represented metaphorically by one particular instance. Or one could say that one member of a set of exemplifications, a hyponym, comes to label the whole set, the superordinate. However, this superordinacy is unconventional:

(20)

|  | *Conventional* |  | *Unconventional* |
|---|---|---|---|
| Superordinates | rodent |  | disloyalty |
| Hyponym |  | rat |  |

The poem in the Introduction to this book, 'An advancement of learning', like many modern short lyric poems which on the literal level recount a personal experience, only achieves literary significance if it can be interpreted in the same way as proverbs, as particular concrete instances of a more general theme, maybe the facing and overcoming of a phobia. It is likely that the poetic theme will be more elusive than the proverbial one, but they both depend on Symbolic Substitution involving unconventional superordinates.

The other kind of symbol involves Analogy: the literal processes in which the entity is involved provide an analogical equivalent to some other hidden processes, generally psychological or abstract:

GW0039    Sooner or later the stealing ceases, for the **love** that was symbolically* stolen in the form of **money or goods** is now given.

GW0207    And towards the end of the century men began to wear, so to speak, the very symbol* of their bashed in **authority**: **the trilby**.

Metonymies, especially of cause and effect, are important in establishing these symbols: wearing clothes and stealing are deliberate actions caused by some inner psychological state. The causal metonymy means there is something indexical about these symbols, just as smoke is an index of fire, because it is caused by it.

Other symbols are not only indexical but iconic, that is to say both Similarity and Analogy are involved (shape of torch and phallus):

GW0039    the psychological meaning of that act of destruction: symbolically*, father's torch represented father's phallus

### 4.5.2. Asymmetric interpretation

Although we located the interpretation of metaphors firmly within pragmatics, our definition does not specify the roles of speaker and hearer. Although the *understood* of the definition can imply both speaker and hearer I have left open the possibility that expressions may be <u>Asymmetric</u>, i.e. intended as metaphors by the speaker but not understood as such by the hearer, or, conversely, not intended as metaphors by the speaker but interpreted as such by the hearer.[5] Though misunderstanding, infelicitous uptake, can occur with all speech acts, utterances like metaphors which are highly dependent on pragmatic inferencing are particularly risky.

With symmetric metaphors the metaphorical intention of the speaker, that the utterance is not, or not simply, an assertion, must be recognized by the hearer, and it must be assumed by the speaker that the hearer so recognizes it (Loewenberg 1975: 335–6). There are several ways in which Asymmetric metaphor might depart from this rule:

(a)    There is no metaphorical intention of the speaker, and no assumption that the hearer recognizes a metaphorical intention, though the hearer believes there was a metaphorical intention.

Examples of expressions which we interpret metaphorically though they are not intended as such are relatively hard to come by or to recognize within the experience of the literarily competent reader. Yet, anyone who has taught practical criticism will find examples of students who tend to overmetaphorize. This stanza from Walter de la Mare's 'The moth' has provoked several interpretations which claim that "moth" is referring metaphorically to a prostitute, and "fan", "swoon" and "face" are referring literally.

| (21) | Lovely in dye and fan, |
| | A-tremble in shimmering grace, |
| | A moth from her winter swoon |
| | Uplifts her face. |

This kind of asymmetry is often exploited for humorous purposes. In the Peter Sellers film *Being There*, a mentally deficient gardener becomes an economic adviser to the US president on the strength of the remark "There will be growth in the spring."

   (b)   There is a metaphorical intention by the speaker and the assumption that the hearer will recognize the metaphorical intention, though the hearer fails to recognize the metaphorical intention.

This kind of asymmetry can also give rise to humour. In the recent film *The Mask*, we have the following dialogue between the psychologist Dr Neuman, author of the book *The Masks We Wear*, and the hero Mr Ipkiss, who possesses the magic mask.

(22)  IPKISS:  Loki? Who's Loki?
      NEUMAN:  The Norse god of mischief. Supposedly he caused so much trouble that Odin banished him from Valhalla for ever.
      IPKISS:  Then he could have banished me with that mask.
      NEUMAN:  I'm talking about mythology, Mr Ipkiss. This is a piece of wood.
      IPKISS:  But your book!
      NEUMAN:  My book is about masks as a metaphor, Mr Ipkiss. A metaphor, not to be taken literally. You're suffering from a mild delusion.

But Asymmetric metaphors may occur less straightforwardly:

   (c)   There is no metaphorical intention of the speaker in the sense that the speaker believes the utterance to be a literal assertion, though the speaker assumes the hearer will recognize a metaphorical intention, and the hearer believes there is a metaphorical intention.

There are plenty of puns, particularly in the popular press and advertising copy, where the literal interpretation is intended rather than the metaphorical one, though one is deliberately lured into metaphorical interpretation.

DT1    Most holiday makers **steered** well clear of the coast as the May Day weekend maintained its usual chill.

(d)    There is a metaphorical intention, in the sense that the speaker does not believe the literal truth of the assertive utterance, though the speaker assumes the hearer will not recognize the metaphorical intention, and the hearer fails to recognize it.

Example (23) is from St John's Gospel. Jesus' disciples had gone off to town to buy food and later returned:

(23)    Meanwhile the disciples were urging him, "Rabbi, have something to eat." But he said, "I have **food to eat** of which you know nothing." At this the disciples said to one another "Can someone have brought him food?" But Jesus said, "It is **meat and drink** for me to do the will of him who sent me until I have finished his work."

(John 4:31–4)

It is hard to see how Jesus, in the context of the disciples returning with food, could have expected most of them to recognize the metaphor. Probably he was trying to separate those of his hearers who could reach a spiritual metaphorical interpretation from those who were damned to literal-mindedness.

We might note in passing that the failure of a hearer to recognize a metaphor can make the hearer seem somewhat foolish, or, alternatively, in case (d), the speaker somewhat pompous or manipulative.

(e)    There is no metaphorical intention on the part of the speaker, and it is not assumed by the hearer that there was a metaphorical intention; nevertheless the hearer refuses to accept the truth of the assertion as a literal statement and therefore interprets it metaphorically.

These are perhaps more interesting cases. One kind are what might be called Impositives (Mack 1975: 248), in which the hearer is likely to refuse the imposition, as with an example like: *Property is theft.* This utterance is an attempt, by the French socialist Proudhon, to redraw semantic boundaries, to redefine the concept of property. One may, of course, reject it outright; but one is still free to attempt a metaphorical interpretation: property resembles theft in that both deprive others of the use or enjoyment of an object. Though there is no metaphorical intention on Proudhon's part, because the statement is axiomatically true and conventional wisdom within a particular socialist subculture, he would surely be aware that this axiom is not accepted by mainstream capitalist culture. Impositives are presumably the Asymmetric version of the symmetric stipulative metaphor, where, in a professional or academic discourse, words are used to

129

refer to concepts more specifically than in ordinary usage, and where, for the duration of the discourse, the speaker willingly accepts the stipulated meaning, e.g.

> (24)  Strain, in a physical object, is deformation of that object under the effect of a force applied to it.

A second example, mentioned earlier (pp. 26–7), was my 3-year-old daughter's referring to the crust of bread on her plate as "shell", which was probably not intended as metaphor. She simply had not realized that the outer surface of the bread had a different conventional label from the outside of an egg. I interpreted this unconventional use of *shell* in much the same way as a deliberate metaphor: using Grounds of Similarity or Analogy to work out what she was referring to.

A clever variation on Asymmetric metaphor occurs in Graham Greene's *The Quiet American*. In this particular case, instead of the utterance being intended as an assertion, it is intended as a lie. Pyle, the "hero", has just rejoined Fowler and Phuong after depositing the libidinous Grainger at a nearby brothel. When asked by Phuong where he has been he replies:

> QA36a  "I've been taking Grainger home."

To which Fowler responds:

> QA36b  "Home?" I laughed.

The laugh suggests that Fowler interprets the lie as a metaphor.

## ■ EXERCISE

*Protestants and Catholics take different views on the metaphorical/literal status of Jesus' utterances as he offered his disciples bread and wine: "This is my body, This is my blood." Catholics believe that the bread and wine in the mass literally change into Jesus' body and blood. Protestants believe they are simply symbols. Can you discuss each sect's views of the other sect's interpretation in terms of Asymmetric metaphor?*

Lest these questions of Asymmetric metaphor seem trivial remember that religious persecution and wars have resulted from these differing interpretations. Catholics believe that Protestants' interpretation of "This is my body, This is my blood" is Asymmetric metaphor (a), an interpretation of a literal statement as metaphorical; and Protestants believe the Catholic interpretation is Asymmetric metaphor (b), a failure to recognize a metaphor. Protestants, of course, interpreted these sayings as perfectly symmetrical metaphors.

### 4.5.3. Subjective interpretation

Asymmetric metaphors which arise because the speaker has a different ideological or physical view of the world from the hearer might be called Subjective metaphors. So, for example, in *The Inheritors* we repeatedly encounter what we interpret as personifying metaphors, but which Lok, through whose mind-style and consciousness the events are related, regards as quite literal.

TI24   The cliff leaned back a little.

The reason for the asymmetry is that Lok's world-view is radically different from ours; our fundamental distinction between animate and inanimate nature does not exist for Lok. In *Herzog* the narrator says:

HZ34   their hunger is for good sense, clarity, truth, even an atom of it. People are dying – it is no metaphor – for lack of something real to carry home when day is done.

Clearly the narrator believes that lack of clarity, sense, and truth literally kills people. He is even willing to admit that we are likely to interpret this metaphorically, which is why he insists on the assertion being literal – "it is no metaphor".

It is often the case that a disagreement in a literary text forces the reader to interpret metaphorically, tempering two extremes.

VG223   "I'm not a child and I don't need seducing."
         "You are a child to me."

We take some metaphorical position on whether the first speaker is a child or not: we might say that, though strictly speaking she is not young enough to be labelled a child, she sometimes behaves like one.

Though it is useful to include Asymmetric Subjective interpretations under the umbrella of metaphor, it may well be that in terms of development and psychology they have more in common with irony. Apparently the understanding of Subjective metaphor, or at least the understanding of the differing subjectivities which explains its existence, is a faculty which, like irony, develops in children later than metaphoric competence (Winner and Gardner 1994: 427).

Gunther Kress (1989: 445–66) has pointed out that Subjective metaphor is often the engine of linguistic change both lexical and grammatical. Metaphors such as *Property is theft* amount to attempts at relexicalization, attempts to create an alternative reality. Kress gives a telling example of how the meaning of the term *invasion* is reclassified by the Australian historian Geoffrey Blainey in his book *A Land Half Won*. He quotes the following passage:

In Central Australia . . . the Pitjantjatjara were driven by drought to expand into the territory of a neighbour.

Several of these invasions might be partly explained by a domino theory: the coastal invasion of the whites initially pushing over one black domino which in turn pushed down other dominoes. But it would be sensible to believe that dominoes were also rising and falling occasionally during the centuries of black history. We should be wary of whitewashing the white invasions. We should also be wary of the idea that Australia knew no black invasions . . . It is possible that many tribes suffered more deaths through tribal fighting than through warfare with the British colonists in the 19th Century.

(Kress 1989: 459)

The application of the term "invasion" both to the actions of the British colonists and to the aboriginal peoples such as the Pitjantjatjara, obviously suggests that their actions were equivalent. But more than this, Blainey changes the meaning of *invasion* in the phrase "the coastal invasion of the whites" so that it no longer involves political entities, but simply geographical ones, like the coast. This makes the white invasion of Australia equivalent to some kind of natural expansion and movement into a different geographical area, something quite different from taking over a political entity belonging to a different human society by the use of military force.

This Subjective metaphor has clear ideological purposes. Kress comments:

In terms of a fuller tracing of the social/ideological process and its linguistic repercussions, I would suggest the following: a process which, up until the late sixties had been classified as 'settlement' ("Australia was settled by . . . " etc.) was at that time challenged by black Australians, and reclassified as 'invasion'. An academic historian who regards himself as politically enlightened takes sides in this contestation, and adopts the politically progressive term 'invasion'. Having taken that step he then attempts (whether aware or unaware is not the point) to reclassify the meaning of that term itself, and to restore it to a safe and conventional account from the white perspective.

(*ibid.*: 460)

We can see here the appositeness of our term *Subjective* metaphor since the explanation for these Asymmetrical metaphors has to be sought in the kind of *subject position* the language user locates or finds himself in (Kress 1989; Fairclough 1989: 38–41).

Kress goes on to point out that these types of reclassification, the uses of terms with contested meanings, open the way to linguistic change, if the term is repeatedly used with the new meaning. The spread of the new meanings will often depend upon whether those who use them have power on their side, for example access to the mass media.

### 4.5.4. Illusion

In some Subjective metaphors the speaker, on the basis of sensory input from the external world, refers to a situation in that world by means of an utterance which is for him a true assertion but which the hearer knows to be false (this is a version of Asymmetric metaphor type (e)). In these cases the lack of symmetry between a speaker's intention and hearer's interpretation is the result of a Subjective Illusion.

In *Lord of the Flies* the line of choirboys in black gowns advancing along the beach gives an illusion of being one organism rather than a collection of individuals, so it is referred to as "the creature" (p. 20). The reader probably participates in the illusion on the first reading of the novel, but on subsequent readings will treat "creature" as a Subjective metaphor produced by Ralph's limited narrative viewpoint. We register the fact that there are sufficient similarities between the line of choirboys and a creature – a continuous single coherent shape of a homogeneous colour – to deceive Ralph.

There has to be some kind of gap between the stance of the author/ narrator and the stance of the character who is experiencing the illusion in order for the readers to be aware of the illusion and therefore interpret it as metaphor. On the initial reading of the *creature* example above this is not the case, because the author/narrator adopts the narrative stance of Ralph, the one suffering from the illusion. However, since the illusion is later dispelled for the boy, and therefore the reader, any rereading of the novel will allow us to treat it metaphorically.

When Subjective Asymmetric metaphors describe inner states we have hallucinations and imaginings rather than simply illusions. In Byatt's *The Virgin in the Garden* Marcus' visions provide us with examples:

> VG119–20   The light then changed. He stopped because it was hard to go forward, there was too much in front and all around him, **light almost tangibly dense** and confoundingly bright. **He stopped in parts**, his body first, then his attention, so that there was a sickening moment when the **inside of the head, the cavern, was striding on beyond the frightened soft eyes and contracting skin**.
>
> **The light was busy.** It could be seen gathering, running, increasing . . . rising in bright intermittent streams of sparks from glossy laurel leaves.

What for us are metaphors in this passage are probably realities for Marcus in his private hallucinatory world.

With Subjective metaphors we have a shift in emphasis from the referent towards the referrer. That is to say the metaphorical interpretation, besides involving Similarity and Analogy, also involves recognizing or inferring the reasons why the speaker's point of view is different from ours, the different ideological subject positions. Whereas with ordinary metaphor the emphasis is simply on challenging the conventions of the referential code, Subjective metaphor is exploited, in addition, for its contributions to the depiction of character (Barthes 1970). The mind-style of the character may be different from our own as in the case of Benjie in *The Sound and the Fury*, who is mentally subnormal, or Lok, who has a Neanderthal way of perceiving things (Leech and Short 1981: 31–6, 202–7).

### 4.5.5. Mimetic and Phenomenalistic interpretation

A further related species of metaphor arises through mimetic artefacts. To admit these into metaphor is, of course, to acknowledge that metaphor can extend to non-verbal expression, straying beyond linguistic texts into the visual and plastic arts. However, we cannot ignore these wider expressions of the metaphorical bent because, when they are referred to in language, they have to undergo a metaphorical interpretation according to our definition.

Trivial examples of Mimetic metaphors are the following, the second describing the burning of a plastic doll:

VG29   The carpet had an oriental **tree** on it.
VG204   But her **stomach perished**. Her vest melted into it.

More complex are cases where there is a verbal description of the way the visual arts portray a myth (which was, perhaps, verbal in origin). In VG137 we have a verbal description of an artistic depiction of Actaeon metamorphosing into a stag, originally from the written text of Ovid.

VG137   She located **a man becoming a stag**, . . . stretched sinews, hardening distorted feet, spreading rib-cage, branching horns, creamy furred dewlap and opening **muzzle-mouth** under a human brow.

The interesting thing about Mimetic metaphor is that its interpretation differs from the more normal kind of metaphorical interpretation. That is to say, in order to interpret "her stomach perished", "a man becoming a stag" or "muzzle-mouth", we would ordinarily translate, by means of Similarity or Analogy, back into concepts which could be true of the world we know. For, example, we would be inclined to interpret "muzzle-mouth" as 'a mouth which resembled an animal's muzzle'. But Mimetic metaphors demand that we imagine a world in which the assertions or descriptions are literally true, e.g. in which it is possible for a man to change into a stag, and during this change, to have something literally half-muzzle, half-mouth.

We are perfectly familiar with this attitude to fictional texts, and Coleridge referred to it as "willing suspension of disbelief" (Potter 1962: 248).

We therefore need to recognize another species of metaphoric interpretation, allowed for in our definition (pp. 108–9) by the phrase *or world*. In this case the reference is unconventional because conventionally we use language to refer to the real world, and in this case we are referring to an imaginary world. Levin (1977) was the first to draw attention to this kind of metaphor and he labelled its interpretation <u>Phenomenalistic Construal</u>.

Phenomenalistic Construal, one must realize, does not simply apply to the portions of fictional texts that are anomalous in some way or contain local metaphors. If the text is fictional then it will be consistently referring to an imaginary world. We have to conclude that the novel itself is a large-scale metaphor. The unconventional referent, the unreal world of the novel, will be interpreted in terms of Similarity or Analogy with the world that we know.

One of the advantages of this insight would be to show how literary texts of a reactive kind, e.g. *Lord of the Flies* as a reaction to *The Coral Island*, seem to work in ways similar to ordinary small-scale metaphors. The argument goes as follows. Some metaphors become Dead and Inactive and are treated as literal items. Similarly some texts and genres become accepted as the normal, reflecting an existing ideology. Part of the function of reactive texts is to question the world-view inherent in the "normal" established text. For example *Lord of the Flies* raises awareness of the western imperialist ideology inherent in the structuring of reality which *Robinson Crusoe*, *The Swiss Family Robinson* and *The Coral Island* provide, by suggesting a new metaphor, an alternative structuring. Here the Christian white boys rapidly degenerate into savages, the most religious of them, the choirboys, degenerating the quickest. Like a good small-scale poetic metaphor, the new Phenomenalistic metaphor which constitutes *Lord of the Flies* brings to light those aspects of our world which we suppress in making use of the conventional referring term.

Fictive texts are Phenomenalistic metaphors positing a different world not a different word. They are Mimetic metaphors as well, providing structures analogous to those we find in the real world, if not imitating that world. In so far as they represent the personal expression of the world-view of the author about the possibilities of human behaviour, a grid-like structure through which we see life schematized by selection, emphasis and ordering, they are Subjective as well. Historically and diachronically one author's Subjective metaphor may become conventionalized and "literal", incorporated into mainstream culture, making it seem the natural way for us to structure our experience. But as illusions can be tested against human activity and found wanting, so conventionalized fictive metaphors may obscure and distort. Does the distorted portrayal of babies in the fictive texts of television advertising contribute to the high incidence of postnatal

135

depression? Ads never depict babies as vomiting or howling, or giving sleepless nights, and even diaper adverts never show excrement or urine. Confronted with such distortion we seek new metaphors which, while less generically predictable, resemble life better.

## 4.6. SUMMARY

The chapter was dominated by a description/definition of metaphor, and the elaboration of its terms and pathways through it, so that the definition (pp. 108–9) in itself forms a summary of the chapter. We distinguished Referential and Colligational metaphors so as to trace the intricate specific differences of the seven pathways through our definition. We briefly discussed three traditional theories of metaphor: Substitution, Interaction and Comparison, deciding that Interaction/Comparison best fitted prototypical Active metaphors, and that Substitution might be useful for the Inactive. I exemplified the differences between Analogy and Similarity as interpretative procedures, and introduced a formula for computing Similarity. Finally we considered less central metaphorical types: Asymmetric metaphor where metaphorical intentions or interpretations do not match across the speaker and the hearer; Subjective metaphors, some of which involve the representation of another speaker's thoughts or representations; and Phenomenalistic/Mimetic metaphors where we are not concerned with local metaphor but with the imagination of an unreal world.

This chapter also picked up two threads from previous chapters:

- The distinction between Active, Inactive, Dead and Buried metaphors was introduced and explored in Chapters 1, 2 and 3, and in this chapter we saw that position on this cline generally correlates with the Substitution/Interaction distinction, which in turn relates to the separability of Topic, Vehicle and Ground.
- The imaginability of Vehicles will depend upon the relative concreteness or abstractness of the Topic and Vehicle. This distinction was introduced in Chapter 1, where we illustrated the Approximative, Transfer, Concretizing cline. It was explored further in this chapter in terms of the choice of Analogy/Similarity as an interpretative strategy.

We have, so far, been taking a rather formalist view of metaphor. Summing up this formalist approach the next chapter provides a theoretical framework, Relevance Theory, within which our different kinds of metaphor can be located. But the next chapter also shifts our point of view to a more functionalist perspective, categorizing the different purposes to which metaphors can be put.

# 5

# RELEVANCE THEORY AND THE FUNCTIONS OF METAPHOR

## 5.1. METAPHOR AND RELEVANCE THEORY

The most active kinds of metaphors demand considerable interpretative work besides the decoding of their semantics. Semantic decoding will simply give us the Vehicle concept. To establish the Topic – what the V-term is referring to – and to explore the Grounds – the Similarities or Analogies on which the metaphor is based – we must employ mental processes beyond those of decoding. In terms of Figure 5.1, metaphorical understanding depends on the processes and principles involved in the interplay between (1), (2) and (3). (1), knowledge of the language, will give us the output of decoding. To add to this we draw on knowledge which we acquire from (2), the surrounding text, and the physical and social situation in which the text is produced. And we also factor in (3), background knowledge about the world, and the society of our language community. The area of linguistics concerned with the inferential principles and processes needed to complement decoding is Pragmatics, and Relevance Theory provides a coherent general explanation of metaphorical interpretation. So in the first half of this chapter I give a sketch of Sperber and Wilson's (1986) theory and suggest how it can be usefully modified to provide a more comprehensive account.

### 5.1.1. What is Relevance? Contextual effects and processing effort

First we need to understand what Relevance means. Information is relevant to you if it interacts with your existing beliefs/thoughts (which Sperber and

1   Knowledge of the language system

2   Knowledge of the context: situation and co-text

3   Background schematic knowledge: factual and socio-cultural

*Figure 5.1* Sources of knowledge in text interpretation

Wilson call *assumptions* (1986: 2)). One product of this interaction is a *Contextual implication*, exemplified below:

You wake up thinking,

(1) If it's raining I won't go to the lecture this morning.

You look out the window and discover,

(2) It's raining.

From existing assumption (1) and the new information (2) you can deduce further information (3):

(3) I won't go to the lecture this morning.

(2) is relevant because, in the context of (1), it produces new information or contextually implies (3).

Creating contextual implications is one kind of Contextual Effect – others are the strengthening or elimination of existing assumptions – and the greater the Contextual Effects the greater the relevance. However, the number and degree of Contextual Effects is only one factor in computing relevance. The second factor is Processing Effort. We need to capture the intuition that in the context of assumption (4), (5) will be more relevant than (6):

You wake up thinking

(4) If it's raining I won't go to the lecture this morning.

Then *either* you look out of the window and see:

(5) It's raining.

*or* you look out of the window and see:

(6) It's raining and the refuse collectors are emptying the bins.

In the context of (4), (5) and (6) have the same Contextual Effects. But (5) is more relevant than (6), because (6) requires more Processing Effort (Wilson and Sperber 1986: 27–30).

The notion of Relevance, then, which is comparative rather than absolute, can be summed up in the following formulae:

(7) Other things being equal the greater the Contextual Effects, the greater the relevance.

(8) Other things being equal, the smaller the Processing Effort the greater the relevance.

Or, alternatively, expressed as a fraction:

$$(9) \quad \text{Relevance} = \frac{\text{Contextual Effects}}{\text{Processing Effort}}$$

This equation makes it clear that if there is no Contextual Effect there will be no relevance, no matter how little the Processing Effort involved.

## 5.1.2. Relevance and implicature

The above examples of Contextual Effects assume, for purposes of illustration, that there are a limited number of existing assumptions. But in real life, of course, this is not the case. We all have various Contextual Assumptions in our short-term memory which have been activated by the situation and the co-text (see (2) in Figure 5.1). In addition we have thousands of unactivated assumptions stored in our long-term memory as factual or socio-cultural knowledge (3). In reaching the Contextual Implications of an utterance we have to choose from among these assumptions those which are most relevant. For example:

(10)    I wake up thinking
        a. If it's raining I won't go to the lecture this morning.
        b. I've run out of eggs for breakfast.

(11)    I open the curtains and discover
        a. It's raining.

We will choose which assumption, (10a) or (10b), to use in the interpretation of (11a) on the basis of relevance: (10a) will be more relevant than (10b).

We must recognize, therefore, that not only is relevance important in measuring Contextual Implications, but also in accessing existing assumptions. This gives us a double-edged definition of an implicature as both Contextual Assumption and Contextual Implication:

(12)    An implicature is a contextual assumption or implication which a speaker, intending her utterance to be relevant, intended to make manifest to the hearer.

Let's look at an example (adapted from Sperber and Wilson 1986: 197) to see how implicatures might operate in practice. Consider the following exchange:

(13)    JOHN:    Would you drive a Mercedes?
        MARY:    I wouldn't drive *any* expensive car.

The most obvious way to make this remark minimally relevant is to access the Contextual Assumption:

(14)    A Mercedes is an expensive car.

from which to derive the Contextual Implication:

(15)  Mary would not drive a Mercedes.

Mary's utterance and (14) here function as premisses in an inferential syllogism to give the conclusion (15).

So far so good, in that we have established some relevance for Mary's utterance. However, the Principle of Relevance states:

(16)  Every act of communication communicates the presumption of its own optimal relevance (after Sperber and Wilson 1986: 158).

We cannot presume on the *optimal* relevance of Mary's utterance if (15) is the only Contextual Implication. To make the Processing Effort involved in decoding her utterance worthwhile we have to arrive at other Contextual Implications, other implicated conclusions. Otherwise Mary would have done better to give the straight answer "No." Here are some extra Contextual Assumptions (17a–d) and Contextual Implications (18a–d) which might make the remark optimally relevant:

(17)  a. A Rolls is an expensive car.
b. A Lexus is an expensive car.
c. A Jaguar is an expensive car.
d. A Rover is an expensive car.

(18)  a. Mary would not drive a Rolls.
b. Mary would not drive a Lexus.
c. Mary would not drive a Jaguar.
d. Mary would not drive a Rover.

Two points need making about (17) and (18). The premisses (17), seem progressively less strong and therefore give progressively less strong implicated conclusions, so that it is doubtful whether Mary could be held responsible for (18d). Second, there is no clear cut-off point on the scale which can help us decide definitely which of these implicatures (18) are valid. The insight that implicatures may be weaker or stronger, and that utterances are often capable of generating a number of weak implicatures, will be important in Relevance Theory's account of metaphor.

### 5.1.3. Metaphor and Relevance

Relevance Theory can give us an insight into the distinctions between literal and metaphorical language, and between Active and Inactive metaphors (Chapter 1). It can also be modified to explain Subjective and Phenomenalistic metaphor (Chapter 4), and metaphorical allusion, and to show the relationship between metaphor and irony.

Sperber and Wilson's scheme for accounting for different illocutionary forces, or what they call propositional attitudes, can be diagrammed as in Figure 5.2. The areas of the diagram which concern us most are the relationship between the propositional form and the thought of the speaker,

140

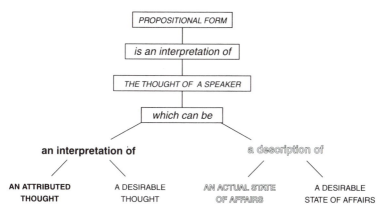

*Figure 5.2* Interpretation: propositions, thoughts and states of affairs
*Source*: From Sperber and Wilson 1986: 232, fig. 3; by permission of Blackwell Publishers

where Sperber and Wilson locate metaphorical processes, and the relationship between the thought of a speaker and an attributed thought, which is where they locate irony.

Sperber and Wilson's argument runs as follows. Every utterance with a propositional form resembles the thought of a speaker. The propositional form interprets the speaker's thought. In some limiting cases propositional form may resemble the speaker's thought completely, but more often there are cases of Approximation because the standard for communication is not truth but relevance (Sperber and Wilson 1986: 233–7). Remember the example of telling your friend the distance from London to Birmingham (section 1.3, pp. 17–18).

Moving along the cline away from Approximation we have Transfer metaphors:

(19)   The room is a pigsty.

(20)   Robert is a steamroller.

(21)      That time of year thou may'st in me behold
          When yellow leaves or none or few do hang
          Upon those boughs which shake against the cold,
          **Bare ruined choirs** where late the sweet birds sang.
                              (Shakespeare, Sonnet 73)

The search for optimal relevance leads the speaker to adopt, on different occasions, a propositional form more or less approximate to her thoughts. Metaphoric and literal utterances do not involve distinct kinds of interpretation: there is a literal–metaphorical cline and what varies is the degree of Similarity between the speaker's thought and the propositional form of the utterance.

In Chapter 1 I demonstrated in detail that the metaphorical–literal distinction is blurred, that metaphorical and literal language is a continuum, that Approximation (hyponymy etc.) is akin to metaphor, and that the same kinds of interpretative process, the search for presumed relevance via Similarity or Analogy, are involved in both literal and metaphorical uses of language. All those arguments reinforce the above arguments of Sperber and Wilson. However, the fact that the literal and metaphorical are difficult to distinguish in the middle of these clines does not mean that the more extreme instances cannot be distinguished. It is quite possible to distinguish Approximation from Transfer metaphors, and Active from Inactive ones.

What distinguishes (19), (20) and (21), which are progressively more Active, is the number and strength of the implicatures they can give rise to. Under normal circumstances (19) gives access to the following implicatures:

> (22)  a.  The word *pigsty* either means 'a pen for pigs' or 'a dirty, untidy place'.
>       b.  This room is not a pen for pigs.

Thus

>       c.  The speaker means 'the room is a dirty, untidy place'.

This interpretation simply involves disambiguation, since, as an Inactive metaphor it has acquired a second conventional meaning. If the speaker intended that the sole implicature should be 'the room is a dirty, untidy place', and yet expected the hearer to access a list of other possible weak implicatures, this utterance could not be optimally relevant. The speaker could have saved the hearer Processing Effort by uttering "The room is dirty and untidy." As it is, (19) is relevant in that it is shorter, so more easily processed than "The room is dirty and untidy", and involves the relatively simple pragmatic strategy of disambiguation.

"Robert is a steamroller" is not so straightforward.

> (23)  a.  The speaker is speaking literally or metaphorically.[1]
>       b.  Robert is not literally a steamroller.
>
> Thus  c.  The speaker is saying metaphorically that Robert is a steamroller.
>
>       d.  Speaking metaphorically involves drawing similarities or analogies.
>
> Thus  e.  The speaker is drawing similarities or analogies between Robert and a steamroller.
>
>       f.  Steamrollers are difficult to stop.
>       g.  Steamrollers are not easily deflected.
>       h.  Steamrollers crush objects.
>       i.  Robert is difficult to stop.
>       j.  Robert is difficult to deflect.
>       k.  Robert crushes people's feelings.
>
> Thus  l.  The speaker is drawing the similarities between Robert and steamrollers that they are both difficult to stop and deflect, and drawing the

analogy between Robert crushing people's feelings and steamrollers crushing objects.

(cf. Sperber and Wilson 1986: 236)

Actually the implicatures (23i–k) are more complex since the words *stop*, *deflect* and *crush* are themselves ambiguous, meaning something different in relation to human behaviour and affect ('prevent', 'distract', 'humiliate') from what they mean in relation to material operations. Even so, the kind of Implicated Conclusion in (23l) is a reasonable pay-off for the Processing Effort involved in decoding the utterance and working out the implicated premises. So that the presumption of optimum relevance is upheld.

The Shakespearean example is even more complex. The following, politically unfortunate, interpretation is based on Empson (1953: ch. 1), and is not one I wholly endorse, especially assumption 37.

(24)    1. Two noun phrases separated by commas can be part of a list or in apposition.

2. Lists have *and* between the last and penultimate items.

3. There is no *and* either before or after "bare ruined choirs".

Thus    4. "Bare ruined choirs" is not an item in a list.

Thus    5. The two noun phrases are in apposition.

6. Two noun phrases in apposition refer to the same object.

Thus    7. "Boughs which shake against the cold" and "bare ruined choirs" refer to the same object.

8. These phrases cannot both be referring literally to the same object.

9. Noun phrases can refer literally or metaphorically.

Thus    10. One of these noun phrases is referring metaphorically.

11. "Leaves", "hang", are literal and belong to the same lexical set as "boughs".

Thus    12. "Boughs which shake against the cold" is referring literally and "bare ruined choirs" is referring metaphorically to the same object.

13. Referring metaphorically involves drawing similarities and/or analogies.

Thus    14. The poet is drawing similarities or analogies between bare ruined choirs and boughs which shake against the cold.

15. Boughs which shake against the cold are bare.

16. Ruined choirs are bare.

17. Choir stalls are made of wood.

18. Boughs are made of wood.

19. Ruined choirs used to have choirboys singing in them.

20. Boughs which shake against the cold used to have birds singing in them.

21. Birds sit in rows on boughs.
22. Choirboys sit in rows in choirs.

23. Choirs are in churches or cathedrals.
24. Boughs are on trees.
25. Churches/cathedrals have pillars with stone vaulting and stained-glass windows.
26. Trees have trunks and branches and leaves.

27. Pillars are round vertical supports for the vaulting.
28. Trunks are round vertical supports for branches.

29. Branches form an arch.
30. Vaulting forms an arch.

31. Leaves in autumn are colourful.
32. Stained glass windows are colourful.
33. The poem was written shortly after the dissolution of the monasteries when stained-glass windows were smashed.

Thus 34. The churches ruined as a result of the dissolution of the monasteries had few stained-glass windows left.
35. When boughs shake against the cold they have few if any colourful leaves left.

36. Shakespeare was homosexual.
37. Homosexuals find choirboys sweet.
Thus 38. Shakespeare found choirboys sweet.
39. The birds are sweet.

THUS 40. The poet is drawing the following similarities between the boughs and choirs: both are wooden, used to have sweet singers in them sitting in rows; and is drawing the following analogies – bough : trunk : branches : leaves : : choir : pillars : vaulting : windows; which themselves depend on further similarities – shape and function of pillars and trunks, shape of vaulting, colour of leaves and windows, etc., etc.

Of course, there is some doubt involved in this inferential process; in other words many of the implicatures are very weak. This is precisely what is required of symbolic cultural objects like a Shakespeare sonnet which is recycled through the same reader many times, and through many readers over the ages, and through many critics influencing those readers. The doubt takes two forms: uncertainty over which are the relevant Contextual assumptions to access; and uncertainty as to the factuality of the assumptions accessed (e.g. 36 and 37). The sensibility of the critic, her ability to posit new implicated premises to throw up new implicated conclusions, depends upon the presumption, if not the generation, of doubt. And the literary historian or biographer will do research to establish the validity of certain historical assumptions, e.g. 33, 34, 36. Communication through poetic metaphors is as risky as it is rich, and the critic, the communicative equivalent of an insurance salesman, is there to initially exaggerate and subsequently minimize the risk.

Several other aspects of this list of implicatures are worth comment. First, we need some kind of inferential process to establish that the two noun phrases are in fact in apposition (1–5), to determine that one is being used metaphorically, and to decide which is metaphorical and which literal (6–12). The next aspect concerns the source of the Contextual Assumptions/ implicated premises. In terms of Figure 5.1, some, but few, of these implications derive directly from knowledge of the language system, as part of the grammar or as semantic features entailed by lexical items – 1, 2, 11, 18, 23, 24. Another potential source of implicated premises, knowledge of co-text, is crucial in contributing 3, 7, 11, 15, 20, 35, 39. Knowledge of situation, which includes knowledge of the time of utterance and knowledge about the addresser, Shakespeare, provides further implicated premises: 33, 36. The remaining Contextual Assumptions are derived from socio-cultural and factual knowledge, invoking such Schemata as: trees (morphology, boughs as habitats for birds, seasonal changes, etc.), cathedrals (history in the sixteenth century, architecture, function of choirs, etc.).

The final aspect worth comment concerns the relative accessibility or salience of these assumptions. The most salient are probably assumptions like 15 and 20 which are evoked from the immediate co-text and context. Less directly accessible are those which depend upon extending the context; for example in 23–35 the choir schema is extended to the cathedral schema which includes a sub-schema for pillars, vaulting, windows, etc. The more the context has to be extended, other things being equal, the weaker the resulting implicated conclusions are likely to be (Sperber and Wilson 1986: 142–51).

The next three chapters consider precisely how aspects of the co-text are used to reduce the risk involved in interpreting metaphors: Chapter 6 – how co-text can be used to signal a metaphor (cf. 9–12); Chapter 7 – how the Topic of the metaphor can be specified or indicated (cf. 1–7); and Chapter 8 – how the Grounds might be indicated or specified by the co-text, as in 16, 20, 35, 39. In terms of Figure 5.1 the question will be: how can the co-text guide us in selecting the Contextual Assumptions in our factual and socio-cultural knowledge relevant to the interpretation of the metaphorical expression? Or, to phrase things differently, how is the risky concentration of information in an Active metaphor reduced by exploiting the redundancy of the surrounding co-text?

### 5.1.4. Irony: echoic utterances

The second area of Figure 5.2 of importance for metaphorical theory is the area in the lower left-hand corner. Here the proposition is an interpretation of the thought of a speaker which can be the interpretation of an attributed thought. Sperber and Wilson (1986: 237ff.) locate echoic utterances, which include irony, on the pathway that leads to this box.

For them an echoic utterance is a means of informing the hearer that the speaker has in mind what X said and has a certain attitude to it. In the case of proverbs X could be people in general: "Don't count your chickens before they hatch." But very often the speaker has a more particular X in mind, as in the following two cases.

(25)  J:   It's a nice evening for a barbecue.
           [you go to the beach for a barbecue and the weather is fine without too much wind]
      M:   Indeed, it's a nice evening for a barbecue.

(26)  J:   It's a nice evening for a barbecue.
           [you go to the beach and there's a thunderstorm and howling gale]
      M:   Indeed, it's a nice evening for a barbecue.

M's utterances are echoic in each case: they inform J that M has in mind what J said, and that M has a certain attitude to it. In the case of (25) this attitude is one of endorsement; and in the case of (26) the attitude is rejection/disapproval. To spell out the relevant assumptions for the case of (26): if (27a–d) are a context in which M makes the utterance, then J might well arrive at the ironic interpretation which generates the Contextual Implications (28):

(27)  a.   If there's a thunderstorm the weather is no good for a barbecue.
      b.   There's a thunderstorm.
      c.   The weather's no good for a barbecue.
      d.   I (J) said it would be a nice evening for a barbecue.

      M:   Indeed, it's a nice evening for a barbecue.

(28)  Implicatures
      a.   M does not believe that it is a nice evening for a barbecue.
      b.   M is echoing my (J's) statement that it would be a nice evening for a barbecue.
      c.   M believes I (J) was wrong to say that it would be a nice evening for a barbecue.

## 5.1.5. A critical look at Sperber and Wilson

As far as the theory goes it furnishes us with a reasonable account of metaphor and irony. However, I wish to argue in this section that Sperber and Wilson's conception of irony and metaphor is too narrow. Let's look at irony first.

Apparently not all cases of irony are clearly echoic. If a student of mine has had a particularly short haircut and, the first time I meet them afterwards, I say to them "Your hair's long" it would be relevant to treat this as irony, but I fail to see how it is echoic. Certainly the attitude to the proposition I have expressed is important, in that I distance myself from the truth of it, but this is simply because it is mutually obvious to myself and the student that the proposition is not true and that I do not believe it is true. This kind of irony belongs in the same category, the same position on Figure 5.2 as metaphor, but in this case the distance between the thought of the speaker and the proposition used to express it is at maximum: I am saying the opposite of what I believe. It would appear that the motive for such irony is sheer playfulness, the deliberate maximizing of Processing Effort, and this suggests we need to qualify our notion of Relevance by making it specific to purpose.

Just as we can have two kinds of irony, one dependent on attributed thoughts and echoic utterance, the other on the diametrically opposed relationship between speaker's thought and the proposition expressed, so we can have two kinds of metaphor. Subjective metaphor, as defined and exemplified in section 4.5.3, depends precisely on attributed thoughts.

LF20   Then the creature stepped from mirage onto clear sand.

In LF20 the illusion of the procession of choirboys being a creature is Ralph's, not necessarily ours. We also established the categories of metaphor, Phenomenalistic and Mimetic. In order to accommodate these we need a further area in Figure 5.1: a description of an imaginary state of affairs.

Better still we can modify and elaborate Sperber and Wilson's Figure 5.2 by building on the simple model of communication we provided at the beginning of Chapter 1 to give us Figure 5.3. This elaborated diagram allows for more delicate and specific distinctions to be made in (A), ACTUAL STATE OF AFFAIRS, of the original figure. This state of affairs may either be actual (A) or imaginary (AI). And, whether real or imaginary, it can include other texts (2) or non-verbal representations such as pictures/models (3). These texts and non-verbal representations would be mediating the thoughts of another person (or the same person on an earlier occasion) (1). These thoughts may, in turn, be describing or interpreting another state of affairs, so that the whole diagram is recursive.

This diagram makes it possible to talk about speech representation in general and speech and thought representation in literature. If a newspaper reports a politician's voicing of her thoughts in a speech then the pathway through the diagram would be 1 → 2 → A → B → C → D. If an omniscient author/narrator represents the thoughts of a character in a novel then the initial part of the pathway will be 1 → AI → B, etc. Only in imaginary worlds do we have direct access to the thoughts of another, without the mediation of text. If I describe a Canaletto oil painting then what I am

1. ANOTHER('S) THOUGHT

2. VERBAL: ANOTHER('S) TEXT          3. NON-VERBAL: ARTEFACT

A. AN ACTUAL STATE                   AI. AN IMAGINARY STATE
   OF AFFAIRS                             OF AFFAIRS

               B. THOUGHT (INCLUDING ATTITUDE)
               C. PROPOSITION
               D. TEXT

*Figure 5.3* An elaborated model of linguistic communication

describing will be a non-verbal representation of Canaletto's perception so the pathway will be $1 \rightarrow 3 \rightarrow A \rightarrow B$, etc.

The last exemplifies Mimetic metaphor. As far as Phenomenalistic metaphor is concerned the pathway will be (A)AI $\rightarrow$ B etc. I have suggested that literary works are generally both Phenomenalistic and Mimetic, so that AI will be a deliberate imitation or Analogy for A, which is why I put A in brackets. The degree of Similarity between A and AI will, of course, vary. The AI of Surrealist, Fantastic, Romance and Mythic literature is very distant from what we expect in A. By contrast, the AIs of realistic fiction, like Lawrence's *Sons and Lovers*, a partly autobiographical work, will be much closer to A.

Subjective metaphor (and some kinds of irony) will, of course, arise when 1 and B do not match, i.e. when the second speaker (e.g. the author) and the second hearer (the reader) do not believe the thoughts represented by the first speaker's (e.g. the character's) text. The kind of reactivity in literary works such as Golding's depends on a large-scale rejection of the validity of the A–AI relationship of other texts and the thoughts of the first author (e.g. Ballantyne in *The Coral Island*) which lie behind them.

## 5.2. FUNCTIONAL VARIETIES

An important criticism of Relevance Theory is that it is not sufficiently explicit about purpose. Relevance only becomes meaningful if we can decide on the answer to the question 'Relevant to what?' We have to locate this principle of communication in social space as part of a genre which reflects purposeful human activity (Martin 1992: 546–73; Swales 1990). In Chapter 10 I will use the Hallidayan framework of genre/register analysis to demonstrate the ways in which genres and types of metaphor interact, according to the Principle of Relevance. Meanwhile we approach the notion of purpose from the opposite end, the functions of metaphor.

We can use Halliday's three metafunctions – the ideational, the inter-personal and the textual – in sketching out the functions of metaphor. The ideational function can be briefly defined as understanding the environment; the interpersonal as acting on others in the environment; and the textual as the providing of resources to ensure that what is said is relevant and relates to co-text/context. The interpersonal metafunction of metaphors is just as important as the ideational, despite the common misconception that metaphor is simply a descriptive device (e.g. Winner and Gardner 1993: 428). The following functions of metaphor are arranged in order according to which of these metafunctions they primarily realize: ideational, interpersonal and textual. I say "primarily" because metaphors fulfil more than one function simultaneously.

### 5.2.1. Filling lexical gaps

We have already seen that one function of metaphors is to fill lexical gaps. These occur when there is no adequate T-term in existence, so that extension or transfer of the reference of an existing word-form plugs the gap. Sometimes it is not simply a question of unavailability, but of processability. For example, we have pointed out the difficulty of finding words to describe time without using metaphors of movement: this is a question of availability. On the other hand, in describing long astronomical distances, although we have the means available, it is difficult to process the figures such as 94,630,000,000,000 kilometres, and so we use the term *light-year*, now conceptualizing space in terms of time.

There are at least three ways in which metaphors are used to plug lexical gaps. In the first case there is absolutely no suitable term available, forcing us to resort to metaphor; metaphor thus becomes a means of word-formation, e.g. *crane*, *mouse*, etc. In the second case although there is a word available it is only approximately adequate. In the following,

PM143    He put his face in the water and half*-gulped, half*-**ate** it.

neither *eat* nor *gulp* exactly matches the action described so the use is only approximate. Instead of describing the action more exactly and at length Golding offers this gap-filling metaphor as an adequate shorthand. The third subspecies are the Precision metaphors in which a process or quality is made more precise by being related, through modification, to a specific first-order entity.

FF184    My cry for help was the cry **of the rat when a terrier shakes it**.

Here "cry" is made more specific by the postmodifying phrase "of the rat", itself made more specific by the postmodifying clause "when a terrier shakes it".

### 5.2.2. Explanation and modelling

When the Grounds of the metaphor become the central issue, metaphors can explain some relatively abstract concept in terms which are more familiar to the hearers. For example, it is common to explain electricity to elementary science students in terms of waterflow through pipes: the abstract concept of voltage becomes water pressure; resistance, the width of pipe; and amperage, the rate of flow. The purpose of this metaphor-model is to highlight the similarities between electricity and waterflow. Actually, dissimilarities should also be stressed, to prevent misconceptions: the flow of electrons is not from positive to negative, but negatively charged electrons flow from negative to positive.[2]

As with the reversal of the time–space metaphors mentioned above (section 5.2.1), the electricity–waterflow metaphor has become reversed in the field of plant physiology, when describing the movement of liquids in plants:

ML16   Many flow equations are closely analogous to Ohm's law which
       describes the flow of electrons, and which we will use as a model.

The idea of metaphor as a scientific model brings us to a slightly different kind of explanation.

At a more fundamental level of scientific enquiry, then, metaphors constitute theories or models (Boyd 1979: 359ff.). Take, for example, the fashionable metaphor of the computer for the human brain. The introduction of this model constitutes a change of theory. It makes predictions which can be tested, thereby initiating a programme of scientific enquiry to find out in exactly what ways the operation of the human brain resembles the workings of a computer. In other words, the Grounds of this theory-constitutive metaphor are initially open-ended, and research is designed to specify them more exactly, by considering the predicted Grounds and attempting to falsify them. Of course, certain psychological phenomena probably cannot be explained in terms of this computer model/metaphor. Scientists will then attempt to propose a new theory-constitutive metaphor which can account for more of the scientific evidence. For example the **wave** theory of <u>light</u> was in some ways inadequate and needed complementing by the **particle** theory.[3]

Explanation and modelling uses of metaphor are not confined to science but are also widespread in myth. For example the Genesis account of creation has the aetiological function of explaining, among other things, why women suffer in childbirth, why men have to work for their living, why humans wear clothes, why snakes have no legs, and why there are seven days in the week. Or consider this account of the tooth fairy addressed to immigrant schoolchildren:

ACE76   In England you put it under the pillow, and a fairy will come and
        give you two and a half p.

Why this myth counts as metaphor is because the Topic (parents substituting coins for teeth) and Vehicle (fairy giving coins in exchange for teeth) share the same effect: the disappearance of the tooth and the appearance of the coin. Clearly the successful deception depends upon this Asymmetric metaphor being unrecognized by the child.

## ■ EXERCISE

*Look at the following passage from A.S. Byatt's novel* Still Life *which describes attempts to provide metaphorical models for a colony of ants. What different metaphors are used, and what might be the different Grounds which differentiate one metaphor from the other? Which are the most useful for Cobb?*

*He spoke of the social life of the ant. He warned against seeing ant life in terms of human life – though the language he spoke was coloured by anthropomorphism. We have named the ants for ourselves: queen, worker, soldier, parasite, slave. We name their social behaviour for ours: we talk of classes and castes. What interested Cobb was the problem of the guiding intelligence of the ant community. How does it assess, as it does, he asked, how many fecundated females it needs? How does it choose whether an egg or a larva shall become a worker or soldier or queen? There is evidence that these choices lie in the genetic inheritance of the egg. But also in the nature of the food fed to the larva by the workers in its very early days. There is determination and some communal choice, but what chooses? A whole colony of ants has sometimes been compared to the aggregation of cells which compose one human being. Is this comparison helpful or distracting? Where does intelligence inhere? Is it more helpful to see the nest as a machine – like a vast telephone exchange, said Christopher Cobb, in the days before the computer – or as Maurice Maeterlinck did, as a community of co-operative virgins, practitioners of an extraordinary altruism, ready to die for the greater good of 'the ideal republic, the republic we shall never know, the republic of mothers'? T.H. White had seen them as inhabitants of a totalitarian labour camp. Now, in 1984, biologists have taken to referring to all organisms, men, amoebae, ants, song-birds, giant pandas as 'survival machines'. They measure the statistical likelihood of altruistic behaviour in baboons and partridges with computer analysis of degrees of kinship and the perpetuation of particular genes. They account for self-consciousness as a product of the self-images the computing brain of the survival machine needs to make in order to be efficient. Can an ant-hill be seen to have self-consciousness? Christopher Cobb urged on the attentive young the need for objectivity (a word now fallen out of fashion). For imaginative curiosity without preconceptions. As though this were possible.*

*(Still Life, p. 195)*

### 5.2.3. Reconceptualization

With theory-constitutive metaphors we are talking not so much about explanation but about reconceptualization. In fact literary metaphors often seem designed to bring about a reconceptualization of experience. They invite us to view our experience from a different perspective by using unconventional terms or unfamiliar categories (Kress 1989). We saw in the Introduction, with the exercise on classifying boxes (Figure 0.1), that there are many possibilities for categorization, depending on what features are selected as critical for our concept. Many poetic metaphors undo the strings of our conventional category packages to induce *defamiliarization*, as for example the Anglo-Saxon expression *mere-hengest* ('horse of the sea') discussed in the Introduction (p. 3). Or understanding the line from Yeats "arrogance and hatred are the wares peddled in the thoroughfares" demands a reconceptualization of arrogance and hatred: as commodities sufficiently in demand that politicians can make their living by producing and selling them.

Some classes of expressions try to do more than effect a momentary reconceptualization. First, there are stipulative or private definitions (see Naess 1952: 267) which bring about a reconceptualization for the duration of the discourse or series of discourses, e.g. "The term *energy* may be applied to the product of the mass or the weight of a body into the square of the number expressing its velocity."

More radically there are attempts to bring about a permanent revolution in thinking, which turn out to be Asymmetric metaphors of the Impositive kind (Mack 1975: 248ff.) such as "Property is theft" (see section 4.5.2).

### 5.2.4. Argument by analogy and/or false(?) reasoning

Argument by analogy seems to have the same purposes as modelling and reconceptualization. These are primarily ideational, as they are ways of interpreting experience, but models and Impositives have an interpersonal strand, are attempts to persuade the hearer to accept them. As Steen points out, "when metaphors are highly appropriate (conceptually) they are also highly persuasive (communicatively) and natural (emotively)" (Steen 1994: 195). With metaphorical analogies used as arguments to justify an action or recommendation, this emphasis on persuasion is even stronger. Whereas with modelling and reconceptualizing metaphors we are concerned with describing the world, "arguments" by analogy seem to be embedded in the sphere of human action on the world. They are arguments for *doing* something.

The text which best epitomizes argument by analogy is John Lyly's *Euphues*:

> EU94 The fine crystal is sooner crazed than the hard marble, the greenest
> beech burneth faster than the driest oak, the fairest silk is soonest

soiled, and the sweetest wine turneth to the sharpest vinegar. The pestilence doth most rifest infect the clearest complexion, and the caterpillar cleaveth to the ripest fruit. The most delicate wit is allured with small enticement and most subject to yield unto vanity.

The context of this speech is as follows. An elderly gentleman has noticed the behaviour of the nobly born Euphues, since his arrival in Naples, and believes he is rapidly becoming a rake. In this speech he is dissuading him from ruining his nobility by indulging himself in vanities, behaving irresponsibly and mixing with the wrong kinds of friends. The utterance has warning for its illocutionary purpose, and its intended perlocutionary effect is persuasion to act or refrain from acting in a certain way.

The passage, at least for the modern reader, has little logical force. As Shaw, talking of such arguments, puts it:

> The acceptance or the rejection of the analogy depends upon the acceptance or rejection of the conclusion, rather than vice versa.
>
> (Shaw 1981: 124)

There may have been more force of "logic" for an Elizabethan audience, given their premiss that there were systematic, divinely designed correspondences between the properties of different orders of existence, in this particular example, minerals, plants, cloth, and human character. Even so, we recognize that this kind of "argument" very often depends upon another means of persuasion besides logic, namely exploiting emotive responses. We have the finest crystal, the ripest fruit, the fairest complexion, the sweetest wine all spoilt in some way, just as, so he is warned, Euphues' most delicate wit is threatened. All the objects spoilt, with the exception of green beech, have positive connotations in themselves, even before they are premodified with evaluative adjectives. So there are two affective thrusts: positive towards the objects, negative towards their spoiling.

## ■ EXERCISE

*Look at Shelley's poem 'Love's philosophy'. What function does metaphor have in it, and how does it resemble the Euphues passage?*

It is (negative) affective response to the process described in the clause, rather than the connotations of the objects referred to, which often carries the burden of persuasion. One typical form is that in which the stupidity of the behaviour in the analogical Vehicle is transferred to the Topical behavioural process:

(29) He told the Conference last week that football hooliganism was exacerbated by press coverage. This was rather like blaming the Meteorological Office for bad weather.

(quoted in Shaw 1981: 125)

Metaphorical reasoning can, of course, be less noticeable and therefore more insidious than in the previous examples which, after all, drew attention to themselves through being signalled as similes. J.R. Martin has noted the way in which surreptitious reasoning or argument works at a subliminal level in the following text:

> I think governments are necessary because . . . **they help** keep our economic system in order for certain things. If there wasn't no Federal Government there wouldn't have been **no one to fix up** any problems that would have occurred in the community. Same with the State government if the SG didn't exist there would have been **no one to look after** the schools . . . The Local government would be important to look after the rubbish because everyone would have diseases.
>
> (Martin 1985: 28)

He comments:

> The writer . . . does not actually say that governments are like parents. But the processes selected to describe what parents do (*help, fix up, look after*) are clearly chosen to portray governments in this way . . . Governments are treated as parents. Everyone understands what parents do and why they are necessary. And if governments are parents, they must be necessary too. Of course the argument sounds absurd when spelt out in this way.
>
> (*ibid.*: 24–5)

Though "*reasoning by analogy*" is something of a smear phrase, we should pause to consider whether in fact there is any other kind of reasoning. The philosopher Condillac admitted that the creation of an abstraction involves the processes of "ceasing to think of the properties by which things are distinguished in order only to think of those in which they agree with each other" (quoted in De Man 1979: 10). This sounds like a description of metaphorical interpretation, apart from the fact that, with metaphor, the deliberate forgetting is not so easy or thorough. Condillac feared that he and other philosophers could not do without these abstractions (or metaphors) and that he was dangerously dependent on them; without them no discourse would be conceivable, and yet they are corruptive. This suggests that philosophical abstractions are likely to undermine the search for logical truths (*ibid.*: 20–1).

What happens, then, to deductive logic if we start questioning the presumed abstractions on which it operates (Hesse 1983: 27–70). Let's consider the so-called logical fallacy known as *affirming the consequent*, taking an example provided by Gregory Bateson (1991: 240):

(30)      Grass dies.
             Men die.
  Thus   Men are grass.

Of course this amounts to metaphorical thinking, and is not sound logic. Whereas the following is logical:

(31)        Men die.
            Socrates is a man.
    Thus    Socrates will die.

But how do we arrive at the concept of 'man' in the first place, and decide that Socrates is one?

(32)        A man is human.
            A man is adult.
            A man is male.
            Socrates is human, adult and male.
    Thus    Socrates is a man.

Is this syllogism (32) any more valid than (30)?


## 5.2.5. Ideology, the latent function

The impossibility of non-analogical reasoning brings us face to face with the relation between ideology and metaphor. We have already mentioned the relationship between metaphor, language and reality in Chapter 1, where we suggested that, just as with metaphor, ordinary language is not a mere reflection of a pre-existing objective reality but a construction of reality, through a categorization entailing the selection of some features as critical and others as non-critical. And we have also, in this chapter, seen how metaphors can consciously be used to construct scientific reality. To narrow this epistemological and ontological perspective to an ideological one, we need to concentrate on the ways in which metaphors are used to construct reality as a means of maintaining or challenging power relations in society.

We have already seen in section 4.5.3, that Subjective Impositive metaphors, like Geoffrey Blainey's use of the word *invasion,* are ideological in origin. I will limit myself here to three more examples for illustrating this wide and important phenomenon. Masako Hiraga demonstrates how in Japanese there is a network of Root Analogies for referring to women (but not men), which can be summed up under the heading WOMAN = COMMODITY. Some of the sub-analogies which contribute to this overarching metaphor are WOMAN = SALES PRODUCT, WOMAN = FOOD (Hiraga 1991: 55). The ideological repercussions of these metaphors are quite clear: commodities are inanimate objects; their sole *raison d'être* is to be used by consumers; they can be bought and then become the property of their rightful owners. All these assumptions construct or defend a system of social relations in which women are passive, powerless, valuable and desirable objects, whose role in society is to be purchased, owned, used, consumed and exploited by men.

## ■ EXERCISE

*Look at the following lexical items for English which realize the Root Analogy* HUMAN = FOOD. *Are they used equally of men and women?*

> *cookie, tart, cream (in my coffee/of the cream* (crème de la crème)), *crumpet, sugar, honey, sweetie, tot?, tasty, dishy, insipid (person), refined, sour, bitter, vinegary*

My second example is taken from an interview of a "middle" manager, Mr Miller, who is trying to stake his claim as a manager rather than a subservient worker. The status and power relations in Miller's company are conceptualized using a spatial metaphor. The interviewer, Gareth Jones, starts by suggesting that there is a line dividing management from below-management and asks Miller where he stands in relation to this line. Miller refuses to accept this spatial conception:

> (33)  MILLER:  If you have to draw a line through the whole company it would be a pretty thick line, you know, it would have two edges, and there would be a fair number of people in it, contained in it.
>
> JONES:  Where would you be – above that thick band or . . .
>
> MILLER:  I don't think so, I'd be in the band and there would be one or two figureheads on the outside – people like Mike for instance and some of the other managers.
>
> (Hodge, Kress and Jones 1979: 82).

By changing the metaphor from "line" to "band" Miller can suggest that he and his peers contained in the band are central to the operational management of the firm and that their superiors are somehow marginal "figureheads". Miller uses metaphor here to define his sense of his own power and status in the company, to meet his personal need to establish an identity in the ambiguous and uncertain environment of middle management.

Third, amongst the Root Analogies listed in Chapter 2 there are a number which express ideological classifications of a somewhat insidious nature. IMPORTANT = FIRST contributes to an ideological interpretation by which *Third World* suggests a less important world. As part of the BAD = DARK analogy, with its items such as *spotless*, emerges the notion that moral goodness is purity, an unmixed or unadulterated state. From this it is but a short step to the notion of racial "purity" and ethnic "cleansing". The pair HUMAN = MACHINE and even the reverse MACHINE = HUMAN probably both contribute to the dehumanizing trends in modern society.

The fact that all the examples of metaphors in Analogy 5.1 functioning

---

### Analogy 5.1 **HUMAN = MACHINE/IMPLEMENT**

Humans or parts of humans are machines/implements or their parts:

*a/your tool, geyser, hulk, machine, mechanical, new broom, robot, waterworks, cog, gear up, mouthpiece, shank, spare tyre, vagina* (B)

To act on a human is like acting on/using a machine/vehicle:

*programmed, adjust, readjust, switch on* (*behaviour*), *turn* (someone) *on, turn on* (*behaviour*), *screw* someone, (*broken limbs*) *mend, override,* (*children*) *in tow*

The functioning of a human is like the functioning of a machine/vehicle:

*drive, input, output, process, rumblings* (*of discontent*), *seize up, run out of steam, under your own steam, What makes you tick?, on automatic pilot*

The state/quality of a human is like that of a machine/vehicle:

*on the scrap-heap, wreck* (cf. *car, ship, plane*)

---

*Key*
(*x*): *x* = part of a phrase in which the metaphor typically participates with this meaning, or an indication of the superordinate class such parts of phrases belong to, e.g. *launch* (*a newspaper*)
(cf. *x*): *x* = the Vehicle, Vehicular domain, Vehicular colligate, e.g. (*emotions*) *run high* (cf. *tide, river*)
(B) = Buried, e.g. SUCCESS = MOVEMENT FORWARDS *progress* (B)

ideologically depend on well-established Root Analogies indicates that ideological metaphor is both highly pervasive and latent. Probably all metaphors express an ideological substratum, of which we are generally unaware. Ultimately ideology and epistemology may be indistinguishable.

If it is their latency that makes ideological metaphors dangerous then we should recognize that replacement metaphors, those taking pathway 1 (Table 4.1 and section 4.2.5), are particularly prone to (mis)lead us.

### 5.2.6. Expressing emotional attitude

Halliday (1994: 118) has suggested that Mental processes can be categorized into three basic kinds: perceptual, cognitive and affective. Imagining should be located in the middle of the triangle formed by these three Mental processes. Perception is of individual experiences, cognition is to do with classes of experience, imagining lies somewhere in between. Concepts are abstractions more or less shared by members of a culture or language group, but images, based on vestiges of perception, can be far more idiosyncratic (see section 3.1.1). Similarly, if images are based on specific experiences which were once actually perceived, they are likely to be associated with the emotions they produced at the time of perception.

One of the major functions of metaphor is to express emotion. In fact MacCormac has suggested that the general illocutionary force of metaphor is producing emotions such as wonder and puzzlement, and the particular emotional effect of the metaphor, its perlocutionary force, will vary across individuals and contexts (MacCormac 1990: 160ff.). Literature, too, has long been associated with the evocation of emotion (Richards 1948), as in Wordsworth's famous dictum "Poetry is the spontaneous overflow of powerful feelings: it takes its origin from emotion recollected in tranquillity." And even poets like T.S. Eliot, who insisted on the importance of cerebration to poetry, nevertheless observe that the best poets "*feel* their thought as immediately as the odour of a rose" (Eliot 1932: 290). So the relative frequency of Active metaphor in poetry (Chapter 10) may be partly due to metaphor's emotional impact and tension.

A good example of this tension is when Cleopatra says, referring to the snake she has applied to her breast in order to commit suicide,

(33)    Dost thou not see my baby at my breast
        That sucks the nurse asleep?

*(Antony and Cleopatra*, 5.2.308–9)

The peculiar character of the metaphor depends on the clashing emotional associations of the Topic and the Vehicle, venomous snakes and babies feeding at the breast.

Metaphorical swearing is the extreme form of expressing emotional attitude in two ways. It is associated with extreme emotions. But, more importantly, the Grounds of the metaphor are entirely affective, and any attempt to build interpretation on conceptual or non-affective Grounds is misplaced. *Hell* and *bugger* are clear examples. *Piss off*, less obviously, is metaphorical because of the creation of affective Grounds; it works by attributing to the hearer the negative emotional attitudes to elimination of bodily wastes.

In our catalogue of Root Analogies emotion tends to be expressed by choosing marginal members of a semantic field. For example in the category IDEAS/INFORMATION/WORDS = LIQUID (section 2.3.6) the prototypical adjective might be *flowing*, so the marginal *turgid* and *slushy* suggest disapproval. The prototypical verb might be to *pour out*, so that *leak* and *meander* are slightly disparaging. Going over the boundary to talk about words as gas often insults the speaker: *hot air, long-winded, windbag*.

### 5.2.7. Decoration, disguise and hyperbole

Reconceptualizing, theory-constitutive and Impositive metaphors are at the radical extreme of metaphorical use. At the other extreme are metaphors used, as it were, to dress up concepts in pretty, attention-grabbing, or concealing clothes, rather than to create a new concept by cannibalizing two existing ones, or giving birth to another body. When used for disguise and concealment they often have an emotive function, though one which is diametrically opposite to that involved in swearing – euphemism, e.g.

(34)   He **fell asleep**.

meaning 'he died'. The main motivation for metaphorical euphemism is precisely to avoid mentioning subjects which have strong emotional associations of a negative kind. Pound (1936) collected a range of euphemisms for death, dying and burial used in American English, many of which are metaphorical: *climbed the golden stair, called to the eternal sleep, crossed over the great divide, answered the last muster*, used for dying; and *planting, cold meat party*, used for funerals (Pound 1936, quoted in Saville-Troike 1982: 201).

## ■ EXERCISE

*Do you think* cold meat party *is euphemistic or not, i.e. does it succeed in disguising the unfavourable affective connotations of funerals?*

Some of our depersonalizing Root Analogies, i.e. those with HUMAN on the left side of the equation, are used for euphemism, to disguise reference to the human body. In Analogy 5.1 HUMAN = MACHINE/IMPLEMENT (p. 157), for example, we have *spare tyre* referring to rolls of belly fat, and *waterworks* for urinary tract.

More sinister is the use of metaphor to prevaricate or avoid responsibility for what one says. Tanaka in her book *Advertising Language* shows how metaphor can be used for covert communication, to make indirect claims for which the advertiser can later avoid responsibility (1994: 40–6).

In the category of decorative purpose we also recognize certain kinds of conventional personification common in eighteenth-century poetry, where they are used almost automatically:

LL   In the soft **bosom** of Campania's vale,
      When now the wintry tempests all are **fled**
      And genial Summer **breathes** her gentle gale
      The verdant orange lifts its beauteous **head**.

The sense that metaphors disguise and misrepresent, even to a greater extent than ordinary language, might well be a reason for avoiding them, or attempting to avoid them. One might, for example, wish to talk precisely and with immediacy about the colour and shape of a plum:

SL164   You may use the word *bloom* for the haze on this plum, and it will
         call up in the mind of any competent reader the idea that the plum is

glistening, overlaid with matt softness. You may talk about the firm texture of the flesh, and these words will not be metaphors, bloom and flesh, as the earlier *cleft* was certainly not a metaphor but a description of a grown declivity. But you cannot exclude from the busy automatically connecting mind possible metaphors, human flesh for fruit flesh, flower bloom, skin bloom, bloom of ripe youth for this powdery haze, human clefts, declivities, cleavages for that plain noun. The nearest colour Alexander could find, in his search for accurate words for the purple of the plum, was in fact the dark centre of some new and vigorously burgeoning human bruise. But the plum was neither bruised, nor a bruise, nor human. So he eschewed, or tried to eschew, human words for it.

In this passage Byatt claims that even lexical gap-filling metaphors, used with the aim of precision, involve a distortion and thus a disguise, a distraction from the immediate impression of the real object. The same is true of all linguistic categorization.

### 5.2.8. Cultivating intimacy

Because the understanding of metaphors depends on shared Grounds, metaphor can become a means of activating the assumptions shared between only two people, or a small group. It is as though, because the meaning of the metaphorical expression lies in the knowledge of the speaker rather than directly in the expression itself, the hearer has to penetrate into this knowledge, explore the mind of the speaker and activate in his own mind the implicated assumptions he thinks are in the speaker's (Cohen 1979). This creates a sense of community. It also excludes those who are unable to penetrate the speaker's mind and access relevant matching information in their own. For example, if I write "Michael Heseltine was Wat Tyler and John Major was Bolingbroke to Maggie's Richard II" some readers can interpret this metaphor because of their knowledge of the Peasants' Revolt against the poll tax, led by Wat Tyler, their knowledge of the way Richard II was deposed by Lord Bolingbroke, later Henry IV, and their knowledge of the political scene in Britain during November 1990. These readers feel included in the community of comprehenders. Whereas those who lack the historical and political knowledge required to make sense of it are excluded.

There is a further aspect of the cultivation of intimacy that might be considered as deriving from metaphorical use. At one extreme of formality or social distance are texts of the scientific, legal or bureaucratic kind which attempt to avoid lexical metaphors altogether. These include texts in what Suprapto calls "standard English for foreigners", English used as a lingua franca "which makes minimal assumptions about shared cultural experiences among its readers" (quoted in Saville-Troike 1982: 107). At the other extreme are texts which, as part of their strategy for creating informality, deliberately mix metaphors in a casual manner (Nash 1980: 155–7). But even carefully constructed and extended metaphors with elaborated Grounds reflect a high degree of communicative collaboration, "a sympathetic communion of reader and writer" who experience some shared enjoyment in "this teasing out of an inwound figurative thread" (Nash 1980: 157).

### 5.2.9. Humour and games

We can, of course, deliberately tease or puzzle our hearer, make the hearer's contribution to the collaboration, the Processing Effort, disproportionate. Such enigmatic metaphors may contribute to any kind of word puzzle, crosswords etc. but they are particularly well represented in riddles. Consider the riddle of the sphinx: "What goes on four legs in the morning, two legs in the mid-day and three legs in the evening?" We can only reach the answer, a man, by giving metaphorical interpretations to the parts of the day (babyhood, middle age and old age) and to the third of the legs, the old man's stick.

### ■ EXERCISE

*Look at the following Anglo-Saxon riddle, in which I have emboldened the V-terms. Can you work out what the Topics are in each case?*

> *I watched four **fair creatures***
> ***Travelling** together; they left **black tracks***
> *Behind them. The support of the bird*
> *Moved swiftly; it **flew in the sky**,*
> ***Dived under the waves**. The **struggling warrior***
> *Continuously toiled, pointing out **the paths***
> *To all four over the fine gold.*

*Clue, if you need it: the key phrase is **the support of the bird**. Think what this might be and how it might have been used in Anglo-Saxon times. The answer is in the footnotes.*[4]

A similar effect to that of the riddle can be discerned in metaphorical puns. These will generally be achieved by the evocation of both Topic and Vehicle in cases where the original metaphor is Inactive, what one might call <u>Revitalization</u>.

(35)   Nero made Rome the **focus** of his artistic attention. (Nash 1985: 144)

DM22   Britain's fastest hairdresser, Alan Cresswell of Tewkesbury Glos, is hoping to **snip** five minutes off his world record today.

In the first of these puns we have more of a riddle since the metaphor is etymologically buried: the word *focus* means 'hearth' in Latin, and Rome became a hearth since it burnt while Nero fiddled. Here the riddling aspect of the humour overlaps with the cultivation of intimacy: only those who understand Latin and are sufficiently familiar with the saying "Nero fiddled while Rome burned" can become parties to the metaphorical conspiracy. There is no such educational snobbery in the *snip* example, but still a momentary double-take.

What is it about metaphorical interpretation which lends itself to these humorous effects? Freud (1963) pointed out that one of the aspects of jokes is the way in which initial confusion is dispelled by sudden illumination. Metaphors whose Topics remain unspecified are suitable candidates for producing this succession of psychological states. The understanding of the riddle, the registering of the pun, the identification of the Topic are all, like getting a joke or seeing the two possibilities in an ambiguous picture, necessarily instantaneous. By contrast the exploration of the Grounds which lead to or from such sudden revelations are quite irrelevant to this specifically humorous effect, this quick fire.

### ■ EXERCISE

*What idioms or inactive metaphors are being Revitalized in the following passage?*

> DT15　*This all means that general managers have cricks in their necks from talking down to the Community Health Councils and District Health Authorities, and up to Regions and the Department. They also have to watch their backs for stabs from the all-powerful health professionals.*

### 5.2.10. Metaphorical calls to action or problem-solving

We have already come across the idea that theory-constitutive metaphors can initiate a programme of research,[5] and that reasoning by analogy can be used to persuade to or against action ('Love's philosophy'; the *Euphues* passage, EU94, pp. 152–3). It's worth developing the point that metaphors can lead to, or be exploited to achieve, action of various kinds. They may be used for problem-solving. Nash (1990: 69–71) gives an example from Paul Gallico's *Poseidon Adventure*, where passengers trapped in the inverted hull of a wrecked ship are trying to escape upwards. Confronted by the jumbled mass of steel which was once the engine room, Scott, the leader of this escape party, provides a metaphorical solution: "Don't think of it as you're seeing it but simply as a mountain to be climbed." Metaphor here has both a reconceptualizing function and also an indirect directive one.

Another example comes from the anthropologist Fernandez, who, in his study of the Fang performative cult of Bwiti, demonstrates the directive function of metaphor in ritual. He shows, for example, that cult members metaphorically classify themselves as Banzie (derived from French *ange* meaning 'angel'), and "some of the dances are imitations of the flying of spirits and hence directly a putting into action of this metaphor" (Fernandez 1977: 114).

Though the perlocutionary effect of many metaphors is action of some kind, stressing the interpersonal speech-act nature of metaphorizing, I am not counting it here as a separate function, but as a by-product of many of the other functions, both interpersonal and ideational.

### 5.2.11. Textual structuring

Metaphor can be used, consciously or subliminally, to structure the development of a text, as the organizing principle which gives the text a lexical cohesion (discussed extensively in Chapter 9). In the following example the explanatory function and the textual structuring function operate simultaneously:

(36)   Entomologists tell us of a strain of ants known to science as the *sanguinea* – a species so martial and imperialist in disposition that they are commonly referred to as army ants, or soldiers. In the insect world their inroads may well be dreaded, as once the disciplined advent of the Roman was a signal of alarm to lesser peoples. For not only do they make war; they are also, it appears, slave owners who prey on unfortunate neighbourhood colonies such as those of the wood ants.

   When a slaving expedition is mounted, the attacking legion of *sanguinea* divides into columns, each led by a scout, approaching the hostile fortress from different directions. Once in sight of their objective they call a halt. Then, while the other detachments maintain a blockade, one unit is sent forward as an assault force. As a rule these invaders easily beat down whatever resistance is offered to them. The wood ant defenders attempt to evacuate their positions, bearing with them the cocoons of their brood, but their line of retreat is cut off by the beseigers, who capture the fugitives while the storm troops continue to scour the fortification.

   (quoted from Nash 1980: 60)

The organizing metaphor here is of ants as an "army" or "soldiers". It develops more specifically when "imperialist" gives the cue for comparison with "legions" of "Roman" soldiers, and this more precise metaphor is rigourously exploited in the second paragraph which spells out the military manoeuvres involved in the "slaving expedition". Notice, however, the slight modification from the specificity of Roman soldiers, to the more contemporary "assault force" and "storm troops". As Nash comments: "The

soldiers began their foray under the eagles and end it under the swastika"
(*ibid.*: 61).


## 5.2.12. Fiction

It is possible, of course, to regard a literary narrative as one whole extended
metaphor. In such extended Phenomenalistic metaphors as literary works
we are invited to imagine a whole world in which what happens is literally
true (section 4.5.5). This contrasts with local metaphors in which we
recognize statements as being literally untrue and interpret them by positing Grounds which will connect the statement with the real world as we
know it. Fiction, like metaphor in general, and unlike lies, does not intend
to mislead (is a flouting of Grice's maxim of quality rather than a violation
of it); and, in so far as it invites interpretation as an Analogy for or Mimetic
representation of the "real" world, it is an extended Phenomenalistic
metaphor.

We can link this construction of a fictional world to the idea that
metaphors are iconic signs *presenting* meanings as well as *representing*
meanings (MacCormac 1990: 192ff.). And this would fit well with the
notion that some metaphors are highly dependent upon imagery for their
effects (section 3.1.1).


## 5.2.13. Enhancing Memorability, Foregrounding
## and Informativeness

It was pointed out in Chapter 3 that metaphorical expressions involving
nouns which refer to imaginable things have a particular vitality. Imagistic
metaphors either intentionally, or as a by-product, enhance memory,
because of their visual nature, as has been experimentally demonstrated
(Honeck *et al.* 1975; Mayer 1983).

It may be useful to consider hyperbolic metaphors here as they grab
attention, if not enhance memorability, by their deliberate exaggeration, a
shifting along a scale of size, quantity or violence. To some extent all
metaphors are hyperbolic, because they give extra weighting to those
features of Similarity, in Tversky's terms (section 4.4.1), which are negli-
gible in conventional linguistic classification. But the following overstate
or exaggerate in a more obvious way:

DM3     then he moved to a private bar upstairs and trouble **erupted**
DM11   Britain's butter **mountain**

These hyperbolic metaphors combine two purposes. They express emotion,
in that the interpreter is expected to transfer to the Topic the sense of

wonder associated with the Vehicle; and they are attempts to attract attention, with the result that they contribute to foregrounding.[6]

Psychological foregrounding is an automatic effect of active metaphors (Van Peer 1986). On the one hand they are, by definition, externally foregrounded, as they involve unconventional reference or colligation. And on the other we are forced to pay them special attention because, all other things being equal, their interpretation is less straightforward than the interpretation of the expressions in the surrounding text; in terms of Relevance Theory, they demand more Processing Effort.

Hopefully we receive a reasonable pay-off for our efforts at interpretation, in terms of the number of Contextual Effects produced. In that case we will have a sense that the metaphorical expression ends up as being highly informative, packing many ideas into a short space. An obvious example is the Shakespearean image we analysed, "bare ruined choirs where late the sweet birds sang".

The information content of Active metaphors can be considered from the more technical perspective of information theory. According to the theory, the more predictable an item the less information it conveys. So that in the word *queen* the letter *u* carries no information, and nor does the word *to* in the sentence *I want to go home*. Active metaphors, again because of their unconventionality, are referentially and/or colligationally unpredictable. No one could be expected to predict the words *tractor* and *icicles* in the lines from Charles Causley "His tractor of blood stopped thumping. / He held five icicles in each hand" (p. 34). As a consequence of their unpredictability they are high in information content. The corollary of this is that they achieve their interpretation by exploiting the redundancy in their co-text/context.

A particularly powerful way of compressing information in a metaphor is allusion to another text through quotation or use of proper name. William Golding chooses the name *Beatrice* for Sammy's first girlfriend in the novel *Free Fall*, a name used by Dante for the heroine of *La Vita Nuova*. This invites the reader who is familiar with Dante's poem to exploit his knowledge of that text and explore the parallels, and ironic differences, between the two narratives.

The kinds of interpretative hints provided by allusions are often the epitome of the sorts of weak Contextual Effect that Sperber and Wilson perceive in literary metaphor. For example, in the same novel, the hero is called Sammy. Sammy is never sure who his father is: before her death his mother suggests from time to time that he is a clergyman (p. 12). On his mother's death Sammy goes to live with the priest, Father Watts-Watt. While at school Sammy becomes obsessed by the story of Moses and the burning bush. Let's consider how these allusions to Samuel and Moses operate.

When we discover that Sammy is going to live with a priest we access the assumptions that the biblical Samuel was also brought up by the priest, Eli. Golding's choice of a name then guarantees the relevance of this assumption, and we can claim that it is strongly enough implicated to turn the allusion into a metaphor. In the case of the Moses story we may access the assumption that Moses was also fostered out, but this time by his adoptive mother, Pharaoh's daughter, back to his real parents. Is the suggestion that Sammy's father was a clergyman strong enough to make the assumption about Moses' fostering relevant? If so we can say that the allusion to Moses implicates that Father Watts-Watt is Sammy's physical father, and that Moses becomes an allusive metaphor for Sammy. But probably the implicatures in the case of the Moses allusion are much weaker than those evoked by the Samuel allusion.

Allusions involving proper names are powerful tools for creating a wide range of weak Contextual Effects because their meaning, in English-speaking cultures, is generally a function of their reference, rather than their sense. So names refer to tokens not types and the schemata which they evoke are particular and individual and consequently much richer than the schemata associated with typed concepts.

## 5.2.14. Summary: metaphoric purposes and the functions of language

We can relate these thirteen common metaphorical functions to the communicative metafunctions of Halliday. Lexical Gap-filling, Explanation/Modelling and Reconceptualization correspond to Halliday's ideational metafunction. The next five functions have a strong interpersonal element: Argument by Analogy seems partly ideational, partly emotive; Expressing Emotional Attitude, Disguise and Decoration are clearly emotive; Cultivation of Intimacy, Humour and Games certainly have a phatic element, the latter being classic ways of cementing relationships between individuals. As we have seen many of the ideational and interpersonal functions have as intended perlocutionary effect a call to action, and this indirect directive function makes them interpersonal. The Ideological function, too, is both ideational and interpersonal: it demands Reconceptualization, but it involves value judgements and depends upon differing subjectivities. Fiction is partly interpersonal and phatic and partly textual, playful in its lack of concern with any real-world reference but involved with the creation of text, almost as an end in itself, so that it distances us from the real world in which we act. Enhancing Memorability, Foregrounding and Informativeness, along with Textual Structuring, seem to be primarily functions which are to do with the organization and presentation of the message, Halliday's textual function.[7]

## 5.2.15. Functions of metaphors and familiarity of the Vehicle

Under the functions of Gap-filling and Explanation/Modelling the Vehicle should be more familiar to the hearer than the Topic, and the same is probably true of Argument by Analogy. Textual Structuring also requires relative familiarity with the aspects of the Vehicle selected to provide textual scaffolding. By contrast with Disguise and Decoration, and Humour/Games the Vehicle may be deliberately less familiar – the exotic comparison, the disguise of the all too familiar processes of excretion, sex, etc., the deliberate strangeness of riddles. Metaphors which function as Cultivators of Intimacy might deliberately take risks by choosing a Vehicle which is slightly unfamiliar to the general hearer, deliberately excluding those with no knowledge of it. To express an Emotional Attitude, one can go either way: refer to Vehicles which are familiar enough to evoke strong feelings, or appeal to the exotica which incite stereotypical feelings of the grotesque, of wonder, of romance, etc. One should not always expect, where emotions are concerned, for the Vehicle to be familiar. Ian Fleming's simile "the skin was grey-black, taut and shining, like the face of a week-old corpse in the river" provoked an objection from the critic Walter Nash: "one is entitled to wonder how many people, including Ian Fleming, might be acquainted with a week-old corpse in the river" (Nash 1990: 125). But the objection is beside the point, as it is when John Donne apostrophizes a particularly intimate part of his mistress' body as "O my America, my Newfoundland".

# 6

# THE SIGNALLING OF
# METAPHOR

## 6.1. INTRODUCTION

The first five chapters of this book discussed the distinction between metaphorical and literal language, and explored the interpretative and functional varieties of metaphor. The remainder of the book considers the contribution of co-text (Chapters 6–9) and social context (Chapter 10) to metaphorical interpretation.

We need this contribution to help interpretation because metaphor is a risky communicative strategy, not always easily interpretable. Eric Cantona, the Manchester United footballer, after being sentenced for attacking a Crystal Palace fan, uttered this gnomic statement:

(1)  When the seagulls follow the trawlers it's because they think sardines will be thrown into the sea.

Though recognized as metaphor, the reporters who he was talking to were not sure what it meant, because Cantona gave no textual guidance for interpretation. ("The seagulls" may, of course, have been referring to them!)

We can start with a simple model of metaphorical production and interpretation as in Table 6.1. Stages (III), (IV) and (V) in this model highlight the interpretative problems of ensuring: that the reader recognizes that 'A' is not referring conventionally, literally (III);[1] that the writer's intended referent, b, corresponds to the reader's postulated referent, c (IV); and that

*Table 6.1* Stages in metaphorical processing

| Writer | | Reader | | |
|---|---|---|---|---|
| I Perceives or creates a resemblance between entities a and b on the basis of feature(s) x | II Forms text using "A" to refer to b | III Realizes that "A" is not referring to a | IV Thinks "A" is referring to c | V Postulates a resemblance between a and c on the basis of features y |

the intended resemblances x, linking the referents a and b, match the resemblances y, hypothesized by the reader (V). In other words the metaphor needs to be recognized (III), the Topic needs to be properly identified (IV), and the Grounds correctly constructed (V). This chapter is about the co-textual means of ensuring stage (III) is successful, and Chapters 7 and 8 concern themselves with stages (IV) and (V).

While we split up these stages for analytic purposes they do not necessarily occur in the numerical order suggested by the model. Often stages (III), (IV) and (V) are interlinked and simultaneous; someone unfamiliar with the term *mouse* for the keyboard attachment could, on encountering the metaphorical term, jointly hypothesize both potential Grounds (V) and potential Topics (IV) in order to home in on the actual Topic. Or the interpretative stages may occur in reverse order, as in allusion by proper name, where Grounds (V), the same name, suggest a metaphorical equation between two texts (III). Or the presence of a potential Topic in the context (IV) might alert us to the metaphorical nature of the reference (III). With model theoretic metaphors, (II) may even precede (I) since the actual Grounds validating the model will be a matter for ongoing research.

As Chapters 6, 7 and 8 give a sketch of the linguistic resources available for guiding the reader at stages (III), (IV) and (V) of this processing model we can give an overview of the kinds of structures they consider in Table 6.2 (cf. Genette, in Petofi 1983: 102 fig. 3). This chapter discusses the signalling of Metaphor (column 4), Chapter 7 the syntactic and discourse structures commonly used for the specification and indication of Topics (column 2), and Chapter 8 (column 3) those structures used to explicate Grounds.

An important point is that, as we move down the table, with signalling and specification becoming less explicit, the Processing Effort, the work left to the reader, increases. Those on the last four rows are, all other things being equal, less certain, generating a wide range of possible weak implicatures. By contrast, the "metaphors" in the first two rows are marked out of existence, sometimes to the extent of becoming a literal comparison or simile, or by being made literal through derivational processes.

We can provisionally make some rough suggestions about how the degrees of specification and marking might correlate with the metaphorical functions which we identified in Chapter 5. These suggestions are represented in Table 6.3, and will be investigated more fully in Chapter 10, where function is seen in relation to genre.

## 6.2. WHICH METAPHORS DO WE NEED TO MARK?

The need to mark metaphors, especially derived and inactive ones, will depend upon whether the social or situational context or the co-text rules

*Table 6.2* The syntactic configuration of metaphor

| V-term | T-term | G-term | Marker | Example |
|--------|--------|--------|--------|---------|
| Yes | Yes | Yes | Yes | One or two tupaia species *run along branches* like* **squirrels**. |
| Yes | Yes | No | Yes | The movement [of the bowels] (is) like* **creamed soup**.<br>The boy was **raven**ous*. |
| Yes | No | Yes | Yes | They pull themselves up into a kind of* *green* **aquarium** under the branches. |
| Yes | Yes | Yes | No | **The bones** of the land, lumps of *smooth grey* rock. |
| Yes | No | No | Yes | A kind of* **autumn** fell over the first grade. |
| Yes | Yes | No | No | Housework is **a treadmill**.<br>**The treadmill** of housework.<br>Housework, **that treadmill**. |
| Yes | No | Yes | No | *Silly* **ass**! |
| Yes | No | No | No | Attach **the mouse** to the keyboard. |
| (Colligation) | Yes | No | No | The **naked** shingles (of the world).<br>Winds **stampeding** the fields. |

out a literal interpretation. We can see this from the evidence of the COBUILD concordance lines for *metaphorical* and *metaphorically*:

GW044     young officers who acquired wives before they had, metaphorically speaking, cut their wisdom teeth

GW0036    and for them the marriage took place in an atmosphere of meta-phorical orange blossom

In both examples the situational context evoked by the text – growing older, and wedding ceremonies – makes probable a literal interpretation of "cutting wisdom teeth", and "orange blossom" respectively. The extreme case will be when the reference is primarily literal, but metaphorical too:

(2)  When the contestants strip off their designer suits to reveal rippling muscularity, they metaphorically* **shed their shackling cloaks** of staid mundaneness.

(*8 Days*, 14 October 1994, p. 48)

This kind of blending of the metaphorical and literal, what I call the *Literalization* of Vehicles, and its literary effect is explored in Chapter 9.

*Table 6.3* Correlations between the functions of metaphors and their marking and specification

| Function | Marked | Specified Topic/Grounds |
|---|---|---|
| Gap-filling for: | | |
| abstracts | No | No T-term exists |
| new object | Only initially | No T-term exists |
| precision | Sometimes | T (G) often indicated |
| Explanation | Usually | Topic/Grounds spelt out |
| Modelling/aetiology | Often (initially) | Topic not pre-existing, G spelt out by research, given in data |
| Reconceptualization | Seldom | Sometimes |
| Impositive | No | T specified |
| Argument by Analogy | Often | T and analogical G both specified |
| Expressing Emotion | No | G unspecified |
| Decoration, Disguise and Hyperbole | No | G and T ignored |
| Cultivating Intimacy | Sometimes | T specified but not G |
| Humour and Games | No | T unspecified (G sometimes) |
| Textual Structuring | Sometimes | G by extension |
| Fiction | No | T unspecified, G = sense of "real" correspondence with life |
| Memorability/Foregrounding/ Informativeness | Seldom | G unspecified, T specified in contradictions |

## 6.3. DOMAIN SIGNALLERS OR TOPIC INDICATORS

We remarked earlier that stages 3, 4 and 5 in Table 6.1, recognition, identification of Topic and Grounds, may occur simultaneously. In fact lexis which <u>Indicates</u> the Topic can simultaneously mark the metaphor. What I have in mind is lexis that points in the direction of the semantic field where the Topic is located, generally by means of an adjective/noun premodifying the V-term. From a rapid survey the most popular domains so marked are those to do with humans:

GW0098  a human* **dowsing twig**
GW253   a <u>human</u>* **Catherine Wheel**

the mind (spirit):

GW0092   mental* **incontinence**
GW0087   intellectual* **stagnation**
GW0113   a kind of psychic* **eddy current**, some sort of spiritual* **diabetic flow**

171

along with metaphors linked with image-schema of the body as container for the mind:

GW0220  inner *speech

TS199   his own interior* road

TS139   his inward* eye on the spire

The popularity of mental-domain Indicators is a consequence of metaphors' Concretizing tendencies. But in principle any labels of fields of human activity and of social or geographical space are likely to function as these markers/Indicators:

GW0205  sexual* monotheism

GW0043  a kind of political* Savonarola

GW0132  One art school in Kent was . . . a kind of cultural* Borstal.

GW0103  Ceylon . . . was a tax* haven, a sort of oriental* Switzerland.

GW220   help to learn rather than relief, a kind of reading* dole

## 6.4. CO-TEXTUAL MARKERS

The body of this chapter considers the relatively explicit markers of metaphor, the words and phrases which seem to occur in the environment of metaphorical V-terms. Table 6.4 gives an overview of the linguistic terms we will be considering in section 6.4, and some provisional suggestion of the kinds of metaphors associated with the specific class of markers. The bolder ticks indicate the typical kind of metaphor marked. (Readers may wish to treat sections 6.4.1–11 as a reference section and read selectively. The subsection of 6.4 in which the marker is discussed is given in parentheses in column 1.)

One reason for looking at these markers is to find evidence supporting the extension of the notion of metaphor to cover the less central kinds such as the Mimetic, Phenomenalistic, Subjective. If the typical markers of the central varieties are used for the less central, then this is some indication that psychologically they are overlapping if not identical phenomena.

### 6.4.1. Explicit markers

The words *metaphor*, *metaphorical* and *metaphorically* are obviously used as markers. We note that they do not apply to all the columns in Table 6.4. However, they can be applied to Subjective metaphors as well as the ordinary Active varieties:

FF222   I saw then in her face, and around the openness of her brow, a metaphorical* light which none the less seemed to me to be an objective phenomenon, a real thing.

It is only in retrospect that Sammy, the narrator of *Free Fall*, acknowledges

the light around Beatrice's forehead as metaphorical. At the time it gave
the Subjective Illusion of being objectively real.

Phrases such as *to change the metaphor* are economical ways of marking
two metaphors:

> DV194 And you could not embark **on the long voyage** of <u>reparation</u> that
> would make all well . . . could not do it because, to change the
> metaphor*, the latest bit of <u>wantonness</u> was only **a bit on the top of
> the pile**.

Synonyms of *metaphor* and *metaphorically* such as *trope* and *figuratively*
occur too:

> MD990 If such a trope* may stand, his special lunacy stormed his general
> sanity.
>
> GW0092 "You have no plan to go to Africa," said the Count. "Sorry, that
> was figurative*." "Figurative*?" "I mean, you're planning to go
> away to forget."

### 6.4.2. *Literally* and other intensifiers

*Literally, actually, really, in fact, indeed, simply, fairly, just, absolutely,
completely, fully, quite, thoroughly, utterly, regular*

The paradox of why *literally* and other intensifiers should be used to mark
metaphor can perhaps best be explained by drawing parallels with the
modality of possibility.[2] The strongest truth claim one can make is one
with no intensification of certainty on this modal scale: *he must be home by
now*, despite the high level of probability of *must*, is less certain than *he is
home by now*, as though the modal is a doubtful speaker's attempt at self-
reassurance. Similarly *literally* implies the need for intensification of the
truth claim. Alternatively *literally* can be viewed as a means of strengthening the metaphorical contradiction:

> GW0010 It is the crowning folly of the Park, and **impregnates**, literally*,
> the whole district about the north end.
>
> GW0052 She lives in a company-owned penthouse and <u>she</u>'s literally* **their
> wholly owned subsidiary**.

There is a related intensification of reference to the metaphorical Vehicle
when, as is frequent, *literally* is applied to idiomatic phrases whose primary
meaning is metaphorical:

> GW0031 By directing electronic waves to her brain, it may, quite literally*,
> **tickle her fancy**.

*Literally*, and frequently-used formulae like *both literally and metaphori-
cally/figuratively*, by drawing attention to literal and metaphorical levels
simultaneously, can give a symbolic thrust to the literal action:

## Table 6.4 The markers of metaphor

| Forms marking metaphors | Kinds of metaphors marked | | | | | | | | Effect on metaphor |
|---|---|---|---|---|---|---|---|---|---|
| | Active | Inactive | Precision | Symbolism | Approximative | Subjective | Mimetic | Phenomenalistic | |
| Explicit markers (1) metaphor/-ically, figurative/-ly, trope | ✓ | ✓ | | ✓ | ✓ | ✓ | | · | Reduce/kill |
| Intensifiers (2) literally, really, actually, in fact, simply, fairly, just, absolutely, fully, completely, quite, thoroughly, utterly, veritable, regular | ✓ | ✓ | | ✓ | ✓ | ✓ | | | Enhance |
| Hedges or Downtowners (3) in a/one way, a bit of, half- . . ., practically, almost, not exactly, not so much . . . as . . ., . . . if not . . . | ✓ | | | | ✓ | | | | Variable: near factive/near contrafactive |
| Semantic metalanguage (4) in both/more than one sense/s, mean(-ing), import | ✓ | ✓ | | | | | | | Revitalize |
| Mimetic terms (5) image, likeness, picture, parody, caricature, model, plan, effigy, imitation, artificial, mock | ✓ | | | ✓ | | | ✓ | (✓) | Reduce |
| Symbolism terms (6) symbol(-ic/-ically), sign, type, token, instance, example | | | | ✓ | | | | | Reduce/create |
| Superordinate terms (7) (some) (curious, strange, odd, peculiar, special) sort of, kind of | ✓ | | ✓ | | ✓ | ✓ | | | Ambiguous |
| Copular Similes (8) like, as | ✓ | | | | ✓ | | | | Kill |

| Marker | | | | | | | | Type |
|---|---|---|---|---|---|---|---|---|
| Precision Similes and other comparisons (8.2) Material verb + like x, the y of a x, y's x; Noun-adj., the x equivalent of | ✓ (large) | | | | | | | Ambiguous Non-factive |
| Clausal Similes (8) as if, as though | ✓ | | | | ✓ | | | Ambiguous |
| Perceptual processes (9.1) seemed, sounded, looked, felt, tasted, + like/as though/as if | | | | | ✓ | | | Ambiguous |
| Misperception terms (9.2) delusion, illusion, hallucination, mirage, phantom, fantasy, unreal | | | | | ✓ | | | Reduce/kill |
| Cognitive processes (9.3) believe, think, regard, unbelievable, incredible | ✓ | | | ✓ | | | | Ambiguous |
| Verbal processes (9.4) say, call, refer to, swear | ✓ | | | | ✓ | | | Asymmetrize |
| So to speak (9.5) | ✓ | ✓ | | | ✓ | | | ?Reduce |
| Orthography (10) " ", . ! white space | ✓ | ✓ | | | ✓ | | | Enhance |
| Modals + Verbal Process (11) could say, might say | | | ✓ | | | | | Non-factive |
| Modals (11) must, certainly, surely, would, probable/-ly, may, might, could, possible/-ly, perhaps, impossible/-bility | | | ✓ | | | ✓ | | Enhance Reduce Kill |
| Conditionals (11) if . . . could, would, might, imagine, suppose | ✓ | | | | ✓ | | ✓ | Reduce/kill |
| As it were (11.1) | ✓ | ✓ | ✓ | | | ✓ | | ?Reduce |

*Notes:* The larger ticks indicate the typical kind of metaphor marked. The subsection of section 6.4 in which the marker is discussed is given in parentheses in column 1.

GW0241   A little boy **comes to grips with** his sex very early, literally* every
         time he urinates.

GW0142   The child has **to look up to** his elders literally as well as meta-
         phorically*.

In GW0241 grasping his penis becomes the symbolic cause of a boy's
adjustment to sexuality. GW0142 is interesting since, by treating looking
upwards as a symbol of respect, it suggests the cause of the metonymy
behind the STATUS = UP Root Analogy.

Examples of all the other intensifiers are too numerous to cite but CEC99
shows multiple marking by intensifiers and superordinates:

CEC99   It's just* frightening, just* really* is absolutely* **dehydrating**. And
        there they are [women's colleges at Oxford] having sort of* grafted
        on this stuff to make themselves feel of equal status and importance
        with the men.

The use of emphasis and amplification relates to both the hyperbolic nature
of the metaphor and the penchant for hyperbole in conversation.


### 6.4.3. Hedges or Downtoners

We can categorize hedges in terms of the increasing degree of Approximation to the literal that they mark, and we can widen Quirk and Greenbaum's
(1973: 218ff.) categories of adjunct to label the positions on the scale:

Minimizers: *a touch, a bit, a little*

GW0127   If you think Lord Longford is a bit* of **a prick** then you draw
         him as one.

DV223    There was a touch* of curiosity in Edwin's face.

Diminishers: *something, in a/one way, somewhat*

PM129    "There is something* **venomous** about the hardness of this
         rock."
         In a way* these officers were **prisoners** themselves.

Compromisers: *rather, pretty much/nearly, more or less, not exactly/*
    *precisely/quite*

(3)      pretty nearly* true desert

(4)      He didn't exactly* block me, but he didn't move either.

(5)      It stood rather* like an old farm dog.

CEC695   They're more or less* **soliciting**.

Approximators: *little more than, almost, nearly, as near as makes no*

*matter, virtually, practically, no more than, or whatever . . . or*
*something*

| | |
|---|---|
| (6) | Cats are, in fact, almost* colour-blind. |
| (7) | It was nearly* dark. |
| TS55 | These people he had to use seemed little more than* **apes**. |
| FF33 | My mother was as near **a whore** as makes no matter*. |
| DV46 | Matty's voice, practically* **of its own accord**, went on speaking. |
| DV150 | Those eyes in Ma Garrett's face were no more than* **reflectors**. |
| CEC249 | **Royal Warwickshire foot and mouth**, or something* |

There are a number of other downtoning formulae which set up a relation between two noun phrases, and these are difficult to locate on our scale, since the phrases related will represent two different degrees of approximation. Using C to stand for relatively close Approximation, and D to stand for more distant approximation/Transfer, the conventional, literal meanings of these phrases is as follows:

| | |
|---|---|
| (8) | *C if not D, C rather than D, D or rather C, not so much D as C,*<br>*half-D half-D, more of/like a C than a D* |

| | |
|---|---|
| (9) | He's earning £50,000 a year, if not* £60,000. |
| GW0206 | a smile lupine rather than* ursine |
| MD1161 | the deliverance or rather* **delivery** of Tashtego |
| FAE406 | He was not so much* elected as **anointed.** |
| PM143 | He put his face in the water and half*-gulped, half*-**ate** it. |

Interestingly enough, where Transfer metaphors, rather than Approximative ones, are being signalled (MD1161, FAE406), there is a strong tendency to override the conventions governing the positioning of C, the more literal item. That is to say, the V-term occupies the C(lose) slot, not the D(istant) slot where we would expect it.

Off the bottom of our scale are intensifiers like *literally*, discussed above, those forms which insist on the factuality or precision of the utterance, like *exactly, precisely,* and others which claim the referents as prototypical members of a cognitive category: *a real/true/regular/veritable . . . .*

Looking back at our list of examples we can see that these Hedges can be used for Transfer metaphors, where the V-term is emboldened, as well as Approximative ones; further evidence, if we needed it, that the Approximative uses of language in "loose talk" are simply part of a continuum which extends to Transfer Similarity metaphors.

### 6.4.4. Semantic metalanguage

*In a/one sense, in more than one sense, in both/every/all sense/s (of the*
*word), import, mean, meaning (of the word)*

These phrases draw attention to lexical ambiguity or polysemy produced by Inactive metaphors. They either demand both literal and metaphorical meanings simultaneously, or, in combination with markers like *metaphorical* or *literal*, exclude one or the other meaning. In that case they may signal active metaphors, as in HSG77.

(10)     I don't like the Singapore **climate** in all senses* of the word.

FF19    Mrs Donovan . . . was not Ma's **weight** in any sense*.

HSG77   <u>its</u> sooty <u>throat</u> (**the big flue**, we mean*, of its wide chimney)

### 6.4.5. Artefacts and Mimetic markers

Obviously the whole range of nouns and adjectives to do with artefacts and acts of imitation and representation can be used to mark or reduce Mimetic (Phenomenalistic) metaphors:

FF83    imitation* **marble**

TS7     the model* **spire**

DV41   Plastics . . . blossomed as a range of artificial* **flowers**.

LF100  the sound of mock* **hunting**

LF163  pretending* to be **a tribe**

Presumably the point of mimesis is to produce the willing suspension of disbelief associated with Phenomenalistic metaphor, if not outright illusion. So it is a short step from here to the marking of Subjective Illusion, hallucination or imagining:

DV2512  She shut her eyes as the image* [of murdering the boy] swept round her . . . She was trembling with the passion of the mock* **murder**.

TI104    The sounds made a picture* in his head of **interlacing shapes, thin and complex**.

DV11    But just now there was so much light that the very stones seemed semi-precious, a version* of **the infernal city**.

More surprising, these prima-facie Mimetic markers can also be used to signal quite ordinary Interactive Transfer metaphors:

GW0100  He places the capsule on her tongue and she closes her mouth. It is all a kind of parody* of a **communion**.

Or even as markers of Symbolic Substitution:

DV249   Its [the rabbit caught in a trap's] passion defiled the night with a grotesque and obscene caricature* of process, of logical advance through time from one moment to the next where the trap was waiting.

## 6.4.6. Symbolism terms

*token, sign, symbol; instance, example, acme, epitome, prototype, the type*

We distinguished two kinds of symbol in section 4.5.1. The more analogical, metonymic or indexical kinds are often marked by *symbol/-ic/-ally*:

LF156     Piggy placed **it [the conch]** in Ralph's hands, and the littluns, seeing the familiar symbol,* started to come back [where the conch symbolizes democratic process and free speech].

LF67     **the stone**, that token* of preposterous **time**

GW0207     To **put on someone else's clothes** is symbolically* **to take on their personality**.

GW0207     James Laver remarks that the tieless Catholic priest is "symbolically* **castrated**".

The other category of symbol occurs when we interpret an actual phenomenon as an exemplification of the class to which it belongs. These attract a different set of markers:

(11)     **Pollock** was an extreme instance*, but **his failure** epitomizes* that of many.

PM207     "**We** are the type* of **human intercourse**."

(12)     It's a very fine example* of traditional architecture.

These are very close to one meaning of the superordinate terms which we discuss in the next section. The difference is that they deconcretize, associating the actual and literal with a higher-order abstract quality, working on the vertical axis as it were; while *kind of* etc. can mean approximation on the horizontal axis.

## 6.4.7. Superordinate terms

In section 1.3 we drew attention to the ambiguity of (*a*) *kind of/sort of*. These forms, along with the less common *type of, form of* are used most frequently in the corpus to mark Approximative or Precision metaphors of the gap-filling kind, but they also mark Transfer and Subjective metaphors. They have a literal use too, of course: identifying hyponym–superordinate relations. Because they are extremely prevalent as markers I will attempt a comprehensive survey and commentary on their functions.

### 6.4.7.1. Marking metaphorical Transfer

Before we turn to the metaphorical types most frequently marked by superordinate terms, we can quickly exemplify the quite ordinary marking of Transfer metaphors.

GW0010     "I have no relish for the country; it's a kind* of healthy **grave**.".

HZ10     A scandal was, after all, a sort of* **service to the community**.

179

## 6.4.7.2. *Lexical Gap-filling*

However, most typically the forms are associated with gap-filling. They often suggest that after an unsuccessful search for a non-existent descriptive lexical item, recourse has been made to Approximation to fill this lexical gap. In GW0052 the word "nameless" is an admission that the search has been abandoned:

GW0052   The longer they sat there, the deeper Kunta sank into a kind of*
         nameless **terror**.

At other times we get several indications of the difficulty of the search:

GW0206   "What's your game?"
         "Why, I just thought I'd sort of*, kind of*, oh, like* **drift** with
         every passion."

This recourse to Approximation tends to appear in dialogue (fictional or otherwise), to meet the demands of spontaneous discourse. From a different angle these forms are used as hesitation strategies, giving the speaker that little extra time she needs to fill the gap, however roughly.

Further evidence of their Approximative nature is found in the patterns of their premodification. It is common to find adjectives which insist that the phenomenon being observed is not typical or prototypical of the category to which it is being allocated:

GW0191   a kind of BIZARRE saint
GW0010   a very ODD sort of outdoor–indoor aura of hush
DV83     a CURIOUS kind of epidemic in the town
GW0199   that PECULIAR kind of melancholy
GW0221   some UNUSUAL sort of – I don't know – gift or faculty or something

We should note, by the way, that these adjectives (in small capitals) can be used as metaphorical markers in their own right, without combining with *sort/kind of*:

MD1137   the STRANGE life-buoy [a coffin] hanging at the Pequod's stern

The most frequent premodifier marking atypicality is *some*:

GW0113   SOME sort of spiritual diabetic flow
GW0225   the third artist, John ,Stalin, SOME sort of kookaburra

It suggests the speaker's lack of familiarity with the entity being described, or a degree of surprise that such entities exist as members of the class. *Some* is used similarly in phrases where it premodifies singular nouns: *that's some pen you've got* (Quirk and Greenbaum 1973: 109).

In keeping with the other function of *sort/kind of*, the marking of hyponymy, premodifiers can suggest specificity rather than vagueness, as though showing the particular subclass that the phenomenon belongs to.

These uses will not necessarily be metaphorical, of course, though we see in GW0104 that a sleeping metaphor is being Revitalized:

> GW0104    It was that **mechanical** sort of* smile that suggested **gears and pulleys**.
> GW0172    Too many rules; it was a **pre-packed** kind of* life.

There are many ambiguities to be resolved in the semantics of interpreting phrases where the noun complement of the preposition *of* is premodified:

> GW0043    this process, a kind of economic osmosis
> LF134      a kind of dentist-chair unreality

The semantic function of *a kind of* could be:

1   simply to reinforce the metaphorical marking which has also been achieved by unconventional colligation;
2   to mark that the interpreted metaphor only approximates to the state of affairs being described, e.g. 'economic osmosis, though that is not exactly the right term for it';
3   to mark that the phenomenon described belongs to a subclass of the phenomena metaphorically labelled, e.g. 'a subcategory of economic osmosis'. In Chapter 1 I suggested that psychologically there might not be much of a distinction between (2) and (3), horizontal and vertical approximation, so to speak;
4   to mark that the phenomenon described belongs to the particular subclass conveyed by the premodifier in the following noun phrase, e.g. 'the particular kind of unreality experienced in a dentist's chair'. Function (4) would, of course, make the examples GW0043 and LF134 equivalent to:

> (13)    an economic kind of osmosis
> (14)    a dentist-chair kind of unreality

It is interesting to note what kind of phenomena typically elude existing lexical categories and demand the extra precision that metaphor can suggest, if not achieve. One especially well-represented area seems to be emotions:

> GW0145    almost with a sort of greed, a hunger
> GW0221    my terror gave way to a sort of sick uneasiness
> GW0092    a kind of crazy sardonic joy

Just as common are attempts to pin down particular qualities of voice:

> GW0100    a sort of growling
> GW0041    a high, snarling caterwaul, a sort of screaming wail
> GW0100    a kind of subdued bark
> GW0122    a kind of throttled yelp

To enhance the specificity of a description so that it borders on uniqueness, lexical gap or Precision metaphors often link *a sort/kind of* with proper names. The three examples below give evidence of the interpretative ambiguities (3) (4): shifting the name before *sort of* might not make much difference to interpretation in GW0022 and GW0087.

GW0001   The driver was a typical easy-going, Charles Bickford sort of*
         Westerner.

GW0022   Here I am, 47 next birthday, longing to be a sort of* Cary Grant
         character.

GW0087   It may be your bloody Sackville looniness, or it may be a sort of*
         George Sand stunt.

One view of the meanings of proper nouns is that, because they are designed for unique reference, they can refer but have no sense – they do not represent a concept. However, proper names can acquire conceptual meanings or senses: a head of department I once worked under was heard to say "I am not Napoleon." This sentence was not a tautology, because Napoleon has acquired the sense 'a tyrannical and powerful leader'. The metaphorical uses of names to add precision contributes to their acquisition of a sense.

GW0184   He is the forgotten and yet the vital character, a sort of* **man from
         Porlock** in reverse.

GW0184 shows how a uniquely referring phrase, *the man from Porlock* – originally a reference to the legendary visitor who interrupted Coleridge's transcription of his dream as the poem 'Kubla Khan' – has now acquired the sense of 'an undesirable factor interrupting a process and thereby preventing an important achievement'. The sense of the concept is sufficiently established by the metaphor, that we can begin to talk about its opposite, what it might be *in reverse*, presumably 'an indispensable catalyst for an important achievement'. Had it no such sense we would have to interpret "in reverse" as the man being turned around or going backwards.

## ■ EXERCISE

*Compare the following two versions of a metaphor: how are they different and which do you prefer?*

(a)  *It would be despair like one can't imagine – a sort of* winter night*

(b)  *It would be despair like one can't imagine – a sort of* winter night,
     (Sunday) at Aberdeen. (GW0087)*

I would guess that most readers, perhaps with the exception of some Scots, would prefer (b), with its humorously irresponsible stereotyping of Aberdeen, to (a), with its rather banal and hackneyed analogy between winter darkness and despair. Slipping in a proper name (or two – we also have "Sunday") gives a degree of precision and imageability lacking in (a).

### 6.4.7.3. *Marking Subjective metaphors*

Occasionally *sort of/kind of* are used to signal Subjective metaphors. These can be of the Impositive variety as in GW0007, or GW0010 which refutes another thinker's Impositive:

GW0007　so laughter is really some kind of* **relief-cry**

GW0010　a soppy notion that all crime is some kind of* **displaced revolutionary activity**

Or they may be Subjective Illusion metaphors, which are being marked by Mental verbs of perception:

GW0206　I seemed to hear a kind of* **high-frequency ping** at the far edge of my mind.

Very typically as Subjective markers *sort of/kind of* occur with Mental processes of cognition, either literally or through the analogy KNOW/UNDERSTAND = SEE:

GW0033　as long as we consider the automobile a sort of* **super-horse**

GW0229　regarding intellectual conversation as a sort of* **rocking horse for a beloved child**

Other common verbs associated with the metaphorical markers *sort/kind of* concentrate on functional Grounds.

GW0205　The lungs functioned as a sort of* **carburettor**.

To summarize: superordinate terms are used to mark lexical gap-filling, Transfer, Subjective and Approximative metaphors. When used for Approximation they may combine with markers for non-prototypicality like *strange*. Conversely, they can create extra semantic precision (notably for emotions and voice qualities), and are used as a device for turning proper names into common nouns.

### 6.4.8. Similes and comparisons

Comparison theories tend to view metaphor as elliptical simile. The reason for doing so is that similes simply make metaphors more explicit by signalling the need for comparison (Table 6.2, row 2), helping us with stage III of Table 6.1. And some kinds of similes are also relatively explicit about the Grounds of the metaphor (e.g. Table 6.2, row 1), helping us with stage V. The major difference between

(15)　Ginseng is a carrot.

and

(16)   Ginseng is like* a carrot.

is that (15) involves a contradiction between conventional categories and is necessarily false in the real world, whereas (16) is not anomalous, in fact borders on tautology. However, similes such as GW0266, because they do not specify Grounds, leave us with the interpretative problem of stage V in our table. So some of the inexplicitness of Interactive metaphor remains:

GW0266   I've heard that cancer is like* opening a bag of feathers in the wind.

The word *equivalent* is often used in more or less the same way as *like*, in the following structures:

T-term + copula + *the equivalent of/equivalent to* + V-term,

for example:

(17)   *The loss of advertising revenue* was the equivalent of*/equivalent to* **a near-fatal heart attack** to the newspaper.

But the word *equivalent* as a marker of metaphor can also be paired with a Topic Indicator or domain signaller (section 6.3). For example:

(18)   Metaphorical expressions are often consigned to the *lexicographical* equivalent* of **a dustbin.**

### 6.4.8.1. Similes as metaphorical frameworks

In cases where similes appear to give the Grounds, the evidence from the corpus suggests two further complications. First, these simile frameworks may be exploited for metaphoric purposes. The Grounds stated in the verb phrase are often only partial: so that the *like*-adverbial allows other Grounds to be exploited or created.

GW0005   I had seen her once before at a Royal Academy private view, *hopping* like* **a raven** in a *black feathered* hat from one gallery to another.

Especially common is the tendency to premodify the V-term to provide extra Grounds:

T125   Here the ravens *floated* below them like* *black* **scraps from a fire.**

Black scraps from a fire presumably float in much the same way as grey scraps; their blackness, irrelevant to the similarity in manner of floating, is nevertheless a further similarity with ravens.

Sometimes the simile simply provides a framework for extra metaphors:

DV165　He *chased* the <u>little boys</u> about and *made noises* like\* **a dog** tormenting **cows**. The little boys responded with *mooing* and shrieks of laughter.

The cows are Vehicles for little boys, with the Grounds supplied by "mooing" in the following sentence. I call these <u>Metaphorizing Similes</u>.

Simile structures using *as* often present an extended simile, introducing an analogy involving four noun phrases which can be paired as T-terms and V-terms respectively.

FF49　He[1] was as *fitted to survive* in <u>the modern world</u>[2] as\* **a tape worm**[1] in an **intestine**[2].

TS43　<u>her body and her dark face</u>[1] *shaken by* <u>the words</u>[2] as\* **a pipe**[1] is *shaken by* **the water that jets out of it**[2]

Syntactic parallelism underlines the metaphorical semantic parallelism, as I have indicated with superscripts, and may be accompanied by lexical repetition to mark the parallel further.

Similes may even go further and disregard any orientation towards the Verb as possible Ground:

GW0010　This morning he glowered down like\* an avenging acid drop.

The verb is anomalous: acid drops certainly cannot "glower"! We need to find further Grounds or Pseudo-grounds: the 'acidity' of his feelings.

To sum up, simile, by alerting the reader to comparisons, spreads a comparative or metaphoric influence beyond the confines of the syntactically located Verb G-terms; in extreme cases we ignore the logic of the syntax/semantics entirely, especially when forced into this disregard by semantic anomaly.

### 6.4.8.2. *Precision similes and other comparisons*

The second complication of simile as a marker is that often these stated Grounds have to be regarded as Ground Indicators, and so interpreted as superordinates, as though the Vehicle gives extra precision or specificity to the Grounds.

GW0005　But when she [his mother] returns <u>he</u> *hangs on* to her like\* **a leech** and refuses to let the other person come near.

GW0010　<u>The outer lead-covered dome</u> *is stretched* almost like\* **an umbrella** on its ribs.

The exact kinds of hanging and stretching are particularized by the V-terms, as though they are filling a lexical gap — the lack of hyponyms for these lexical verbs. We call these <u>Precision</u> similes.

*As if/though* similes also confer precision on the meanings of the preceding clause. But they often combine this function with the marking of Phenomenalistic/Subjective metaphor, at least in fictional texts.

TI142    *His head hair was sleek* as if* **fat had been rubbed in it**.
FF242    *The room was shuddering slightly*, as if* **a tunnel on the underground lay below**.

Genitive constructions and compounding are interpreted as Precision comparisons, but they are rather more contradictory than similes, for they do not seem to signal the metaphor out of existence:

FF184    My cry for help was *the cry* of* **the rat when the terrier shakes it**.
TS109    He made his **bear's*** *way* down the ladder, **paw** after **paw**.
TI138    *Their legs and arms* were **stick**-*thin*.

## 6.4.9. Foregrounding consciousness and attitude: Mental and Verbal processes

From this point in the chapter onwards we will be concentrating on Subjective metaphors. We can relate their subjectivity to the notion of deixis. Deictic terms are those like *me*, *here*, *today*, whose meaning is incomplete unless we know who is speaking, and where and when. So deixis is of three kinds: person, place and time. Anything which foregrounds difference of speaker/thinker/perceiver (personal deixis: pronouns etc.) and position (place deixis: location adverbials) and time (temporal deixis: tense, time adverbials) will make possible the recognition of different perspectives, possibly giving rise to a misfit between these perspectives which is then resolved metaphorically.

The major method for introducing the subjective element necessary for signalling these Asymmetric metaphors is to foreground the processes of thought, perception, and speech, what Halliday calls Mental and Verbal processes (section 3.1.3). The ensuing sections consider how overt representation of these processes, along with modality, become effective metaphorical markers.

### 6.4.9.1. Similes and Mental processes of perception

*seem, appear, feel like, taste like, sound like, look like*

*Seem/appear* are used to modulate statements which an individual character believes, if only for a moment, to be literally true. With them the author signals to the reader that he should have doubts about the truth of the statement.

PM25    Inside his head it seemed* that **the pebbles were shaking** because the movement of his white hand forward and back was matched by the movement of his body.

186

Formulae such as the general *seem like/as if* and the more specific *look like*, *feel like*, *taste like* and *sound like* are common in any sample of concordance data. For example, out of my random sample of 370 concordance lines for *like*, more than 12 per cent combined with perceptual verbs in this way.

GW0005   Sipping a drink through a straw may make it seem* like a treat.
TI181   She *sounded* like* **a whole party of people**.
GW0010   His mouth *tasted* like* **a vulture's crotch.**
GW0001   those parkas that *look* like* **balloons** but weigh about an ounce

### 6.4.9.2. Misperception terms

*illusion, mirage, phantom, fantasy, spectre, chimaera, imagine (-d/-ation/ -ary)*

By definition Subjective Illusion metaphors depend on misperception. A number of nouns and adjectives are available as a way of marking the possibility of illusion.

TS133   He had a moment of fantasy* when the stone seemed* as soft as a pillow.
TI113   The air round Lok echoed with the phantom* screaming.

Unless the characters themselves use the term we cannot be immediately sure that they have not succumbed to the illusion. Though in PM166, where Pincher does, the irony is that the rock is far from fixed, its existence having been conjured from memories of a decayed tooth by his obsessively prehensile imagination. (For a summary of the plot of this novel see 6.4.11.)

PM166   "Optical illusion*." For of course the rock was fixed.

### 6.4.9.3. Mental processes of cognition

We have already noted a number of uses of these verbs of cognition in conjunction with *sort/kind of* in section 6.4.7. They are strongly associated with illusion (TS30), or something similar – imaginings (TS13) or delusions (LM205) (section 4.5.4).

TS30   He thought* their faces **were monstrously deformed** until he saw they had drawn cloths over their mouths.
TS13   thinking* that the thin sound of mattins was **the slow breathing of the drugged body where it lay stretched on its back**
LM205   I sometimes think even a hummingbird **leaves her tail in the air**.

What appears to be a marking of Subjective Illusion in PM78, however, turns out to be, in the context of the novel, a marker of reality, since the rock, as we mentioned, if it is anything, is a decayed tooth.

PM78    He looked solemnly at **the line of rocks** and found himself thinking* of them as <u>teeth</u>.

Other examples suggest a thought process akin to treating an object as a metaphorical symbol:

TS156    <u>The thing [the spire]</u> I thought* of as a stone **diagram of prayer**.

### 6.4.9.4. Reporting or Verbal process verbs

By foregrounding the act of utterance through reporting clauses we draw attention to the transition from the internal mental world to the outward material world. This transition carries the potential for metaphorical speech acts, or Subjective uses of language, which the hearer/reporter may wish to distance himself from.

MD1150    One voyage . . . calls* them the wondrous "**whiskers**" inside the whale's mouth.

GW0119    when she did meet "Old **Dungheap**", as her father referred* to <u>the Lord Provost</u>

MD1317    You almost swear* that **play-wearied children lie sleeping in these solitudes**.

The difference between these Verbal process verbs and the idiomatic *so to speak/in a manner of speaking* is that the former usually specify the sayer.

### 6.4.9.5. So to speak/in a manner of speaking

*So to speak* signals Active original metaphors and Inactive metaphors equally:

GW0120    He was a skinny witty old negro. He was, so to speak*, in **the semi-finals** of <u>life</u>.

GW0022    But that's only **the tip of the iceberg** so to speak*.

The phrase is also associated with the Revitalization of inactive metaphors, making us aware of double meanings, of puns:

GW0205    We might as well enjoy it **to the hilt**, so to speak*. Get on with it. Clem did, *thrusting* himself *into* me savagely.

This last example probably is intended to revitalize the classically buried metaphor of the vagina, meaning 'sheath' in Latin. It is not simply signalling an Inactive idiomatic metaphor (*to enjoy something to the hilt*) but making us aware of the extent of Clem's penetration, or, to put it less sexistly, the speaker's enclosing of Clem.

Distinctively this phrase seems to be a favourite for marking explanatory lexical gap-filling in popular science texts:

GW0176    the energy that had, so to speak*, been **trapped** in the black hole; and those atoms, so to speak*, **cave in**

The same text also manifests a coyness about the use of metaphor, as though *so to speak* is used to mark any ordinary use of Inactive meta-phorical language which is not strictly scientifically true:

GW0176    bulky electrons that are **brought together in contact**, so to speak*; there is an electron **surface**, so to speak*, to the book and an electron **surface** to the table

Turning from metalanguage of utterance to metalanguage for the language code, *word* often occurs in the environment of metaphorical gap-fillers:

FF199    There was no bush to the outward eye, and only to dwell on **this bush** – for bush will do as well as any other word*.

DV142    Of course there was **a bit of warm pleasure** in it, and on her side **a faintly pleasurable contempt** for them both, as she said to herself, putting words* to what wouldn't really go in to them.

Incidentally, the last example exploits the LANGUAGE = CONTAINER and EMOTION = LIQUID analogies (Figure 2.1).

### 6.4.10. Orthographic devices

Both in advertising and news reports, though not in literature (Bauer 1983: 42), it is common for inverted commas to mark off V-terms, whether inactive or not:

DM32    David Pleat yesterday labelled Belgian star Nico Claesen "a misfit"*.

DT7    some Western observers suspect that many figures had been "padded"* for so long

DT4    Another young soldier had a bone broken by the "toothpaste tube"* treatment.

Inverted commas/italics are ambiguous. On the one hand the primary speaker uses them to mark off someone else's speech which she is men-tioning and embedding in her utterance, as in DM 32, with its clear reporting verb *labelled*. On the other hand they mark off a metaphor from the literal language around it (DT 7). In some cases they may be doing both (DT 4).

### ■ EXERCISE

*In a news report in the* Daily Telegraph *(DT6) we have the summary: "He expected a 'full-fledged' treaty." This is followed by a lengthier quotation:*

*"'I expect a treaty, a full-fledged treaty on medium range missiles', Mr Vorontsov said."* *Why, do you suppose, is the word* treaty *not included within the first set of inverted commas?*

We have seen that both reporting verbs of direct and indirect speech and inverted commas are associated with metaphorical marking. This evidence supports my argument that Relevance Theory's account of metaphor and irony needs expanding, to allow for another kind of metaphor, the Subjective, which shares echoic properties with certain kinds of irony (section 5.1.5). Whether quotation or metaphor or both simultaneously are being marked by inverted commas and reporting clauses, they indicate a propositional (referential) attitude of something weaker than belief or acceptance.

We saw in section 3.2.4 that Burying or hiding of metaphors can be facilitated by incorporating the metaphorical V-terms into larger units, by affixation, compounding, creating phrasal verbs, and using idioms, in other words by the use of prefabricated lexical items stretching at least beyond the single morpheme. Conversely, one of the ways of alerting the reader to these unobtrusive metaphors is to disturb the easy flow of affixed forms or fixed idiomatic phrases, by punctuation and the use of white space. Advertising copy regularly uses sentence fragments or minor sentences without a verb.

GH214   Stilton. Enjoy it all the year.* Round.

The full-stop and gap following disrupt the idiomatic phrase *all the year round*. White space may also be used to separate a suffix or divide a compound:

GH76   OUT STANDING
         *furniture*

Exclamation marks, too, seem to make the reader take a second look for a pun:

GHL16   Lose yourself – find yourself!

The juxtaposition of idioms only superficially antonymous, "lose yourself" ('become absorbed in') and "find yourself" ('discover your true identity'), works together with the exclamation mark to disturb our automatic processing. The use of exclamation marks might be associated with hyperbolic metaphors for some language users:

BOC171   "Spent the night with Q" it was true wasn't it. Besides I put in an exclamation mark to show . . . they always called it the exaggeration mark.

## 6.4.11. Modals and conditionals

Metaphor shares with the modalities of possibility and usuality the fact that neither make absolute truth claims about what they state. So modality has a widespread use in marking metaphor, often marking it out of existence. But what kinds of metaphor are modals usually associated with?

First, they are associated with gap-filling Approximative metaphors, when they modify some kinds of verbs of speaking:

DV21　They could* be said to have converged on each other, though Matty was going up and Mr Pedigree was going down.

TS212　I've still a residue of, what shall* I call it, disbelief perhaps*.

Or, simultaneously with marking gap-filling, they can hint at Illusion metaphors:

FF187　The power of gravity, dimension and space, **the movement of the earth and sun and unseen stars made** what might* be called **music and I heard it.**

At other times they simply draw attention to a metaphorical pun, i.e. a Sleeping metaphor:

GHL19　And dare* we say you will actually come back **the richer** for it. [That is, after paying for and going on a holiday on the Orient Express!]

P40　**Food for thought**, you might* say.

Other modals or conditionals put forward the unrealized possibility of an illusion.

PM179　A madman would* see the gulls as **flying lizards.**

PM108　At ten thousand feet the rock would* be **a pebble.**

LF13　He might* have been **swimming in a huge bath.**

The conditionals *could* and *would* underline that the proposition would be true or believed (or at least disbelief would be suspended) if there were some hypothetical change of circumstances, either of consciousness (PM 179), or observational perspective (PM108), or state of the world (LF13, PM103):

PM103　If* I were **that glass toy that I used to play with** I could* **float in a bottle of acid: nothing** could* **touch me then.**

To illustrate the link between Subjective and Phenomenalistic metaphor we can consider the following example where there is a protracted use of conditionals, but without any accompanying *if*-clause. We might supply *If anyone had ever been there to perceive.*

DV72–3　Yet every other sense would* have been well enough supplied with evidence. Human feet would* have felt the soft and glutinous texture, half water half mud, that would* rise swiftly to the ankles and farther, pressed out on every side with never a stone or splinter. The nose would* have taken all the evidence of vegetable and animal decay, while the mouth and skin – for in these circumstances it is as if the skin can taste – would* have tasted an air so heavy with water it would* have seemed* as if* there was doubt as to whether the whole body stood or swam or floated.

The author only has to introduce into this world a mediating perceiving consciousness, technically a *deictic centre*, for the modals/conditionals to be unnecessary and for us to have a fictional text rather than a hypothetical one. Fictional worlds are hypothetical, of course, but the pretence that they are not hypothetical is maintained, at least in traditional literature. If alternatives are mentioned, as in the following passage from *Tess of the D'Urbervilles*, when Tess and Angel Clare part after their disastrous honeymoon, one is generally marked as hypothetical:

> TD246–7 Had Tess been artful, had she wept, become frantically hysterical in that lonely lane, notwithstanding the fury of the fastidiousness of which he was possessed, he would probably not have opposed her.

However, a modernist writer like John Fowles in *The French Lieutenant's Woman* (1969) introduces two alternative endings, and we can read either as "what might have been" within the phenomenalistic world of the novel.

The transition between Subjective Illusion and Phenomenalistic metaphor is important near the beginning of *Pincher Martin*. This is the story of Christopher Hadley Martin, a Second World War naval officer, who drowns in the sea after the cruiser on which he serves is torpedoed. He drowns somewhere between pages 8 and 10 of the novel. The next 190 pages constitute Pincher's imagination of his own six days' survival, in which he kicks off his seaboots on page 10, swims to an isolated rocky island, and somehow manages to stay alive. In the last chapter, beginning on page 202, his body, with feet surprisingly still in seaboots, is picked up from the Hebridean island where it has been washed ashore.

The unwary reader feels tricked at the end of this novel on reading that the seaboots were never kicked off, and that pages 9–201 are Pincher's Subjective Illusion, with the "island" constructed out of the remembered sensations of a decaying tooth. Most British readers took this illusion to be a Phenomenalistic metaphor, i.e. true of the fictional world, so much so that, when published later in America, it had to be retitled *The Two Deaths of Christopher Martin* to give an extra clue. However, careful readers would anyway have noticed the use of modals which mark the Illusion:

> PM8 Could* he have controlled the nerves of his face, or could* a face have been fashioned to fit the attitude of his consciousness where it lay suspended between life and death, that face would* have worn a snarl. But the real jaw was contorted down and distant, the mouth was slopped full . . . There was no face but there was a snarl.

In the last sentence of this passage, and subsequently in the novel, the hypothetical nature of the snarl is immediately forgotten as it is no longer marked by modals/conditionals.

We should not, of course, confine markers to verbs since there are also modal adjectives, adverbs (and even nouns). We could position these, just as we did intensifiers and downtoners, on a scale of likelihood (Figure 6.1).

LF63    the glittering sea **rose up moved apart in planes** of blatant impossibility* . . . Piggy discounted all this learnedly as mirage* . . . at midday the illusions* merged into the sky

DV13    What had seemed impossible* and therefore unreal* was now a fact and clear to them all.

### 6.4.11.1. As it were

Lastly the phrase *as it were*. It is associated with conditionality, because it represents an abbreviated form of *as if it were*, and it is associated with the hypothetical because the *were* is subjunctive in mood. It marks both Subjective Illusion (DV110), Inactive (CEC522), and slightly more Active Transfer metaphors (DV231), though "volume" is little more than a nominal corresponding to the hackneyed *read* as in *reading a palm*.

DV110    They disappeared instantly as it were* **into thin air**.
CEC522   It's Tom Walker's own **field**, *as it were*, so to speak*.
DV231    He looked into his own palm, *pale crinkled*, **the volume**, as it were*.

## 6.5. FACTIVITY AND THE EFFECTS OF MARKERS: AN AMBIGUITY IN PROPOSITIONAL ATTITUDE

We have now completed our survey of marking devices, summarized in Table 6.4 (pp. 174–5), and it will be useful to make some general

| High | Scale of likelihood | | | Low |
|---|---|---|---|---|
| Certain | Probable | Possible | Improbable | Impossible |
| | Probably | Possibly | Improbably | Impossibly |
| Certainty | | | Improbability | Impossibility |
| Sure | Likely | | Unlikely | |
| | | Perhaps | | |
| | | Maybe | | |

*Figure 6.1* Scale of likelihood

193

comments. First, we need to say something about the last column, which has to do with factivity.

It has been traditional to distinguish three kinds of presupposition – the factive, non-factive and contrafactive. With the factive the presupposition is that the embedded proposition is true (19a), with the contrafactive that it is not-true (19b), and with the non-factive there is no presupposition about its truth one way or another (19c):

(19)   a.   It's amazing that the sailors survived ⇒ the sailors survived
      b.   If the sailors had survived ⇒ the sailors did not survive
      c.   I hope the sailors survived ⇒ the sailors may or may not have survived
      (the symbol "⇒" means 'presupposes that')

By taking the marking devices we surveyed and categorizing them as factive, non-factive or contrafactive we can decide whether they actually mark metaphor or turn metaphors into literal language. I have presented my intuitions on this in the right-hand column of Table 6.4. Contrafactives include the explicit markers, copular similes, mimetic terms, conditionals, negative modals, misperception terms (though the latter may not kill Asymmetric metaphors) and perhaps the minimizers and diminishers from among the hedges/downtoners. All marking of metaphor does something to reduce metaphoric strength and reader's work but contrafactives are the most extreme in their effects, at least reducing if not killing the metaphors, turning the utterances into literal comparisons.

By contrast, factives – most obviously the intensifiers – come closest to enhancing or energizing the metaphors. Close to factivity will be those modals which are high on the scale of probability.

Turning to the apparent non-factives, clausal and Precision similes, perceptual and cognitive process terms, medium-level modals of possibility and superordinate terms, we may wonder whether *non-factive* is actually the right word for all of them. Clausal and Precision similes, cognitive and perceptual process terms seem ambiguous between factivity and non-factivity, as I shall show.

## ■ EXERCISE

    (a)   *It seems as if the weather is improving.*
    (b)   *For a long time the earth seemed to be spherical.*

*What do you think the speaker believes about the statements "the weather is improving" and "the earth is spherical"?*

It is very difficult to locate *appear/seem, sound/look like*, or indeed *like* occurring separately, in one definite area on the scale of factivity. One presuppositional meaning can be paraphrased 'according to the (perceptual) evidence available it is probable that', which would locate these markers on the boundary between the factive and non-factive, or even on both sides of the boundary as in (20):

(20)   like the unflagging Calvinist he is

A second presuppositional meaning could be paraphrased 'people (have) mistakenly believe(d) that', which would make the markers contrafactive.

> NSJL25   The feedback loops linking life with its environment are so numerous that, at first, it seemed* that there was little hope of quantifying them or understanding them. But we can make an abstraction of the essence of it.

We can systematically link this ambiguity of our Non-factives to the notion of Subjective metaphor and deictics of time, person and place. With these Non-factives it is crucial, first, to distinguish to whom it seems or appears that such is the state of affairs and, second, to indicate the time at which it so appeared, which is why past tense often resolves the ambiguity towards a contrafactive presupposition. *It seems to me* thus becomes almost factive, whereas *it appeared to our ancestors* is more likely contrafactive. In Subjective Illusion metaphor we are invited to reject the thoughts of the character as a true description, and to interpret them metaphorically by seeing what qualities or aspects of the real state of affairs led to the illusion that is the thought of the character. Perhaps we could take these ambiguities in metaphorical markers as some kind of evidence of a blurring of the distinction between fact and fiction, a recognition of the mediation and distortion of language categories and the way they impose themselves on our thinking. At least we can count this as further evidence that Sperber and Wilson's theory on metaphor (Figure 5.1) should be developed to include a further category of metaphor, the Subjective, which is akin to echoic irony (section 5.1.5).

Superordinate terms are also ambiguous in several ways as we discovered in section 1.4. They are not always contrafactive for they are used to mark literal superordinate-hyponymy relations. This ambiguity means that they, like the other "non-factives", have little weakening effect on metaphors.

The remaining marking devices seem to achieve other effects besides weakening or energizing. Symbolism markers both mark and in a sense create the metaphor by doing so, alerting us to the abstract or thematic overtones of the text or the action. While semantic metalanguage is commonly used for drawing our attention to Inactive metaphors.

## 6.6. SUBJECTIVE METAPHORS AND FANTASTIC LITERATURE

We have seen in this chapter that foregrounding perceptual, cognitive and Verbal processes and introducing non-factivity by modals and conditionals are major devices for marking Subjective metaphors.

> TS38   Say* if you like that the building floats. It is a manner of speaking*. It may* be so.

It is common to discuss such devices in narrative theory. Recently Simpson has developed a theory of narrative point of view in which one dimension is labelled negative, and which is identified precisely by the kinds of marking modal devices we have discussed (Simpson 1994: 58–60). And Labov (1972), under the heading of comparators, one of the evaluative resources which interrupt narrative clauses, includes negatives, modals, quasi-modals, and comparatives. These devices also overlap with *words of estrangement:*

> Expressions of this type occur in the text when the narrator takes an external point of view in describing some internal state that he cannot be sure about.
>
> (Uspensky, quoted in Fowler 1977: 92)

However, in the corpus I have analysed, especially Golding's texts, we can put more emphasis on the *internal* point of view and make useful reference to Todorov's work on *fantastic literature* (1970: ch. 2). This is literature in which the reader, who identifies himself with a character and his fictional point of view, nevertheless hesitates in his attitude to the nature of the event. The question the reader asks, and cannot quite resolve, is whether the events perceived by the character are real or the fruit of imagination or illusion. Todorov points out various properties of the fantastic text: figurative language is often taken for literal; the text cannot be reread; there is frequent use of modalization, and of imperfect (past) tense. We have already mentioned the contribution of tense to increasing the degree of non-factivity of Subjective metaphors (*seem, appear*); we have devoted various sections to modal verbs; but we should note that Todorov includes under the heading of modalization the projecting clauses involving Mental processes of perception and cognition: *it seemed, I had the idea that, I had the feeling, I believed myself* (*ibid.*: 42) – we covered these in sections 6.4.9.1 and 6.4.9.3.

## 6.7. PROMISCUITY OF THE MARKERS

One criticism I have had of my approach to metaphor is that I have defined it too broadly, especially when straying into areas of non-central varieties like the Mimetic and Subjective. My decision to do so arises from experience of textual analysis, where I think the broader conception becomes inevitable. But a close look at the distribution of markers across metaphoric categories in Table 6.4 validates my judgement. With the exception of symbolism terms, perceptual process terms and misperception terms, all the other categories are quite unashamedly promiscuous with the variety of metaphors they mark. Particularly telling is the use of Mimetic terms to signal ordinary Active Transfer metaphors, and the reverse, of explicit markers like *metaphorical* itself to apply to Subjective and Phenomenalistic varieties.

## ■ EXERCISE

*As a way of considering together various of the markers, you might like to discuss the following passage from D.H. Lawrence's 'St Mawr' (p. 5). What are the markers used, and what kinds of metaphors do they apply to?*

> *She with her odd little museau, not exactly pretty, but very attractive; and her quaint air of playing at being well-bred, in a sort of charade game; and her queer familiarity with foreign cities and foreign languages; and the lurking sense of being an outsider everywhere, like a sort of gypsy, who is at home anywhere and nowhere: all this made up her charm and her failure.*

# 7

# THE SPECIFICATION OF TOPICS

## 7.1. INTRODUCTION

At the end of Chapter 1 we introduced the two clines of Marking and Explicitness. Taken jointly these two clines stretch from explicit literal comparison to inexplicit metaphor. Chapter 6 discussed how metaphors can be marked by simile and other markers of comparison (Table 6.1, stage III). This chapter deals with one aspect of explicitness – how the indeterminacy or open-endedness of metaphorical meaning can be diminished by explicitly specifying the Topic (Table 6.1, stage IV (p. 168)). It attempts two main things: first, to give an overview of the syntactic resources available; and second, to demonstrate how the syntactic choices made, with their options for ordering and clausal ranking of V-term and T-term, and so on, will affect the interpretations of metaphors; specifically, how lexical metaphor will impinge on grammar by introducing or enhancing ambiguities in the meanings of syntax.

There is certainly a need for an in-depth investigation of the syntax of metaphor though Brooke-Rose (1958) and Genette (1970) were pioneers in the field and some useful recent work has been done by Stockwell (1992a). Much of the psychological research on metaphor ignores syntax at its peril, but the neglect spoils some of the insights of linguists too. For instance, Lakoff and Johnson (1980) fail to take it into account when discussing metaphorical mixing. They claim that what makes the following examples of mixing permissible and impermissible respectively is that the two metaphorical schemata involved do or do not share entailments.

(1) **At this point** our argument doesn't have much **content**. (Lakoff and Johnson 1980: 92)
(2) **The content** of the argument **proceeds** as follows. (*ibid.*: 95)

It seems equally likely that it is the intimacy of the syntactic bond between subject and verb in (2) which makes for a sense of mixing, whereas (1) only has a distant bond between prepositional complement and object of the same clause (see also Low 1988: 132). We may not accept the exaggerated emphasis put upon syntax by Lecercle:

> The core of metaphor is indeed syntax, and the role of semantics is only negative – we temporarily forget that there might be semantic constraints and let syntax speak.
>
> (Lecercle 1990: 153)

But at least we can settle for the more measured claims of MacCormac that the creation of metaphor, though cognitive, is accomplished by means of a linguistic procedure, and that the syntactic realization will affect the semantics (MacCormac 1990: 116–17).

### 7.1.1. Ferris' Meaning of Syntax

In order to hold any useful discussion on the syntax of metaphor we need a general theory of the meaning of syntax, and, when discussing Vehicle, Topic and G-terms which are nouns and adjectives, I shall use the rather elegant theory developed recently by Ferris (1993).

Ferris makes a primary distinction between equation and qualification. Equation occurs when the referent of one noun phrase is the equivalent of the referent of another, and will allow reversal:

(3a)   the prime minister, John Major
(3b)   John Major, the prime minister

or

(4a)   John Major is the prime minister.
(4b)   The prime minister is John Major.

Qualification is the introduction of an element that the speaker believes to be relevant to the identification of an entity, but without the equivalence associated with Equation:

(5)   the green bottles
(6)   The bottles are green.

Qualification is of two kinds, Ascription and Association. The distinction is clear in Ferris' examples:

(7a)   a meteorological expert
(8a)   romantic novelists
(9a)   French wine
(10a)   a reliable student

Examples (7a) and (8a) are associative qualifications, and (9a) and (10a) are ascriptive qualifications. The test for Ascription is whether these phrases can be reformulated in clauses with the Copula *to be*, i.e. predicatively, with the same meaning as the original phrase:

199

(7b)    The expert is meteorological.
(8b)    The novelists are romantic.
(9b)    The wine is French.
(10b)   The student is reliable.

Examples (9a) and (10a) pass this test and are ascriptive, but (7a) and (8a) are associative because they fail it.

So we have the primary Equation and Qualification distinction, and the subcategorization of Qualification into Association and Ascription. There are two kinds of Ascription, adjectival and <u>Class-inclusion</u>. Examples (5) and (6) are adjectival, but (11) and (12) are Class-inclusion Ascriptions:

(11)    the politician John
(12)    John is a politician.

But a further concept is crucial in teasing out the meaning of syntax and this is the notion of assignment. The absence and presence of assignment is what distinguishes (3a) from (4a), (5) from (6), (9a) from (9b), (10a) from (10b) and (11) from (12). <u>Assignment</u>, then, is the making explicit, through predication, of a relation between an entity and another entity, or an entity and a property. We have already noted that Assignment is impossible with Associative Qualifications, as in (7b) and (8b); Associative Qualifications can only be used attributively as part of the noun phrase, (7a) and (8a). Figure 7.1 sums up Ferris' scheme.

### 7.1.2. Equation, Ascription, Interaction and Substitution

The distinction between Equation and Ascription corresponds in part to the Interaction and Substitution theories of metaphorical interpretation. Take the case of a metaphor interpreted according to Substitution.

(13)    Thomas is a monkey.

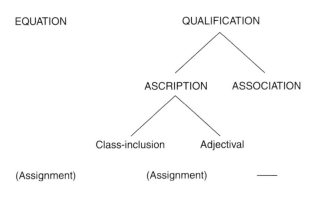

*Figure 7.1* Semantic relations within syntax

200

Here all that is happening is that the V-term is substituting for the meaning 'mischievous'. So we have a simple case of Ascription, in which the property 'mischievous' is assigned to the entity referred to by "Thomas". On the other hand, with a metaphor like:

PQ199   A committee is **an animal with four back legs**. (Le Carré)

we are forced to consider the Vehicle before going on to decide exactly which properties of this curious creature (if any) are actually being ascribed to committees. In this a sense of Class-inclusion, if not Equation, seems essential to the interaction, though by stage V of Table 6.1 we will still end up ascribing Grounds to the committee. We shall see that metaphor deliberately introduces a tug-of-war between the possible semantic meanings of syntax, and the first case is the tension between Ascription and Class-inclusion and Equation.

### 7.1.3. The applicability of the term *Topic*: specification and Indication

We have already seen that the application of the label *Topic-term* is not entirely unproblematic. Whenever the purpose of a metaphor is the filling of lexical gaps, we are unlikely to have a Topic-specifying term at all; the absence of such a term is the reason for the use of metaphor in the first place. The concrete metaphorical lexis for abstracts (Chapter 2 *passim*) often gives us the impression that metaphors are not so much labelling a pre-existing unnamed concept, but rather constituting a new concept; it is difficult to find a literal paraphrase which would do for the Topic, let alone a single literal lexical item.

With these Gap-filling metaphors the most we can expect in the way of interpretative guidance will be Topic Indication (already discussed in section 6.3.4). In Topic Indication, e.g. verbal **diarrhoea**, the T-term does not refer precisely to what is referred to unconventionally by the V-term, but indicates the general area, the conceptual–semantic field in which the Topic is located.

A further problem arises if we admit that many metaphors result in Assigned Ascriptions. Inactive metaphors, which are paradigm cases of Ascription (13), were discovered not to have independently variable Topic and Ground (section 4.3.4). If we want to be absolutely precise we should go further and admit that in cases involving Class-inclusion, too (e.g. PQ199), the subject of the clause does not strictly refer to the same entity as the complement. Topic Indication can perhaps be widened in its meaning to cover such cases.

This chapter will basically be a survey of the most common syntactic structures used for guiding the reader to the identification of the Topic. Table 7.1 gives an overview and the reader may like to use the following

*Table 7.1* Types of syntactic Topic specification

| Syntactic construction | Example |
| --- | --- |
| Copula (7.2) | The eye was **a raindrop** |
| Apposition (7.3) | The eye, **a raindrop** |
| Genitive (7.4) | **The raindrop** of an eye |
| Noun premodifier (7.5) | The **raindrop** eye |
| Compounds (7.6) | The eye-**raindrop** |
| Blends (7.7) | The re**ye**ndrop |

*Note*: The relevant sections of this chapter are given in parentheses.

sections as a reference manual (the relevant sections are given in paren-thesis). Tables 7.2, 7.3 and 7.4 supply more detailed summaries.

## 7.2. COPULA CONSTRUCTIONS

We have already mentioned the elementary distinction between Equative and Ascriptive uses of the Copula. Put simply Equatives identify or state the equivalence of the referent of one expression with the referent of the other, whereas Ascriptive uses qualify the referent of the first phrase with some property or properties in the second. Equative structures answer questions like *Who is John?* whereas Ascriptives answer questions such as *What is John (like)?* or demands of the sort *Tell me something about John.* Adjectives are the most prototypical Ascriptive complements.

| (14) | John is fat. | Ascriptive (Adjectival) |
| | John is a manager. | Ascriptive (Class-inclusion) |
| | John is Mary's husband. | Equation |

Class-inclusion statements, with noun phrases as the complement, while still Ascriptions, are closer to Equation, because, instead of ascribing a single property they, as it were, ascribe a bundle of properties. Most copular metaphors, but by no means all, are Class-inclusion Ascriptives.

The traditional test of equativeness is reversibility, providing the intona-tion pattern is preserved (Lyons 1977: 472–3). MD1099 is equative by that criterion:

MD 1099    **that gold watch** he sought was the innermost life of the fish →
the innermost life of the fish was **that gold watch** he sought

But when metaphor is involved, distinguishing Ascriptives and Equatives is not always certain. On the one hand equation between two unique referents is difficult to maintain, since the V-term has to evoke the concept or image of its conventional referent, and this will be different from the referent of the T-term. Since there is no unconventionality about the reference of this

202

T-term, and it precedes the V-term, it is much better for identifying the actual referent than the V-term is. On the other hand it is only if the two incompatible referents are felt to be equated that the metaphor can achieve the contradiction necessary for strong metaphorical force. LF165 provides a good example of this tension:

LF165   the log . . . was **his throne**

It is quite easy to take an Ascriptive Class-inclusion interpretation and select the functional component of the meaning of throne [for a ruler to sit on]. However, the example is permutable to ***his throne*** *was the log*. And Equation would underline the ironic distance between two images: a log, bare and rough; and a throne, precious and perhaps jewel-encrusted.

A further important distinction relevant to the Copula constructions is that between analytic and synthetic statements. What an analytic statement does is give information about the meaning of the first noun phrase.

(15)   A car is a vehicle.

Whereas a synthetic statement gives information about a state of affairs in the world:

(16)   The car is a 1965 Ford Consul.

It would seem that use of the present simple tense is a necessary condition for making an analytic statement, though not a sufficient one as (16) demonstrates. Where metaphor is concerned, some Copula metaphors have a particularly strong metaphorical force because, at the initial stage of processing, they seem to be making analytic generalizations which are true for all time and all places.

PQ86   Sex is only **the liquid centre of the great Newberry Fruit** of friendship. (Jilly Cooper)

PQ91   An autobiography is **an obituary in serial form with the last instalment missing**. (Quentin Crisp)

### 7.2.1. Equatives

A number of interesting tendencies emerge from the relatively few structures equatively specifying the T-term. First, Equatives are common when the detailed correspondences in an extended metaphor or allegory are being identified.

TS8   The model was like a man lying on his back. The nave was **his legs placed together**, the transepts on either side were **his arms** outspread. The choir was **his body**; and the Lady Chapel where now the services would be held, was **his head**.

Equations are possible because, once the metaphor has been set up, as it is in the initial clause, the typical (other) parts of the Topic and Vehicle entities become given information and therefore are referred to by definite noun phrases. That is to say, "A man" evokes the schema for a man's body with its "legs", "arms", "body" and "head".

Second, Equative uses are often associated with Subjective metaphors. This could be at the point where a Subjective Illusion is being dispelled:

LF20    **The bat** was <u>the child's shadow</u>.

TI139    **It [the white bone mask]** was <u>skin</u>.

Previously Ralph had mistaken the shadow for a bat, and Lok the skin of the face for a bone mask. And the reader, seeing the world from their fictional point of view (Leech and Short 1983: 174–5), shared the illusion. This means that previous occurrences of "the bat" and "the white bone" had been taken as literal. Their givenness accounts for their thematic position, first in the clause, and also demonstrates their reversibility,

In other examples the Subjective nature of the metaphor, the individual and idiosyncratic world-view, is explicitly pointed out by the "our" and "in her mind":

FF229    <u>Mr Carew and Miss Manning</u> were our **Adam and Eve**.

TS137    <u>I</u> was **the church** in her mind.

Moreover, subjectivity is evident in those startlingly original and self-conscious metaphors in dictionaries of quotations (PQ86, PQ91 above) or in advertising copy.

GH200    <u>Style</u>. <u>It</u>'s **your sixth sense**.

It goes without saying that Assignment is vital for making these personal and original *bons mots*; such quasi-analytical statements need the explicitness and certainty of predication to be noticed as the outrageous semantic mistakes or Impositives they are. One could contrast this with the surreptitiousness of a non-assigned equivalent:

(17)    Style, your sixth sense, is something you need when choosing to shop at Ikea.

It's easy to overestimate the number of Equative Copula metaphors because superficial examples often turn out to be as much metonymic as metaphorical.

FF116    You are my sanity, Beatrice.

PM115    Speech is identity.

These probably depend upon cause-and-effect metonymy: you are the cause of my sanity, speech causes me to have identity.

## 7.2.2. Ascriptives

## ■ EXERCISE

*What meanings could you give to the following utterances (a) and (b)? Do they have different interpretations? If so, why?*

(a)  *Encyclopaedias are stone quarries.*
(b)  *Stone quarries are encyclopaedias.*

By far the highest proportion of Copula metaphors are non-equational by the criterion of reversibility, four-fifths in the corpus I examined, and are Class-inclusion statements[1]. Their V-term occurs as complement; the identification through reference will already have been achieved by the T-term subject; and the V-term will be referring to an image or concept or class rather than to an actual literal thing in the context. The V-term will be conveying new information, or at least reminding us of associations of the Topic which are less than obvious, and the ultimate stage of interpretation will involve ascribing it to the entity referred to by the T-term.

As new or refurbished information is being ascribed to the Topic in most cases, it is hardly surprising that reversals of similes and metaphors give different meanings (Ortony 1979a: 190). In (a) an interpretation might be that encyclopaedias contain solid facts, like rock, that can be constructed into arguments (buildings), but that the extraction of these facts is a laborious process. While (b) might suggest that geological and palaeontological facts are stored in the rocks of a quarry just as facts in general are stored in an encyclopaedia. As we shall see in Chapter 8, normally the Grounds of the metaphor are more closely associated with the Vehicle than with the Topic (section 8.6; see also Verbrugge and McCarrell 1977).

Though this Ascription of properties, or Grounds, pushes the metaphor in the direction of Substitution, it is still the case, with Active metaphors, that these properties will be selected on the basis of an interaction between Topic and Vehicle. For instance, taking an earlier example, if we substitute *his mind* as the T-term in:

LF10   The beach was a thin **bowstave**.

the interpretation will be quite different: maybe the Grounds would be that he easily becomes "tense" and is in danger of "cracking up", so the word *thin* is then interpreted as mental fragility.

As it stands, the example gives plenty of evidence of the Ascriptive or descriptive effect of these kinds of Copula metaphors; it is only the extra new information provided by the V-term that prompts us to form an image of a particular beach: a thin strip of sand which curves out to headlands at each end (see my interpretation in section 4.4.2).

## ■ EXERCISE

*Look at lines 2–5 of the following poem. What reasons can you give for treating the copulas specifying the Topic as Equative or Ascriptive?*

> When I was a child I thought
> The new moon was a cradle
> The full moon was granny's round face
>
> The new moon was a banana
> The full moon was a big cake.
>
> When I was a child
> I never saw the moon
> I only saw what I wanted to see.
>
> And now I see the moon
> It's the moon
> Only the moon and nothing but the moon
>
> May Wong

### 7.2.3. Abstractness of Topic and Vehicle and Ascription/Equation

The semantics of Ascriptive metaphorical Copula constructions will be affected by the degree of abstractness of the Topic and Vehicle. Quite common are copulas in which the T-term is more abstract, a higher order of entity, and the V-term is a thing, first-order entity. The interplay between higher-order Topics and first-order Vehicles actually exaggerates the general tension we have noted between Equation and Ascription. This is especially the case when the Topic is a non-specific abstract entity, like 'life' or 'being good'.

> TS58    The renewing life of the world was **a filthy thing, a rising tide of muck** so that he gasped for air.
>
> TS190   Life itself is **a rickety building**.
>
> DV167   Being good is just **another tangle**.

In one respect these are Ascriptive because the Vehicles supply specificity, reify and crystallize vague notions into hard and definite objects, and in the process they will be ascribing or attributing properties. Yet in another respect the very fact that the entities are of different orders of abstraction means that there can be no real similarity between Topic and Vehicle, and any Grounds are likely to depend upon Analogy. So the Copula metaphor becomes a means of equating two of the terms in a four-term analogy. A discussion of TS58 will make this Equative tendency clear.

In William Golding's *The Spire*, Jocelin implements his vision of replacing the tower on the (Salisbury) cathedral with a spire. The builders have to excavate the foundations to ascertain the feasibility of the project and they dig a pit which, in the long rains of chapter 3, begins to fill up with foul, muddy, slimy water. Jocelin's suppressed sexuality becomes apparent in the process of digging and building, what is, after all, a phallic symbol. In this context, what is happening in example TS58, besides Ascription, is that a symbol is being identified and labelled, equatively. To paraphrase:

(18)   The literal rising tide of muck which has been described as filling the pit and making the earth creep is to be interpreted as a symbol of the renewing life of the world, the sexual drive.

What we have, then, is the identification of the corresponding points on the allegorical (symbolic) and literal planes.

(19)   pit : rising tide of muck : : sexual drive : renewing life of the world

I conclude that Ascription and Equation are both important to these Copula metaphors, in which the Vehicle, as part of a mini-allegory, represents a concrete symbol of a relatively abstract Topic.

When we shift to cases where neither Topic nor Vehicle are first-order entities or things, rather than exaggerating the tension between Ascription and Equation, the distinction disappears. Whereas first-order entities/concepts are bundles of several properties/features, nominalized verbs and adjectives are more austere in their semantic representation, and often reduce to one (or two) feature(s).

PQ141   Insanity is a kind of* **innocence**. (Graham Greene)
PQ300   Small is beautiful. (F.E. Schumacher)
HZ10   But a scandal was, after all, a sort of* **service to the community**.

We should also glance briefly at the cases where Vehicles are a higher order of entity than the Topics.

FF89   Was I an **expiation**, not of the one blow, but of numberless . . . uneases and inadequacies . . .?
TS120   The building was **a diagram of prayer**.

In FF89 and TS120 the Vehicles are interpretable as events or processes: either because they are nominalizations (expiate → expiation) or because their semantics involves something like a verb, what has been called a *down-graded predication* (Leech 1974: 149–54), e.g. diagram = a figure which illustrates an action, process or object; prayer = act of praying. What is interesting here is that changing the nouns back into a more congruent verbal form actually destroys the metaphors:

(20)   Did I expiate numberless inadequacies?
(21)   The building diagrammed praying.

The sense of possible equivalence is lost at the same time as the reification.

207

## 7.2.4. Other statives/Relational processes

Besides the use of the Copula *to be* there are a number of other Relational process verbs to do with states or changes of state which can be employed for guiding the reader to the Topic. Like the Copula most of these have the T-term as subject and the V-term as complement.

PQ218    The car has become **the carapace, the protective and aggressive shell** of urban man. (Marshall McLuhan)

TS62    Yet the purity of the light . . . seemed **a tiny door** at an infinite distance.

PM109    Then the rock will become **a hot-cross bun**.

LF210    The stick in his hand became **a crutch** on which he reeled.

LF168    The circle became **a horseshoe**.

Very often *seem* and *become* assign Subjective metaphors, dependent on the perception of the character whose fictional point of view we are adopting, as in TS62, and PM109 where Pincher is imagining how his rock striped with a cross of seaweed would look to a pilot from above. Other uses of *become* can be called transformational or non-transformational, according to whether the Topic maintains its entityhood (PQ218, LF210), or ceases to exist (LF168). The circle ceases to be a circle when it becomes a horseshoe so the Topic is Indicated not specified.

*Make*, componentially [cause [become]], tends to be used non-transformationally, in T-term subject, V-term object/complement constructions (LF12). More often, however, with *make* and *turn* a prepositional phrase is used and a prepositional complement provides the V-term slot, as in PM134, MD1234, or the T-term slot as in TS16.

LF12    The palms that still stood made **a green roof**.
PM134    He made the lobster into **a hand** again.
MD1234    He had turned the horizon into **one star-belled tambourine**.
TS16    They've made **a game** of my whole life.

Prepositions can (Ferris 1993: 148) in fact, act as a shorthand for the Copula (MD 1297, FF151) or the verb *to become* (FF214).

MD1297    He has a stick of a whale-bone's jaw for **a wife**.
FF151    I could see this war as **the ghastly and ferocious play of children**.
FF214    a black gown gnawed into **a net** by acid

Ditransitive verbs, too, may be employed for T-specification with the object as T-term and the object complement as V-term.

PQ159    I find Cambridge **an asylum** in every sense of the word. (Housman)

Having discussed the Copula, we now turn to the second major syntactic resource for specifying Topics, Apposition.

## 7.3. APPOSITION AND OTHER PARALLELISM

To understand the nature of Apposition we have to extend Ferris' binary division between Assignment and non-Assignment into a ternary one. We can then account for the differing degrees/kinds of syntactic bond in:

(22)   a.      Incest is a game the whole family can play.
       b.      The incest game the whole family can play.
       PQ136   Incest, the game the whole family can play. (Graffiti)

PQ136, a case of Apposition, displays a minimum bonding between the two noun phrases, and the Copula, involving assignment, the maximum.

### ■ EXERCISE

*Which of the noun phrases in this poem by Ezra Pound, including the title, are actually in Apposition to each other, i.e. are referring to the same thing?*

*In a station of the Metro*

> *The apparition of these faces in the crowd;*
> *Petals on a wet, black bough.*

Apposition punctuated with commas, because of its minimal syntactic bonding, demands more work from the reader than the other means of Topic specification, and can give equal prominence to T-term and V-term. Since metaphorical coreference often has to be inferred – noun phrases separated by commas could be part of a list, and which phrases are coreferring is not always certain as in the Pound poem – the conventional referent of the V-term is likely to be strongly evoked.[2] The two apposed structures will be syntactically equivalent, and one can be omitted without damage to the larger syntactic structure. However, when apposed phrases are punctuated with dashes or parentheses, rather than commas, the bracketed noun phrase is less important.

(23)   So pop down to your nearest Mitsubishi **boutique** (sorry showroom).
       (*Wheels* April 1994: 22)

Quirk *et al.* (1985: 1308–16) distinguish seven types of non-restrictive appositive relation: Appellation, Designation, Identification, Reformulation, Attribution and Inclusion, and Table 7.2 summarizes their survey. We will look at these in turn. The first four of these are labelled equivalent, or equative in my terms, Attribution is Ascriptive, and Exemplification and Particularization are inclusive relations, reversing the order of class-inclusion statements that are so common with the copula.

Given the tension between Equation and Ascription which complement V-terms create, we might wonder whether Quirk's taxonomy for literal

*Table 7.2* The semantics of literal and metaphorical Apposition

| Type of Apposition | Noun Phrase₁ | Noun Phrase₂ | Cue | Examples literal and metaphorical |
|---|---|---|---|---|
| Appellation (equative) 'naming' one-to-one correspondence (3.1) | Definite Less specific | Definite More specific | optional: *that is* | *the company commander, that is Captain Madison* when he thought of **his tool**, <u>Roger Mason</u> |
| Identification (equative) no one-to-one correspondence (3.1) | Indefinite Less specific | More definite and specific | optional: *namely* | *a company commander, namely, Captain Madison* **a rug of the softest Turkey,** <u>the tongue</u> |
| Designation (equative) reverse of appellation and identification (3.2) | Definite More specific | Definite Less specific | optional: *that is to say* | *Captain Madison, that is to say the company commander* <u>Director Matt Busby,</u> **the Godfather of the club** |
| Reformulation (equative meanings) rewording of lexical content (3.3) | Synonym, equivalent or related meaning | Synonym, equivalent or related meaning | optional: *in other words* | *an ophthalmologist, in other words an eye doctor* the using of people, the well-deep wish, **the piercingness**, – the what? |
| Attribution (ascriptive) equal to non-restrictive relative clause (3.4) | | Indefinite | optional: no article | *Robinson, leader of the democratic group* <u>The conch</u> was silent, **a** *gleaming* **tusk**. |
| Exemplification (inclusive) (3.5) | More general | More specific | optional: *e.g., for instance* | *They visited several cities, for example, Athens and Rome* <u>a kind of absorbing</u>, **a kind of drinking** |
| Particularization (inclusive) (3.5) | More general | More specific | essential: *especially, particularly* | *the children loved the animals, especially the monkeys* |

*Notes*: The subsection of Chapter 7 in which the type of Apposition is discussed is given in parentheses in column 1. The italicized examples in column 5 are literal; those in roman type are metaphorical.

Apposition can apply to metaphors. Provided we follow the rules for definiteness (column 2), and modify the specificity criterion to include the criterion of successfulness of reference (column 3), the taxonomy will be useful, if sometimes difficult to apply.

### 7.3.1. Appellation/Identification

At first glance one doubts whether with two definite apposed noun phrases, the first the T-term and the second the V-term, it would ever be the case that the second would refer more specifically or successfully than the second. But in fact it is quite possible, theoretically.

(24)   the man with 50,000 hairs on his head, the semi-coot

Unless we happen to know that the normal head of hair has, let's say, around 100,000 individual hairs, so that having 50,000 makes you half bald, the first phrase will be less helpful in picking out the referent in a room full of people, than the second; a good example of relevance not truth being the yardstick for communication.

In practice T-term ^ V-term Appellation/Identification certainly applies in cases where the T-term is a pronoun:

TS89    Let <u>him</u> settle it, **my slave** for the work.
TS208   "Fall when <u>you</u> like, **me old cock!**"
        [referring, among other things, to the spire as phallic symbol]

Or where the V-term identifies a subset of the class referred to by the T-term, but without being Exemplification:

DV47    sink down through <u>all noises and all words</u>, down through <u>the words,</u>
        **the knives and swords**

Here it is not words in general, but those which are hurtful, scandalous or malicious that are identified by "knives and swords". In this case, strictly speaking, the T-term will be an Indicator rather than a specifier.

More obviously Appellation/Identification applies when the first of the noun phrases is the V-term:

TS68    when he thought of **his tool**, <u>Roger Mason</u>
MD1111  **my private table** here, <u>the capstan</u>
MD1151  For carpet to the organ we have **a rug of the softest Turkey**,
        <u>the tongue</u>, which is glued, as it were*, to the floor of the mouth.


### 7.3.2. Designation

I have shown that it is possible for the V-term to be more specific and refer more successfully than the T-term, thereby giving us Appellation or Identification Appositions. But it is more normal for the Topic-specifying term to refer exactly and successfully, leaving the second noun phrase, the less specific V-term, to designate (or ascribe).

DM1     <u>Employment Secretary Lord Young</u>, **the spearhead of the Tories'**
        **General Election campaign**
DM31    <u>Director Matt Busby</u>, **the Godfather of the club**

FF123   How did <u>that good girl</u>, **that uninscribed tablet** receive these violations?

### 7.3.3. Reformulation

The most obvious cases of Reformulation are those in which a number of V-terms are used to approximately fill a lexical gap, though none being, as it were, exactly the right shape to do so. In this case the absence of the T-term is what makes the speaker flounder around for words. In a famous passage from *The Four Quartets*, T.S. Eliot reflexively illustrates the very phenomenon he describes with a string of apposed verbs:

FQ19                                   Words strain,
            Crack, and sometimes break, under the burden,
            Under the tension, **slip, slide, perish,**
            **Decay with imprecision, will not stay in place.**
            **Will not stay still.**

As Widdowson points out:

What these verb phrases represent is a number of features of some non-existent verb, aspects of a concept for which the code provides no lexical item.

(Widdowson 1975: 42)

The desperate obsessive search for the right expression, metaphorical or otherwise, sometimes results in extremes of what has been called *over-wording* or *overlexicalization* (Fowler 1991: 85, 103, 109, 144; Fairclough 1989: 115, 119):

DV187   And she saw that what they missed out of their experiments in magic which gave them little or no result, was just **the stinky-poo** bit, the breaking of rules, the using of people, the well-deep wish, **the piercingness**, the – what?

The marking of Reformulations may not always be quite as desperate as this final anguished *what?* Compare the *or rather* and *I mean* in MD1161 and CEC 528.

CEC528   You might actually get **three duds**, I mean, <u>three people whom you didn't want</u>.
MD1161   <u>the deliverance</u>, or rather **delivery** of Tashtego
            [Tashtego has just been rescued after falling into the belly of the whale, so that *delivery* is a rather apt gynaecological metaphor.]

One point about Quirk *et al.*'s category of Reformulation is its concern with semantics as much as with text-external reference. That is to say the second term and its meaning refers back to the first term and its meaning. It may be that there is an element of Reformulation about many metaphors, especially analytical Copula metaphors with a Subjective, Impositive function, such as *Property is theft* where we are being asked to modify our semantic concept of property.

### 7.3.4. Attribution

With Attributive (Ascriptive) appositives the second noun phrase will be indefinite or at least less specific than the first.

LF18    <u>The conch</u> was silent, **a** *gleaming* **tusk**.
TS104    And <u>the young man</u> laughed back, **a** *good* **dog**.

Sometimes the article in the second phrase will be omitted entirely:

PQ142    Had a look at <u>the alligators</u>. Just *floating* **handbags** really. (Trevor Griffiths)
TI22    **the bones of the land** showed, <u>lumps of</u> *smooth grey* <u>rock</u>
PM18    <u>Her periscope</u> . . . , **eye of a land creature** that has defeated the rhythm and necessity of the sea.

In cases of Attributive Apposition Grounds will often be specified in the second noun phrase, as in all but the last example. This facilitates the Ascriptive tendency, by-passing full interaction and taking us quickly to stage V of Table 6.1.

### 7.3.5. Inclusion

There are a number of metaphorical appositions which seem examples of Inclusion, but which do not fit neatly into Exemplification or Particularization.

DV108    It was a kind of* <u>absorbing</u>, a kind of* **drinking**, a kind of*.
DV9    It was <u>a glare</u>, **a burning bush**, through or beyond which the beams were sketched more faintly.
FF202    **a journey on the wrong track**, <u>a huge misunderstanding</u>

The Vehicles here are all more particular examples of the abstract Topics, which they symbolize. The T-terms, in fact Topic Indicators, will therefore be G-terms too.

### 7.3.6. Other appositions

Given that noun V-terms have more metaphoric force than other parts of speech, I've so far concentrated discussion on noun phrases. However, T-specifying Apposition is not confined to them.

### 7.3.6.1. Verb Apposition

The Apposition may involve simply the head of the verb phrase, the lexical verb:

TS131    The whole tower was **talking**, **groaning**, <u>creaking</u>, **protesting**.

or the whole verb phrase (in Chomskyan terms), the predicate:

FF133    I <u>am wise in some ways</u>, **can see unusually far through a brick wall**.

### 7.3.6.2. Adjectival Apposition

Adjectives can be apposed:

DT6    Their rounds have been **open-ended**, <u>without a final date</u>.
LF149    **wedded to her in lust**, <u>excited</u> by the long chase
FF231    **a dirtier**, <u>wickeder</u> more shameful trick

### 7.3.6.3. Clauses and sentences

And even whole sentences are apposed for comparison if not for metaphor.

FF116    **I'm on rails.** <u>I have to.</u>
FF10    **I tick.** <u>I exist.</u>
FF113    <u>She baffles me still</u>, **she is opaque.**
GH235    <u>**You don't use Wedgwood because you are short of mugs. You don't buy AEG just to do the washing up.**</u>
MD1102    <u>**Out of the trunk the branches grow; out of them twigs. So, in productive subjects, grow the chapters.**</u>

[Double marking by underlining and bolding indicates comparison rather than metaphor.]

## 7.3.7. Recognizing Apposition: schemes for tropes

The problems of interpreting Apposition, caused by the weakness of the syntactic bond and the need to infer coreference, become more severe as the distance between apposed terms increases. Two ways of guiding the reader to recognize the Apposition are apparent in the above examples.

The first way is to exploit Inactive metaphors or Root Analogies and our examples show just how common this is: UNDERSTAND/KNOW = SEE (FF133, FF113), TIME = (MOVEMENT THROUGH) SPACE (DT6), BAD = DARK (FF231), PURPOSE = DIRECTION (FF116). To put the same thing another way, the syntactic links here are so tenuous and distant that it is only Inactive metaphors which will work: anything more original would have to have its Topic specified more explicitly with stronger syntactic cement.

The second prompt for recognition of these T-terms is by using parallelisms or schemes: phonological (MD1161, DV47, DV38), morphological (LF149, TS131, FF231), lexical or syntactic (FF113, FF116, FF10, GH235). What happens is that the parallelism on the phonological and grammatical level suggests a parallelism of semantics or reference, so that the metaphoric play becomes doubly determined both by meaning and grammar (Lecercle 1990: 164ff.); we forgo the range of grammatical and phonological options in order to point out the semantic equation.

### 7.3.8. Conjunctions

■ **EXERCISE**

*In which of the following two sentences do you detect conjoined T-term and V-term noun phrases? Can you explain why?*

> *LF41   The simple statement brought light and happiness.*
> *FF67   The lady with the leathery coat brought in a bucket of coal and some*
> *advice.*

Before leaving Apposition we can point out that noun phrase V-terms and T-terms may actually be linked by the conjunctions *and* and *or*, giving a juxtaposition of coreferring noun phrases similar to Apposition. Recognition is going to be even harder here, notably with *and* since we naturally assume two different referents. So again recognition depends upon Root Analogies EMOTION = LIGHT (LF41), FREEDOM = SPACE TO MOVE (FF238), UNDERSTAND = SEE (TS209):

> FF238   Here we met officially in <u>suits</u> and **constraint**.
> TS209   the **formless** and <u>inexpressible</u> mass that lay in his mind
> DV38   **a sediment** or <u>remainder</u>

Note that LF41 and FF238 are examples of zeugma or syllepsis; an abstract and concrete are conjoined as objects of the same verb, or complements of the same preposition. *Or* often indicates Reformulation, where reference is to meanings as much as to the world.

We now pass to the third main syntactic resource for Topic specification, the genitive.

### 7.4. GENITIVES

This structure is a favourite syntactic pattern for specifying the Topic of active metaphors, both in the Golding corpus (Goatly 1983); and in poetry (Brooke-Rose 1958: 288); and in adverts and popular science (Chapter 10, Table 10.1). Perhaps the reason is that, unlike Copulas and many Appositions, the V-term precedes the T-term, with the result that the momentary delay in specifying the Topic intensifies the reference to the Vehicle; any Interactive filtering out of the features of the Vehicle is not possible until the T-term is specified. And yet the delay is only momentary, for the T-term comes quickly after the V-term, guaranteeing the right choice of Topic. In addition, as we noted with the Copula (Identification and Appellation Appositions), there is more of a sense of Equation when the T-term comes second.

Traditionally the *of*-construction is considered equivalent to the Genitive *'s* construction, with the noun phrase following the *of* functioning as a modifier of the other head noun, just as the noun + *'s* does. But Halliday (1994: 195–6) has noted the ambivalence *of*-structures. And Sinclair (1989: 140), working with concordance data, suggests that the second noun is often semantically the head noun; the relative status of the first noun is variable, only sometimes becoming equal to the second noun phrase.

| (25) | NP$_1$ | NP$_2$ | Meaning |
|---|---|---|---|
| | *a number of*<br>Premodifier | *logistic support ships*<br>Head | (Partitive) measure |
| | *The growth of*<br>Head | *a single-celled creature*<br>Head | Subjective |

He suggests two criteria for deciding which is the head: the noun whose omission does most damage to the meaning; and the noun which provides

*Table 7.3* The metaphorical semantics of the *of*-Genitive

| Type | Head | Semantics | Example | Transform | Ambiguity |
|---|---|---|---|---|---|
| Appositive | 2 | NP$_2$ or NP$_1$ | **the taut wire** of the horizon | the horizon, (or) a taut wire | Equative or Ascriptive? |
| (Partitive of) shape/measure | 1 + 2 | NP$_2$ the shape/ size of NP$_1$ | **trunks** of ice | ice the shape/ size of trunks | Which is head? |
| Partitive (possessive) | 1 + 2 | NP$_1$ is part of or belongs to NP$_2$ | **the hinges** of his legs | the hinges are part of his legs | |
| Analogic | 1 + 2 | NP$_1$ : Y : : X : NP$_2$ | **the rags** of my self-respect | rags : [clothes] : : X : self-respect | Which is head? |
| Subjective | (1) 2 | NP$_2$ does NP$_1$ | **the whisper** of rain | the rain whispers/ whispered | ?Appositive |
| Objective | (1) 2 | NP$_1$ is done to NP$_2$ | **the ruin** of his skull | his skull is/was ruined | ?Appositive |
| Origin | 1 | NP causes, produces or accompanies NP | **the worms** of loathing | worms cause loathing | ?Appositive |

the principal reference point or anchor to an object in the physical world (Sinclair 1989: 140). (Presumably subject–verb concord could also be decisive: *a lot of students is taking this exam.)

Disagreeing a little with Sinclair, I would suggest that when the 's-Genitive or noun premodifier is the unmarked form, e.g. Partitive (Possessive) and Origin, in the equivalent *of*-phrase the first noun alone is the head as in Table 7.4.

We will now discuss the categories of Genitive in Table 7.3, which represent a re-think of Quirk *et al.* (1985: 249–51, 321–6, 1275–85), and introduce a new category, the Analogic Genitive. All these *of*-Genitives, except Appositive, are best viewed as examples of Associative Qualification, in Ferris' terms (see Figure 7.1) and are cases of Topic Indication rather than specification.

### 7.4.1. Appositive Genitives

The semantic category which is most obviously important for Topic specification is the Appositive Genitive. In this category the second noun phrase certainly has equal if not greater status as the head, since by Sinclair's criterion, it refers principally and more successfully to an object in the world. The other criterion of damage to meaning is difficult to apply: of course omitting the T-term damages the literal meaning, but omitting the V-term destroys the metaphorical meaning entirely.

CEC99  She was a sort of colourless **mouse** of a <u>woman</u>.
without V-term = she was a woman
without T-term = she was a mouse

We might want to suggest that these are equivalent either to (a) Designation appositions (where the first phrase is definite) which amounts to Equation (PQ36, PQ179); or to (b) Attribution (where the first is indefinite (LF38)) which amounts to Ascription.

PQ36  We roll back the lid of **the sardine tin** of <u>life</u>. (Alan Bennett)
PQ179  Every revolution evaporates, leaving behind only **the slime** of <u>a new bureaucracy</u>. (Kafka)
LF38  **a shrimp** of <u>a boy</u>

*Table 7.4* Heads and premodifiers in marked Partitive and Origin Genitives

|  | *Marked* |  | *Unmarked* |  |
|---|---|---|---|---|
| Partitive (Possessive) | *the key* | *of the back door* | *the backdoor* | *key* |
| Origin | *a sonata* | *of Beethoven* | *a Beethoven* | *sonata* |
|  | Head | Postmodifier | Premodifier | Head |

### 7.4.2. (Partitive of) shape/measure

When a T-term as second noun phrase is obviously a mass noun indicating a substance, and the Grounds of the metaphor are interpreted as shape or size, we have what Quirk *et al.* call the *typical partitive* (1985: 250):

TI186    a little **half-moon** of <u>earth</u>
TI82    congealed **trunks** of <u>ice</u>
FAE318    a large gin with just **a rumour** of <u>tonic</u>

Ice, water, and tonic are substances, not solid things, so that the metaphor imposes a shape (TI186, TI82) or a measure (FAE318) on inherently shapeless and dimensionless substances (Quirk, personal communication). Consequently the second noun phrase is a Topic-Indicating term, not a strict specifier. Incidentally, there is no equivalent *'s*-Genitive for the examples of these structures.

It is interesting to apply Sinclair's criteria of (a) damage to meaning and (b) principal reference to the world of physical objects to these metaphors. Omitting the second noun phrase does great damage to the literal meaning; but omitting the first would do away with metaphorical meaning and with reference to objects entirely.

### 7.4.3. Partitive Genitives

Here the Topic will be part of the entity referred to by the second noun phrase.

FF235    in **basements** of the forest
TS204    **the hinges** of his legs
PQ94    (<u>Catalonia</u>) is **the nose** of the earth. (Salvador Dali)

It should be possible to arrive at the Topic by asking the question: "What part of the entity referred to by the second noun phrase resembles the conventional referent of the first noun phrase?" Or one could set up an analogy for FF235 in which the Topic is X:

(26)    basement : building : : X : forest

The two noun phrases are of equal head status: unlike Appositives, the second noun phrase, although referring successfully to the larger thing in the world, does not specify exactly the Topic but Indicates it. We can see this from PQ94 which specifies the true T-term "Catalonia" quite independently. The first noun phrase therefore refers more exactly. On the other hand omitting the second noun phrase, the Topic-Indicator, would do great damage to the literal meaning. These remarks apply equally to Analogic Genitives.

### 7.4.4. Analogic genitives

When we are forced to resort to this kind of four-term interpretation we have another Genitive category, the Analogic. Though this is not mentioned in Quirk's taxonomy, it is recognized as important by Sinclair (1989: 143–4), and analogy is indispensable when we are considering relatively concrete initial Vehicles paired with relatively abstract Topic Indicators.

FF94   the **rags** of my self-respect

An interpretation can be diagrammed thus:

(27)   a. rags : Y : : X : self-respect
       b. rags : [clothes] : : X : self-respect

The Lexical Gap-filling function is apparent in these examples, the paraphrase of the nebulous Topic being 'whatever in relation to self-respect, rags are to clothes' .

### 7.4.5. Subjective and Objective Genitives

Subjective and Objective Genitives can be transformed into clauses, so that the first noun phrase is often a nominalization – by conversion or suffixation – of an underlying verb.

Subjective

| | |
|---|---|
| **the faint whisper** of rain (DV50) | the rain whispered |
| **the coils** of cruelty (FF115) | cruelty coiled |
| **the enlacement** of canal and railway (DV216) | canal and railway enlace |
| **the screen** of grass (LF114) | the grass screened |
| **a cradle** of warm flesh (TI39) | the warm flesh cradled |

Objective

| | |
|---|---|
| **the ruin** of his half-raw skull (DV18) | his skull was ruined |
| **the wreckage** of that childhood (DV17) | that childhood was wrecked |

We saw in section 3.2.4.2 that the effect of nominalization, especially of the Improper kind, is to confer the status of a thing, a permanent entity possessing more semantic features than the equivalent verb. And that such a thing, being imaginable, can take part in a more Interactive metaphorical interpretation. While verbs underlie all seven of these examples the last four are inclined to be understood as Improper nominalizations and thus Appositive Genitives: *the grass, a screen*; *the warm flesh, a cradle*, etc. By contrast, the first three are more equally poised between a Subjective/Objective and an Appositive interpretation.

Strictly speaking, in DV216, DV18, LF114, and TI39, the Topic Indicators, the second noun phrases are the heads, because they refer to things – canal, railway, skull – or substances – grass, flesh – and so are the principal anchors to the physical world. However, when the second noun phrase is abstract (FF115 and DV17), or when the first noun phrase could be referring improperly to a thing, as in the last four, we are justified in giving head status to the first noun phrase.

### 7.4.6. Genitives of Origin

The Genitive of Origin is something of a rag-bag term for the remainder of semantically elusive Genitives, and should correspond to Association in Ferris' categories. It resembles the Subjective and Objective Genitives because a verb seems to be lurking somewhere in the deep structure, though we have to guess exactly which verb in each separate case. Often this metonymic relationship is one of cause, production, effect or accompaniment:

| | |
|---|---|
| **the long wolfhowl** of the man's flight (TS90) | the wolfhowl accompanies the flight |
| **a nightmare** of starvation and torture (DM5) | starvation etc. causes a nightmare |
| **the rose** [= blushing] of indignation (LF27) | indignation causes the rose |
| **the luminous wall** of his myopia (LF187) | myopia produces a luminous wall |
| **the worms** of loathing (P112) | worms produce loathing |
| **the granite** of my immobility (FF172) | immobility is the effect of the granite |
| **some pit** of destroying consummation | the destroying consummation is the effect of the pit |

Generally speaking, the first noun phrase anchors us to a thing in the world and therefore appears to have head status, more than the relatively abstract T-indicator. However, there is a tendency for the last three Vehicles to be reinterpreted as a symbol of the abstract property referred to by the second noun phrase. Granite symbolizes immobility, worms symbolize loathing, pits symbolize destructive consummation. In doing so these Genitives of Origin transform themselves into Appositive Genitives, apparently of the Attributive/Ascriptive type. But they may even go further to achieve the status of an Equation as in 'the pit symbolically represents/equals destructive consummation'.

### 7.5. PREMODIFICATION

As we shift to structures internal to a noun phrase, this is a convenient place to discuss aspects of Ferris' theory of prenominal or Attributive Qualification, a structure which, without Assignment, has the role of helping to identify the referent of the noun phrase. Attributive Qualification will either be Ascriptive or Associative. If a noun is Associative in prenominal/attributive position, the phrase cannot be transformed into an equivalent predicative Assignment clause.

(28)    a sea monster → *the monster is sea

220

This is because Associative qualifiers have a different referential locus from the head of the noun phrase (Ferris 1993: 41–2). Ascriptive qualifications, however, have only one referential locus, thus they can be used predicatively, with assignment:

(29)   the naughty children → the children are naughty
(30)   Chancellor Kohl → Kohl is Chancellor

While this may be clear-cut for literal premodification, the question arises of how lexical metaphor will affect the meanings of this syntactic structure. Live metaphors, by definition, involve more than one referential locus, the Vehicle as well as the Topic. So Active metaphorical premodifying nouns have an Associative relation with their head noun.

(31)   the sausage hands → *the hands are sausage

But contrast this with Inactive metaphors:

(32)   the chestnut hair → the hair is chestnut

As we have said before, initially perceived as Associative or Equative, metaphors often end up, by stage V of interpretation (Table 6.1), or by Lexicalization, as Ascriptive.

In fact Ferris recognizes that the distinction between Association and Ascription is weakened by processes of lexical extension, word-formation and Burying: e.g. the *bovine* in *bovine behaviour* is difficult to categorize decisively as Associative or Ascriptive and *Platonic love* is unlikely to mean 'love of Plato', so that both can be used predicatively (Ferris 1993: 32–3).

The further complication with noun premodifiers is that, though as premodifiers they obviously do not assign, they resemble Apposition and can therefore be equatively related by transformation. So *the hands are sausages* works better than *the hands are sausage*. One reason for entertaining an Equative relationship is that it is hard to see how Active V-term premodifying nouns can fulfil the typical semantic role of attributive Qualification: aiding in identifying the referent of the noun phrase.

It is worth exploring in more detail this potential for a clash between Qualification and Equation. Premodifying noun V-terms, because they precede the T-term, may be momentarily misclassified as the head noun, since, unlike corresponding adjectives, they have no suffixes. Moreover, as in Apposition, the two nouns occur in close proximity (even closer than the Genitive), and often very little in the way of Grounds is explicitly provided. These factors position such metaphors high on the scale of Contradictoriness. On the other hand, once the syntactic position of premodifier becomes clear, so does the qualifying nature of the interpretation: premodifiers can, according to the syntactic–semantic rules, only qualify, not equate.

FAE143   a **plum** seat
MD1068   however **baby** man may brag of his science and skill

| DT5 | a **cat** <u>burglar</u> |
| MD950 | and Doughboy, the steward, thrusting his *pale* **loaf of bread** <u>face</u> from the cabin scuttle |
| AL | the **raindrop** <u>eye</u> |
| MD1173 | **portcullis** <u>jaw</u> |

We can say more about the interpretative potential of these structures if we consider the general principles of syntactic and semantic ordering within the noun phrase. Syntactically, whenever a premodifier is a noun it will appear in a slot adjacent to the head noun. Semantically, this adjacent position is occupied by classifiers which indicate a certain sub-class of the thing referred to by the head. So we would expect "portcullis" in MD1173 to behave like a classifier: to subclassify among the class of jaws. Since with metaphor, the two classes are semantically incompatible, this should produce a strong sense of contradiction. However it seems that the test for classifiers, that they do not accept degrees of comparison, does not work with "portcullis". *He had a very portcullis jaw* seems reasonably acceptable, though less than the Inactive *She had very orange hair*. The fact is that the divide between epithet and classifier, never a very clear one (Halliday 1994: 184–5), is transgressed by the metaphorical process which, apparently assigning to classes, ends up by ascribing features from one entity to another. And these ascribed features may be susceptible to treatment as scalar adjectives, which is why they can take degree adverbials like *very*. So metaphor breaks the gradable/non-gradable distinction.

There is another reason why the adjacent-to-head position is significant. It seems to be a semantic principle that unsuffixed epithets occurring close to the noun head very often describe colour or shape (Vendler 1968: 119ff.). It is therefore no coincidence that at least half of our examples, certainly the last three, depend upon Grounds involving shape or colour.

For the sake of comprehensiveness we should also mention that the order of T-term and V-term can be reversed, with the V-term coming second:

(33)   Europe's <u>butter</u> **mountain**
(34)   the <u>killing</u> **shit**

Often these structures are equivalent to the *of*-Genitive with a (Partitive of) Shape/Measure meaning (section 7.4.2), e.g. *a mountain of butter*; or to the Copula, e.g. *Killing is shit*. As we saw in section 6.3 this is also a favourite structure for Indicating Topics, e.g. *a tax haven*.

## 7.6. COMPOUNDS

In many ways Compounds are semantically equivalent to noun-premodifier + head noun structures. What distinguishes them is a tendency for Compounds to be more easily reversible (→), suggesting a more thorough Equatability.

TI25     The weed-**tails** were very long → the tail-weed
PM177    A chunk of rock**leaf** had fallen → the leafrock

MD1304   these coffin-**canoes** → the canoe-coffins
PQBU57   my **sword**-pen → my pen-sword

Very likely "equatability" is the wrong word; the compounding makes clear that only one entity is involved, one referential locus. This means that, as we saw in the case of premodifying V-terms, there both are and are not two referential loci (cf. Bauer 1983: 30). As with the word *cotton-wool* the compound may reflect an indecision about which criterion, substance or appearance to give primacy when referring to the stuff: to all appearances cotton-wool is wool, but, in substantial fact, it is made of cotton.

## 7.7. BLENDS/PORTMANTEAUX

At a level still more intimate than compounding, are Portmanteau words like (the somewhat Antipodean) *reyendrop*, *brunch* and *smog*. These are rather minimalist specifications of Topic–Vehicle, since the submorphemic units *sm* and *og* stand for the whole words *smoke* and *fog*. Often they have a gap-filling purpose and are Approximative metaphors referring to a substance which is halfway between one category and another, or simultaneously a member of both categories. So that in CEC701 and GH12 it is impossible to say which are the Topics and which the V-terms partially provided: *hilarity* or *hysterics*, *hygiene* or *genius*.

CEC701   I so nearly burst into **hilarics**.
GH12     a touch of sheer **Hygenius** (from a Hygena kitchen ad)
GW0143   he thought we had the same **whoroscope**, so to speak

The semantic intersection of overlapping categories is enhanced by a graphological/phonological overlap (Bauer 1983: 235–6), which symbolizes it iconically, and which is underlined in (35).

| (35) | hyste**rics** | **hilar**ity | **hilarics** |
|------|------------|------------|------------|
|      | hyg**iene** (hyg**en**a) | **gen**ius | **hygenius** |
|      | w**hor**e | **horo**scope | **whoroscope** |

## 7.8. TOPIC SPECIFICATION ACROSS DIFFERENT
## PARTS OF SPEECH

So far in considering the specification and Indication of Topics, our T-terms and V-terms have belonged to the same word-class; indeed we have concentrated on nouns. It is perfectly possible, however, to mix word-classes by using nouns which refer to processes:

TS203   the sick **fire**
TS190   Father Adam **scratched** his voice into the evening air

Some of these will rely on nominalizations:

TS89   But then the silence **was slashed** by <u>a fierce yell</u>.

TS68   <u>death</u> of the ancient Chancellor who **had tottered through his last door**

TI178   Into his uncertain silence the tribe **spilled** their <u>murmur</u>.

While on the subject of cross word-class specification or Indication, we note that Topics can be indicated in a rudimentary sort of way through the actual noun colligates of metaphorical verbs and adjectives, according to the pathway 7 (Table 4.1) that we sketched out in Chapter 4. Or, from another point of view, the actual verb or adjective V-term suggests an extension of the V-term, through conventional colligates (pathways 5, 6 and 7), and the actual colligates are T-terms for these suggested V-terms. Furthermore in section 3.1.3 we showed how the specificity of the conventional colligate gives definition to the metaphor and makes it more imageable, more prone to Vehicle-construction.

## 7.9. CONCLUSION AND SUMMARY ON TOPIC SPECIFICATION/INDICATION

Table 7.5 sums up the main findings of this chapter, and includes, for comparison purposes, the similes and suffixed forms discussed elsewhere. Column 3 indicates the order of the T- and V-terms, the semantic relations of Equation, Ascription and Association obtaining between the nouns, noun phrases, and whether Assignment is involved or not. The direction of Ascription is conveyed by the arrowhead, and in cases of Equation it will be double-headed. Most of these are quite straightforward, but let me explain the more complex cases. As far as adverbial similes are concerned one quality of the Vehicle is ascribed to the Topic by means of the Ground verb phrase which itself is both ascribed and assigned to the Topic subject. With noun premodifiers the prima-facie relationship of Association can be reinterpreted, under the pressure of metaphor, as Ascription or Equation. The same is true of Apposition, except that the reinterpretation tends more towards the Equative.

The ordering of these elements might be important, though this would have to be established by psychological tests.[3] The greater the distance between T- and V-term the correspondingly greater the effect might be. In Relevance Theory terms, the effect would be of forcing the reader to access Contextual Assumptions about the Topic before these Contextual Assumptions were later made co-textually explicit. In cases where Subjective Illusions are dispelled, distance between the initial V-term and the disillusioning V-term is likely to be great, but this takes us beyond the sentence level which this chapter is confined to.

I hypothesize that the Genitive construction would give rise to different

*Table 7.5* The syntax of Topic specification and Indication

| Syntactic construction | Example | Order + semantics | Distance | Syntactic prominence | Contradiction |
|---|---|---|---|---|---|
| Adverbial Simile | The eye shone like a raindrop | Assign and Ascribe<br>T ←— G ←— V | 3 words | T + G | None |
| Copula Simile | The eye was like a raindrop | Assign and Ascribe<br>T ←— V | 3 words | T + V equal | None |
| Suffixed premodifier | The raindrop-like eye<br>(The cavernous mouth) | Ascribe<br>V —→ T | 1/2 word | T | None |
| Noun premodifier | The raindrop eye | Associate (Ascribe/<br>Equate)<br>V (<) —→ T | 0 words | T (V) | Moderate |
| Copula | The eye was a raindrop | Assign and Ascribe<br>T ←— V | 2 words | T + V equal | High |
| Apposition | The eye, a raindrop | Associate/Equate<br>(Ascribe)<br>T ←→ V | 1/0 words | T + V equal | Low |
| Genitive | The raindrop of an eye | Ascribe/Equate<br>V ←→ T | 2 words | V (T) | Moderate |

psychological processes from the other syntactic formulations, for three reasons: (a) the V-term comes first; (b) it is separated from the T-term by two or more words; and (c) syntactically it is more prominent than the T-term, at least if analysed according to traditional conceptions of which is the head noun. Contrast this with the premodifying structure, in which the V-term comes first but separation and syntactic prominence do not apply. The prominence of the V-term in *of*-genitives makes it unique, as can be seen from column 5 (Table 7.5), where we can observe the relative syntactic prominences of V- and T-terms in these structures.

### 7.9.1. The cline of Contradictoriness

We are now in a position to sum up our rather scattered comments on one of the metaphorical clines we introduced in Chapter 1, the cline of Contradictoriness, which corresponds to the tensive or controversional impact of metaphor (4.3.2).

### ■ EXERCISE

*Which of the following do you find most contradictory?*

(a)  *Life is a box of chocolates.*
(b)  *Nudity is a form of dress. (PQ29)*

Notice that this cline is quite independent of the cline of Approximation; indeed, since opposites have to belong to the same semantic field it probably has an inverse relationship. So that I guess you would find (b) more contradictory than (a).

Various syntactic-semantic factors contribute to this cline. First, there is the question of Assignment or non-Assignment, exemplified by the difference between oxymoron, *the new ancient faces*, and paradox, *the child is father of the man*. Table 7.4 shows that Apposition, where the syntactic link is tenuous and coreference has to be inferred, gives rise to the least contradictory metaphors. The Genitive and premodifiers will have relatively moderate contradiction levels because they do not involve Assignment. So it is the Copula which holds out the possibility of the greatest overt contradiction.

Among the Copula metaphors we made more delicate distinctions. We noted that the Equative are more contradictory than the Ascriptive. And that Ascriptive metaphors can either be synthetic and particular – suggesting some temporary contingent contradictoriness – or analytic and generic – suggesting a more universal one, often a redrawing of semantic boundaries (section 7.2).

If we look at column 6 we notice the levels of contradiction involved in the structures. In the case of similes there will be little or no sense of contradiction because these have been marked out of existence. So a further factor in the scale of Contradictoriness is the kind of markings involved (see Table 6.4). Explicit markers, copular similes, mimetic terms, conditionals and negatived modals, do away with contradiction altogether, while most of the other markers reduce it to some extent. But intensifiers, as their name suggests, can sharpen the contradiction. Suffixed forms, not only those in -*like*, but others like *cavernous* (row 3) tend to be less contradictory, first, because denominalization reduces the strength of the image, and second, because they are often Inactive. In this respect the cline of Activity and the cline of Contradictoriness overlap.

The final contradictoriness factor is the specificity of the semantic contrast. In section 3.1.3 we noted that the specificity of the conventional colligate would sharpen image potential and therefore lead to a tensive clashing of semantic features, whereas the more general selectional restriction violations give less tension. When a meaning with only one semantic feature clashes with its opposite, as is the case with oxymoron and paradox, we have very high degrees of semantic tension.

### 7.9.2. Summary: lexical metaphor and ambiguity in syntactic meanings

An obvious point which has emerged time and time again in the survey of Topic specification is that metaphor introduces extra ambiguity into the meaning of syntactic structures, or sharpens existing ambiguities; the metaphoric cat, as it were, disturbs the syntactic-semantic pigeons. These ambiguities are worth summarizing here.

First, and overarching, we noted the general tug-of-war between Equation and Ascription, notably in Copula constructions where the complements are V-terms. Equation disappears into Ascription to an even greater extent when the Topics are higher-order entities, since we have the sense that the V-term is conferring qualities on an abstract concept. And the whole Equation–Ascription distinction seems to dissolve when both Topic and Vehicle are abstract.

With *of*-Genitives of the Appositive variety we are similarly torn between Equation and Ascription. And we saw that the ambiguity about which noun phrase is the head is complicated by metaphor. But a more interesting ambiguity arises because Subjective and Objective Genitives can be reworked as Appositive Genitives, especially when Improper nominalization is involved; as can Genitives of Origin when the concrete Vehicle becomes a symbol of the abstract Topic. These interesting cases represent a move from Association to Equation/Ascription.

Turning to noun premodifiers we noted a momentary ambiguity about which noun is head, and observed Association turning into non-assigned Equation and then Ascription. Finally, lexical metaphor seems to introduce a similar ambiguity between classifiers and epithets, and undoes the gradable–ungradable distinction.

# 8

# THE SPECIFICATION OF
# GROUNDS

## 8.1. INTRODUCTION

To see how far we have come in exploring the contribution of co-text to the risky business of metaphorical interpretation, we should take another look at Table 6.1, reproduced here as Table 8.1.

In Chapter 6, I discussed ways of marking metaphor, helping reduce the risk that stage III never happens, and in Chapter 7, I described the major syntactic apparatus for specifying and Indicating Topics, to reduce the risk of a potential mismatch between the writer's b of stage I and the reader's c at stage IV. A third means of risk reduction is to provide Grounds, to ensure that the x of stage I matches the y of stage V. The commonly used syntactic resources for guaranteeing this fit are the subject of this chapter.

### 8.1.1. The applicability of the concept of Grounds

It is worth repeating, before we begin, that the distinction between Topic and Grounds is not applicable to all metaphors. First, consider Inactive metaphors receiving a Substitution interpretation. The unconventional referent of the V-term, the Topic, amounts to the feature automatically selected by a secondary convention from the Vehicle, a feature which is, in fact, also the Ground. In:

(1)   Thomas is a monkey.

*Table 8.1* Stages in metaphorical processing

| Writer | | Reader | | |
|---|---|---|---|---|
| I Perceives or creates a resemblance between entities a and b on the basis of feature(s) x | II Forms text using "A" to refer to b | III Realizes that "A" is not referring to a | IV Thinks "A" is referring to c | V Postulates a resemblance between a and c on the basis of features y |

the meaning 'mischievous' is both the actual concept referred to by "monkey", the Topic, and also the Grounds of the original metaphor.

Second, in the case of concrete Vehicles filling gaps for abstract concepts the Vehicle will often constitute the concept, which will therefore have no antecedent features which can function as Grounds. These Grounds will be external to both Topic and Vehicle since they will involve analogical relationships, not inherent similarities. In the phrase *the rags of my self-respect* there can be no real Similarity between the concrete rags and the abstract self-respect. Even when both Topic and Vehicle are concrete, e.g. with the computer hardware term *mouse*, Grounds become purely incidental and marginal once the term has filled the gap.

Incidentally, just as we used the term Topic Indicators, so we will need a term <u>Ground Indicators</u> where the Vehicle is seen as lending specificity or precision to the G-term.

### 8.1.2. The degrees of association of Grounds with Topic and Vehicle

Theoretically, features used for Grounds may display three degrees of association with the Topic and Vehicle referents (concepts): necessary, expected or possible. Let's refer back to our analysis of the Shakespearean metaphor (5.1.3),

> (2) those boughs which shake against the cold,
> *Bare* ruined **choirs** where late *the sweet* birds *sang*

Some Grounds will be necessary properties of Topic or Vehicle. Boughs are inherently made of wood. Other Grounds are expected: we can expect choirboys to frequent choirs (the place in the church), and we expect birds to perch on boughs and sing. The explicit Ground [bare] is not exactly expected of choirs – it might even be unexpected but it is certainly possible.

This range of relationships between Topic, Vehicle and Grounds is diagrammed in Table 8.2 (though the distinction between the expected and possible is often a matter of degree, certainly not as clear as the definite line suggests).

We could locate the Ground [wooden] in box 4, [songsters] in 5, and [bare] in 9. The latter allocation is slightly problematic: from the previous co-text we know that the season is winter, so that the given information makes the bareness of the boughs expected, moving the example upwards into (or perhaps above) box 6. This kind of effect of co-text is so powerful in literature that we will need to interpret the expected, row B and column Y, as contingent: an expectation which is not part of the semantics or decontextualized connotations, but which has been introduced by preceding textual description. I shall use the term <u>Ground Reminder</u> when interpretation depends upon previously given co-textual information.

*Table 8.2* Grounds: degrees of association with Vehicle and Topic

| Association with Topic | Association with Vehicle | | |
|---|---|---|---|
| | *Necessary* (X) | *Expected (contingent)* (Y) | *Possible* (Z) |
| *Necessary* (A) | 1 | 2 | 3 |
| | the *quick* . . . <u>patter</u> of hoofs, **a castanet** sound | **the screen** *that conceals* <u>*the working of things*</u> | the transepts . . . were **his arms** *outspread* |
| *Expected (contingent)* (B) | 4 | 5 | 6 |
| | Let <u>Roger Mason</u> settle it **my slave** *for the* work | the flies made a *dark* **cloud** around the head | the letter was still there like a *white* **tray** |
| *Possible* (C) | 7 | 8 | 9 |
| | The *faint* **whisper** of <u>rain</u> | **the bones** of the land . . . lumps of *smooth* . . . <u>rock</u> | <u>Ralph</u> *launched* himself like **a cat** |

One problem with this rather neat scheme for classifying Grounds, besides the fact that these box allocations are untested intuitions, is that degrees of semantic association and degrees of psychological association rarely coincide. Certain Grounds like [wooden] in our last example (2), are relatively general features of boughs; although semantically necessary, they may not be psychologically salient (McCloskey 1964: 220–1; Verbrugge and McCarrell 1977: 500, 527–8). That is, they will have a low rating θ on Tversky's *f*-scale (section 4.4.1).

### 8.1.3. Preposed and postposed Grounds

Another important distinction is the relative order of G-term and V-term. When G-term occurs first in the sequence I will call it <u>Preposed</u>, and when it follows, <u>Postposed</u>. Preposed Grounds tend to pre-empt a full Interactive interpretation, preventing the potential mismatch between x and y at stage V of interpretation (Table 8.1). While Postposed ones may eventually involve the abandonment of an interim interpretation. In Relevance Theory terms the Contextual Assumptions we use to find Grounds will be immediately co-textual with Preposed Grounds, but initially non-co-textual with Postposed ones. Increasing distance in Postposed cases and decreasing distance in Preposed cases accentuate these differential interpretative tendencies.

In this chapter I will first survey the syntax of Preposed G-terms and then proceed to the syntax of Postposing. An overview of the Ground-marking devices is given in Table 8.3 and readers may wish to read the sections 8.2 to 8.3.6 selectively.

Table 8.3 Syntactic resources for specifying Grounds

| Construction | Example | Order | Prominence | Comments |
|---|---|---|---|---|
| Adverbial Simile | a rock standing like a fort | T ^ G ^ V | G-term | Often restrictive uses: but ambiguity with (Quasi)-Literal |
| As preposition Simile | empty as a bubble | G ^ V | G-term | Ambiguity of degree specification |
| As conjunction Simile | looking at it all over as a **mother** might examine **her baby** | G ^ V | G- & V-terms equal | Possibility of double T and V, with Gs as analogic relation |
| As if/though Simile | His head-hair was sleek as if **fat had been rubbed in it** | G ^ V | G-term | Associated with Phenomenalistic Similes |
| so that conjunction | the ivy spread upwards and downwards in a dark tangle so that **they might have been sitting in a bush on the ground** | G ^ V | G- & V-terms equal | Associated with Subjective Similes: then have to be in columns X or Y |
| Prenominal adjective + V-term | a pack of painted **niggers** like you | G ^ V | V-term | Restrictive use possible; process V-terms → box 7. Boxes 5 & 8 common |
| Prenominal adjective + T-term | **a thatch** of silver hair | G ^ T | T-term | Must be in columns X or Y |
| Of-genitive | They had in their bodies the bending grace of **a young bough** | G ^ V | G-term | Restrictive interpretation |
| Genitive | Mary Michael turned her **swan**'s neck | V ^ G | G-term | Restrictive interpretation |

| Type | Example | | Term | Notes |
|---|---|---|---|---|
| Prenominal noun + G-term | The **fish 'n' chip** *smell* of the engine oil **cherry**-*red* | V ^ G | G-term | Restrictive: noun head is general perception or colour/shape word |
| Postnominal prepositional phrase | **sausage** hands *with discolorations of* <u>red and blue</u> | V ^ G | G-term | Mostly box 8 G-terms nominalized |
| Postnominal verbless clause | <u>I</u> am **an album of snapshots**, *random* | V ^ G | V-term | Non-restrictive: assignment |
| Postnominal non-finite clause | the lobsters wore **armour** *to protect them* | V ^ G | V-term | Tendency to column X |
| Verb phrase/predicate | Overhead **the cannon** *boomed* again | V ^ G | Equal | Less noticeable than relative clauses; must be in column X or Y to be recognized |
| Relative clause | <u>the heat</u> became **a blow** *that they ducked* | V ^ G | V-term | Non-restrictive despite *that*. Combine easily with copula and *of* T-terms |
| Adverbials as Gs for verb V-terms | the building **sweating** now *with damp* | V ^ G | V-term | Tendency to column X |

## 8.2. PREPOSED GROUNDS

### 8.2.1. Premodification

One frequent and noticeable way of specifying Grounds is by adjectival premodification of the V-term. The following examples indicate how the matrix in Table 8.2 can be used, and how the placing in the columns and boxes corresponds to positions on the continuum between Interaction and Substitution interpretation.

*8.2.1.1. Column X*

DV50 the *faint* **whisper** of ra<u>i</u>n
LF162 a *thin* **trickle** of <u>sm</u>oke
LF 72 <u>The smoke</u> was a *tight* little **knot**.

I am tempted to locate these Grounds in column X, since whispers are necessarily faint, trickles must be thin, and to make a knot string has to be tied tight. The only problem is that the adjectives in prenominal position are notoriously semantically relative, which means their meanings are often defined restrictively in relation to the noun they qualify. A small elephant will be bigger than a big mouse. This means there is no tautology in saying "a big elephant": it may simply mean 'big even in relation to your average-sized elephant'. Similarly the meaning in DV50 could be 'faint even as whispers go'.

These examples feature V-terms whose semantic specifications involve processes or functions, i.e. deverbal nouns *whisper*, *trickle*, or results of actions, *knot*. So their semantic specification is relatively lean compared with thing-referring nouns. This is one reason the specified Grounds seem to be both logically necessary and psychologically salient.

■ **EXERCISE**

*Do you hypothesize any other Grounds besides those specified, when interpreting DV50, LF162 and LF 72?*

Their Grounds could fall within box 7. And if the Grounds specified were the only ones, this would mean the metaphors were hardly Interactive at all: the interpretation would work by simple Substitution of the Ground for the Vehicle: 'faint rain', 'thin smoke'. Perhaps, however, there are unstated Grounds which would redeem these examples: a single line of string extends from a knot, just as a single line of smoke extends upwards from a smoky fire on a calm day; the rain communicates something, if only its human-like presence. However that may be, these Preposed Grounds in box 7 tend towards Substitution–Ascription, rather than

Interaction–Equation. The Vehicles would appear to have a decorative function, or to provide foregrounding, to induce the heightened aesthetic experience associated with imagery.

### 8.2.1.2. Column Y

The Grounds in the following examples inhabit column Y as expected features of the Vehicle: lips are prototypically pink (LF17), and asses (PM53) and niggers (LF199) are stereotyped, unjustifiably, as stupid and painted.

LF17     between the point [of the conch], worn away into a little hole, and the *pink* **lips of the mouth**

PM53    *Silly* **ass!**

LF199   a pack of *painted* **niggers** like you are

In which row do we locate the Grounds? LF17's probably belong in B, box 8, as we could well conceive a conchshell mouth as yellow, white, grey or even brown. The Grounds of PM53 and LF199, however, are Ground Reminders: Nathaniel, the silly ass of PM53, has just been described as balancing precariously on the ship's rail, and the preceding co-text of LF199 makes it clear that Jack's tribe have daubed their faces and bodies with coloured clay. Contingently, therefore, their Grounds belong in box 5.

There is a significant shift when we compare the examples of column X and column Y. As we move to column Y and the degree of association between Vehicle and Ground becomes less necessary and more contingent, we find a corresponding increase in degree of association between Ground and Topic. We expect this if Grounds are to link Topic and Vehicle. Correspondingly, a high degree of association between Topic and Ground is evidence of Interactiveness in the metaphorical interpretation.

### 8.2.1.3. Column Z

TI221   there were eyes like *green* **fires**

FF22    two *dark blue* **pillars** . . . **the coppers**

TS27    **the letter** was still there like a *white* **tray**

There is something unsatisfactory about the way these Grounds are ascribed to Vehicles with which they have no antecedent association. So, in order to maintain a more satisfying Interactiveness we can easily posit further unstated Grounds: [brightness] (TI221); [height], [shape], [immovability] (FF22); [flatness] (TS27). As we would predict, there must be a relatively high degree of association between Topic and Grounds in these cases for them to function as Grounds at all: eyes are more likely to be green than sparks, policeman to be dark blue than pillars, letters to be white more than trays. So they belong in box 6.

To sum up. Grounds specified by adjectival premodification of V-terms seem to inhabit boxes 5, 6, 7 and 8, box 8 being the most common location. Grounds in boxes 6 and 7 are less satisfactory from an Interactive viewpoint, and it is common to involve further unstated Grounds in their interpretation.

It is also possible, though not so common, to have G-terms premodifying T-terms.

DV70    the secretary had **a thatch** of *silver* <u>hair</u>
TI22    **the bones** of the land showed, lumps of *smooth grey* <u>rock</u>
TI43    lights ran to and fro along the edge or **leapt** in a *sudden* <u>sparkle</u>
LF53    the *quick hard* <u>patter</u> of hoofs, **a castanet** sound, seductive, maddening
        [boxes 1 and 4]

In this position adjectives must have either an expected or necessary degree of association with the Vehicle. So that *silver* in DV70 is doubtful as a G-term. Bones are prototypically smooth and grey, however (box 8). *Leap* (TI43), being a momentary verb (Quirk and Greenbaum 1973: 47), entails suddenness, while *sparkle* combines momentariness with continuation (the borderline of boxes 1 and 4).

### 8.2.2. *Like*-similes: adverbial and prepositional phrases

Simile, as we saw in Chapter 7, marks metaphor out of existence, and lacks the initial contradictoriness of metaphor. Nevertheless it makes explicit aspects of comparison necessary for metaphor, and does so to varying degrees.

(3)     the spire looked like a hammer [box 9]
(4)     the spire smashed the roof like a hammer [box 8]
LF17    the conch mooed like a cow

Example (3) indicates Grounds in a rather loose way, using one of the sense-specific phrasal verbs *look like, sound like, feel like, smell like* and *taste like* to draw attention to the general perceptual area of Similarity. In (4) the Ground is conveyed more specifically: it is the smashing of an object which provides the link between hammer and spire. Of course, if the colligational link becomes so uniquely specific as in LF17 we move over to extended metaphor, off our matrix altogether into an impossible area for the Topic, somewhere below box 8 or box 5.

We should not be surprised that simile is often used restrictively to convey extra precision to meanings, since this is a major metaphorical function (5.2.1). We can, in fact, distinguish two basic kinds of interpretation of Ground-providing similes: the <u>Precision</u> and the (Quasi-)Literal. With the Precision or restrictive variety the Vehicle, in a way, provides a non-existent hyponym; the Vehicles furnish the verb (adjective) meaning with extra specificity, the *like* introducing a manner adverbial.

LF215  Ralph *launched himself* like **a cat**. [box 9]

(I'm ignoring the Inactive metaphor "launched himself" for the present analysis.)

G-terms in these cases Indicate rather than specify. If I say "Peter shook his head like a dog just emerging from water" our sense is that *shaking one's head* usually means something different predicated of a human being than predicated of wet dogs. There will be a tendency for any interpretations whose Grounds we locate in box 9 to be treated as Precision interpretations, particularly in the case of verbs with few selectional restrictions, i.e. with a very wide range of colligational distribution, like *stand*:

LF31  a rock, almost detached, *standing* like **a fort**

Literal interpretations are those which simply make/imply two propositions where the Topic and Ground share the same property or participate in the same process:

LF189  "I'll *have to be led* like **a dog**, anyhow."
(5)  Paul teaches like me.

Example (5) can mean 'Paul is a teacher and I am a teacher', rather than the Precision 'Paul teaches in the same manner as me'. With Literal simile interpretations we simply have an explicit comparison, of two states of affairs which are true simultaneously, but of different entities.

Many examples are quite ambiguous as between a Precision and Literal interpretation, especially examples to be found in boxes 7 and 8.

LF155  Ralph *was kneeling* by the remains of the fire like **a sprinter at his mark**. [box 8]
LF167  The chant lost its first superficial excitement and began to *beat* like a **steady pulse**. [box 7]

## ■ EXERCISE

*Paraphrase the ambiguous meanings which are possible in LF155 and LF167. Why are examples in boxes 7 and 8 particularly prone to this ambiguity?*

### 8.2.3. *As*-similes: prepositional phrases and conjunctions

When similes take the form of (*as* +) adjective + *as* + noun phrase another ambiguity arises. Are we simply making a Literal simile? Or are we making claims about the degree of the property conveyed by the adjective, being precise in terms of position on the scale? (Traditionally the latter is known as *comparatio*.) In other words do we understand TS106 to mean 'they were soft and smooth and warm to the extent that a young body is'?

TS106    They [the rounded downlands] were *soft* and *warm* and *smooth* as **a young body**. [boxes 8, 5 and 8 respectively]

Examples of adjective G-terms which find themselves in box 7 because the Grounds are both logically necessary and psychologically salient features of the Vehicle, suggest a scalar interpretation, e.g.

FFl7    I crawled . . . , *empty* as **a soap bubble**

Moreover, when similes have a double *as* the scalar interpretation is natural. For example we have proverbial similes like *as black as pitch, as green as grass*, and *as smooth as a millpond* in which Grounds are highly salient – though perhaps not always logically necessary – features of Vehicles.

When *as* is used as a (subordinating) conjunction linking two clauses a further category of simile emerges which I shall call Quasi-Literal. While Literal simile interpretations make comparisons between two states of affairs in the same temporal and spatial context, with a consequent interchangeability between Topic and Vehicle, in Quasi-Literal ones the Vehicle participates in states of affairs in some other hypothetical context, an unrealized world. In the following examples we detect a progressive distancing from the Topic context in the simile adverbial clauses:

PM47    **the few birds and the splashes of their dung** *were visible* as **the patches of foam** *were visible* on the water

TI203    he seized a branch *and struck* again and again at the log as **Tanakil** had *struck* at **Liku**

TS41    they must have cut slices and *piled* them, as **children** playing at chequers will *pile* one **counter** on another

FF57    Mercifully you cannot see it, as **Moses** could not see it though he asked to.

TS55–6    He caressed it gently, cradling it in his arms and *looking at* it all over as a **mother** might *examine* **her baby**.

PM47 is Literal since both dung and foam are visible at the same time in the same context. The tense in TI203 shows that the comparison is between the present and the past, so temporal context is not shared. In TS41 we have a comparison between a probable state of affairs in the novel, and typical behaviour of children in the world (of that novel), rather than as in TI203 and FF57 a token of behaviour. In FF57 the comparison reaches out to the context of another (fictional) text, the Old Testament. TS55–6 is more thoroughly Quasi-Literal than the others; the *might* signals that it is entirely unreal or hypothetical.

## 8.2.4. Phenomenalistic and Subjective Grounds

Since *might* is often used as a Subjective marker this is a convenient point to discuss the ways in which Subjective Grounds are specified. With the clauses introduced by *as though/if* we move even further away from the world of actual happenings into a hypothetical or unreal world, which can only be described as very iffy:

TI22     After these jerks *he would lean on* his thorn bush as though **he were sliding down it.**

TI12     He *opened his eyes again* as if **he were waking out of a dream.**

TI107    they [*the cries*] *were cut off suddenly* as though **someone had clapped a hand over her mouth**

The first clauses in these examples give perceptual evidence for the less than real/certain state of affairs in the second clause. If that state of affairs were real, rather than imaginary in a Phenomenalistic way, then the first clause would provide Grounds for that reality.

Conjunctive links between Grounds and Phenomenalistic metaphors can also be made by *"so that"*, and *"X was so* + adjective + *that"*:

TI137    the ivy *spread upwards and downwards in a dark tangle* so that they might* have been **sitting in a bush on the ground**

TI176    **they had consumed each other** rather than <u>lain together</u> so that *there was blood on the woman's face and the man's shoulder*

The unreal state of affairs in the V-term clause may be due to the narrator's misperception (TI137), but in TI176 it results from the character's misperception, giving us a Subjective metaphor/simile. And many of the previous examples taken from *The Inheritors* can be interpreted Subjectively, since Golding exploits this tension between Lok's Neanderthal fictional point of view and the modern world-view of writer and reader. Here *so that* might mean 'so that Lok perceived it to be the case that . . . '. Subjective construal is clear in TI176 (strictly a case of Postposed Grounds), where Lok describes the new people's creative, ecstatic, almost sadistic love-making, a phenomenon beyond his experience or comprehension. For these Grounds to produce an Illusion of a Subjective kind there must be a reasonably high degree of association between Vehicle and Grounds (Table 8.2, columns X or Y): e.g. cannibalism and being covered in blood.

To sum up: in our discussion of Ground-specifying similes we noted two major structures: (a) prepositional phrases as adverbials introduced by *like* and *as*; and (b) *as* (*if/though*) as conjunction, co-ordinating or subordinating clauses. We found that (b) was associated with Subjective metaphor especially of the Phenomenalistic variety.

### 8.2.5. *Of*-genitives

We have already dealt with this construction as a means of supplying Topics. But Ground Indicating terms can also figure as the first of the two noun phrases linked by *of*:

FF24    <u>His moustache</u> seemed of *the texture* and *whiteness* of **swan's feathers**. [boxes 9 and 8, respectively]

FF184   <u>It</u> *struck with the frantic writhing and viciousness* of **a captive snake**. [box 8]

TI143   They had in <u>their bodies</u> *the bending grace* of **a young bough**. [boxes 8/9]

TI138   <u>It</u> was more *the colour* of **the big fungi**, the ears that the people ate. [box 9]

These certainly demand Precision interpretations. Grounds are generally conveyed by derived forms – nominalizations of adjectives ("whiteness", "viciousness"), or of verbs ("writhing"), or nouns with some adjectival equivalent ("grace", cf. *graceful*). Sometimes they may be general nouns associated with perceptual properties, e.g. touch ("texture") or sight ("colour") which is likely to locate them in box 9. (At least, they are not salient, though they may be logically necessary.)

We have now completed our survey of Preposed G-terms, and found that the main structures are premodifying adjectives, *like* and *as* structures introducing adverbials, and the genitive construction. The main points to emerge are:

- Vehicles are often important in giving Precision to the Grounds and in such cases strictly speaking we have Ground *Indication* rather than specification.

- Precision interpretations with Ground Indication enable us to use some of the unlikely boxes in our figure, for example those in column X, without necessarily implying redundancy or tautology.

- We discovered that the uses of *as* and *like* can be categorized as
  Literal
  Quasi-Literal
  Phenomenalistic/Subjective
depending upon the degrees of shared context, actuality and typicality of the Topic and Vehicle.

We will now pass to a consideration of Postposed Grounds.

## 8.3. POSTPOSED GROUNDS

### 8.3.1. V-term premodifiers with G-term heads

The first two categories of syntactic structure for Postposed Grounds, premodifying nouns and 's-Genitives, are transformational equivalents of preposed structures:

DV125  in the way that did not suit <u>him</u> [Stanhope] or his **hawk**'s *face*. [cf. the face of a hawk]

FF55  the **fish 'n' chip** *smell* of <u>the engine oil</u> [cf. the smell of fish 'n' chips]

So we might compare the effects of the preposing and postposing versions. One' possible difference, it seems to me, is that contradiction is stronger with preposing: while a man cannot literally be said to have the face of a hawk, even less can he be said to have a hawk's face. This extra Contradictoriness may arise from the V-term occurring first, giving a momentary primacy and importance to the noun. A similarity is that, whether preposed or postposed, modifiers can be used descriptively to fill lexical gaps by giving extra Precision to sensations and perceptions.

With Postposed Grounds the need to give more specificity to colour and shape lexis is evidenced by the productivity of suffixed compounds ending in *-shaped* and *-coloured* (FF64, LF94), as well as by compounds which have a more specific colour word as their second element (FF157, DV133):

FF64  he moved away, sat down in a **mother**-*shaped* **chair** by the dead fire

LF94  no one had seen the **mulberry**-*coloured* **birthmark** again

FF157  **cherry** red

DV133  **smoke**-grey hair

## ■ EXERCISE

*In which column of the matrix in Table 8.2 would you place the Grounds of FF157 and PM19?*

*PM19  <u>it [ the sea-water ]</u> was **bottle**-green*

FF157 is in Y if not X, whereas PM19 is closer to Z. While FF157 can be interpreted as 'the redness of a cherry' PM19 has to be paraphrased 'the green of bottles when they are green' because bottles can be many other colours.

### 8.3.2. Verbless clauses

When we turn to verbless clauses, typically Postposed adjectives, we notice a further contrast with the Preposed forms.

PM132–3  <u>I</u> am **an album of snapshots**, *random*, a whole show of trailers of old films.

FF29  **the transparency** which is <u>myself</u> floats through life like **a bubble**, *empty* of guilt, *empty* of anything

Postmodifying adjectives, unlike the premodifying ones we discussed in section 8.2.1, involve Assignment (Ferris 1993: 51–3, 147–50) – one argument, I suppose, for calling them clauses. So they are non-restrictive

241

and not semantically relative. Compare *I am a random album of snapshots* with *I am an album of snapshots, random . . ..* This means that Postposed adjectives can *specify* Grounds whereas Preposed ones might be *Indicating* them. Notice too how, with the Postposed examples, the metaphor can produce a strong initial sense of contradiction, an enigma only later followed by a resolution as in PM132–3 and FF29.

### 8.3.3. Non-finite clauses

It is obvious enough that Assignment is involved where the Postposed clause contains a verb, the case in this and the following sections 8.3.3 to 8.3.6.

> TS107    the great house, **the ark**, the refuge, **a ship** *to contain* all these *people*
>
> PM175    the lobsters wore **armour** *to protect them* from the enormous pressure of the sky

There is a tendency for non-finite clause Grounds to be in column X or row A. In PM175 the verbs make explicit a process which is integral to the meaning of the noun V-term, e.g. the process of protection is the whole purpose of armour. In TI134 we have an example of how the Grounds can be used to work out a Topic, stage V of Table 8.1 guiding us to stage IV.

> TI134    **their seeds were in his nose,** *making him* yawn and *sneeze*

Lok, after a sleepless night, has caught a cold, an experience he has never had before, and so he believes, in a Subjective metaphor, that fluffy seeds are blocking his nose. We work out this Topic from the symptoms he gives, translating, so to speak, from the mind-set of Lok into our own. But we can only do so because there is a high degree of association between Grounds and Topic, sneezing and having a cold.

FF36 is a marvellous example, already discussed at length (section 4.4.2), of how the similarity on which the metaphorical interpretation depends is built *in situ*, as it were, rather than relying on prefabricated associations: we see amoebas in a quite different light, poised between unlimited evolution and ultimate primitiveness.

> FF36    <u>We</u> are an **amoeba**, *perhaps waiting to evolve . . . perhaps not.*

There is little expectation here, especially about the first half of the Grounds, so the example belongs near to box 9.

### 8.3.4. Relative clauses

A particularly frequent way of specifying Grounds is the relative clause. Traditionally a distinction is drawn between restrictive (Precision) and non-restrictive relative clauses. The non-restrictive type is semantically equivalent to a co-ordinated clause, while the restrictive type provides Precision by identifying a subset from the set identified by the noun phrase it postmodifies.

(6) Non-restrictive
The Bible, which has been retranslated, remains a bestseller. = 'The Bible has been retranslated and remains a bestseller'.

(7) Restrictive
The woman who is approaching us seems to be somebody I know. = 'Out of the set of women the one approaching us is somebody I know'.

(Quirk *et al.* 1985: 1247)

A traditional grammatical rule states that the relative pronoun *that* cannot precede the non-restrictive variety (*ibid.*: 1257).

## ■ EXERCISE

*Do you think this grammatical rule applies in DV18?*

DV18    *It seemed that a word was* **a golfball** *of a thing* that he could just about manage to get through his mouth *though it deformed his face in the passage.*

However, it seems quite easy to find examples of V-terms qualified non-restrictively by relative clause G-terms introduced by *that*.

LF63    the heat became **a blow** *that they ducked*

I cannot believe that in LF63 and DV18 we are being invited to pick out one instance of a blow or of a golfball from a set. LF63 seems to mean 'the heat became a blow and they ducked it'. And surely in DV18 we are not being asked to identify particular kinds of golfball which can function as Vehicles of the metaphor in distinction to other kinds that cannot. Extra evidence of their non-restrictive nature is the lack of definiteness – proto-typically restrictive uses will have a cataphoric definite article implying the more definite subset created by the relative clause which follows. e.g. *the books that are lying on the table*.

This evidence suggests there is something special about the semantics of lexical metaphor which overrides a rule which may be perfectly valid for literal language. If we think about it, how could a relative clause specifying a G-term be restrictive in any case? In Active metaphors, the Vehicle is, after all, not actually being referred to by the noun phrase, so that the question of using the relative clause to narrow down and identify the referent from a subset of Vehicles does not arise. The very idea that the relative clauses could be used to distinguish among different instances of the Vehicle seems a non-starter and yet the use of *that* suggests that this is what is going on. This seems another instance of metaphor creating semantic tension between syntactic and lexical semantics.

When Grounds belong in column X the semantics of the relative clause cannot be restrictive in any case, as in FF23.

FF23    I could not catch **this particular signature** of being *which made her unique.*

DV16    **The screen** *that conceals the working of things* had shuddered and moved.

DV16 is worth considering as a candidate for box 2, so far unfilled by any of our previous examples. It illustrates how noun V-terms hold on to their metaphorical life more tenaciously than verb V-terms. Actually "conceals" is the V-term of a Tired metaphor. We interpret according to Substitution: the metaphor loses little by being reduced to a paraphrase 'that which conceals the working of things', so the distinction between Topic and Grounds disappears. I locate it in box 2 rather than box 1, since screens can be designed for purposes of protection as well as concealment: riot police use transparent plastic screens.

### 8.3.5. Specification by verb phrase (predicate)

A rather subtle structure involves predicating a verb of a V-term which could also be literally predicated of a T-term. Usually the T-term is not stated, so that the Ground may guide us to the Topic, e.g. in PM163, in the same way as it did in TI134.

PM163    "Why drag in good and evil when **the serpent** *lies coiled* in my own body?"

LF157    Overhead **the cannon** *boomed* again.

LF270    the **rose** of indignation *faded* slowly from his cheeks

TS138    for **his angel** was a great weight of glory to bear and *bent* his spine

The unstated Topics are the gut (PM163) (symbolically reducing evil in general to greed in particular), thunder (LF157), and blushing (LF270). This last example is on the borderline of Ground specification and extension of metaphor since *fade* is ambiguous between 'lose colour' and 'diminish'. TS138 is Subjective: Jocelin believes in an angel bending and spreading warmth through his back, but the reader has doubts: it seems likely that he is suffering from spinal tuberculosis and its associated symptoms, spinal curvature and "gargoylism". (This medical term probably suggested to Golding the choice of spinal tuberculosis as the disease Jocelin mistakes for an angelic inspiration to add a spire to a medieval cathedral.)

We might note that these predicative Grounds can also be Preposed:

TI19    Liku took the little Oa from her mouth and *rubbed* **her mop** of
hair against Lok's thigh.

FF140   I got the cigarette into the flame and *sucked* at the white **teat**.

As we would predict these predicate G-terms must either be in column X or
Y to be recognized.

Now that we have looked at predicate and relative clause structures we
should distinguish their semantic effects. First, the relative clause, unlike
predicates, operates at a different rank from the Vehicle, and is a separate
clause, part of the noun phrase. This means that it is more detachable and
recognizable as a discrete constituent where its Ground-specifying function
becomes more obvious. By contrast the predicate structure smuggles in the
Grounds surreptitiously. The predicate makes possible a barely noticed
transition from the metaphorical to the literal level: e.g. "boomed" in
LF157 acts like a common chord between two keys enabling a smooth
modulation.

Second, relative clauses will combine more easily with the Copula (or
other Relational process verbs) and *of*-genitive when these latter are used
for Topic specifications, e.g. LF63, DV18 (p. 243), FF23 (p. 244) or
LF167:

LF167   They were glad to touch the brown backs of **the fence** *that hemmed in*
the terror and made it governable.

### 8.3.6. Prepositional phrases

Prepositional phrases are less common than clauses for Postposed specification of Grounds, whether these are verbless clauses specifying with
adjectives (section 8.3.2), or verb clauses (sections 8.3.3–5.). This is
because Grounds tend to involve single properties and so are more readily
conveyed by verbs or adjectives. As a result the relatively few examples of
prepositional phrase postposed Grounds are nominalizations of verbs
(TS89 and FF69) or adjectives (FF111 and LF7) in the noun phrase
complementing the preposition:

TS89    Let him [Roger Mason] settle it, **my slave** *for the work*. [box 4]

FF 69   I see now the **sausage** hands *with discolorations of red and blue*.
[box 8]

FF111   there were huge **desert** areas *of silence* [box 8]

LF7     the long scar was **a bath** *of heat* [box 8]

TS89, in box 4 rather than 8, is the exception: work is an intrinsic part of
the role of slave, and Roger, the master mason supervising the erection of
the spire, is strongly associated with work by contingency.

## 8.3.7. Grounds of verb V-terms

We have completed our survey of Ground specification for noun V-terms, and we now shift our attention to verbs. As we would expect, the means of qualifying a verb meaning, which is a property, will probably be adverbials, either adverbs or prepositional phrases.

LF167   the centre of the ring **yawned** *emptily*

TS53   the building **sweating** now *with damp*

TI171   the flames came **squirting** *out of* the top of the pile

TI115   the log stayed where it was and the man in the back end **dug** his **brown leaf** *into* the water every now and then

Perhaps one reason noun metaphors could have verb predicates providing Grounds (8.3.5) was the ease with which verb metaphors become Inactive. But as I suggested in section 3.1.5, prepositions and adverbs have an even more slippery hold on metaphoric activity, so that they in turn can provide Grounds. In LF27 we could say that "rose" has the G-term "faded" which is in turn given the G-term "slowly", so that as we progress through the clause we gradually subside to the literal level (a process that is almost iconic of fading).

LF27   the **rose** of indignation *faded slowly* from his cheeks

Since verbs are, compared with nouns, rather lean in their semantic specifications, representing properties (single features) rather than entities (multiple features), it is not surprising that many of their Grounds fall into or close to column X. So there is something tautological about LF167 and TS53. As a result the Topic–Ground distinction tends to disappear, and we could easily paraphrase by omitting the Vehicle or the Ground:

TS53   → the building sweating,

LF167   → the centre of the ring was empty

However a full Substitution interpretation can be avoided if other Grounds can be postulated, for instance in LF167 [wideness] might be a further Ground. Let's look at the rather interesting example TI115. Lok is describing to us an activity with which we as readers are familiar, but which he has never encountered: one of the new people paddling a canoe. In fact he has never seen a paddle which he mistakes for a brown leaf, so the metaphor is Subjective. We could formalize the interpretation as in (8) at three levels:

| (8) | T-terms | The man | [stuck] | his | [paddle] | *into* | *the water* |
|---|---|---|---|---|---|---|---|
| | V-terms | (The man) | **dug** | (his) | [spade] | *into* | [the earth] |
| | V-term | | | | **brown leaf** | | |

Besides the Grounds provided overtly – digging with a spade and paddling with a canoe involve putting both paddle and spade *into* a substance – there are many other possibilities for Grounds: the shape of a paddle and the shape of a spade; the repeated downward movement of both; and displacement of the relatively solid substance into which they penetrate.

## 8.4. PSEUDO-GROUNDS

<u>Pseudo-grounds</u> occur when what appears to be a G-term is in fact ambiguous, and one of the meanings is colligationally compatible with the V-term, while the other is not. Of course it will appear to be a G-term, precisely because it is an Inactive verb or adjective metaphor which has become Lexicalized, whereas its noun .V-term is relatively Active. In this sense we could take "faded" in LF27 as a Pseudo-ground. Usually the reason the Pseudo-G-term is ambiguous and Inactive is that it expresses a Root Analogy as in the SOUND = TOUCH synaesthesia of TS136, the ACTIVITY = MOVEMENT FORWARD of DV133. At other times the ambiguity is less obviously metaphorical, as in TI12. In fact "stretching", because there is no conventional Root Analogy behind the ambiguity, seems to be a successful pun.

TS136   the scream was short and *sharp*, like the cruel **blade of a knife**
DV133   as if the algebra was **glue** *they were stuck in*
TI12     the water was . . . **waking up**, *stretching* on the right into wildernesses of impassable swamp

These Pseudo-grounds may be Preposed or Postposed with quite different effects. With the Postposed the preceding V-term alerts us to the metaphor and may revitalize the Inactive metaphor contained in the pseudo-Ground (DV133). When Preposed we may hardly notice Pseudo-grounds as they make an imperceptible ramp upwards to the more obviously metaphorical noun phrase (TS136). But look how in LF83 the rather inert idiom, *lost in thought*, picks up some metaphorical momentum from the V-term "a maze" (itself perhaps unconsciously related to or punning on *amaze*).

LF83   He *lost* himself in **a maze** of <u>thoughts</u>.

I compare cases of Pseudo-grounds with cases of genuine predicate

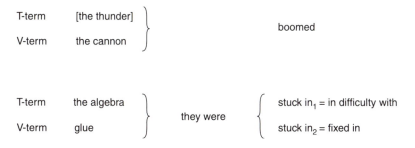

*Figure 8.1* Predicate Grounds and Pseudo-grounds

Ground specification in Figure 8.1. In the genuine case *boomed* has only one meaning, but with the Pseudo-ground I have indicated the double meaning by subscripts.

## 8.5. GROUNDS AT GREATER DISTANCES

Though there is no scope for a thorough investigation of Grounds functioning across sentence boundaries in this chapter, to some extent the next chapter will take up the issue when it deals with extended metaphors. As I have pointed out, in metaphors whose Grounds depend upon Analogy, extension itself constitutes Grounds, as in TI50.

> TI50    Delicately he sampled the air, *drawing a stream into* his nostrils and *allowing it to remain there until* his blood *had warmed it* and the scent was accessible. He performed miracles of perception in **the cavern** of his nose.

(In TI50 the features of the Vehicle which provide Grounds depend on the contingencies of the previous context. We have to remind ourselves of the cavern which Lok's tribe inhabit, with its fire that draws in the cold air from outside and then warms it.)

The greater the distance between V-term and G-term the more important will be the distinction between Preposed Grounds and Postposed Grounds. Since the metaphorical V-term is more foregrounded than the G-terms, it is unlikely that Preposed Grounds in TI50 could be perceived as readily as the Postposed ones in FF49.

> FF49    Philip became my **shadow**. Living *near* the toughest of the lot he was protected. Since *he was so close I could not run after him.*

For another example look at FF241. I would expect rather different processing of the metaphor for the text as it stands compared with a hypothetical minimal text made up of the second sentence followed by the eighth, (2) ∧ (8), where the distance between Preposed Ground and Vehicle is shorter; and in turn differences between hypothetical texts comprising sentences (8) ∧ (2) and (8) ∧ (1) ∧ (3) ∧ (4) ∧ (2), where the Grounds are Postposed with variation in distance (Lim 1993).

> FF241    The three tall glass windows on our left were too big for frequent cleaning, so that although they let the light in they qualified it [1]. There were no pictures or hangings, though the *light-green* room cried out for both [2]. There was little enough fabric anywhere [3]. There was only a scatter of heavy round tables, chairs and one or two sofas arranged by the farther wall [4]. There was a scatter of women too, but left random as the furniture [5]. One held a ball of string [6]. Another stood looking out of the middle window, unnaturally still like the ungainly statue on the lawn [7]. Nurse knew her way about this **aquarium** [8].

## ■ EXERCISE

*Read through TS94 quickly.*

> TS94  *The laugh came out and the tower sucked it up. That was bad, he*
> *thought. I mustn't do that again. He looked back at Roger Mason, but*
> *the master builder was following the workmen, ascending methodically,*
> *heavily, ladder after ladder. Jocelin craned back, and watched him*
> *climb where the square chimney with its geometrical birds was soaring*
> *to heaven height.*

*Now, without reading from the beginning again, see if you can remember*
*any Grounds for the V-term ten words from the end.*

In TS94, the distance between Preposed G-terms and V-term is so great that
I wonder whether a reader reading at normal speed, rather than a punctilious
textlinguist, would detect "sucked it up" as G-terms for chimney.

Increasing distance creates problems for Postposed Grounds too. The
longer the distance the more likely it is for the reader to construct interim
Grounds out of his own head without textual support. And in this case there
is always the risk that these will be contradicted or overridden by the
Grounds finally provided, cancelling out an existing Contextual Implication, with a resulting waste of Processing Effort. The following seems to be
a good example:

> DV81  So then there was a kind of* confused **charade** in which Edwin Bell,
> his privates still *concealed by* fists as well as *clothes*, ducked and
> wove through the saried marketeers, followed as closely as possible
> by Pedigree while *both of them talked at once as though silence would*
> *allow something else to be heard*, something deadly. *It turned in the*
> *end* – when they had reached Sprawsons and there was a clear
> danger of Pedigree coming right upstairs, past the solicitor's office,
> right up to the flat – *into a naked avowal*, a terrified prohibition from
> Edwin Bell.

When the V-term "charade" first appeared I first interpreted it along the
lines of 'a ridiculous and awkward series of actions which draw the attention of onlookers, without them being able to guess the purpose or meaning'. The actual Postposed Grounds depend on the fact that in the parlour
game of charades dressing up is common; that in the version that allows
speaking the correct strategy is to mention the syllable without giving it
undue prominence – for both speakers to talk at once would be an excellent
tactic; that eventually the acting team has to state the intended word
conveyed by the action/dialogue of the playlet, the "naked avowal".
Though some of these specified Grounds coincide with my initial ones
the others are less strongly associated with the Vehicle than the interim
ones were, so they give quite a different emphasis to the interpretation.

We note that in DV81 the V-term is introduced at the beginning of the paragraph, and placing it there or at the end gives it a macrothematic prominence, which might alert us to the possibility of Grounds; as though the initial or final sentence uses a Vehicle to sum up the scattered Grounds elaborated in the body of the paragraph. In fact one solution to the problems of Grounds at a distance is to state the V-term both at the beginning and the end of the text, as in (9), an advert for Meyer kitchenware. The visual accompanying this ad (Plate 1) has a saucepan filled with dark blue crystals (meant to be sapphires, though probably copper sulphate). One Ground depends upon the knowledge that sapphires and jewels in general are produced or "formed" or "tempered" at very high temperatures.

### The jewel in our crown

(9)  Our Tensl range of cookware, like most *precious* things, *doesn't reveal all its secrets at first glance*. Its elegant *good looks* serve to disguise a formidable *strength and durability*.

Formed from *beautiful*, heavy-gauge, Profinish aluminium, Tensl cookware heats evenly, to eliminate hotspots and ensure burn free cooking.

*Tempered* by a specialist process, the surface of the metal actually changes – to resemble *the structure* of **sapphire** – one of the *hardest* and *most beautiful precious* stones on Earth. Profinish will not taint the colour or flavour of even the most delicate of sauces, and by incorporating stainless steel handles and *heat tempered* Cook 'N Look lids, the Tensl range is always a joy to use.

The result is a range of cookware that is unsurpassed for *durability and beauty* of design. For these reasons we are quite happy to give each piece of Tensl cookware a lifetime guarantee.

Once you let **the jewel in our crown** take pride of place in your kitchen you will discover the secret of truly successful and enjoyable cooking.

(GH159, my boldening and italics)

## 8.6. SUMMARY: THE POSITIONING OF G-TERMS

First, let's summarize our findings about the positioning of Grounds in the boxes on our matrix Table 8.2.

● Column Y boxes 5 and 8 are the most interactively satisfactory and the most common, at least as far as the Golding corpus is concerned. The reason that boxes 5 and 8 are so popular lies in the reconceptualizing nature of metaphor. That is to say, if we are attempting an unconventional classification, then we will not highlight those features which are already critical for conventional classification, which will be in row A. A separate reason for the popularity of box 8 is the ultimately Ascriptive nature of many metaphors.

Though Y is a straightforward choice, columns X and Z are altogether more problematic.

*Plate 1* Advertisement for Meyer cookware; courtesy of Meyer (UK) Limited

251

- Column Z is impossible in some cases: G-terms which premodify T-terms and predicate G-terms with V-term Subject/Object must be in columns X or Y to be recognized. However column Z box 9 is a possibility for Precision or restrictive interpretations.
- Grounds in column Z box 6 and in column X box 7 are less satisfactory from an Interactive point of view, and in those cases it is common to involve further unstated Grounds in the interpretation.
- Column X cannot, by definition, accommodate Precision/restrictive interpretations, and the Grounds in box 7 have decorative tendencies.

Besides the findings on the semantic nature of the Grounds, this chapter also made other important observations:

- There is a trend for Phenomenalistic and Subjective metaphors to be associated with *as if/though* similes and *so that* clauses.
- To add to our inventory of syntactic–semantic ambiguities introduced by metaphor (7.9.2) we have the non-restrictive/restrictive ambiguity with *that* relative clauses.
- We demonstrated that the Postposed Grounds which involved Assignment were unlikely to be restrictive.
- We showed that whether Grounds are Preposed or Postposed makes considerable differences to interpretation when they are distant from the V-term, and this may lead to irrelevant Processing Effort.

This chapter was organized according to the distinction between Postposed and Preposed Grounds. And Table 8.1 also gives an indication of the relative syntactic prominence of V-term and G-term in the different structures surveyed. The psychological processing differences brought about by these distinctions would be an interesting area of empirical research.

## 8.7. OVERVIEW OF THE CLINES OF METAPHORIC FORCE

Since we have now completed our discussion of the contribution of syntax to metaphorical interpretation, we should take another look at our clines of metaphoricity as in Figure 8.2 (a repetition, for convenience sake, of Figure 1.4). Chapter 1 illustrated in some detail clines (1) and (2); at the end of Chapter 6 we summarized our findings on the Marking cline (3), and at the end of Chapter 7 we brought together our scattered comments on Contradictoriness (4). But we can now summarize our findings on cline (5), Explicitness.

Table 6.2 which we introduced at the beginning of Chapter 6, reproduced here as Table 8.4, provides a reasonably neat summary of how syntactic structures can add more or less explicitness to the metaphor, so that the risk of misinterpretations is kept to a minimum. But to integrate our comments with the findings of the present chapter we could relabel this cline in terms

(1) Approximative Similarity ——————————— Distant Similarity/Analogy

(2) Conventionality ——————————— Unconventionality

(3) Marking ——————————— No Marking

(4) Non-contradictoriness ——————————— Contradictoriness

(5) Explicitness ——————————— Inexplicitness

*Figure 8.2* Five metaphorical clines

*Table 8.4* The syntactic configuration of metaphor

| V-term | T-term | G-term | Marker | Example |
|---|---|---|---|---|
| Yes | Yes | Yes | Yes | One or two tupaia species *run along branches* like* **squirrels**. |
| Yes | Yes | No | Yes | The movement [of the bowels] (is) like* **creamed soup**. The boy was **raven**ous*. |
| Yes | No | Yes | Yes | They pull themselves up into a kind of * *green* **aquarium** under the branches. |
| Yes | Yes | Yes | No | **The bones** of the land, lumps of *smooth grey* rock. |
| Yes | No | No | Yes | A kind of * **autumn** fell over the first grade. |
| Yes | Yes | No | No | Housework is **a treadmill**. **The treadmill** of housework. Housework, **that treadmill**. |
| Yes | No | Yes | No | *Silly* **ass**! |
| Yes | No | No | No | Attach **the mouse** to the keyboard. |
| (Colligation) | Yes | No | No | The **naked** shingles (of the world). Winds **stampeding** the fields. |

of Vehicular prominence as opposed to Ground or Topic prominence. Clearly the lower we go down Table 8.4 the more prominence, in one sense, is given to the V-term, because the other T-terms and G-terms disappear.

Turn now to Table 8.5. In some cases, as well as V-terms, T-terms (columns 2 and 4) and/or G-terms (columns 3 and 5) are present. In these cases we can pick out the syntactic structures which give more prominence

*Table 8.5* Vehicle prominence in syntax

| Structure | Syntax T/V | Syntax G/V | Order T/V | Order G/V |
|---|---|---|---|---|
| Genitive | √ | | √ | √ |
| Postnominal verbless clause | | √ | | √ |
| Postnominal non-finite clause | | √ | | √ |
| Relative clause | | √ | | √ |
| Adverbials for verb V-terms | | √ | | √ |
| Suffixed premodifier | | | √ | |
| Noun premodifier | | | √ | |

to the V-term (ticked), through syntactic prominence (columns 2 and 3), or order (columns 4 and 5). We notice again why the *of*-Genitive might be a very popular construction in creating prominence of these kinds (Brooke-Rose 1958: 288).

However, note that order is somewhat equivocal as a criterion for prominence. Prominence by occurring first, which is what has been marked in the table, might be outweighed by the principle of end-weight, which states that the focus of the most important new information will be the end of the clause (Halliday 1994: 299–300).

As Sperber and Wilson (1986: 215–17) point out, the most felicitous expressions will be those where the most relevant information is the most prominent. This prominence would presumably involve syntactic prominence or end-weight focus. For example there is something ironic or playful about smuggling in the most unexpected or startling information in a parenthesis:

> (10) Browning was an adept at rhyme, but Tennyson was not without moments of burlesque agility (he once found an apt rhyme for the name Friswell). (quoted from Nash 1980: 148)

A third aspect of Vehicle prominence was explored in Chapter 3 where we noted the importance of imagery in metaphorical processing. The hypothesis was that noun phrase V-terms can involve imagery more directly than other word-classes, which can only do so through Vehicle-construction. Remember too that in investigating cline 2, in Chapter 1 we noted that the difference between Active and Inactive metaphor is precisely that Active interpretations make the Vehicle more prominent, wiring it in series, as it were, with the Topic/Grounds. In Chapters 6, 7 and 8 we have investigated the local means by which text raises awareness of metaphorical language use, and guides the interpretation of the metaphor. The next chapter takes a wider perspective on the effect of co-text on interpretation, by considering the ways metaphors interact in texts. We shall also see that in the Phenomenalistic metaphor constituted by the imaginary world of literary texts, the Vehicle achieves an extreme prominence.

# 9

# THE INTERPLAY OF
# METAPHORS

## 9.1. INTRODUCTION: OVERVIEW OF THE FRAMEWORK

In this chapter I show how a theoretical framework can be built up to explain the interplay between metaphors within texts. In fact, in the interests of psychological realism, it ought to be extended in this way, since metaphoric processing depends upon both local and global metaphoricity and they interact with each other (Steen 1994: 119). The texts which provide my main examples are *Macbeth*, *Paradise Lost* (Book 1), *The Rainbow* by D.H. Lawrence and six early novels of William Golding. After a schematic overview of the interrelations and other complicating processes (section 9.1), I illustrate each interrelation in turn (sections 9.2–9.7). I then focus on three complicating processes, compounding, literalization (section 9.9) and overdescription (section 9.10), and relate the last two to symbolization (section 9.11), one of the distinctive features of literary texts.

The framework I propose for studying the interplay of metaphors, defines the interrelation of metaphors according to two factors – the semantic/real world relations of their separate Topics and Vehicles, coupled with the co-textual relations between their corresponding V-terms and T-terms. Figure 9.1 diagrams these relations.

First, and simplest, is the Repetition of a metaphor. This occurs when a V-term is repeated, referring to the same Topic on each occasion.

Next follow the complementary pair Multivalency and Diversification. In Multivalency the V-term is again repeated, but the Topic differs with each repetition. With Diversification, by contrast, the Topic remains the same, but the V-terms differ. Note that Diversification rules out any syntactic relation between the two different V-terms, which would amount to Mixing.

Extension generally occurs when the V-terms belong to the same lexical set. More specifically in Articulated Extension there is a syntactic link between the two V-terms, which parallels the relation between the two Topics, hence the term *Articulated*. This syntactic relationship is indicated

255

in Figure 9.1 by a vertical line. Extension can become allegory: <u>Allegory</u> proper when the Topics are specified, <u>Quasi-allegory</u> when not.

The remaining two kinds of relationship are <u>Mixing</u> and <u>Modification</u>. Mixing occurs when two V-terms are put into a syntactic relationship with each other, while their conventional referents, the Vehicles, can contract no such corresponding relationship to each other in the world, hence the horizontal line breaking the vertical in the bottom right corner of Figure 9.1. So, though the two Topics can relate, and their T-terms could articulate, the two V-terms are, as it were, dislocated.

In Modification the relationship between the two V-terms is best conceived as a lexical one. One V-term may be the hyponym, superordinate, or synonym of the other, for example; or more vaguely, the V-terms may be members of the same lexical set.

These seven kinds of relation between metaphors are further complicated by three other processes. The first of these, <u>Literalization</u> of Vehicles, occurs frequently in all of the main texts cited. A lexical item may be used literally at one point in the text and at another point as a V-term. Sometimes <u>Reversal</u> may even occur, in which the two referents involved in the metaphor remain the same but exchange Vehicle and Topic roles. In the second process, <u>Overdescription</u>, descriptive details, insignificant in terms of character or plot, are spelt out with what seems unnecessary frequency or prolixity. The third process is <u>Compounding</u> metaphor, by enclosing one metaphor inside another already established one. Let's look at these interrelations and complicating processes in more detail (Figure 9.1).

## 9.2. REPETITION

PM66    They [anemones] lay like a handful of **sweets**.
PM66    His finger closed over a **sweet**.

DV18    It seemed that <u>a word</u> was an object . . . *round and smooth*, a **golfball** of a thing that he could just about manage to get through his mouth.
DV23    The **golfballs** emerged from his mouth.

R436    She had the **ash** of <u>disillusion</u> **gritting under her teeth**.
R437    Always she was **spitting out of her mouth the ash and grit** of <u>disillusion</u>, of <u>falsity</u>.

## ■ EXERCISE

*What do you notice about the degrees of explicitness in the first two pairs PM66, PM66 and DV18, DV23?*

The first two sequences illustrate a widespread feature of repeated metaphors: the law of diminishing signalling/specification. Metaphors tend to be

REPETITION
| Vehicle 1 | Topic A |
| Vehicle 1 | Topic A |

MODIFICATION
| Vehicle 1 | Topic A |
| Vehicle 2 | Topic A |

(where there is a lexical set including V-term 1, V-term 2 etc.)

DIVERSIFICATION
| Vehicle 1 | Topic A |
| Vehicle 2 | Topic A |
| Vehicle 3 | Topic A |

MULTIVALENCY
| Vehicle 1 | Topic A |
| Vehicle 1 | Topic B |
| Vehicle 1 | Topic C |

LEXICAL EXTENSION
| Vehicle 1 | Topic A |
| Vehicle 2 | Topic B |

(where both V-terms and T-terms are members of the same lexical sets)

ARTICULATED EXTENSION
| Vehicle 1 | Topic A |
| &#124; | |
| Vehicle 2 | Topic B |

MIXING
| Vehicle 1 | Topic A |
| + | |
| Vehicle 2 | Topic B |

*Figure 9.1* Types of metaphoric interplay

marked when they first occur, so that the first of the sequence is often a simile, as in the first pair. And Topic or Grounds will have a fuller specification on the first occurrence, with reduced specification on subsequent repetitions, as in the second sequence.

Simple Repetition of Active metaphors is relatively infrequent in *Macbeth*, and *The Rainbow*. It is usually almost immediate and involves Articulated Extension of the metaphor as in R436, R437. Apparent repetitions separated by many pages are often more like Multivalency, in R147/R187 brought about by a contents/container metonymy.

R147    And he had felt so secure, as though <u>this house</u> were **the Ark** in the flood, and all the rest was drowned.

R187    <u>She</u> was **the ark**, and the rest of the world was flood.

The borders between Repetition and Modification are also unclear on occasions:

R320a    <u>She</u> was *cold and unmoved* as **a pillar of salt**.

R320b    <u>She</u> was *bright* as **a piece of moonlight**.

R322     But hard and fierce <u>she</u> had fastened upon him, *cold* as **the moon** and *burning* as a fierce **salt**. Till gradually his warm, soft iron yielded, and she was there, fierce, corrosive, seething with his destruction, seething like some cruel *corrosive* **salt** around the substance of his being.

"A pillar of salt" and "salt" are not quite a repetition: "salt" is part of the postmodifier in R320a and "pillar" seems more vital to the interpretation and more relevant to the Grounds than "salt". In addition the Grounds in R320a, which might include [coldness], are contradicted in R322 by the G-term "burning". There is a similar change of phrasing with "a piece of moonlight"/"the moon", accompanied by a change of Grounds in R320b, R322, though the G-terms "bright" and "cold" are less contradictory.

## 9.3. MULTIVALENCY

One cause of Multivalency is a lack of lexical resources necessitating the multiple use of the same lexical item to refer to different Topics. In Golding's *The Inheritors*, for example, Lok, from whose narrative viewpoint most of the novel is related, has a limited vocabulary, communicating by gesture and telepathy as much as by word of mouth, and on at least one occasion the same V-term *snake* is forced into gap-filling service twice, referring first to locks of hair (TI154), and second to a whip (TI209):

TI154    All at once the petals fell in black **snakes** that hung over her shoulders and breasts.

TI209    The old man stood by them and a dead **snake** hung from his right hand.

One of the effects of the use of multivalent Vehicles is the creation of a sense of equivalence between the Topics referred to:

TI135    The farthest reaches of <u>the river</u> burst into **flame**.

TI171    <u>The people</u> were like the **fire**.

TI199–200    The scent of <u>the honey</u> rose out of it like **the smoke and flame from a fire**.

This three-way Multivalency that uses the V-term <u>fire</u> to refer to water, the new people, and honey, makes possible comparisons between these three Topics:

TI195    The people are like the **honey** in the round stones, the new **honey** that smells of dead things and **fire**.

TI197    The new people are like a wolf and **honey**, rotten **honey** and the **river**.

TI198    Terrible they might be as the **fire** or the **river** but they drew like **honey** or meat.

Multivalency can, then, help create or prepare the way for metaphoric parallels between two or more Topics.[1] But it can also bring about or suggest certain thematic equivalences. In *Macbeth* the equivalences produced are often ironic.

M1.5.64     LADY MACBETH:   Look like the innocent flower,
                   But be the **serpent** under it.
M3.4.28     MACBETH:   There the grown **serpent** lies; the worm that's fled
                   Hath nature that in time will venom breed,
                   No teeth for the present.

Lady Macbeth advises her husband to feign innocence while planning the regicide of Duncan. The use of the same Vehicle to refer to the dead Banquo, M3.4.28, reminds us of their equivalence. Macbeth views Banquo as the same kind of threat to himself as he was to Duncan. Both, too, are party to the witches' prophecy which foretells that Banquo's son, Fleance (the "worm"), will reign on the throne once occupied by Macbeth. So, besides the Macbeth–Banquo equivalence, the multivalent *serpent* suggests the analogy:

(1)    Macbeth : Duncan : : Fleance : Macbeth

Similar thematic equivalences appear in *The Rainbow*:

R342    Ursula could not help dreaming of **Moloch**. Her god was not mild or
        gentle, neither Lamb nor Dove.
R350    If she could destroy the colliery and make all the men of Wiggiston out
        of work, she would do it. Let them starve and grub in the earth for
        roots, rather than serve such a **Moloch** as this.

Ursula, during the few weeks visiting her pit-owning uncle Tom Brangwen, develops a certain maturity – "It was in these weeks that Ursula grew up" (R351) – and Lawrence implies that in doing so she rejects her false concept of God (as Moloch), just as she rejects the coal-mining industry of Wiggiston. He also suggests a cause-and-effect relation between the two. The belief in an active, proud god, separate from the universe, results in the kind of enslavement to the machine epitomized by the colliery.

## 9.4. DIVERSIFICATION

Diversification is the opposite of Multivalency, multiple Vehicles with an identical Topic. My extensive illustration of different Vehicles for language in section 2.3.6 should remind us that Diversification and Multivalency can also be applied to the lexicon, as well as texts.

Table 9.1 shows very clearly the workings of Diversification in William Golding's *The Inheritors* by listing the main Vehicles that are variously applied by the Neanderthal tribe to the new people, *homo sapiens*.

Few of the diverse Vehicles applied to the new people have identical

Table 9.1 Diverse Vehicles for the new people in William Golding's
The Inheritors

| Topic | Vehicle | Ground | Page |
|-------|---------|--------|------|
| | cat | same smell, same teeth | 77, 98 |
| | water | horrifying, daring, inviting | 126 |
| | fire | made of yellow and white | 171 |
| | famished wolf in a tree | skill and malice | 194 |
| | honey-drink | inflicting pleasure and pain | 194 |
| | river and fall | nothing stands against them | 195 |
| the new | Oa | patient creativity | 195 |
| people | wolf | dangerous | 197 |
| | honey | attractive | 197 |
| | forest fire | fearful | 197 |
| | meat | attractive | 198 |
| | fire | terrible | 198 |
| | river | terrible | 198 |
| | hollow log | destructive | 198 |
| | winter | destructive | 198 |

Grounds specified. This might suggest that one possible reason for using Diversification is to highlight different aspects of the Topic on different occasions. Similarly diverse Grounds appear in the following sequence from Macbeth:

> M5.3.40   Can'st thou not minister to a mind diseased,
> **Pluck from the memory a rooted sorrow,**
> **Raze out the written troubles of the brain,**
> **And with some sweet oblivious antidote**
> **Cleanse the stuffed bosom of the perilous stuff**
> **Which weighs upon the heart?**

In M5.3.40, the curing of Lady Macbeth's mental disease is viewed from a number of different perspectives: the eradication from the memory of a sorrow that is deeply and long established, the complete removal from the brain of troubles that have acquired the permanence of writing, the cleansing of the bosom packed with poisonous material which is dangerously depressing the heart. However, in other cases of Diversification Grounds are shared.

## ■ EXERCISE

*Consider these diverse V-terms applied to Satan's legion of angels in* Paradise Lost. *How many lexical sets do they belong to, and what are they?*

> PL301   *His legions, angel forms, who lay entranced*
> *Thick as autumnal **leaves** that strew the brooks*
> *In Vallambrosa, where the Etrurian shades*
> *High overarched embower; or scattered **sedge***

260

> *Afloat, when with fierce winds Orion armed*
> *Hath vexed the Red Sea coast . . .*

PL337
> *Yet to their general's voice they soon obeyed*
> *Innumerable. As when the potent rod*
> *Of Amram's son in Egypt's evil day*
> *Waved round the coast, up called a pitchy cloud*
> *Of locusts . . .*

PL768
>                                    *As bees*
> *In spring time, when the son with Taurus rides,*
> *Pour forth their populous youth about the hive*
> *In clusters . . .*
> *. . . So thick the airy crowd*
> *Swarmed, and were straitened; till the signal given*
> *Behold a wonder! they but now who seemed*
> *In bigness to surpass earth's giant sons*
> *Now less than smallest dwarfs, in narrow room*
> *Throng numberless, like that pygmean race*
> *Beyond the Indian mount, or faerie elves . . .*

"Sedge" and "leaves" might be allocated to the same lexical set of vegetation. "Bees" and "locusts" to the set of insects. "Dwarfs", "pygmies" and "faerie elves" to a set of mythological humanoids. In which case we have three clusters of modified V-terms applied diversely to the same Topic. The problem arises, that, in cases where the diverse Vehicles share Grounds one can always isolate this Ground to produce a (spurious?) lexical set. So that bees, locusts, dwarves, pygmies, faerie elves can be classified as belonging to the set of small creatures. In which case one has Modification rather than Diversification.

There are two kinds of Diversification, therefore. In one type the Grounds are relatively diverse, as in Table 9.1. and M5.3.40. The motive for Diversification with diverse Grounds is often lexical gap-filling: Lok is struggling to express in his limited vocabulary the feelings incited by his experience of the new people; Macbeth is attempting to put his finger on different aspects of psychiatric therapy, and uses the metaphors to nudge his hand in the right direction. In the other kind of Diversification the Grounds are identical, as in the PL337 and PL768, where smallness and numerousness seem to be shared, and the sharing of Grounds provides a certain thematic unity to the text. If, as we have seen, Diversification with shared Grounds is close to Modification, then Diversification with diverse Grounds borders on Mixing.

## 9.5. MODIFICATION

We can discuss methods of modifying Vehicles applied to the same Topic in three sections. The first, lexical relations, illustrates the role of synonymy, polysemy, hyponymy, and superordinacy in achieving Modification.

The second, lexical sets, considers more radical Modifications. And in the third we discuss more particularly Modification through changes of scale and axis.

### 9.5.1 Lexical relations

It seems unlikely that pure synonyms would be used in close metaphorical sequences when Repetition is always an option, but there are a few examples which are quasi-synonymous.

> TS166   down in the **vaults**, the **cellarage** of my mind
> R435     She was sick with this long service at the inner commercial **shrine**.
> R436     College was barren, cheap, a **temple** converted to the most vulgar, petty commerce.

One should note, however, that "temple" (R436) achieves a quite different effect from "shrine" (R435) because it functions, potentially, as an allusion to the gospel story in which Christ drives out the money-changers from the temple in Jerusalem. Exact lexical repetition is necessary for allusions to function effectively.

Modification may also occur through the use of hyponyms (LF153, LF157) and superordinates of the first-occurring Vehicle (M1.3.108, M1.3.145).

> LF153     The thunder went off like a **gun**.
> LF157     Overhead the **cannon** boomed again.

> M1.3.108   The Thane of Cawdor lives: why do you dress me
>                 In **borrowed robes**?
> M1.3.145   New honours come upon him,
>                 Like our **strange garments**, cleave not to their mould
>                 But with the aid of use.

### 9.5.2 Lexical sets

Table 9.2 exemplifies Modification within lexical sets in *Pincher Martin* (PM), *The Rainbow* (R), Book 1 of *Paradise Lost* (PL) and *Macbeth* (M). The labels for lexical sets in the first column are not entirely adequate. There is, for example, something more specific about the items in the mammal category: small, carnivorous mammals with sharp teeth. This suggests that as the lexical set gets wider the Grounds which are shared between the metaphors become prominent. By contrast we recognize a couple of anomalies in the animal set applied to Macbeth. *Lamb* is ironic, since lambs are neither poisonous nor carnivorous; it is no accident that this Vehicle is used by Malcolm when he is dissimulating to Macduff, and constitutes part of the first lie he ever told in his life (M4.3.130–1). *Cat* also

*Table 9.2* Modification within lexical sets

| Lexical set | Vehicle | Topic | Reference |
|---|---|---|---|
| cleaning | scouring, sweeping | searching | PM52 |
| insects | spider, daddy-longlegs, mantis | Nathaniel | PM70, 100, 185 |
| film | snapshots, trailers | memories | PM133 |
| capture | net, chain, tie down | naming | PM86–7 |
| mammal | kitten, ferret, weasel, stoat | Millicent, Skrebensky | R198, 199 |
| ruler | sultan, emperor | Satan | PL348, 378 |
| bird of prey | eagle, owl, kite | Macbeth | M1.2.35, 4.2.11, 4.3.217 |
| animal | lion, serpent, cat, lamb, bear, hound | Macbeth | M1.2.35, 1.5.64, 1.9.45, 4.3.54, 5.9.2, 5.9.3 |

stands out, a contemptuous use of the word by Lady Macbeth for her husband's cowardice in hesitating to kill Duncan and thereby become king (lion).

In this connection we should also be aware that, for the Elizabethans, there was a chain of correspondences between lexical sets, so that analogies would be made from one to the other. According to this correspondence:

(2)   king : man : : eagle : bird : : lion : beast (Tillyard 1963: 42–3)

### 9.5.3 Scale and axis Modification

The third means of Modification is so common in Golding as to be distinctive of his style.

> FF25  It [the alarm clock] was an early make, round, on three short **legs**, and it held up a bell like an **umbrella** . . . The **umbrella** became a **head**, the clock beat its **head** in frenzy, trembling and jerking over the **chest** of drawers on three legs until it reached a point where the **chest** would drum in sympathy.

FF25 illustrates scale Modification: the Vehicle first applied to the clock is a human being, holding an umbrella, the bell, and standing on three short legs. But later in the extract this human being is expanded in scale, so that the clock, including the bell, becomes a head, and the drawers below it, reviving a Dead metaphor, are the chest. One might wish to regard this kind of Modification as dependent on one particular kind of synecdoche or meronymy: the first Vehicle for the clock is the whole human being, the second Vehicle for the clock is the head, part of a human being.

One of the conventional correspondences that the Elizabethans perceived was between the microcosm, the little world of man's body, and the state or the "body" politic. This is a particular kind of scale or synecdochal Modification. It does not operate straightforwardly in *Macbeth* but in conjunction with Literalization. For example, the description of Banquo's murder in M3.4.26 prepares us for the microcosm/body politic correspondence in M4.3.39:

| | |
|---|---|
| M3.4.26 | Ay, my good Lord, safe in a ditch he bides, |
| | With twenty trenched GASHES on his head; |
| M4.3.39 | I think our country sinks beneath the yoke: |
| | It weeps, it bleeds; and each new day a **gash** |
| | Is added to her wounds. |
| | [GASHES is in small capitals as it is a literal use of the V-term.] |

## 9.6. EXTENSION

Extension is generally achieved when neither Vehicles nor Topics are repeated but when several Vehicles belong to the same semantic field, the same domain, and when the Topics share a semantic field too, the same realm. In lexical terms this will mean the V-terms belong to one lexical set and the T-terms belong to another distinct lexical set. Usually the Vehicles in an extended metaphor will all be connected to some consistent image or schema. PL670 is an example of Extension, dependent on lexical sets to do with the semantic field of the body:

| | |
|---|---|
| PL670 | There stood a hill not far whose grisly top |
| | **Belched** fire and rolling smoke; the rest entire |
| | Shone with a glossy **scurf**, undoubted sign |
| | That in his **womb** was hid metallic ore. |

Since scurf (dandruff) and womb both have a part–whole relationship with a body we might call this particular kind of Extension Synecdochal.

In some cases the extension is not merely lexical but also syntactic:

| | |
|---|---|
| M4.3.61 | your wives, your daughters, |
| | Your matrons, and your maids, could not **fill up** |
| | **The cistern** of my lust |

This is an Articulated Extension as there is a syntactic relationship between the two V-terms.

## ■ EXERCISE

*Look at DV46. Can you integrate the Vehicles so that they become an extended metaphor? What image or schema do you supply to do so?*

*DV46    He was waiting for the right moment to **wrap up** his silence, **roll** it into
a weapon and **hit** Matty **over the head with it**.*

Often noun metaphors help to create the recognition of the extended
metaphor. In the exercise the colligate of the verbs has to be supplied to
construct the Vehicle image of a newspaper on which the Extension
depends. The most widely recognized category of metaphorical Extension
is allegory. In <u>Allegory</u> proper both V-terms and the T-terms are specified.
So, for example, in the famous medieval allegory *Piers Plowman* the
process of farming provides an extended analogy for the functioning of
the church (Passus XIX, lines 253ff.) and the four horses ploughing the
field are labelled as equivalents for the four evangelists Matthew, Mark,
Luke and John. In the case of Golding and Lawrence, however, there is a
tendency towards <u>Quasi-allegory</u>, by which I mean extended metaphors in
which the literal Topic level is not or cannot be specified.

### 9.6.1. Allegory

First of all consider two allegories in which the main Topics are specified:

TS8    <u>The model</u> was like **a man lying on his back**. <u>The nave</u> was **his legs
placed together**, <u>the transepts</u> on either side were **his arms outspread**.
<u>The choir</u> was **his body**; and <u>the Lady Chapel</u>, where now the services
would be held, was **his head**.

TS8 is only a small-scale Allegory, depending for its development on
Synecdochal relations between parts of the Vehicle and parts of the Topic.
We notice that Golding carefully provides all the Vehicle and T-terms
(though it is left to the reader, at this stage in the novel, to consider that a
spire is being built and supply the extra corresponding Vehicle, i.e. a
phallus).

*On Wenlock Edge*

On Wenlock Edge the wood's in trouble;
    His forest fleece the Wrekin heaves;
The gale, it plies the saplings double,
    And thick on Severn snow the leaves.                    4

'Twould blow like this through holt and hanger
    When Uricon the city stood:
'Tis the old wind in the old anger,
    But then it threshed another wood.                      8

Then, 'twas before my time, the Roman
    At yonder heaving hill would stare:

265

The blood that warms an English yeoman,
    The thoughts that hurt him, they were there.    12

There, like the wind through woods in riot,
    Through him the **gale** of <u>life</u> blew high;
The **tree** of <u>man</u> was never quiet:
    Then 'twas the Roman, now 'tis I.    16

The gale it plies the saplings double,
    It blows so hard 'twill soon be gone:
Today the Roman and his trouble
    Are ashes under Uricon.    20

(*Note*: Wenlock Edge is a steep hill in Shrophire, and the Wrekin is another wooded hill close by. *Plies* means 'bends', *holt* a small wood, *hanger* the wood on the side of a hill.)

The allegorical potential of this Housman poem only becomes apparent in lines 14 and 15, where the tree = man, gale = life equations are made explicit. Line 17 then proceeds to articulate these two Vehicles, though substituting "saplings" for "tree". On re-reading the poem we interpret the action of the gale on the wood as an extended metaphor for the effects of life on man and may be tempted to fill in, as follows, the parts of the Topic which are not specified:

(3) | *Vehicle* | *Topic* |
|---|---|
| The wood's [disturbed] | = Mankind's in trouble |
| The gale plies the saplings double | = Life bends young people double with age/pain |
| 'Twould blow like this through holt and hanger when Uricon the city stood | = Life disturbed people in the same way in Roman times, however well-established (holt) or precarious (hanger) their existence |
| But then it threshed another wood | = The people who suffered in Roman times no longer exist |
| It blows so hard 'twill soon be gone | = Life is so painful it will soon be over |

## ■ EXERCISE

*Does this Allegory depend upon lexical Extension or syntactically Articulated Extension, or both?*

In fact it depends upon both. Syntactically, in lines 3, 5, 13–14, 17; lexically, by the set "wood", "saplings", "holt", "hanger", "tree".

Incidentally, the last equivalence in this Allegory contradicts the earlier equation by shrinking the time-scale to the period of the individual's, the persona's, life. The "speaker" in the poem pursues the Grounds that gales in the real meteorological world do blow themselves out quickly, in order to present a hint of optimism: though life is disturbing and painful, or perhaps because of it, it will soon be over for me.

### 9.6.2. Quasi-allegory

We can turn to a Quasi-allegory, now, in which the T-terms are less easy to identify.

R437–8    That which she was, positively, was dark and unrevealed, it could not come forth. It was like a seed buried in dry ash. This world in which she lived was like a circle lighted by a lamp. This lighted area, lit up by man's completest consciousness, she thought was all the world: that here all was disclosed for ever. Yet all the time, within the darkness she had been aware of points of light, like the eyes of wild beasts, gleaming, penetrating, vanishing, and her soul had acknowledged in a great heave of terror only the outer darkness. This inner circle of light in which she lived and moved, wherein the trains rushed and the factories ground out their machine produce and the plants and the animals worked by the light of science and knowledge, suddenly it seemed like the area under an arc-lamp, wherein the moths and children played in the security of a blinding light, not even knowing that there was any darkness, because they stayed in the light.

But she could see the glimmer of dark movement just out of range, she saw the eyes of the wild beast gleaming from the darkness, watching the vanity of the camp fire and the sleepers; she felt the strange foolish vanity of the camp, which said "Beyond our light and order there is nothing", turning their faces always inward towards the sinking fire of illuminating consciousness, which comprised sun and stars, and the Creator, and the System of Righteousness, ignoring always the vast darkness that wheeled round about, with half-revealed shapes lurking on the edge.

Yea, and no man dared even throw a firebrand into the darkness. For if he did he was jeered to death by the others, who cried, "Fool, anti-social knave, why would you disturb us with bogeys? There *is* no darkness. We live and move and have our being within the light, and unto us is given the eternal light of knowledge, we comprise and comprehend the innermost core and issue of knowledge. Fool and knave, how dare you belittle us with the darkness?"

Nevertheless the darkness wheeled round about, with grey shadow-shapes of wild beasts, and also with dark shadow-shapes of the angels, whom the light fenced out, as it fenced out the more familiar beasts of darkness. And some, having for a moment seen the darkness, saw it bristling with the tufts of the hyena and the wolf; and some, having given up their vanity of the light, having died in their own conceit, saw the gleam in the eyes of the wolf and the hyena, that it was the flash of the sword of angels, flashing at the door to come in, that the angels in the darkness were lordly and terrible and not to be denied, like the flash of fangs.

## ■ EXERCISE

*What might the light, the darkness and the wild beasts be Vehicles for? Can you and your fellow students agree on the Topics of these allegorical Vehicles?*

Some of the Topics in this extended metaphor are perhaps easier to guess than others. It seems that the light stands for some kind of scientific, rationalist, objectivist materialism which is none the less accommodated to a religious moral code. The darkness and its beasts are, however, more enigmatic. They might represent the unconscious, the id; animal desire and instinct. However, in a process that I call <u>Compounding</u>, a further V-term, "the flash of the sword of angels", is superimposed on "the gleam in the eyes of the wolf and the hyena", suggesting that the darkness too has a spiritual or religious dimension. Of course, there would be something perverse about making the Topic of darkness explicit, as conventionally it symbolizes ignorance, and part of the elaboration of the Quasi-allegory is that hardly ever is a firebrand thrown into this darkness to find out what lurks there. To discover the Topic would be to dispel the Vehicle.

In R437–8 the development of the Quasi-allegory into a narrative is dependent on the exploiting of actual syntactic articulation as in the under-lined passage. The wild beasts' eyes gleam from the darkness; they watch the vanity of the camp fire and the sleepers; the sleepers turn their faces inwards towards the sinking fire etc.

We have seen that in discussions of extended metaphors and allegories it is useful to consider two questions: (a) whether the Extension is dependent solely on lexis, or whether it involves syntactic Articulation, either actual or potential, as well; and (b) to what extent the T-terms are specified in parallel with the V-terms.

The question also arises of how Grounds are established in extended allegorical metaphors. You will recall that Grounds can be of three kinds depending on whether they depend on Similarity, Analogy, or Analogy which gives rise to Similarity (section 4.4). In cases where the Topics of the Allegory are specified there need be no Similarity between individual Vehicle–Topic pairs. In the Housman poem 'On Wenlock Edge', there is no intrinsic Similarity between a tree and a man, apart from the rather trivial one, from a metaphorical perspective, that they are both living beings. But the relationship between the tree and a gale provides an Analogy for the relationship between man and life. This Analogy can then give rise to a Similarity: the action of the gale on saplings and of life on young humans is similar in that both humans and trees are bent double by the process. However, it is perfectly possible for there to be some Similarity established between individual pairs of Topics and Vehicles, quite independent of the Allegory. So in TS8 (p. 265) transepts do resemble arms, quite apart from their relationship with other parts of the church/body.

In the case of indeterminate Topics used by Lawrence the Vehicles fulfil some kind of Gap-filling function, referring to relatively recondite and abstract psychological processes. So their obscurity pre-empts intrinsic Similarity, nor can they give rise to Similarity through Analogy. These psychological processes are conceptualized by having an extended metaphor imposed upon them; the analogy is imputed or attributed but there are no similarities to be recognized as a result of this imposition. We might conclude that in extended metaphors some Vehicles and Topics are born Similar, some achieve Similarity through Analogy, and some have Analogy thrust upon them. In these latter kinds of extended metaphors, the *thrust upon* kind, the distinction between Ground and Vehicle can disappear. The Ground is provided by the Extension of the Vehicle or metaphor.

At the end of this section on Extension, what can we say about the contrasting allegorical styles of our four authors? There is a marked difference between the metaphoric extension in Golding and in the other texts under consideration. I do not have space here to show adequately the extent of the consistency in Golding's allegories in *The Spire* or *Lord of the Flies*. But we cannot attempt to read Milton, or even the Housman poem, in the same way (we remember how the allegorical consistency was deliberately sacrificed in the latter). And to pin down Lawrence's symbols with a single allegorical label would be entirely misguided. To demand a label for what, for example, in *The Rainbow* or *Sons and Lovers* is symbolized by the moon would be crying for the moon.

## 9.7. MIXING

The term *mixed metaphor* is usually pejorative, implying a careless writer. Because in many cases one or more of the metaphors is Inactive, the writer has ignored the Vehicles of the metaphor, but the reader has evoked them, and tried to interpret them as an extended metaphor.

(4)  Sino-Indian **thaw** continues, though still at a **snail**'s pace . . . Indonesia was "ideologically ready" to **reopen** economic **ties** with China . . . Suharto may have **softened** his **stance** in order to appear more statesmanlike. One important **obstacle** to **forging closer ties** with China is Indonesia's relatively **warm ties** with Vietnam.

(*Far Eastern Economic Review*, 19 May 1988, p. 42)

269

In this example using *tie* as a synonym for *relationship* creates some ludicrous juxtapositions, if we reactivate the metaphor by evoking the Vehicle image of a rope tying two objects together: *reopen ties* then acquires a meaning opposite to that intended, "warm ties" seems nonsensical, and "forging closer ties" only makes sense if we conceive the rope as a metal cable. Along with the incongruity of "thaw" and "snail" this makes the whole passage a little ridiculous.

Our definition of Mixing, it will be recalled, places it in contrast to syntactic or Articulated Extension. In (3) we see V-terms syntactically articulated with each other even though their conventional referents, the Vehicles, either have no such relationship in the world we know ("softened his stance") or, if they do, a relationship which provides a distraction from the intended meaning ("warm ties"), or a contradiction to it ("reopen ties").

There are two factors, therefore, which are relevant to the perception of metaphorical Mixing. One is the strength of syntactic bonding and syntactic proximity between the two V-terms. The other is the degree of activity of the metaphor.

> R49 Sometimes a high moon, liquid-brilliant, scudded across a hollow space and took cover under electric brown-iridescent cloud-edges. Then there was a blot of cloud and shadow. Then somewhere in the night a radiance again, like a vapour. And all the sky was **teeming** and **tearing** along, a vast disorder of flying shapes and darkness and **ragged fumes** of light and a great brown circling halo, then the terror of a moon running liquid-brilliant into the open for a moment, hurting the eyes before she **plunged** under **cover** of cloud again.

In the phrase "ragged fumes of light" two incompatible V-terms have close syntactic bonds, i.e. the relation of noun head and premodifier. "Ragged" should be applied to a flexible solid substance of some kind, typically cloth. "Fumes" must apply to a gaseous substance. We also have the example "plunged under cover". This is quite a close syntactic relationship between verb and prepositional complement of the adverbial. In addition the verb *plunge*, though slightly Inactive, is revitalized in the context of *liquid* and *scudding*. And "cover" is being used in the sense of a hiding place for a hunted animal, contrasted as it is with "the open". So the Mixing and the bombarding with disparate Vehicles is extreme. However, we sense that the disorder being described by Lawrence here is the very motivation for this metaphorical Mixing – to mirror a rapid succession of physical impressions and their accompanying emotions.

One of the closest syntactic bonds and a potentially proximate one is between subject and verb. There are three tactics which authors can employ to reduce the incongruity of such a mix. One is to increase the distance, the number of intervening words, between the two V-terms, by for example, using an *of*-genitive postmodifying the subject noun head.

LF58    The **trickle** of smoke **sketched** a chalky line up the solid blue of the sky.

This postmodifying *of*-phrase facilitates a reading in which the second noun is interpreted as the head of the noun phrase and thus the subject of the clause, psychologically, at least, downranking the initial noun to premodifier status, e.g. *the smoke sketched a chalky line* (see section 7.4). At the very least this construction reasserts the literal level of language use before the second V-term occurs.

A second tactic is to place one of the V-terms in a syntactic structure operating at a different rank from the other, for example a relative clause.

LF152    Up there, for once, were <u>clouds</u>, great bulging **towers** that **sprouted** away over the island.

This structure also employs the first tactic mentioned above, this time introducing a relative pronoun to intervene between subject and verb.

A third tactic places the less Active V-term first, typically the verb. The passive exemplifies all three of these tactics, initial verb, distance and downranking (PM30 is a near equivalent to a passive):

PM30    The rock that had saved him was **lathered** and **fringed** with leaping **strings** of foam.


## 9.8. COMPOUNDING OF METAPHORS

Compounding of metaphors occurs when the V-term of an already established metaphor becomes the T-term in a new second-order metaphor. Let's begin with two clear examples:

LF7    The <u>scar</u> was a **bath** of heat.
R198    She seemed to snuggle like a <u>**kitten**</u> within his warmth while she was at the same time elusive and ironical suggesting the fine **steel** of her <u>**claws**</u>.

By page 7 of *Lord of the Flies*, Golding has already established *scar* as a label for the long, thin clearing that the crashing aeroplane's fuselage scrapes in the jungle. It is almost as though this word is used to fill a lexical gap, for it quickly becomes accepted as the most normal lexical item to refer to the clearing. Now that the word has been Lexicalized, as it were, it can be used as the Topic-term of the new metaphor. In R198 the primary metaphor is established more locally. But providing the reader has accessed the kitten schema, of which claws will be part, then there is no real sense of Mixing when these claws are compared with steel. Another tendency can be observed in all these examples: a conventionality about one or other of the Vehicle–Topic pairings (e.g. *a bath of heat*, cf. *sunbathe; steel claws*). In this respect Compounding resembles Mixing.

271

Our final example, M5.5.24, seems, on first acquaintance, to be a case of deliberate Mixing rather than of Compounding:

M5.5.24   Life's but a **walking shadow**.

However, once we co-textualize the sentence in the rest of the speech it becomes apparent that both "shadow" and "walking" are part of lexically extended metaphors permeating the whole:

M5.5.19       Tomorrow, and tomorrow, and tomorrow,
              **Creeps** in this petty **pace** from day to day
              To the last syllable of recorded time;
              And all our yesterdays have **lighted** fools
              The **way** to dusty death. Out, out, brief **candle**!
              Life's but a **walking shadow**; a poor player,
              That **struts** and frets his hour upon the stage,
              And then is heard no more; it is a tale
              Told by an idiot, full of sound and fury,
              Signifying nothing.

The juxtaposition of these two V-terms creates a hinge on which to hang the two extended metaphors: time elapsing = walking; life = shadow. Such Compounding of two already established metaphors is, in fact, one means of amalgamating extended or repeated metaphors.

We have now discussed all the major kinds of metaphoric interplay. We next turn to consider a number of processes which make interesting complications for their operation.


## 9.9. LITERALIZATION OF VEHICLES

David Lodge has suggested that modern writers working within what he calls "the metonymic mode", that is, preserving in their prose the kinds of relationships between entities which we find in the real world, tend to use metaphor in a particular way.

> We would expect the writer who is writing within the metonymic mode
> to use metaphorical devices sparingly; to make them subject to the
> control of context – either by elaborating literal details of the context
> into symbols, or by drawing analogies from a semantic field associated
> with the context.
>
> (Lodge 1977: 113)

Neither Milton, Golding, nor Shakespeare seem to be working within this mode, though Lodge does classify Lawrence's writings as basically metonymic (*ibid.*: 61). Nevertheless all these writers display the tendencies to "make them subject to the control of context".

The following section demonstrates the means used to achieve the Literalization of metaphoric Vehicles; and, most importantly, describe the general effects achieved by this Literalization, and how it might affect the kinds of metaphoric interplay we have been considering up to now.

### 9.9.1. Means of Literalization

One of the most effective methods of achieving Literalization of V-terms is the <u>Reiteration</u> of a V-term lexical item which is used literally in the co-text. (From now on the item will be in small capitals when used literally.)

TS55    He had the model of the cathedral brought and stood against the north-west PILLAR, spire and all, to encourage them.

TS62    Roger and Rachel Mason, Pangall and his Goody, like four **pillars** at the crossways of the building.

PL27    Say first, for heaven hides nothing from thy view
Nor the DEEP tract of hell

PL125    So spake the apostate angel, though in pain,
Vaunting aloud, but racked with **deep** despair

M1.7.54    I have given suck and know
How tender 'tis to love the babe that MILKS me

M4.3.97    Nay, had I power, I should
Pour the sweet **milk** of concord into hell

There are also plenty of examples of reverse Reiteration in which the lexical item is used as a Vehicle first and later as a literal item:

FF113    Even though she enjoyed being herself innocently as a young **cat** before the fire . . .

FF128    A car had caught a CAT and taken away about five of its nine lives.

M1.6.3                This **guest** of summer,
The temple-haunting martlet, does approve
By his loved mansionry, that the heaven's breath
Smells wooingly here.

M1.6.24    We are your GUEST tonight.

PL18               O Spirit, that dost prefer
Before all temples the **upright** heart and pure

PL221    Forthwith UPRIGHT he rears from off the pool
His mighty stature

Under what circumstances will the Reiteration be noticed? The first factor is the proximity of the Reiteration (e.g. M1.6.3, M1.6.24). Second, the centrality of the literal referent, or its semantic field, to the plot or setting of the narrative: *The Spire*, with the cathedral as its exclusive setting, centres on the building of a spire in place of a tower and the doubts about whether the pillars will be strong enough to support it. In much the same way the *Paradise Lost* examples relate to the main narrative event and setting – the fall of the angels from heaven into the deep pit of hell. Third, as we shall see, the image schema of verticality extends the metaphor throughout the whole of Book 1. Fourth, an image may be presented so powerfully that it is difficult to forget; the impact of M1.7.54 is achieved by the violent emotional contrast between this tender image of suckling a child and the sequel:

M1.7.54     I would, while it was smiling in my face
                 Have plucked my nipple from his boneless gums,
                 And dashed the brains out, had I so sworn
                 As you have done to this.

In conjunction with these four factors we have to consider the order in which the items appear. In the case of FF113 and FF128 it is difficult to claim that the Reiteration would be noticed. The incident of the squashed cat, FF128, presents a powerful image which is unforgettable. But the preceding FF113 is a little unobtrusive simile, so the lexical Reiteration is noticeable only when we read the novel a second time. Unless the term is part of a metaphorical Extension, its Reiteration is less likely to be noticed when the literal use comes second. In other words Reiteration is more detectable in the case of L ^ M than of M ^ L.

A less obvious means of achieving Literalization of Vehicles is when there is no verbatim Reiteration, but the use of a synonym, hyponym or superordinate:

FF59–60   He ran ahead and came back like a **puppy**, for all the world as if I
          were the master . . . I stopped again and used the wall that the DOGS
          used.

FF59–60 is an interesting little example. The context is that Sammy, the narrator, is about to take up the dare, suggested by his friend Philip, of spitting on the altar of a church. The V-term "puppy" occurs first followed by the literal term "dogs". By pointing out the ironic falsity of the Philip–puppy comparison with a contrafactive *as if*, Sammy in fact suggests the validity of the Sammy–dog comparison.

In *Paradise Lost* Book 1 the transitive verb *raise* is used consistently as a V-term (lines 22, 42, 98, 528, 551), whereas the intransitive quasi-synonym *rise* is used consistently in a literal sense (lines 10, 210, 329, 545, 546, 711). Milton asks God to "raise" what is low in him, talks of Satan "raising" war in heaven, of Satan "raising" (i.e. stirring up) other devils to fight, "raising" their fainting courage, and the way music was used to "raise" the temper of heroes. But describes how the world "rose" out of chaos, Satan had not yet "risen" from the lake of hell, the devils' banners and spears "rise" into the air, and how Pandemonium "rises" out of the earth.

As we saw when considering Extension and Modification, potential Articulation through various kinds of metonymy often occurs between members of lexical sets. There is some such potential Articulation or metonymical relation of process and result behind the Literalization in the following pair:

FF23  I think he must have been, so to speak, **the fag-end** of a <u>craftsman</u>.
FF25  As I remember him and his breathing it occurs to me that what he had
      was LUNG CANCER.

The two relevant lexical items belong to the smoking schema and are both products: smoking results in both fag-ends and lung cancer.

In *Macbeth* the V-terms link to literal schemas of horse-riding, and drinking to a remarkable degree. Horse-riding appears in the play on a literal level in various aspects. Banquo goes on his last ride with Fleance. When Duncan announces his intention to spend the night at Macbeth's castle, the latter rides as quickly as possible to reach there before the king, who races after him. On arrival at the castle Duncan asks:

M1.6 22  Where's the Thane of Cawdor?
         We coursed him at the heels, and had a purpose
         To be his purveyor; but he rides well
         And his great <u>love</u>, sharp as his **spur**, hath holp him
         To his home before us.

Before the invocation of night we have a description:

M3.3.6  Now SPURS the lated traveller apace
        To gain the timely inn.

These literal references to spurring on and to overtaking, are balanced by metaphorical references:

M2.3.110  The expedition of my violent love
          **Outrun** the pauser, reason.

M4.1.144  Time, thou anticipatest my dread exploits:
          The flighty purpose never is **o'ertook**
          Unless the deed go with it.

And there are several more general Vehicles related to horse-riding:

M1.9.21  . . . or heaven's cherubins, **hors'd**
         **Upon the sightless couriers** of the air
         Shall blow the horrid deed in every eye
         That tears shall drown the wind. I have no **spur**
         **To prick the sides** of my intent, but only
         **Vaulting** ambition, **which o'er leaps** itself
         And **falls** on the other –

Drinking (of wine) takes place on the literal level. Lady Macbeth drinks it to make her bold, when she gives drugged wine to the grooms who she is attempting to incriminate (M1.9.64–5; 2.2.1). The porter has been carousing on the night of the murder (M2.3.25) and describes the equivocating nature of drink at some length. In this context appear:

M1.9.35    Was the hope **drunk**
Wherein you dressed yourself? Hath it slept since?
And wakes it now to look so green and pale
At what it did so freely?

M2.3.95    The **wine** of life **is drawn and the mere lees
Is left this vault to brag of**.

The V-terms are even more tightly controlled by Literalization in *Paradise Lost* Book 1 as may be seen if you consult the first 50 lines. The lexical set which controls many of the V-terms in Book 1 is the vertical axis. Milton establishes this initially by talking about the mountains of "Oreb" and "Sinai" where God spoke to Moses, telling him how the world "rose out of chaos", and of "mount Sion", the site of the Temple in Jerusalem. We then switch over to the metaphorical level where Milton claims that his verse "with no middle flight intends to soar above th'Aonian mount" (the home of the muses). He proceeds to talk metaphorically, describes morality in terms of this axis, "upright heart", asks God to "raise and support" his "low" nature, laments the "fall" of man who was so "highly" favoured, describes the rebellion of Satan, how he "stirred up", "raised impious war", due to his ambition to be "above" his peers and equal to "the most high". He then returns to the literal level, describing the casting of the rebel angels "down to bottomless perdition".

We have seen many examples of how the use of hyponyms, superordinates and synonyms, and Vehicles from lexical sets represented literally in the co-text can achieve Literalization which is equivalent to Modification. We earlier showed how Literalization was achieved by Reiteration. We now consider the effects that Literalization might have on the interpretation of both the V-terms and of their literal equivalents.

### 9.9.2. Effects of Literalization

Some effects of Literalization are on the interpretation of the metaphor: the Revitalizing of metaphors, and the blurring of the literal–metaphorical distinction.

#### 9.9.2.1. Revitalizing

One of the defining features of an Inactive metaphor is that the Vehicle is no longer manifest when the term is used. As was pointed out in Chapter 1, one of the most obvious consequences of this is the existence of pairs of lexical items which share the same phonological or graphological form but which differ in meaning: we may regard them as homonymous or polysemous. When an Inactive metaphor is used, and the preceding or immediate co-text literalizes it, then the Vehicle is likely to become more manifest. In such cases we may talk of the metaphor being Revitalized. For example:

DV164    There was a mutual expansion of pupils.

In this context of Sophie visiting her gymnastic-teacher boyfriend, the phrase *expanded pupils* belongs simultaneously to two semantic fields; sexual excitement (cf. *dilated pupils*) and physical education – we notice a parent's exhortation "Build him up, Masterman" at the foot of the same page. The phrase has a double reference, but this in no way enables us to construct the Grounds of the original metaphor, and the pun seems gratuitous; we still feel that the coincidence of one form for two concepts is arbitrary. By contrast in GW0031 Grounds of Similarity/Analogy could be evoked:

GW0031    By directing electronic waves to her brain, it may, quite literally*, **tickle her fancy**.

### 9.9.2.2. Blurring the literal–metaphorical distinction

Literalization often makes possible an almost imperceptible movement from the metaphorical to the literal level (or vice versa) within mid-sentence:

FF6    I have hung all systems on the wall like a row of useless **hats**. They do not fit . . . the Marxist **hat** . . . the Christian **biretta** . . . Nick's rationalist **hat** . . . There is a SCHOOL CAP too. I had no more hung IT there, not knowing of the **other hats** I should hang by it.

"Biretta" and "Marxist hat" have no literal existence in the world of the novel. But "school cap" does. So that in the last sentence of the example the "it" refers back to a literal use, whereas "the other" refers back to metaphorical ones. By backward reference Golding blurs the literal–metaphorical distinction further.

In some cases of Literalization it may be impossible to decide whether to process at the metaphorical or the literal level.

PL679    Mammon, the least erected spirit that fell
From heaven, for even in heaven his LOOKS and **thoughts**
WERE ALWAYS DOWNWARD BENT.

In PL679 we have an instance of zeugma. "Downward bent" has to refer literally as an attribute of "looks", and metaphorically as an attribute of "thoughts". Describing the relationship between the pregnant Lydia and Brangwen, Lawrence writes:

> R63   He had learnt to contain himself again, and he hated it. He hated her that
> she was not there for him. AND HE TOOK HIMSELF OFF ANYWHERE.

Are we to take this last sentence as metaphorical, an indication of a mental state, as the immediate context might suggest? Or is it to be understood literally in the wider context of "He went out more often to the Red Lion again" (R64)? Probably both.

### 9.9.2.3 Symbolism

The most important effect of the Literalization of Vehicles is on the literal lexical items. The literal term and the schema to which it refers acquire symbolic status from the presence of the same item used as a Vehicle. So, for example, in *Paradise Lost* Book 1 the description of the temples of the devils who subsequently attempt to lure the Jews from worship of God typically involves references to hills, "that opprobrious hill" (l. 403), "that hill of scandal" (l. 416), or mountains, "the offensive mountain", or height, "his temple high-reared in Azotus" (l. 463). These hills or high places become symbols of other attempts to revolt against God, though on a smaller scale than the original revolt in which Satan "trusted to have equalled the most high" (l. 40). A variation on the theme of lesser revolt is the building of Satan's palace in hell, Pandemonium: "the fabric huge rose like an exhalation" (l. 710) until "the ascending pile stood fixed her stately highth" (l. 722). Satan's upwards movements are the first stirrings in a plot to continue this revolt by bringing about the fall of man: "with head uplift above the wave" (l. 192); "upright he reared from off the pool" (l. 221); "then with expanded wings he steers his flight" (l. 225). In the context of PL111 they also become symbolic of the attempt to avoid shame and preserve pride even in adversity:

> PL111        To BOW and sue for grace
> With suppliant knee and deify his power
> . . . that were **low** indeed,
> That were an ignominy and shame **beneath**
> This DOWNFALL.

And the flying symbolism carries over into the similes involving bees (l. 768), and locusts (l. 338).

In Golding's *The Spire* we are given a clear example of how Literalization leads to symbolism. In an example already discussed in section 7.2.3 the literal muddy pit dug in the cathedral which stinks and creeps is emphatically identified as a symbol of Jocelin's subconscious and its repressed desires for Goody.

> TS158   Then an anger rose out of some **pit** inside Jocelin. He had glimpses in
> his head of a face [Goody's] that dropped daily for his blessing, heard
> the secure sound of her singing in Pangall's kingdom. He lifted his

chin, and the word burst out over it from an obscure place of indignation and hurt.

"No!"

All at once it seemed to him that the renewing life of the world was
a filthy thing, **a rising tide of muck**, so that he gasped for air.

This symbol is taken up in the thematic pattern of the novel by which the
higher the spire is built the more Jocelin discovers about his unconscious
motives. As Roger's wife, Rachel, puts it: "Child, a spire goes down as far
as it goes up." The symbol is explicitly underlined towards the end of the
novel when Jocelin has achieved more self-knowledge and asks:

TS213   What is a man's mind, Roger? Is it the whole building, cellarage and
        all?

The widespread tendency in Golding to create a symbolic level operating in
parallel with the literal level is what allows critics to regard his novels as
fables, or even allegories. This is not surprising. We have already had an
excellent example of Literalization of Vehicles leading to an allegorical
interpretation in Housman's poem 'On Wenlock Edge'.

## 9.10. OVERDESCRIPTION

I have shown, elsewhere, how unrelentingly repetitious is the description of
the gale and its effects on the wood in the Housman poem (Goatly 1990).
We are unlikely to be interested in the description for its own sake at the
literal level. Similarly the amount of descriptive detail and attention lav-
ished on the processes of medieval building in *The Spire* and on the state of
the boys' clothes in *Lord of the Flies* appear somewhat superfluous.

For another example in *Macbeth* we notice the literal references to night,
and descriptions or invocations of night and darkness. There are the two
famous invocations:

M1.5.50     Come, thick Night,
            And pall thee in the dunnest smoke of Hell
            . . .
M3.3.46     Come, seeling Night,
            Scarf up the tender eye of pitiful Day,
            And with thy bloody and invisible hand,
            Cancel and tear to pieces that great bond
            That keeps me pale!

There are descriptions of a tempestuous night (M2.3.55) and of a day which
is preternaturally dark (M2.4.6). References to the setting of the sun, "that
will be ere the set of sun" (M1.1.5), and "the fog and filthy air" (M1.1.12)
set the scene for the play. The first is taken up, when Lady Macbeth denies
the possibility of another sunrise for Duncan: "Never shall sun that morrow

see" (M1.5.60). By the end of the play she has to have "light by her continually" (M5.1.21) and Macbeth begins "to be aweary of the sun" (M5.5.49). In a similar way one could continue by pointing out the over-description of flowers and the moon etc. in Lawrence.

Though the elaboration of literal description in this area seems on the surface irrelevant, not producing the kinds of Contextual Effect that would make its processing worth the effort, we can recover or salvage its relevance by interpreting it at what Barthes calls the semic level (1970: 97ff.). In other words, Overdescription becomes relevant if what is described does not simply remain at the referential level, as a description of context, but becomes symbolic of a theme. Literalization of Vehicles and Overdescription often work hand-in-hand to create this symbolic level in the text. For instance, we saw that a large dose of Overdescription is useful to ensure that Reiteration is noticed by the reader.

## 9.11. SYMBOLISM AND THE COMPLICATIONS OF METAPHORIC INTERPLAY

It is worth taking a wider perspective and defining, in relation to literary theory, more exactly what might be meant by Symbolism or Symbolic Level as we have used these terms when describing the general effects of Literalization.

How the thematic level and the literal levels of meaning are connected to each other by symbolism has been clearly set out by Hasan (1989). The literal level she calls *verbalization*. If we ask ourselves what the text is about at this level, then our answer depends upon our understanding of language. The higher level she calls *theme*. The answer to the question, "What is this text about?", will, at the thematic level, be more abstract. So, in the well-known Robert Frost poem 'The road not taken', at the level of verbalization the answer will be that the poem is about someone choosing to go down one road in the hope of coming back to the other, but never being able to do so. At the thematic level the poem might be about the limitations and immutability of human choices (*ibid.*: 97). Bridging the gap between these two levels of meaning is the level of Symbolic articulation. This presumably depends upon some such metaphorical process as I have described as symbolic substitution in section 4.5.1. An important feature of this level of Symbolic articulation is that not all literal details of the text will contribute to the theme. What guides us in choosing which descriptive details to treat symbolically is the process of foregrounding (*ibid.*: 98).

The particular kind of foregrounding which I have concentrated on has been Overdescription, the elaboration of descriptive detail. This foregrounding is achieved partly by repetition, but also by lack of relevance, at the level of verbalization, to the purposes we recognize in a literary text. But obviously metaphor is itself a device for foregrounding and the fact that a lexical item has been used metaphorically carries over to help foreground its literal use. To that extent the metaphoric interplay we have been considering and Literalization are both foregrounding devices. Compounding and Revitalization are both reassertions of foregrounding: in Compounding a secondary metaphor provides a further level of foregrounding; in Revitalization we have an attempt to re-foreground metaphors which have become so well established that they have faded into the background.

The observation that the literary text has two levels of meaning, two senses of Topic, one at the level of verbalization and one at the level of theme, has far-reaching consequences for our model of interplay. It invites us to reverse or invert the Topic and Vehicle relation. Language used literally at the level of verbalization, which have, up to now, been treated as comprising T-terms, can now be used as symbolic V-terms for a thematic Topic. Using Housman's 'On Wenlock Edge' as an example, one could diagram the relationship as in Figure 9.2.

At the verbalization level the poem is clearly about the effect of a gale on trees. At the thematic level the poem is obviously about the effects of life on humankind. Until now we have assumed that Topics should be defined at the level of verbalization. But precisely what is achieved by symbolization through Literalization and Overdescription, is the reversal of the roles of Topic and Vehicle, and the equation of Topic with theme. We should remember that not only Literalization and Overdescription have a part to play in this symbolization process. The very fact that the language of literary text is generally interpreted as an extended Phenomenalistic metaphor, referring to a world to which it does not conventionally refer, is an equally important factor. If literature holds a mirror up to nature, it laterally and literally inverts the Vehicle–Topic equation.

We can relate these comments to the observations at the end of Chapter 8, where we saw that different syntactic patterns, different word-classes and different levels of activity combine to give Vehicles more or less prominence. In Phenomenalistic literary texts, where the world presented is a large-scale Vehicle for a thematic Topic, Vehicle prominence reaches

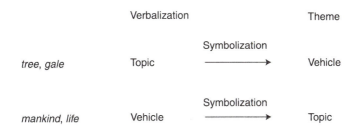

*Figure 9.2* Symbolization and the interchange of Topic and Vehicle

281

its zenith. We will see in the final chapter how novels and poetry, and to some extent advertising, demand and exhibit more Vehicle prominence than other genres.

## ■ SUGGESTIONS FOR FURTHER WORK

*Look at the last three paragraphs of the* New Scientist *passage (pp. 321–2) and the last stanza of the poem 'On the farm' (pp. 326–7). Using the framework introduced in this chapter, explain as carefully as possible how the metaphors interrelate to each other.*

# 10

# METAPHOR IN ITS SOCIAL CONTEXT

## 10.1. INTRODUCTION

We have almost completed our survey of the language of metaphor, considering the literal–metaphorical distinction (Chapter 1), the contribution of Concretizing metaphors to the lexicon of English (Chapters 2, 3), the various semantic and functional varieties (Chapters 4, 5), and the ways in which co-text enables the signalling, interpretation and interplay of metaphors (Chapters 6, 7, 8, 9). But to frame our sketch, constraining the portions of the jigsaw to fit together, we need to consider metaphor in its larger social context. This involves integrating the relatively decontextualized Relevance Theory, which we relied on in Chapter 1, and discussed more fully in Chapter 5, with a developed model of social context.

Sections 10.2 to 10.4 work towards a model of text interpretation by merging Hallidayan concepts of genre/register with Relevance Theory through a development of the model for discourse interpretation in Fairclough's *Language and Power* (1989). Section 10.5 shows that, once Relevance is defined in terms of social context we can explain: how metaphors are detected and disambiguated (section 10.5.1); how contextually determined purposes affect interpretation (section 10.5.2); what counts as adequately relevant (section 10.5.3); and how time constraints will impinge on interpretation (section 10.5.4). Finally, in section 10.6, I report rough statistical results of wide-ranging text analysis to draw up a metaphorical profile of six genres, according to the dimensions of metaphor discussed in the earlier chapters of the book.

## 10.2. DEVELOPMENT OF RELEVANCE THEORY: THE NEED FOR A SOCIAL DIMENSION

An interesting reaction to the appearance of *Relevance: Communication and Cognition* (Sperber and Wilson 1986) was Clark's review 'Relevance to what?', where he argues that verbal communication is a means of social action:

> People talk . . . as a means of doing things they can only do collec-
> tively – arguing, instructing, negotiating business, performing rituals,
> telling stories, gossiping, planning.
>
> (Clark 1987: 714)

He emphasizes that the particular kinds of collective action for which
language is used must be factored in if the concept of Relevance is to
have any substance. I believe that Register/Genre Theory can show how the
socio-cultural context of an utterance selects and constructs goals and
purposes, and that, bringing together the two theories might result in a
fruitful cross-fertilization.

Let's remind ourselves of what we mean by *Relevance* as discussed in
Chapter 5. The formula we arrived at was:

(1)   Relevance = $\dfrac{\text{Contextual Effects}}{\text{Processing Effort}}$

The notion of genre enables us to estimate the amount of Processing effort
possible or presumed to be possible to the (speaker) hearer. Just as important, the nature and range of Contextual Effects may be specified more
exactly if we have some theory of contexts. It will determine the Contextual
Assumptions most accessible to the interlocutors, one aspect of what Halliday calls "meaning potential".

To take a simple example: if a sales assistant in a butcher's shop is
interacting with customers the most accessible Contextual Assumptions are
those from the Field/schema/script of sales encounter. So, presuming on
optimal relevance, she will interpret the utterance "Two lamb chops" made
by a person entering the shop, as a sales request, rather than a descriptive
assertion about the contents of the meat display cabinet. In Sperber and
Wilson's terms the Contextual Assumption provided by the sales encounter
schema:

(2)   A person entering the shop wishes to buy something

interacts with:

(3)   The person entering the shop has uttered the sentence *"Two lamb chops"*

to produce the contextually implicated conclusion:

(4)   The person entering the shop wishes to buy two lamb chops.

This is the most relevant interpretation, in fact the default one in this highly
conventionalized socio-cultural context.

Apart from Relevance Theory's lack of social dimension, it can be
criticized along other lines. It seems to assume, following Grice, that
linguistic exchanges aim for the most efficient transfer of information,
with the minimum processing (Grice 1975). But I think that certain genres,

like pastimes – puzzles, jokes, riddles – and some kinds of test, are deliberately designed to increase Processing Effort.

## ■ EXERCISE

*Consider the following written text.*
*Tick the best answer, (a), (b), (c) or (d).*

> *Lexical items are:  (a) usually (b) never (c) always (d) sometimes*
> *more than one morpheme long.*

For instance, genres such as multiple-choice tests and crosswords exploit the Principle of Relevance by creating Contextual Assumptions which are ultimately irrelevant in terms of the answer, but which are nevertheless relevant in their distractive and puzzling function. The distractors (a), (b) and (c) have, at least superficially, no relevance in terms of strengthening or eliminating existing assumptions or producing new Implicated Conclusions. For a good examinee they will contradict existing assumptions but leave them unaffected. Adjustments need to be made to the notion of Relevance according to the specific purposes of specific genres.

## 10.3. HALLIDAY'S SOCIAL DIMENSION: A THEORY OF CONTEXTS AND PURPOSES

One way of describing the features of the social context is Register Theory, which Halliday and Hasan explain as follows:

> A register is a semantic concept . . . a configuration of meanings that are typically associated with a particular situational configuration of Field, Mode and Tenor. It will, of course, include the expressions, the lexico-grammatical and phonological features, that typically accompany or realize these meanings.
>
> (Halliday and Hasan 1985: 38–9)

We must then go on to subsidiary definitions of Field, Tenor and Mode.

> Field = what is happening, the nature of the social action that is taking place; what it is that the participants are engaged in, in which the language figures as some essential component.

> Tenor = who is taking part, the nature of the participants, their statuses and roles: what kinds of role relationships obtain among the participants . . . both the types of speech role that they are taking on in the dialogue, and the whole cluster of socially significant relationships in which they are involved.

285

Mode = what part the language is playing, what the participants are expecting the language to do for them in that situation: the symbolic organization of the text, the status that it has and the function in the context, including the channel (is it spoken or written or some combination of the two?) and also the rhetorical Mode, what is being achieved by the text in terms of such categories as persuasive, expository, didactic and the like.

(Halliday and Hasan 1985: 12)

Field defines the kind of purposive and co-operative social action which Clark (1987) mentioned. As in the butcher's assistant example, identifying the Field makes some assumptions more accessible than others: those stereotypically associated with the context by socio-cultural convention, organized so that they form a script or schema for the particular activity.

Tenor involves social relationships. It gives us a further kind of purpose besides that of co-operation in an activity, such as acquiring and maintaining role and status, though the two purposes are often interdependent. For example, certain activities in a specific culture, such as education, will create status differences between teacher and pupil; service encounters position subjects as buyers and sellers. It is this social purpose and social positioning which Sperber and Wilson ignore.

Halliday's Mode partly involves the rhetorical purposes which language takes on in the context of the larger purpose defined by Field. One important distinction is between constitutive and ancillary Modes. In the constitutive Modes discoursal acts constitute the Field, whereas in the ancillary the language activity is less central, a by-product of the main activity. Literature is at the constitutive end of the spectrum, not typically related to any social activity beyond itself, and we laugh at people who misinterpret it as ancillary, like Don Quixote reading romances as an instruction manual. Similarly, pure conversation or chat is more or less an end in itself. Chatting and chatting-up are quite different. (Perhaps conversation's self-sufficiency of purpose is why some theorists regard it as a pre-genre rather than a genre proper (Swales 1990: 58–9).) At the other extreme are ancillary Modes like the language of ballet lessons, where the text only has meaning in relation to some other physical activity identified by the Field. Spoken registers tend to be more ancillary in Mode, written more constitutive.

## 10.4. RELEVANCE AND SOCIAL SEMIOTICS IN FAIRCLOUGH'S MODEL OF TEXT INTERPRETATION

But how do we integrate Hallidayan notions of social context and a pragmatic theory like Relevance into a model of communication? The only model I am familiar with which attempts this integration is Fairclough's, as expounded in his influential book *Language and Power* (1989). Figure 10.1 shows his debt to Halliday, as will become clear when I explain it.

Starting at the top of Figure 10.1, Fairclough sees human activity divided up and structured into different social spaces or social orders. These orders are generally structured institutionally, and institutions will have fairly well-defined concepts of what kinds of situations and activities can take place within them.

For example, if you are a university student, your social space might be divided up into five main areas:

(5)     Education    Part-time work    Family    Badminton    Courtship

Most of these, probably the first four, will, literally, be associated with a place or building, and will be more or less institutionalized. Education will be linked to the university institution where you are a student. And a university will have a number of distinct discourse situations open to students, which operate within it either centrally or less centrally, e.g. tutorial, seminar, lecture, library private study, student common-room chat, etc. Moving to the bottom right of the diagram, the four aspects of the Discourse Type – Content, Subjects and Relations, and Connections – correspond to the features of the situation on the left, which are reworkings

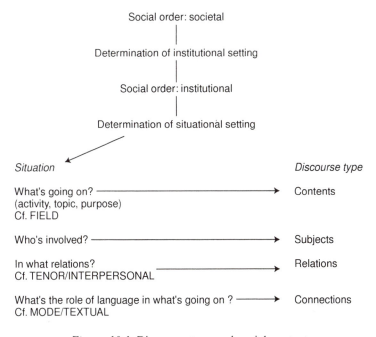

*Figure 10.1* Discourse type and social context
*Source*: Adapted from Fairclough 1989: 146, fig. 6.2; by permission of Addison Wesley Longman Limited

287

of Halliday's categories of Field, Tenor and Mode respectively. As far as Field is concerned, obviously the different situations will have different purposes: for example, a lecture might have the purposes of giving information, explaining theory, providing an overview of a topic, stimulating interest/entertainment, demonstrating analysis; whereas the tutorial demands the processing of information and theory, by allowing problem-solving, application of a theory to data, questioning and testing of ideas and theory, discussion, argument etc. At the interpersonal level of Subjects and Relations the roles of participants are quite different in a lecture than a tutorial. In their Subject positions as the lectured, students are obliged to keep silent most of the time, but as tutees are expected to talk. Lecturers are entitled to lengthy monologues, but tutors should keep their mouths comparatively shut. Tutorials are cosier affairs than lectures and Relations can become more friendly and intimate, or more overtly hostile and antagonistic, than in the semi-public lecture. In both lectures and tutorials, discourse is constitutive, of course, but plays different rhetorical roles; persuasion and argument are more common in tutorials, while exposition is prevalent in lectures.

I shift now to a second diagram of Fairclough's which I have modified and present as Figure 10.2. This diagram models the interpretation of both text and context, text at levels 1–4, and context at levels 5 and 6. It is crucial to my theoretical framework, and I shall spend the next few paragraphs explaining it and integrating my model of metaphorical interpretation within it.

The model divides into three columns. On the right is a list of areas which need interpretation, ranging across context and text/utterance. On the left are the interpretative procedures (members' resources or MR) which are available to readers/hearers. These resources come from various sources: from our experience as members of society/institutions (level 6) and as readers of texts (level 5); from our knowledge of the kinds of discoursal and other activity that goes on in the world, and the internal organization of such discourse/activity (level 4); from pragmatic principles (levels 2b and 3); and from knowledge of a particular language (levels 1 and 2a).

We envisage the act of interpretation taking place in the middle column. The double-headed arrows at each level, and linking the context and text/utterance, indicate that the levels do not operate in isolation. As I shall demonstrate, a metaphor will be interpreted in different ways according to the social context in which it is located. Indeed, Relevance, (one of) the pragmatic principle(s) operating at levels 2 and 3, will be computed in different ways depending on the situational context – the purposes inherent in the Field and Tenor and the processing time available as an aspect of Mode, which are part of the situational context operating at level 6.

Interpretative procedures
(members' resources)

Interpreting

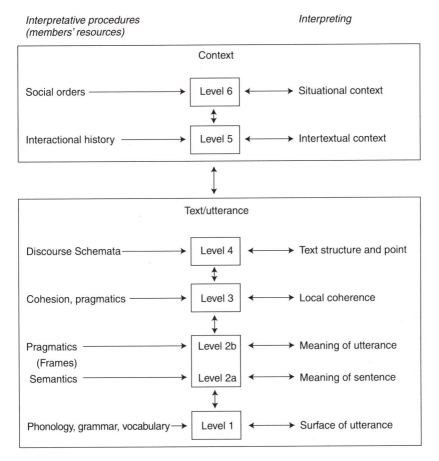

*Figure 10.2* A model of text interpretation
*Source*: Adapted from Fairclough 1989: 146, fig. 6.1; by permission of Addison Wesley
Longman Limited

### 10.4.1. A sample analysis of metaphor using the model

To make this model clear and relate it to metaphor let's work through an
example. In the first chapter of *Life on Earth* (1979), David Attenborough
describes the evolution of life. At this point he has just given an account of
Darwin's discoveries and the publication of his theory in *The Origin of
Species*. He continues:

[1] It [natural selection] remains the key to our understanding of the
natural world and it enables us to recognize that life has a long and
continuous history during which organisms, both plant and animal,
have changed, generation by generation, as they colonized all parts
of the world.

[2] The direct, if fragmentary, evidence for this history lies in the archives of the earth, the sedimentary rocks. [3] The vast majority of animals leave no trace of their existence after their passing. [4] Their flesh decays, their shells and their bones become scattered and turn to powder. [5] But very occasionally, one or two individuals out of a population of many thousands have a different fate. [6] A reptile becomes stuck in a swamp and dies. [7] Its body rots but its bones settle in the mud. [8] Dead vegetation drifts to the bottom and covers them. [9] As the centuries pass and more and more vegetation accumulates, the deposit turns to peat. [10] Changes in sea level may cause the swamp to be flooded and layers of sand to be deposited on top of the peat. [11] Over great periods of time, the peat is compressed and turned to coal. [12] The reptile's bones still remain within it. [13] The great pressure of the overlying sediments and the mineral-rich solutions that circulate through them cause chemical changes in the calcium phosphate of the bones. [14] Eventually they are turned to stone, but they retain not only the outward shape that they had in life, albeit sometimes distorted, but on occasion even their detailed cellular structure is preserved so that you can look at sections of them through the microscope and plot the shape of the blood vessels and the nerves that once surrounded them.

(Attenborough 1979: 14)

I will use this passage to illustrate Fairclough's model, level by level, concentrating on and beginning with sentence (2) which contains the metaphorical expression "the archives of the earth". Though I work from level 1 upwards this is simply an analytical convenience; in real processing the levels interrelate simultaneously.

At level 1 we will use our knowledge of the language to interpret the surface level of the utterance by recognizing the letter- and word-shapes in the sentence, how the words combine into phrases or groups – for example, nominal groups (NG), verbal groups (VG), prepositional groups (Prep.G) – and how these groups take on the syntactic roles of subject, verb and adjunct:

the direct if fragmentary evidence for this history (NG) ——→ subject
lies (VG) ——————————————————————→ verb
in the archives of the earth, the sedimentary rocks (Prep.G) —→ adjunct

At level 2 of interpretation we first of all use semantic knowledge, 2a, accessing the meanings of the words and phrases, for example what "sedimentary rocks" and "archives" mean, as well as the meanings of the syntax. There are a number of ambiguities here: the forms "direct" and "fragmentary" represent both literal and Inactive metaphorical meanings; postmodifying prepositional phrases like "for this history" and "of the earth" are notoriously ambiguous or vague; "earth" and "lies" are ambiguous. If we take "lies" as indicating a stative process of an Existential or Relational kind, 'is', rather than a verbal one meaning 'tells an untruth', the meanings conferred by the syntax will have the subject as existent and the adjunct as a circumstance of location, the place where the evidence exists.

We also need to invoke pragmatics here (2b). Disambiguation will be essential. But so will reference assignment. Even if the coreference of "the archives of the earth" and "the sedimentary rocks" is established by grammatical rule through Apposition (see my analysis of Shakespeare in 5.1.3) we still have to decide which of the two phrases is referring literally and which metaphorically.

I have added *frame* to the interpretative procedures operating at this level. Frames refer to the structures in which we organize and store knowledge of objects and things, so strictly speaking they may operate at the contextual level. Nevertheless they are crucial at this level in helping with reference assignment and disambiguation. For example our real-world knowledge stored in the Frame for 'evidence' suggests that there is not always enough of it, it is often incomplete, and this would prompt us to interpret "fragmentary" metaphorically.

At this second level we also have to try to work out what kind of speech act this is, and what kind of attitude the writer has to the proposition expressed. Supposing two possible propositions emerge:

(6)   The evidence that life has a long history and has changed during that history exists in the libraries of the earth.

(7)   The evidence that life has a long history and has changed during that history exists in the sedimentary rocks.

Assuming the utterance is an assertive speech act, which of these propositions is the writer asserting, which is he most likely to believe, or which is most relevant to the point of his discourse? We seek answers to these questions and resolutions to the other ambiguities by exploiting resources from higher levels.

Level 3 will help us with at least four of the difficulties left unresolved at level 2. We have a good example in sentence (2) of how a cohesive device can create local patterns of coherence. The demonstrative adjective "this" refers us back to the phrase in (1) "a long and continuous history during which organisms . . . have changed". So, first, the phrase "of this history" becomes less ambiguous once we recognize this backward reference. Second, trying to disambiguate "fragmentary" at level 2 led us to select the inactive metaphorical meaning. However, after reading the paragraph, we realize that the evidence is literally fragmentary as well, consisting of bits and pieces of rocks. Third, both from the text before our sentence and the remainder of the paragraph with its references to "great periods of time" we deduce that' 'lies" does not mean 'tell an untruth'. The writer is not, after all, a creationist believing that the fossils in the earth were simply put there to test fundamentalist Christian beliefs. Fourth, as we read through the rest of the paragraph and decode the words "coal" (11) and "sediment" (12) we resolve the indecision about whether "the archives of the earth" or "the sedimentary rocks" is referring literally, in favour of the latter. "The archives of the earth" then becomes a V-term. Fifth, we disambiguate "of the earth" as a Partitive interpretation (see section 7.4.3) since only part of the earth, the sedimentary rocks, regularly contains information about the past.

It is difficult to exemplify level 4 as we can only look at a small part of Attenborough's book. But coherence relations are crucial for understanding the structure of the second paragraph. To understand the metaphor "archives of the earth" we must recognize that the remainder of the paragraph is an elaboration of the Grounds: the fact that knowledge and evidence is stored in the sedimentary rocks just as it is in libraries. Only at the end of the paragraph do we find details of the knowledge that the sedimentary rocks preserve, the outward shape and the structure of blood vessels and nerves of extinct species. Our sense of discourse schemata includes such a typical paragraph structure, where a point is made in the first or "topic" sentence, and elaborated afterwards; if a Vehicle is mentioned at the beginning we expect Grounds later (cf. section 8.5).

Interactional history, level 5, is obviously a resource which feeds into these stereotypical notions of discourse structure (level 4), and I have rearranged Fairclough's diagram to make this clear, by placing boxes 4 and 5 in proximity. In the case of reading the book *Life on Earth*, the reader may well have had more specific interactional history with relevant previous texts such as the television series, and knowledge or images from those might contribute to his interpretative resources.

At level 6 we come back to Figure 10.1. Reading a book in the genre of very popular natural history is quite different from studying, for example, a scientific paper. It is a leisure activity, and the writer occupies a Subject position of both informant and entertainer. But the entertainment has its limits: we would not expect him to indulge in fantasy or science fiction and we expect assertions which are relevant to a description of the "real" history of life. Also, from both intertextual and social experience of this genre, we would not expect much irony. Relations will be different from a scientific paper too, and we can see textual traces of the attempt at informality and *easification* (Fairclough 1989: 221–2) in the short snappy sentences (6), (7) and (8). But we are not reading this text too carefully, as we would a poem, so that the awkward *not only . . . but even on occasion* structure in the last sentence probably passes unnoticed.

292

## 10.4.2. Integrating a Relevance-based model with Fairclough's

The whistlestop tour through Fairclough's model oversimplifies it, and I would recommend the reader who wants to explore further to read pages 142–54 of Fairclough (1989). Nevertheless it gives us an indication of a wider framework in which we can locate the model of metaphorical interpretation which I developed earlier. To show how they fit together let's reconsider the example in the light of Figure 5.2, reproduced here as Figure 10.3. David Attenborough, no doubt relying partly on previous texts (1 and 2), and perhaps models and diagrams of some kind (3), is moving from A to B to C to D to compose his text. As both Fairclough and Sperber and Wilson would agree, text is merely a trace of the thought of the author and a cue to the reader in reconstructing that thought. What the example demonstrates is how resources at higher levels (2b to 6) can be exploited by the reader as he moves in the reverse sequence from D through C to hypothesize B. Level 1 simply gives us the output of graphology, morphology, lexis and syntax. Level 2a, semantics, is a process of decoding this lexis and syntax. The Principle of Relevance, at levels 2b and 3, guides our use of other resources from levels 3–6 to turn the output of decoding into a fully explicit propositional form B, by, for example, resolving ambiguities and assigning reference. And it also enables us to hypothesize the author's attitude to the proposition (probably non-ironic assertion) and any necessary implicated conclusions, such as the Grounds of the metaphorical Apposition "the archives of the earth, the sedimentary rocks".

## 10.5. CONTEXT AND THE INTERPRETATION OF METAPHOR

Having sketched in a possible theoretical framework for integrating Hallidayan socio-linguistics and Relevance Theory I will now illustrate more specifically how the contextual variables in the social situation that is Field (what's going on), Tenor (who's involved in what relations) and Mode (the role of language), impinge on metaphorical interpretation. The six registers

1. ANOTHER('S) THOUGHT

2. VERBAL: ANOTHER('S) TEXT      3. NON-VERBAL: ARTEFACT

A. AN ACTUAL STATE      AI. AN IMAGINARY STATE
   OF AFFAIRS                   OF AFFAIRS

B. THOUGHT (INCLUDING ATTITUDE)
C. PROPOSITION
D. TEXT

*Figure 10.3* An elaborated model of linguistic communication

293

which I have selected for comparative purposes are Conversation, National News Reports, Popular Science articles, Magazine Advertising of consumer goods, Modern Novels and short Modern English Lyric Poetry.

We begin with an attempt to describe the contextual configuration of Field, Mode and Tenor for each variety.

Conversation

> Field: social interaction, conversation (a Field or end in itself; if subordinated to other purposes ceases to be conversation)
> Tenor: interlocutors; close to equal; social distance: medium to intimate; has largely phatic function (which overlaps with Field)
> Mode: language role: constitutive; channel: phonic; medium: spoken, with visual contact/feedback; small group or dyadic; processing time close to identical for speaker and hearer; rhetorically multifunctional (phatic?)

National News Reports

> Field: publishing (selling), newspapers, giving/receiving information and forming opinion about recent events of, or in the, public interest; ?entertainment
> Tenor: editorial team as writers, any literate members of country of publication as readers; unequal: editorial team knowledgeable authority, reader dependent on writers for information; readership not entirely assured, tending to read selectively; social distance: near maximum (identified but unknown journalist to unknown readers) but synthetic personalization in popular press
> Mode: language role: constitutive rather than ancillary (but related to economics of publishing, politics and the democratic process); channel: visual; medium: print/graphics; mass; processing time greater for addresser than addressee, but addresser still working to severe time pressure and addressee might skim etc.; rhetorically expository (persuasive or manipulative)

Popular Science

> Field: publishing magazines/books; investigating the physical properties of the universe; hypothesizing, justifying and/or explaining scientific theories/findings
> Tenor: journalist/scientist to magazine/newspaper/book reader; hierarchical: identified (eminent) expert authority as writer to non-expert readers (efforts made to explain the difficult in more comprehensible language); social distance: near maximum
> Mode: language role: rather constitutive but dependent on scientific research; channel: visual; medium: print/graphics; processing time for addresser greater than for addressee (based on meticulous and

time-consuming research); designed to be read carefully but probably only once: rhetorically expository

## Magazine Advertising

Field: economic, buying and selling; description and recommendation of product as persuasion to buy/information-gathering and decision-making about purchases

Tenor: company/advertising agency to reader; hierarchic: advertiser less powerful than potential buyers who are non-assured, perhaps reluctant addressees; social distance maximum but extreme synthetic personalization (often the ad promises that buying admits reader to a social group)

Mode: language role: ancillary to selling (but often read as constitutive?); channel: visual; medium: print with heavy reliance on graphics/visuals (and in phonological patterning often reflective of spoken); mass; addresser processing time disproportionately greater than addressee processing time, though possibility of (accidental) repeated processing; read/looked at selectively; rhetorically persuasive

## Modern Novels

Field: publishing books; entertainment, aesthetics, literature; creation of a fictional world and fictional characters, which more or less reflect society and psychology – thereby exploring themes of interpersonal/ social significance; exciting emotions of identification, sympathy or antipathy towards characters; and of suspense and curiosity in the reader

Tenor: author to unknown reader, but complicated by internal levels of narrators and characters as addressers; hierarchic: author is specially talented and skilled; reader is any literate interested member of the public; author varies in terms of assumed knowledge of the mental processes of characters; author in control of the withholding, revealing, and ordering of information; social distance between author and reader: maximum but, through being an implied narrator and relying on characters as narrators, is overlaid with fictional intimacy, disclosure of intimate details of thoughts and feelings

Mode: language role: entirely constitutive; channel: visual; medium: printed to be read; aspiring to reach a mass public; rewritten in several drafts, but usually one linear reading; processing time for addresser relatively large in proportion to reading time; rhetorically entertainment, imparting pleasure

Modern English Lyric Poetry

> Field: entertainment, aesthetics, literature; expression of/responding to emotion/beauty; (re-)creation of and reflection on an individual experience as a means of exploring themes of universal significance
>
> Tenor: poet to unknown reader; hierarchic: poet as unique voice to any poetry-reading member of public; but presumption of undivided attention from reader; social distance: maximum but, through implied poet/persona, overlaid with fictional intimacy, self-disclosure, vicarious sharing of experience
>
> Mode: language role: entirely constitutive;[1] channel: visual/aural; medium: printed to be spoken; mass; rewritten in several drafts and designed for rereading; processing time for addresser and addressee large in proportion to text processed; rhetorically entertainment, imparting pleasure

Having spelt out these contextual configurations we can proceed to present a number of hypotheses concerning the interpretation of metaphor in these registers.

### 10.5.1. The contribution of Field to metaphorical interpretation

An obvious hypothesis here would be that the detection (disambiguation) of a metaphorical meaning as opposed to literal meaning will depend on the principle of Relevance in relation to the Contents associated with Field.

Take the sentence *I shot an eagle*. If uttered at the end of a hunting expedition it will probably have its literal meaning. In the clubhouse after a round of golf the chances are the same verb phrase would have a metaphorical meaning ('two under par'). The literal meaning, if accessed in the clubhouse, would not be relevant to the Field, playing golf, and the nonliteral meaning would be selected. Since the metaphor here is Sleeping it is simply a question of disambiguation. However, taking a top-down approach one could even suggest that the influence of Field at level 6 (Figure 10.2) is so strong, that ambiguity does not arise and the choice of the metaphorical meaning is automatic. In other words, ambiguities in the code are overridden by the meaning potential of the social context.

Many early theories of metaphor stressed the role of semantic deviation in detection (Levin 1977). Deviant colligation, that is, semantic contradiction, or deviant collocation – lexical items which fail to fit into the major lexical sets represented by the text – were seen as signals. While this is a possible approach (see *colligation* in my definition on pp. 108–9 and in section 4.2.4), in fact metaphors are primarily deviant in their reference, and any collocational deviance occurs because they do not conventionally refer to the Contents of the Field. Colligational and collocational deviance are simply secondary by-products. Those theorists who admitted metaphor as basically pragmatic, like Grice (1975), thought of it as primarily a flouting of the maxim of Quality: the maxim that one should tell the truth or not make claims for which one lacks evidence. However, I am arguing that it is better diagnosed in terms of the maxim of Relation; that is, in terms of apparent irrelevance to Field Content.

Let's consider some examples from other varieties which illustrate the influence of Field on the detection of metaphor.

> CEC528   You might actually get three **duds**, I mean three people who you
>          didn't want.

The "conversation" in which these metaphors occur is actually an informal discussion of various candidates for a teaching post, and the current teaching needs of a department. Since the speakers are aware that the Field of discourse is educational administration not shooting, "duds" cannot have its literal meanings.

However, the following is an interesting contrasting example of a more Active metaphor from a news report:

> DT4   He had been subjected to "toothpaste tube" treatment. This involved a
>        corporal taking a rod or bar to him as he lay in bed, slamming it on the
>        bottom of the bed and then slamming progressively upwards until he had
>        his knees beneath his chin. When the rod reached him it was brought
>        down on his body.

Since the Field content is the treatment of privates by army officers, it gives us no guidance as to whether "toothpaste tube" is being used literally or metaphorically. Presumably toothpaste tubes are widely available in army camp life, and we could well imagine some kind of torture involving literal toothpaste tubes (though I won't suggest any exercises on this). This is one of the reasons the lexical item has to be explicitly marked as metaphorical with inverted commas. In fact, marking of metaphors typically takes place where the Field provides no clues for disambiguation, as we saw in section 6.2.

In the case of metaphors in advertising language the simple incongruence to Field (Content) as a means of marking metaphor undergoes an interesting complication. In GH123, for example, although "steps" is straightforwardly given its Sleeping metaphoric meaning, the co-presence of "walk" in the context re-activates the alternative literal meaning.

> GH123   Master the four basic **steps** of this recipe and you'll be able to **walk**
>         the more exotic stir-fry dishes.

Perhaps we can formalize this Revitalization according to the deductive logic of Relevance Theory as follows:

> (8)   a.   The advertisement is selling cooking utensils by promoting the recipes
>            that can be cooked with them.

    b. The word *step* either means 'a stage in a process' or 'the movement of a leg in walking'.

    c. Recipes involve stages in processes.

Thus d. *Step* means 'stage in a process'.

    e. *Walk* as a transitive verb usually means 'to perform easily' but it can mean 'move forward by taking steps'.

    f. Recipes involve performing a sequence of processes.

Thus g. *Walk* means 'perform easily'.

    h. Making steps is part of walking.

Thus i. The writer also intends us to notice the meanings 'move the leg in walking' and 'move forward by taking steps' as secondary meanings of *step* and *walk* respectively.

In GH155 the pun actually exploits two aspects of the Field: first, the metaphorical meaning of "splash out" relates to the position of advertising in the economic process of buying and selling; second, the literal meaning of *splash*, though probably not the phrasal verb *splash out* (section 3.2.4.3), relates to the goods being sold – bathrooms.

> GH155  A beautiful new bathroom from Graham makes freshening up a positive pleasure. But with interest free credit as well it feels even better. Because that means you won't have to **splash out** too much.

In poetry too we often have a metaphorical relation of one aspect of Field content with another aspect of the same content. In 'An advancement of learning' (see Introduction, pp. 10–11) the persona of the poem describes the flow of the river thus

> AL  The river **nosed** past

We might formalize the interpretation as follows:

(9)  a. The poet has said "the river nosed past".

    b. We speak literally of animals nosing past, not rivers.

    c. In saying "the river nosed past" the poet is not speaking literally, but metaphorically.

    d. The only animals mentioned in the co-text are rats.

Thus e. The poet is comparing the river with rats.

    f. The poet is obsessively afraid of rats.

    g. When people are obsessively afraid of something they misidentify other entities as the thing they are obsessed with.

Thus h. The poet compares the river with rats because of his obsessional fear of them.[2]

The detection of metaphor by irrelevance to the Field Contents becomes, therefore, more complex in adverts and poetry. The tendency to extend metaphors and thereby evoke minor Fields distant from the primary Content is especially pronounced in poetry and literature as we demonstrated at length in Chapter 9. In 'An Advancement of Learning' we have "established a bridgehead", "trained on me", "retreated" which all have meanings associated with the schema for warfare.

### 10.5.2. The contribution of Field/Tenor purpose to metaphor interpretation

A second hypothesis is that the kinds of Implicated Conclusions will be determined by the principle of Relevance in relation to the purposes inherent in Field and Tenor.

To use a simple example, the kinds of Implicated Conclusions to be found in a biology class will be different from the kinds of implicated conclusions to be discovered in conversation. Consider examples (10) and (11):

(10)   The kidney is the sewer of the body.

(11)   A:   Do you want to go on a boat trip on the river?
       B:   What, on that sewer?

Because conversation, both in Field and Tenor, has a strongly interpersonal and affective function, we could look for Implicated Conclusions of an attitudinal emotive kind in interpreting (11). Whereas in (10), where the Field is scientific education, and the social distance of the Tenor is greater, we expect metaphor to be explanatory and ideational rather than affective and interpersonal.

Before our more detailed survey of our six registers it will be useful to provide a sketchy overview of how the functions of metaphor (see Chapter 5) relate to the six registers being considered. See Table 10.1.

#### 10.5.2.1.  Conversation

As Table 10.1 shows, the kinds of metaphorical function associated with conversation are generally of an interpersonal nature, though there are often affective-laden expressions of opinion of an ideational type which can be Subjective Impositives. This accords with our labelling of Field as *social interaction* and Tenor (in section 10.5) as *phatic function*.

### ■ EXERCISE

*Identify the metaphors in the following conversational text, and discuss what functions they perform.*

CEC98–9   *I've got a thing anyway about academic women – I think something ghastly happens to them – but these women you know untouched by human hand it's just frightening just really is absolutely dehydrating.*

Table 10.1 Metaphorical functions in different genres

| | Conversation | National News Reports | Popular Science | Magazine Advertising | Modern Novels | Modern English Lyric Poetry |
|---|---|---|---|---|---|---|
| **Ideational** | | | | | | |
| Ideology | x | x | x | x | x | x |
| Filling Lexical Gaps | x | x | x | | x | x |
| Explanation/Modelling | | | x | | | |
| Reconceptualization | ?x | | x | | x | x |
| Argument by Analogy | ? | | x | ?x | | |
| **Interpersonal** | | | | | | |
| Expressing Emotion | x | ?x | | x | x | x |
| Decoration/Disguise | x | x | | x | x | x |
| Hyperbole | x | x(pop) | | x | x | x |
| Cultivating Intimacy | x | | | x | x | x |
| Humour and Games | x | x(pop) | | x | x | ?x |
| **Textual** | | | | | | |
| Textual Structuring | | | ?x | x | x | x |
| Memory/Foregrounding/Informativeness | | x(pop) | ?x | x | x | x |
| Fiction | | | | x | x | x |

Besides the hyperbole in this example of conversation (cf. Crystal and Davy 1969: 114), it is also common for jokes to be incorporated in chat.

CEC43    A: You know **the safest oral contraceptive**, do you?
         B: What?
         A: The two phonemic cluster "No."

(adapted)

Besides the fact that jokes, *qua* jokes, have a mainly interpersonal function we talk of *sharing* jokes, and when we hear a good one feel something of a burden until we have passed it on to our intimate friends – this particular joke cultivates intimacy in two additional ways. First, it will only be fully understood by those who are aware of what phonemes are. And second, it probably conveys negative attitudes to casual sex. It therefore cultivates intimacy with a, perhaps, rather small section of society – those linguists who disapprove of casual sex.

Though most of the spontaneous metaphors in conversation are Tired and Sleeping, their particularity and imageability have a phatic function. If I say

CEC520    There are certain areas of the syllabus which the students **queue up** for.

using "queue up" instead of "prefer", my hearer is invited to form a mental image. Such particularization can be interpreted interpersonally as a symptom of involvement, or affect (Chafe 1982; Tannen 1989: 24–7 and ch. 5).

### 10.5.2.2. National News Reports

The widespread use of hyperbole in the popular press matches one of the Field functions, entertainment, and is obviously a bid to attract the attention of a non-assured readership. Hyperbolic metaphors present Vehicles which are larger scale, more extreme, or more violent than the Topics to which they refer:

DM16–17    Did she [Fergie] keep **ice-cool**? . . . She shook out her **mane** of red hair . . .

We have already mentioned (section 3.1.3) the widespread use of violent Material process metaphors for Verbal and other processes in newspaper language (Fowler 1991: 144–5). This is both hyperbolic and a way of forming opinion (one of our Field Purposes) by constructing undesirable groups like soccer "hooligans" as an enemy. Also notable is the kind of wordplay in headlines which gets attention through Colligational non-referential metaphor.

IE7    The truck stops here, bitter boss tells ex-wife.

IE7 is the headline for a story of a husband who, forced to close down his road haulage business because of the unfavourable terms of a divorce settlement, parks his six lorries in front of his ex-wife's house and throws away the keys. He is reported as saying "the ball's in her court now", which suggests a metaphorical idiom underlying the headline.

(12) Topic     The truck stops here
     Vehicle   The [buck] stops here

However, serious newspapers, with their informative rather than entertainment priorities, generally discourage metaphorical processing.


### 10.5.2.3. Popular Science

Popular Science emphasizes the explanatory and reconceptualizing functions, as part of the ideational element. Explanatory comparisons entail the explicit spelling out of the Grounds of what would otherwise be metaphors, generally by Extension, deliberately by-passing the need for implicatures with their attendant uncertainties.

> NSLG1   Snake bites illustrate both the strengths and the weaknesses of the antibody system. On the positive side, the body can *manufacture* antibodies to *fit* any chemical – neither the horse nor its ancestors need to have encountered a cobra before. This chemical feat is not achieved by producing "**tailor-made**" antibodies to *suit* each new chemical as might be expected. Instead the body generates a vast number of "**off-the-peg**" antibodies with an almost infinite *variety of "shapes and sizes"*. One of these *is bound to fit* any new antigen.

Since science is actually a Field of activity devoted to making explicit theoretical models or metaphors (Boyd 1979; Kuhn 1979), providing the metaphorical Grounds in the co-text is essential to its *raison d'être*.

As far as reconceptualization is concerned, an article by James Lovelock is especially significant. It presents an alternative theory-constitutive model/metaphor, Gaia theory, hypothesizing that the earth is an organism which *regulates* its own environment, to replace the conventional theory that living organisms only *adapt* to it.

> NSLJ28   I see the world as **a living organism** of which we are a part; not the **owner**, nor the **tenant**, not even a **passenger on** that obsolete metaphor "**spaceship earth**".

The fact that new discoveries are being retailed in the Popular Science genre creates a need for new lexis, often supplied metaphorically. In the Introduction (pp. 1–2) I quoted many metaphorical items from indexes to a book on Chaos theory and popular natural history.

### 10.5.2.4. Magazine Advertising

In advertising we have to recognize the importance of interpersonal functions and relate this to the Field which is selling. Punning is a widespread technique and strengthens the emotional bond between customer and product by the association of pleasurable experiences with the latter. A particularly interesting example is the advertisement for Anglia Building Society (P71) (Plate 2). The logo for this company is a triangle which appears prominently in the ad. The copy reads:

P71   If buying a house seems a **vicious circle**, try Anglia.

A slight change of pronunciation gives us *triangular*!

These puns have both a decorative function and, more important, a phatic one: decorative, in the sense that the understanding of the ambiguity which gives rise to the humour is not necessary for understanding the main point of the copy; phatic, in the sense that one of the purposes of humour is to lower the psychological defences, to open the way for closer contact and intimacy.

So humour becomes a tool for synthetic personalization – addressing a mass audience as though talking to them intimately as individuals (Fairclough 1989: 217ff.). Synthetic personalization may also lie behind the personifying tendency of ads; the product can be promoted as a human being, capable of solving problems for the customer. This represents a triumph for the ideology of consumer capitalism (Dyer 1984: 77–84) as we exchange real political power for purchasing power, and products become powerful and considerate agents which remove our problems. So washing-up liquids are *kind* to hands, cold remedies are *gentle*, shampoos "tackle dryness from two angles", "ward off further drying out threats from hairdryers" and help anyone "get their hair out of trouble" (GH142–3). Cars are frequently humans:

(13)   Our 2.5 **family** is eagerly waiting for yours. (*Punch*, May 1987, p. 29)

Given the obvious interpersonal slant of these ads it would be facetious to look for many rich ideational implicatures from personification, beyond those of rather vague, positively affective user-friendliness or helpfulness.

### 10.5.2.5. Modern Novels

Novels and poetry, both being literature, share some purposes in common. They both demand exact description to give a reality effect, so some metaphors will be highly perceptual, highly visual. This is the case in the first four metaphors in the following extract, which is set in the National Gallery in London.

*Plate 2* Advertisement for Anglia Building Society, published 1986; courtesy of Nationwide Building Society

VG11–12    She extended her hands. In one was a greenish square of mirror glass, possibly a tiny bathroom tile. In the other was a **crushed strawberry** cloakroom ticket with 69 on one side and LOVE stamped on the other in mauve ink.

"Pressed on me by a **platinum** blonde **Pocahantas** and **a cowboy** in a green eyeshade. Is it a joke, or an earnest message?"

"Both," said Alexander. "All our earnest messages are couched as jokes and we take them deadly seriously. We frame them and cover our gallery walls with them. The great British sense of humour, cross-fertilized by American self-consciousness, the Latin absurd and the Oriental **fingersnap** or educative **blow on the ear.**"

Novels are more interested than poetry in the cut and thrust of conversation as social interaction, so that clashes of Subjectivity and Impositive statements are common. The whole of Alexander's speech, including the metaphors, is Impositive polemic about British attitudes to art, and implies a contradiction of the presupposition of the first speaker's question. Foregrounding with the striking turn of phrase makes paradoxes quite common in literature, as in *we take them* [our jokes] *deadly seriously*. There is also the space for polyvalence and indeterminateness of metaphorical interpretation in novels and poetry. As coy ritual objects capable of rereading they should not yield all their meanings first time. Such obscurity is exemplified by the last two metaphors, which I don't understand.

## 10.5.2.6. Modern English Lyric Poetry

Short lyric poetry recreates individual experience in an aesthetically pleasing way, and attempts to share an emotional response as a reflection of self-disclosural Tenor. So, many of the metaphors, besides describing vividly and exactly the physical properties of the experience, present aesthetically pleasing images, and evoke strong emotions.

In 'An advancement of learning' (see Introduction, pp. 10–11) the succession of military metaphors such as "he trained on me" and the lines with their synaesthetic metaphor "Something slobbered curtly, close, **Smudging** the silence" have a strong emotional component, underlined by the phonological patterning. While "He **clockworked** aimlessly a while" probably meets the demand for vivid and exact description of the visual experience. While "The **raindrop** eye" combines exact description with a pleasurable aesthetic experience.

## 10.5.3. Genre and adequate Relevance

One of the grey areas in Relevance Theory is in what number and kind of Contextual Effects are necessary in order to achieve a relevant interpretation. There seem to be three possibilities here, as pointed out by Levinson

(1989: 463), and the specification of genre will help us to decide what counts as an adequate level of relevance.

In the first case Relevance has a predetermined value, and contexts will be expanded until this value is satisfied. This applies to genres like jokes, crossword puzzles and riddles, where we go on accessing Contextual Assumptions until the solution clicks. Let's take another look at the two-phonemic cluster joke. It can be interpreted along the following lines:

(14) a. The speaker has conveyed the proposition "the two phonemic cluster 'No' is the safest oral contraceptive".
   b. The two phonemic cluster 'No' is not an oral contraceptive.
   c. Therefore the speaker is not speaking literally.
   d. In saying "No is an oral contraceptive" the speaker is speaking metaphorically.
   e. Speaking metaphorically involves making comparisons or analogies.
   f. Contraceptives prevent conception as a result of sex.
   g. Saying *no* when offered sex will also prevent sex and therefore conception.
Thus h. The speaker is making a metaphorical comparison between saying *No* when offered sex and a contraceptive.
   i. *Oral* when used of contraceptives means 'taken by mouth'.
   j. *Oral* can also mean 'of the mouth'.
   k. Saying *No* involves movement of the mouth.
Thus l. The speaker intends us to be aware of both meanings of *oral*.
   m. The speaker has said *No* is the *safest* contraceptive.
Thus n. The speaker believes that abstaining from sex is safer than using contraceptives.

Provided the hearer is aware of the generic conventions of jokes, and the joke has been adequately signalled, he will assume that, once any reasonably likely implicated conclusion such as (14h) has been reached, there is no need to continue generating weaker Implicated Conclusions such as (14n). So with jokes, like crossword puzzles, Relevance has a fixed value and contexts will be expanded until that is reached. However some jokes, as well as being jokes for purely humorous effect, are also designed to make a point, and this might be interpreted as one of them, justifying the extra effort of continuing up to (14n).

In some genres, like poetry, we will set this predetermined value almost infinitely high, so that we can go on processing live metaphors and generating multiple meanings for as long as we wish. In this case we can have extra or secondary interpretations. The interpretation of the Shakespearean metaphor "those boughs which shake against the cold, bare ruined choirs where late the sweet birds sang" given in section 5.1.3. is already very rich. But this does not prevent us generating other interpretations which we can entertain simultaneously. Since in the original *choirs* was spelt *quires*

Shakespeare might be referring to the sheets of paper on which he wrote his poems, and by implication the poems themselves, which are now ruined, and in which he used to sing before he became bitter about his lover's unfaithfulness.

A second way of computing relevance will be to see it as a comparative measure so that the best of the competing interpretations are selected. For example Lakoff and Turner (1989: 28) give a quite different interpretation to the Shakespearean metaphor in which they take the referent of *choir* to be a wooden choir loft, a gallery at the back of a church. Under this interpretation a different set of implicatures is generated so that, if we accept Lakoff and Turner's interpretation we cannot preserve the idea that the pillars in the nave of the church are like tree trunks, with the vaulting on the roof the intersecting branches. We have to choose between one or the other.

A third way of assessing adequate relevance is to "assume that processing costs will have a threshold value, so that the first available Contextual Assumption which yields any effect will be automatically selected".[3] This is probably observable in most conversational metaphors. In CEC102 the speaker is talking about the way she adapted to and joined in common room talk in an Oxford college:

CEC102    I sat there all the time thinking this isn't me – and I was really – I don't know how much of a **chameleon** I was being in this common room conversation – you know – expressing great animate – animated interests in these theories

The meaning 'changing to suit one's surroundings' is an obviously relevant implication which the surrounding speech makes quite explicit anyway. With Tired metaphors like this, the computation of Grounds is almost automatic, so that we take the first available interpretation to yield any Contextual Effect. There would be no question of trying to elaborate by suggesting the speaker was looking in two directions at once, or considered the ideas she listened to as flies with their negative associations of disease, even though these interpretations might be relevant to the Field Content.

There are many symptoms of the ways in which the genre affects the amount of Processing Effort that can be presumed upon in metaphorical interpretation. Limiting ourselves to two areas we can consider the interplay of metaphors and the uses of allusion.

Journalism is notorious for its Mixing, suggesting that we should process quickly and easily, ignoring metaphors, their original Vehicles and their attendant ambiguities as much as possible. Certainly the writer of the following copy did not have in mind juice made out apples which had been stored in a cellar:

IE3    a **windfall** of £2 million from the **foundation** for sport is being **pumped** into the West London studio to take them out of receivership

Literary texts, as we demonstrated fully in Chapter 9, usually control carefully the interplay between metaphors. Even when they are Mixed, or Diverse, successful literature often manages the transitions effectively by various ambiguities and the sharing of Grounds. Lines 3–5 from 'An advancement of learning' (Introduction, pp. 10–11) illustrate this:

> The river **nosed** past,
> **Pliable, oil-skinned, wearing**
> **A transfer** of gables and sky.

Noses are pliable, the paints used in transfers, the sheets of children's pictures, are oil-based. One reading of "oil-skinned", 'with a skin of oil', reminds us that oil is thicker than water and therefore "pliable" applies to it more literally; the alternative reading 'covered with an oilskin' suggests the clothing used by sailors which is literally "pliable" and designed for "wearing".

A second symptom of the different degrees of Processing Effort is the way allusion is handled across genres. In an advertisement for the Mitsubishi Cordia car we have the slogan "The Shape of Cars to Come", echoing, with variation, the title of H.G. Wells' tract *The Shape of Things to Come* (1933). In advertisement allusions one is simply required to register the familiarity of the phrase rather than to explore the extra Grounds derivable from comparing the two texts. So, the pessimistic tone of Wells' work would be quite inappropriate to the optimistic hype for a new model of car.

Contrast this with a metaphorical allusion taken from the Popular Science 'Gaia' article:

NSLJ25   Planetary control would require the existence of some kind of **giant Panglossian nanny** who had looked after the earth since life began.

The metaphor alludes to the character Pangloss in Voltaire's *Candide* (1759) who repeatedly claims that we live in the best of all possible worlds. Lovelock does not allow the allusion free rein to wander over whatever Grounds it wishes, but in two other areas of the text actually quotes or adapts the words of Pangloss: "This is the best of all worlds, but only for those who have adapted to it"; "we live on 'the best of all possible worlds'". In this Popular Science text the other possible implicatures we might initially generate for the metaphorical allusion will be discarded in favour of the one explicitly endorsed.

Compare both these examples with the processing of the title of the poem 'An advancement of learning' which, as we noted earlier, is an allusion to the work of Francis Bacon. Unlike the allusion in the Cordia advert, the allusion in this poem has a good deal of relevance, as the first section of Bacon's work is devoted entirely to disposing of objections to learning, just as the persona disposes of his objections to encountering rats. However, unlike the Lovelock allusion, we have to postulate these Grounds without help from the text. We noted earlier (section 5.2.11) how Golding's allusions in *Free Fall* often repay large investments of Processing Effort, as in the use of names like *Sammy* and *Beatrice*. This allusive care is a hallmark of literary genres.

### 10.5.4. Processing Effort and processing time

If Processing Effort is dependent on processing time, to understand what is adequately relevant we must consider the temporal dimensions of each genre, as entailed by Mode. In other words, we have a further hypothesis: the amount of Processing Effort as part of the value of Relevance will depend upon the time available for processing within each genre.

Basically the length of production and processing time, determines the possible kinds of metaphoric effects, and correlates with the kinds of purpose to which metaphors are put in different registers.[4] More exactly, two aspects of time are relevant to the question of the relation between Mode and metaphorical purpose. The first aspect is simply a measure of the time available for production and processing. The second aspect concerns the symmetry or asymmetry between production and processing time in any particular Mode or register (Chafe 1982: 36–8). I diagram my intuitive sense of the relationships in Figure 10.4, where the relative length of production time is represented by the length of the lines on the left, and the length of processing time by the lines on the right.

Since conversation is largely spontaneous, production and processing time are extremely short, and more or less symmetrical. This predicts that Inactive metaphors will be common. The jokes/riddles which incorporate Active metaphors in their interpretation (CEC43, p. 301) are, of course, not spontaneous at all but echoic, and probably allow the hearer a substantial pause to guess the answer.

In National News Reports there is considerable time pressure on the producers to meet edition deadlines, so that, among our written genres, they take the least time to compose. Although the permanence of the medium makes leisurely processing possible, in practice a news report will be skimmed and scanned or read partially and quickly. The relative speed of both production and processing time accounts for the fact that writers are careless enough to produce mixed metaphors and yet generally "get away with it".

Popular Science, with less frequent deadlines, has more time at its disposal to control its metaphors. In a sense, too, the time spent on the research reported counts as production time, since scientific research is often devoted to exploring what exactly are the metaphoric Grounds on which a model or theory is based. So theory-constitutive or explanatory metaphors are very carefully selected, signalled and their Grounds are

| Genre | Addresser time | Addressee time |
|-------|----------------|----------------|
| Conversation | — | — |
| National News Reports | —— | — |
| Popular Science | —— | — |
| Magazine Advertising | ——— | — |
| Modern Novels | ——— | —— |
| Modern English Lyric Poetry | ———— | ———— |

*Figure 10.4* Relative times for processors in different genres

elaborated at length. The reader has the time to stop and think carefully, and backtrack if need be. However, because of their explicitness, the reading of these articles is more straightforward and less time-consuming than poetry, which leaves the reader to identify metaphors and generate Implicated Conclusions with less co-textual help.

Advertising copy is composed with a good deal of time and labour, but read rapidly, if at all, so that processing time is wildly asymmetric. Metaphors, therefore, are carefully selected and combined, but, acknowledging the speed of processing, attract attention and produce the kind of quick-fire effect associated with puns, where speed is the essence of the humour. We are seldom invited to explore Grounds and, as we noted, allusions in ads are seldom "milked" to the extent they are in poetry or literature.

Novels are rather variable as a genre, and one might want to distinguish the popular from the literary. On the whole they are certainly composed with more time and care than journalism, but I suspect less time per word than ads and poetry. Reading takes more time than ads and newspapers (Zwaan 1993), but writing and reading time will still be asymmetric. Probably literary novels demand more time than Popular Science, so that metaphors can afford to be more suggestive and the Grounds less neatly packaged. Such novels can exploit allusion to as great an extent as poetry, presuming a leisurely pace of reading and allowing for rereading. This suggests a novel can be engaged with at different levels, with different degrees of processing. I read *Animal Farm* (1954) when I was 11, simply as a fable, and *Gulliver's Travels* (1726) is often presented as a children's classic.

Poetry is the most time-consuming, both from the production and processing standpoints. Much of the work of recognizing the metaphor and hypothesizing Topics and Grounds is left to the reader. The poet makes little allowance for superficial reading and assumes the poem will be reread and lived with over a period of years, perhaps a time-span even longer than its slow composition. One might, on one's death-bed, see a new meaning in the compound Shakespearean metaphor:

> In me thou seest the glowing of such fire
> That on the ashes of his youth doth lie,
> As the death-bed, whereon it must expire,
> Consumed by that which it was nourished by.
>
> (Sonnet 73)

## 10.6. ASPECTS OF METAPHORICAL EXPRESSIONS IN DIFFERENT GENRES: A SURVEY AND SUMMARY

We've now given many examples of how Relevance Theory and a developed notion of social context can be brought together to explain metaphorical interpretation. But to go beyond exemplification and find general patterns I have made a rough statistical survey of our six genres based on a number of diverse texts within each genre.[5] My purpose was to investigate how they compare according to the dimensions of metaphor investigated in Chapters 1 to 9.[6] This final section of the chapter, therefore, constitutes a summary and tying together of the lines along which we described metaphor in each of the preceding chapters, as Table 10.2 makes clear.

Table 10.2 shows the statistical patterns I discovered in the above genres. The most reliable and significant of the statistics are presented in bold. Figures in larger font are reliable enough, but figures in shaded areas need to be viewed with some caution, either because my own interpretation was involved or because the sample was too small.

Let's consider each column in turn. The first column gives the percentages of Active metaphors. Notable are the low figures in National News Reports, partly explained by short processing time. Quality papers use Active metaphors even less than popular ones, with the *Financial Times* only using one. Rather surprising are the relatively high percentages in Conversation, possibly inflated by performance "mistakes" or slips of the tongue that I have processed, asymmetrically, as metaphors, e.g. *she slapped on the brakes* [slammed], *what turned you on to this job* [put you on]. Not surprisingly Modern English Lyric Poetry provides the highest percentage, and either Magazine Advertising or Modern Novels come second highest depending upon whether one includes Revitalized metaphor in ads (the figures in parentheses). Metaphor is used deliberately in Popular Science, and Tired metaphor kept to the minimum.

Column 2 shows whether Active metaphors belong to the Transfer, Concretizing or Approximation variety. To consider the Transfer/Concretizing distinction first. I took all the Active metaphors with noun and verb

Table 10.2 A metaphorical profile of six genres

| Genre | Column 1 | Column 2 | Column 3 | Column 4 | Column 5 |
|---|---|---|---|---|---|
| | | | Chapter | | |
| | 1 & 2 | 2 | 3 | 3 | 4 |
| | ACTIVE M as % OF TOTAL | TRANSFER CONCRET. APPROX. | WORD-CLASS ACTIVE M | WORD-CLASS INACTIVE M | REFERENCE/ COLLIGATION |
| Conversation | 10% | Tran. 59%<br>Conc. 41%<br><br>Appx. 6% | N 35%<br>V* 58%<br>Adj. 6%<br>Adv. 0% | N 22%<br>V 48%<br>Adj. 24%<br>Adv. 6% | 22% |
| National News Reports | 4% | Tran. 61%<br>Conc. 39%<br><br>Appx. 1.7% | N 65%<br>V 22%<br>Adj. 13%<br>Adv. 0% | N 36%<br>V 45%<br>Adj. 16%<br>Adv. 4% | |
| Popular Science | 18% | Tran. 97%<br>Conc. 3%<br><br>Appx. 0.2% | N 58%<br>V 35%<br>Adj. 7%<br>Adv. 0% | N 34%<br>V 47%<br>Adj. 16%<br>Adv. 3% | 49% |
| Magazine Advertising | 22%<br>(31% rev) | Tran. 83%<br>Conc. 17%<br><br>Appx. 3% | N 62%<br>V 30%<br>Adj. 12%<br>Adv. 1% | 43% 28%<br>24% 48%<br>24% 22%<br>3% 2% | 53% |
| Modern Novels | 28% | Tran. 64%<br>Conc. 36%<br><br>Appx. 2.7% | N 56%<br>V 21%<br>Adj. 21%<br>Adv. 1% | N 25%<br>V 50%<br>Adj. 20%<br>Adv. 6% | 23% |
| Modern English Lyric Poetry | 56% | Tran. 57%<br>Conc. 43%<br><br>Appx. 1.6% | N 41%<br>V *49%<br>Adj. 15%<br>Adv. 1% | N 14%<br>V *57%<br>Adj. 22%<br>Adv. 7% | 63% |

| Genre | Column 6 | Column 7 | Column 8 | Column 9 | Column 10 |
|-------|----------|----------|----------|----------|-----------|
| | | | Chapter | | |
| | 4 | 6 | 7 | 8 | 9 |
| | SUBJECTIVE | SIGNAL | T SPECIFIED | G SPECIFIED | EXTENSION SYMBOLIZE |
| Conversation | 6% | 30%<br><br>Simcomp 14% | | | E 2.5%<br><br>S 0.2% |
| National News Reports | 4% | 39%<br><br>Simcomp 23% | | | E 3%<br><br>S 0.15% |
| Popular Science | 7% | 14%<br><br>Simcomp 21% | Gen 41%<br>Cop *41%<br>App 4%<br>Prem 15% | G's 60%<br>Definite Similes: 67% | E 13%<br><br>S 1% |
| Magazine Advertising | 2% | 12%<br><br>Simcomp 10% | Gen 32%<br>Cop 27%<br>App *15%<br>Pre *27% | G's 40% | E 23%<br><br>S 1.6% |
| Modern Novels | 9% | 8%<br><br>Simcomp 32% | Gen 52%<br>Cop 30%<br>App 5%<br>Pre 13% | G's 40%<br>Definite Similes: 52% | E 19%<br><br>S 5% |
| Modern English Lyric Poetry | 8% | 2%<br><br>Simcomp 13% | Gen 41%<br>Cop 21%<br>App *26%<br>Pre 12% | G's 36%<br>Definite Similes: 68% | E 30%<br><br>S 10% |

*Note*: The figures in parentheses include revitalized metaphor.
*Source*: The texts used for statistics in this table are to be found on pp. 345–6 in the References.

313

V-terms and calculated percentages of the total for each genre. The result-ing figures can be seen to correlate with Field, both from the Activity and Contents dimensions. The highest percentage of Transfer active metaphors are found in Popular Science; since the Field Content is description of the physical properties of the universe, rather than abstract theorizing, there is little scope for Concretizing Analogy. The next highest percentage of transfers is with advertisements where, similarly, Contents are physical products. Modern Lyrics have the highest percentage of Concretizing metaphors because the Field contents are partly the abstract *themes of universal significance*. The last six lines of Yeats' 'Prayer for my daughter' exemplify this tendency:

> For <u>arrogance</u> and <u>hatred</u> are **the wares**
> **Peddled** in the thoroughfares.
> How but in custom and in ceremony
> Are innocence and beauty born?
> <u>Ceremony</u>'s the name for **the rich horn**,
> And <u>custom</u> for the **spreading laurel tree**.

This Concretizing is balanced by the need to recreate a physical experience of some kind, demanding the vivid imagery of transfer metaphors. The percentages suggest that Modern Novels tip the balance in favour of physically descriptive Transfer metaphors, rather than the Concretizing and symbolic ones of poetry.

I also give some rough figures for relative occurrences of Approximative metaphors. These are calculated as a percentage of all Inactive and Active metaphors for each genre. The difficulty here is that we have no reliable test for whether a description is approximative or not. Consequently I count as approximative only those cases where the approximation is marked, e.g. "about fifty", or where round figures, e.g. "£150,000", suggest inexacti-tude. Not surprisingly, Conversation comes top, followed by Magazine Advertising. The spontaneity of conversation leads to imprecision, and there is little pressure to be accurate because Field-wise Conversation is generally constitutive, so information exchanged is not usually the basis for important transactional decisions. Often imprecision in Conversation is a matter of exaggeration rather than understatement, which fits with its phatic, entertaining, attention-grabbing nature. The frequency of approx-imation or hyperbole in Magazine Advertising reflects, too, this fore-grounding function; the desire to make exaggerated claims which, however, have to be downtoned for the sake of advertising standards, sometimes with devastating results: "Virtually every Hygena kitchen has passed the toughest tests". God help us if we bought one that got away! In contrast with Conversation and Ads, Popular Science, with the lowest figure, prides itself on meticulous accuracy of information. News Reports claim the same kind of accuracy, but the figures are boosted by the approximations which occur in directly quoted speech, as are the Modern Novel percentages. Modern Lyric Poetry tends to be very sparse with Approximative metaphors, apart from the occasional hyperbolic Approximation in Ted Hughes, or gesture towards a conversational tone in Philip Larkin and Edward Thomas. If a poet were constantly to signal imprecision, this might be an admission of poetic failure, the ability to find the *mot juste*. After all, it is the words which *create* the Phenomenalistic poetic or fictional world; that a world is being *described* is an extra fiction.

Columns 3 and 4 show the word-class of the V-term, column 3 for Active metaphors, column 4 for Inactive. The Advertising boxes are divided into three – Active, Revitalized and Inactive – to allow for the high proportion of Revitalizing puns. As predicted by the hypotheses in Chapter 3, the more Active the metaphor the more likely it is to be nominal. The only exception to this is in Conversation, due to slips of the tongue, all verbs. In Modern Lyric Poetry verbs are more common than nouns as V-terms of Active metaphors; the general metaphoric heightening in poetry spills over beyond the more obvious thing-referring nouns to verbs, either allowing for Vehicle-construction, or as a result of metaphorical Extension. Conversation is the genre with the highest number of Inactive adjectival V-terms, and shows a much greater difference than other genres between the Active, 6 per cent, and the Inactive, 24 per cent. This reflects the plethora of affective adjective metaphors like **poor**, **bored**, **tough**, **smooth**, **shattered** and adjectives attached to abstract nouns, e.g. **long** *time*, which are often hyperbolic – a **huge** *affair*, **enormous** *disparity*. These confirm that the expression of affect as an element of the interpersonal function is particularly pronounced in Conversation.

The figures in column 5 are percentages for Active verb and adjective V-terms, and depend on the primary distinction between purely referential uses and those colligations to which evocative Vehicle-construction is relevant. The figures reflect the care with which Active metaphors are used in Adverts, Popular Science and above all Poetry, and tend to correlate with the figures for metaphorical Extension (column 10): Extension actually provides the conventional colligate/collocate, in many cases.

Column 6 gives rough figures for Subjective metaphors, both the Impositive and perceptual. The low figures for News Reports convey the impression of value-free objectivity, rather than personal comment, and most of the few examples occur in quoted speech. The highish figure for Popular Science reflects the number of times disputed or doubtful theories are mentioned in the texts. The highest figure for Modern Novels arises from the representation of conversational disagreements, probably exaggerating the number found in actual conversation for dramatic purposes.

Most significant are the top bold figures in column 7: the percentage of Active metaphors which are marked in each genre. The inverse rank order for these figures matches exactly the rank order of the figures in column 1.

The greater the likelihood of Active metaphor occurring in a particular genre, the less likely is that genre to signal Active metaphors. We are primed to expect Active metaphor in genres in the following decreasing order: Modern Lyric Poetry, Modern Novels, Advertising, Popular Science, Conversation and News Reports. The figures below concern similes and other comparisons, which signal metaphors or downgrade them to explicit comparisons. Modern Novels and Popular Science are higher than we would expect compared with the top figures. This suggests that the literariness of Novels depends much more than Modern Lyric Poetry on the use of similes and points to the need for Popular Science to make explicit comparison as part of the descriptive/explanatory nature of its Field.

Column 8 considers in detail how Topics are specified in Active noun V-term metaphors, considering the Genitive, the Copula (and similar constructions), Apposition and Premodification. (There is not enough data to give meaningful figures for Conversation and News Reports.) Noticeably the Genitive construction is very important for reasons we've suggested (section 7.9). The high number of appositives in Modern Lyric Poetry and Advertising require comment. It may be that Modern Poetry favours the Apposition construction, inexplicit in its simple juxtaposition (Frye 1957: 123–4). Certainly, it makes for brevity, a possible reason for its frequent use in ads, where space costs money. The high incidence of the Copula in Popular Science, indicates that this genre is more particular about making its metaphorical equations through Assignment, rather than relying on the vaguer associative Genitive and Appositive constructions.

Our ninth column deals with the specification of Grounds for Active metaphors. (The figures given at the top are for G-terms occurring in the same sentence as the V-term.) What is significant is the higher percentage of Grounds given in Popular Science texts, reducing the risky indeterminacy associated with metaphor. The lower figures deal with similes. (Similes are divided into two groups: (a) those where *like* and *as* simply signal a metaphor, or vaguely indicate Grounds, e.g. *look like*, *sound like*, or are metaphorizing similes (section 6.4.8.1); and (b) those which give a more definite Ground indication/specification: "Like **cows** they clattered new shiny bells around their necks", "it was as hot and public as a **market place**". The percentages are for group (b) as a percentage of the total.) Precision uses of similes and comparisons appear equally important in Poetry and Popular Science. Novels, on the other hand, seem less precise and exploit Metaphorizing Similes more. Or, comparison with column 7 suggests that similes in Novels are often used simply to satisfy the need to mark metaphors in that genre.

Our last column deals with the interplay of metaphors, giving figures for Extension and Symbolism. The low extension percentages for Conversation and News Reports reflect time constraints, an aspect of Mode, and the high numbers for Ads and Modern Lyric Poetry reflect the slow and leisurely time frame of composition.[7] Figures for Symbolism show that this is more important in literature, to satisfy the need for universal thematic significance (section 9.11). These higher figures for Modern Novels and Modern Lyric Poetry match neatly the higher figures of Concretizing metaphors in these genres, as seen in column 2.

Table 10.2 more or less summarizes the whole book. But we should, to finish, say a little about four of our clines of metaphoricity and how they relate to genre. (See Figure 1.4, repeated here as Figure 10.5. Our findings on the cline of Contradictoriness have already been summed up in section 7.9.1.)

Column 1 deals with the second scale, the basically diachronic one by which what were once Active metaphors become Lexicalized in the dictionary. We realize that we can expect more Active metaphors in Modern Lyric Poetry and Novels than in News Reports and Conversation. Steen has also demonstrated that the largest difference between journalistic and literary metaphors is their relative conventionality (Steen 1994: 193, fig. 8.1, Factor 1). From column 6, dealing with the third cline of Marking, we noted that signalling varies inversely with these expectations.

Column 2 addresses the first cline, the question of Approximation, Transfer and Concretizing Analogy, migrations between progressively distant Vehicle and Topic domains. The concrete Contents of the Field in Advertising and Popular Science privilege Transfer over Analogy. In Conversation the Mode demands on processing time make approximation common. But in News Reports, despite the tight time deadlines, the need to give a patina of reliability excludes frequent use of obviously Approximative metaphors. Concretizing Analogy and Symbolism (column 10) is demanded by Modern Novels and Modern Lyric Poetry in order to satisfy the Field requirement of the pursuit of universal themes.

Lastly, the scale of Explicitness. We noted that Popular Science favours Copula Topic specifications more than the other genres (column 8) and is more careful than the other three to specify Grounds (column 9). Taken

(1) Approximative Similarity ———————————— Distant Similarity/Analogy

(2) Conventionality ———————————————— Unconventionality

(3) Marking ———————————————————— No Marking

(4) Non-contradictoriness ———————————— Contradictoriness

(5) Explicitness ———————————————— Inexplicitness

*Figure 10.5* Five metaphorical clines

317

together with the figures of columns 1 and 6 these findings suggest that News Reports and Conversation avoid the risky business of unspecified and unmarked Active metaphors, with their potential for generating a large number of weak implicatures or uncertain Grounds. While Popular Science, though using Active metaphors more than News Reports and Conversation, is explicit in metaphorical expression, thereby reducing the need for implicatures. By contrast Modern Lyric Poetry, and to a lesser extent Modern Novels, delight in giving extra implicative work to the reader, by lack of marking, by using Appositions and Genitives, and by specifying Grounds less often and less clearly. This is in line with Gentner's (1982) findings that what counts as a good literary metaphor is rich evocativeness, and what counts as a good scientific metaphor is conceptual clarity. The conclusion must be that the cut-off point for generating relevant implicated Grounds varies from genre to genre.

## 10.7. POSTSCRIPT: FURTHER RESEARCH

I hope this book has gone some way towards remedying the relative neglect of the textual aspects of metaphorical language. While it was being written, another book by Gerard Steen (1994) was published which takes a rigorous psychological approach to metaphorical interpretation. Particularly relevant to this chapter are his findings on the perceived differences between Literary and Journalistic metaphors (1994: 71–2, 207). For further research I would suggest that the hypotheses about the influence of language and textual specification which have been arrived at in this volume, especially Chapters 2, 3, 7, and 10, along with the responses of readers to some of the exercises scattered through this book, will encourage more linguistically informed, psychological research.

I hope, too, that, since language and metaphor are closely involved with each other, this book has given some insights into the nature of the English language, the structure of its lexicon, word-formation, syntax, semantics, and the pragmatic principles employed to understand it. I learnt most of what I know of the linguistics of English through the study of metaphor, and I hope my thoughts on this trope stimulate an interest in the way language works both in literary and non-literary texts.

## 10.8. SUGGESTIONS FOR FURTHER WORK

I began this book with an invitation to text analysis. And I end in the same way. Below are extracts which are more or less typical of the generic patterns of Table 10.2. You might work through them with that table in mind, identifying the metaphors, commenting in any way on their activity level, their classification, the ways in which the text guides interpretation, and their functions in relation to context. I give brief notes of my own following the passages.

### 10.8.1. Conversation

A:   I don't think the printed word has had its day any more than the people who run the Open University think the printed word has had its day

B:   no they're using it –

A:   but it's a question of gearing the various modes of communi-  5
cation together to make a sort of combination thing because the eye is as important as the ear is as important as the eye – reading – so you can look at television and you can listen to sound presentations and you can look at print and illustrative material  10

B:   there is

A:   but it's a question of what you use – when – for what purposes

B:   there is a change though the number of really quite bright young people there are around today who have virtually never read a book – and are quite well-informed  15

A:   that's right but it's still not true to say that print has had its day because they are disadvantaged – they can't make references you see

B:   no

A:   because – well – obviously television is something which goes  20
past like film and you can't refer back

B:   linear entirely

A:   yes quite – the unfortunate McLuhan seemed to think that print was linear which was about the most stupid mistake anybody could possibly have made  25

B:   oh he got all back to front – rubbish to McLuhan

A:   absolutely hopelessly back to front yes completely dotty

(CEC: 262–3)

- Only one Active metaphor "gearing" (l. 5), a Verb V-term; many Inactive ones: "had its day" (l. 3), "rubbish" (l. 26), "dotty" (l. 27), often exploiting Root Analogies: "run" (l. 2), "bright" (l. 13), "you see" (l. 18) "goes past" (l. 20–1), "back to front" (l. 26).
- All these are analogical.
- High numbers of approximations marked by intensifiers and downtoners "really", "quite" (l. 13), "virtually" (l. 14), "about" (l. 24), also sometimes marking metaphors
- Other metaphorical markers such as "sort of" (l. 6), "as" (l. 7), "seemed" (l. 23).

- Adjectival Inactive metaphors noticeable: "back to front", "dotty" (l. 27).
- Referential rather than colligational.
- Subjective metaphors: McLuhan's Impositive view (ll. 23–4) and the speaker's refutation of it (ll. 24–5).
- No Extension.
- Emotive Grounds "rubbish" (l. 26) and hyperbole (ll. 24–5, 27) serving the interpersonal function.

### 10.8.2. National News Reports

*Summer rail strike threat looms*

Another summer of rail misery is in prospect after a second union decided to ballot its members on one-day strikes over pay.

Jimmy Knapp's Rail Maritime and Transport Union joined the train drivers union Aslef in rejecting British Rail's "final" three per cent offer.                                                                    5

BR urged its 77,000 workers involved in the dispute not to inflict more "misery" on rail travellers after last year's signal-workers strikes. Personnel director Paul Watkinson said it was "generous" compared with other public sector workers and called on rail employees to think "long and hard" before voting to 10 strike.

BR will write to its workers explaining the offer in full. Mr Watkinson said he was confident the vast majority would reject industrial action. The railway's recovery from recession and last summer's strikes was "fragile" and would be damaged by 15 another dispute.

RMT general secretary Mr Knapp said the union's target remained six per cent.

A three per cent rise would add £55 million to BR's pay bill. Mr Watkinson said he had a "gut feeling" the unions were 20 willing to settle for a rise around the current inflation rate of 3.3 per cent.

But he still insisted that the current offer was "fair and final".

(*International Express*, 1–7 June 1995, p. 6)

- High number of Inactive metaphors, "strike", "looms" (headline), "in prospect" (l. 1), "inflict" (l. 7), "long and hard" (l. 10), "in full" (l. 12), "recovery" (l. 14), "fragile" (l. 15), "damaged" (l. 15), "target" (l. 17), "gut feeling" (l. 20), "settle" (l. 21), "rise", "current", "inflation" (l. 21), and this leads to Mixing (ll. 20–1).
- These are mostly Concretizing analogies.

- Frequent marking even of Inactive metaphors, usually by quotation marks.
- Subjective metaphors/lies are in quotes too: " 'final' " (l. 4), " 'misery' " (l. 7), " 'generous' " (l. 9), " 'fair and final' " (l. 23).
- Higher percentage of Inactive noun metaphors than in other genres: "strike" (headline), "prospect" (l. 1), "recovery" (l. 14), "target" (l. 17), "gut feeling" (l. 20), "rise", "inflation" (l. 21).
- Hyperbole in attention-grabbing headlines.
- Some colligational metaphors/Extension: "fragile", "damaged" (l. 15).

### 10.8.3. Popular Science

Lymphocytes are so called because they are abundant in the lymphatic system, a network of vessels that drains fluid (lymph) from the
tissues. The fluid derives from blood serum that oozes through the
walls of the capillaries. Lymph contains no red cells and lacks many
of the proteins of blood, so it appears pale and watery.                    5

But it contains many white cells because these too migrate through
the capillary wall. Lymph eventually flows back into the circulatory
system via the thoracic duct. As it travels through the lymph vessels,
it is filtered by the lymph nodes, which contain large numbers of
lymphocytes ready to fight infection.                                       10

Concentrations of lymphocytes also occur in other places, such as
the tonsils, and in areas of the gut wall known as Peyer's patches.
These lymphatic tissues help to defend the areas of the body where
infection can easily enter.

Lymphocytes all originate from stem cells in the bone marrow.  15
Some then migrate to the thymus where they mature into T cells (the
'T' means thymus-derived). As the T cells mature, an important
process occurs known as "thymic education", which prevents the
immune system from attacking the body's own cells. Exactly what
happens during thymic education is still uncertain. Many immunol-   20
ogists believe that any Th [T-helper] cells with receptors that bind to
the body's own molecules are destroyed. This process is called clonal
deletion. Others disagree and believe that the educative process may
lie with the T cells, or elsewhere.

B cells mature in the bone marrow rather than the thymus, and  25
auto-immune B cells are not eliminated. Because the T cells do not
allow these auto-immune cells to proliferate, they normally produce
no ill-effects.

If lymphocytes are thought of as a police force, patrolling the
body, then the primary lymphatic organs are the police training  30
colleges where they originate and learn their skills. The secondary

lymphatic organs are the local police stations where they congregate and deal with suspect antigens.

*(New Scientist,* 24 April 1988, p. 4)

- Higher numbers of Active metaphors compared with News Reports and Conversation: "'thymic education'" (l. 18), "clonal deletion" (ll. 22–3), "police force", "patrolling" (l. 29), "the police training colleges" (ll. 30–1), "learn their skills" (l. 31), "the local police stations" (l. 32), "deal with suspect" (l. 33)
- All are Transfer metaphors, no Concretizing Analogy or Approximation.
- The large number of Active metaphors, six in all, and Inactive: "network" (l. 2), "wall" (ll. 4, 7) "stem", "marrow" (l. 15), "marrow" (l. 25) relative to other genres.
- Subjective hypothesizing involving disputed theories is noticeable (ll. 19–24).
- Strong tendency to mark: "known as* 'thymic education'" (l. 18), "is called* clonal deletion" (ll. 22–3), "If lymphocytes are thought of* as a police force" (l. 29).
- Preference for Copula T-term specification: "the primary lymphatic organs are the police training colleges" (ll. 30–1), "The secondary lymphatic organs are the local police stations" (ll. 31–2).
- Explication of Grounds important: "where they congregate and deal with" (ll. 32–3), "where they originate and learn" (l. 31).
- Extension a possibility: "fight" (l. 10), "defend" (l. 13), "attacking" (l. 19), "education" (ll. 18, 20), "educative" (l. 23), "the police training colleges" (ll. 30–1), 'learn their skills' (l. 31), "police force", "patrolling" (l. 29), "the local police stations" (l. 32), "deal with suspect" (l. 33).
- Explanatory function for Active metaphors and lexical gap-filling for both Active and Inactive.

## 10.8.4. Magazine Advertising

*You never know what's around the corner*

If all of a sudden you're looking at family cars, congratulations.

Because with the money you'd have spent on an ordinary five-door car, you can now buy a five-door Volkswagen.

For £6,844 you can be the proud owner of a Volkswagen Golf C.

A 1.3 litre, 55bhp, five-door, bundle of joy.

Delivered with a stereo radio cassette. A height adjustable driver's seat. Rear seat belts. Adjustable seat belt mounts. Child proof locks. And above all delivered with everything that makes a Volkswagen a Volkswagen.

Every passenger is protected by a reinforced safety cell. There are crumple zones front and rear. Dual-circuit brakes and self-stabilizing steering help stop the car in a straight line in an emergency.

And then we protect what protects you.

We pump 265 lbs of wax into doors and cavities.

We bond with rust inhibiting adhesives.

We put zinc between wing and bodywork.

We bolt with galvanised bolts.

We then wrap your Volkswagen in at least seven pounds of paint.

In a world where you never know what's coming next, isn't it comforting to drive something as predictable as a Volkswagen.

**5-door Golf**

(Volkswagen ad appearing in *GH*: 38–9)

(See also Plate 3)

- Highish number of Active metaphors: "fresh edition of cucumbers", "Europe's kitchen garden", "A 1.3 litre, 55bhp, five-door, bundle of joy".
- These mainly Transfer metaphors (cucumber = newspaper, car = baby), the product being concrete, and are usually nominal.
- To realize the phatic function Revitalization and punning common, creating lexical Extensions: "you never know **what's around the corner**", "what's **coming** next", "**delivered** with a radio cassette", "**delivered** with everything that makes a Volkswagen a Volkswagen", "We **bond** with rust inhibiting adhesives", "We then **wrap** your Volkswagen in at least seven pounds of paint".
- Most of these Revitalizations fail to explore the Grounds (except perhaps for "wrap").
- They also exemplify the personification/synthetic personalization of the product.
- Positive emotions transferred to the product by *the car = baby* metaphor

323

*Plate 3* Advertisement for Dutch cucumbers; courtesy of CBT (Centraal Bureau van de Tuinbouwveilingen in Nederland)

("congratulations", "proud owner"). But does it work for cucumbers = newspapers? "No news is good news".

- Both main Active metaphors extended throughout the copy.
- Colligational Vehicle-construction important: "fresh edition of [news-papers]", "your daily [newspaper] Dutch", "then wrap your [baby] Volkswagen in [a blanket] seven pounds of paint", "the proud [father] owner", "we [parents] bond with [a child]", etc.
- Metaphors often make Subjective claims about product: "they're good news indeed".
- Little signalling, maintaining the attention-grabbing surprise.
- Apposition common: "A 1.3 litre, 55bhp, five-door, bundle of joy".
- Topic is normally provided by the pictures.

### 10.8.5. Modern Novels

How then, can I trust my memory concerning that particular Sunday afternoon? Memory does not serve me, I had nothing to remember then. Julia was a nine-year-old girl; I was eighteen. I did not know that she would leave the pulpit, turn into a whore, and then the mistress of an African chief in Abidjan. I did not know that we     5
would become lovers, and that she would become one of the pillars holding up my life. I knew nothing about Arthur, who was then eleven, and less about Jimmy, who was then seven, who would become Arthur's last and most devoted lover. Who could know that then? Beneath the face of anyone you ever loved for true –   10
anyone you love, you will always love, love is not at the mercy of time and it does not recognize death, they are strangers to each other – beneath the face of the beloved, however ancient, ruined and scarred, is the face of the baby your love once was, and will always be, for you. Love serves then, if memory doesn't, and passion, apart  15
from its tense relation to agony, labours beneath the shadow of death. Passion is terrifying, it can rock you, change you, bring your head under, as when a wind rises from the bottom of the sea, and you're out there in the craft of your mortality alone.

(James Baldwin, *Just Above My Head*, p. 71)

- Large number of Active metaphors: "she would become one of **the pillars** holding up my life" (l. 6–7), "ruined" (l. 13), "**the baby** your love once was" (l. 14), "Passion is terrifying, it can **rock** you" (l. 17), "**bring your head under**" (ll. 17–18), "Passion . . . **labours** beneath the shadow" of death" (ll. 15–16), "in **the craft** of your mortality" (l. 19).
- Analogy quite high; all the above except "ruined".
- A number of Active adjectives, e.g. "ruined".
- Subjective categorical statements (ll. 10–15).

- Not much signalling: "as* when a wind rises from the bottom of the sea, and you're out there in the craft of your mortality alone" (ll. 18–19).
- Popularity of Genitive: "**shadow** of death" (l. 16), "in **the craft** of your mortality" (l. 19).
- Extension quite frequent: "she would become one of the pillars holding up my life" (ll. 6–7), "bring your head under, as when a wind rises from the bottom of the sea, and you're out there in the craft of your mortality alone" (l. 17–19).
- Symbolism important: "**beneath** the face of the beloved . . . **beneath** the shadow of death", "Passion . . . can . . . **bring your head under**" (cf. *Just **Above** My Head*).

### 10.8.6. Modern English Lyric Poetry

You may also want to consider 'An advancement of learning', quoted in the Introduction (pp. 10–11).


*In a station of the Metro*

The apparition of these faces in the crowd;
Petals on a wet, black bough.

(Ezra Pound)


*On the farm*

There was Dai Puw. He was no good.
They put him in the fields to dock swedes,
And took the knife from him, when he came home
At late evening with a grin
Like the slash of a knife on his face.                          5

There was Llew Puw, and he was no good.
Every evening after the ploughing
With the big tractor he would sit in his chair,
And stare into the tangled fire garden,
Opening his slow lips like a snail.                             10

There was Huw Puw too. What shall I say?
I have heard him whistling in the hedges
On and on, as though winter
Would never again leave those fields,
And all the trees were deformed.                               15

And lastly there was the girl:
Beauty under some spell of the beast.
Her pale face was the lantern
By which they read in life's dark book
The shrill sentence: God is love.                                    20

(R.S. Thomas)

- High number of Active metaphors: "And stare into the tangled fire **garden**" (l. 9), "And all the trees were **deformed**" (l. 15), "Her pale face was **the lantern** / By which they read in life's **dark book** / The shrill **sentence**: God is love" (ll. 18–20).
- Analogical metaphors frequent: "life's dark book" (l. 19), "beauty under some spell of the beast" (l. 17).
- Large number of verb metaphors: "read" (l. 19), and in "An advancement of learning" (AL): "clockworked", "plastered", "trained", "sickened", "bunched".
- Vehicle-construction appropriate: (AL) "dirty-keeled [boat] swans", "the river [rat] nosed past", "he [guns] trained on me".
- Subjective statements quite common: "There was Dai Puw. He was no good" (l. 1).
- No markers except similes which are frequent, and tend to be Precision, definite in their Grounds: "Opening his slow lips like a snail" (l. 10), "whistling . . . as though winter / Would never again leave those fields" (ll. 12–14).
- Topics are often specified: "fire" (l. 9), "her face" (l. 18), "the girl" (l. 16), "life" (l. 19).
- Genitive occurs: "life's dark book" (1.19).
- Apposition (see "In a station of the Metro") is well represented; "And lastly there was the girl: / **Beauty** under some spell of the beast" (ll. 16–17).
- Extension is common: "Her pale face was the **lantern** / By which they read in life's **dark book** / The shrill **sentence**" (ll. 18–20)
- Literalization and Symbolization high: "And took the KNIFE from him, when he came home / At late evening with a grin / Like the slash of a knife on his face" (ll. 3–5); (AL) "established a bridgehead", "crossed the BRIDGE".

## 10.9. ENVOI

Allow me, at the last, a metaphor of my own, but not my own since it is permeated by Root Analogy. Metaphors are hills and mountains on the flat literal landscape. They are more noticeable and take longer to cross than the flat land. But in crossing them we obtain a different perspective, an alternative viewpoint. Divers and astronauts give us a more inclusive picture of this "flat" land on which we walk. From a submarine perspective this land is a plateau on the top of a hill. We feel unstable, all at sea without the firm land of conventional metaphor beneath our feet. Astronauts tell us that the familiar world we fondly imagine to be flat, is, in fact, more or less spherical. The metaphorical mountain chains and the hills which seemed exceptional and noticeable are merely exaggerated or steeper versions of the natural curve of the globe. Language is more metaphorical, less literal than we are accustomed to think. Look at the front cover as you close the book.

# NOTES

## INTRODUCTION

1 I use the term *refer* in its everyday sense, rather than in the sense which distinguishes it from predication. In other words, I opt for the possibility of saying that predicates refer to concepts (Searle 1969: 118) . More discussion of reference as it operates in my definition is found in Chapter 4.

## 1 METAPHORICAL AND LITERAL LANGUAGE

1 This was a preoccupation of Bakhtin (see Holquist 1990: 146–8).
2 When a child goes through such an experience, it will produce a permanent change in her cognitive categories, whereas when adults respond to metaphors of, say, a literary kind, no such changes are introduced; indeed, the tension between the two concepts needs to be maintained for them to interact, and for them to go on interacting when the text is reread.
3 For evidence in the psychological literature see Gibbs (1984), Hoffman and Kemper (1987).

## 2 METAPHOR AND THE DICTIONARY: ROOT ANALOGIES

1 On my Figure 2.1, the map of Root Analogies, I have indicated my indebtedness as follows. When the Root Analogy is followed by a number in brackets this indicates where it, or a synonymous analogy, was first identified or discussed. (1) refers to Lakoff and Johnson (1980); (2) refers to Johnson (1987); (3) refers to Lakoff and Turner (1989). In the case of Johnson (1987), very often the analogy is not explicitly stated but may be inferred from his discussion of image schemata.

(1) Lakoff and Johnson (1980): Argument is War (p. 4); Ideas (meanings) are Objects (p. 10); Communication is Sending (p. 10); Happy is Up (p. 15); Conscious is Up (p. 15); Health is Up (p. 15); Control is Up (p. 15); More is Up (p. 15); Good is Up (p. 16); Status is Up (p. 16) Known is Down (p. 20); Mind is an Entity (p. 27); Mind is a Machine (p. 27); Place for the Event (p. 40); Theories (and Arguments) are Buildings (p. 46); Ideas are Food (p. 46); Ideas are People (p. 47); Ideas are Plants (p. 47); Understanding is Seeing (p. 48); Emotional Effect is Physical Contact (p. 50).
(2) Johnson (1987): Sane is Balanced (p. 88); Responsibility is Weight (p. 89); Justice is Straight (p. 90); Amount is Dimension (pp. 90, 123); Activity is

Travel/Path (pp. 113–14); Important is Central (p. 124); Process is Movement (p. 115); Purpose is Direction (p. 115); Cause is Connection (p. 118).

(3) Lakoff and Turner (1989) (pp. 221–3): Bad is Black; States are Locations; Change of State is Change of Location; Dispassionate is Cold; Important is Central; People are Plants; Important is Big; Lust is Heat/Passionate is Hot; People are Machines; Purposes are Destinations; Progress is the Distance Travelled; Seeing is Touching; Time Moves.

2  I am prepared to make my data available for students and researchers in disk form. Please e-mail me on <goatlya@nievax.nie.ac.sg>.

3  Sweetser (1990: 33–8) gives an etymological analysis of this area, including UNDERSTAND/KNOW = SEE, AFFECTION = PERCEPTION, and the structures of metaphors of perception.

4  See Lakoff (1993: 220) for discussion of event structures as cognitively characterized in terms of space, motion and force.

5  Gibbs (1992) presents convincing experimental evidence for the claim that the figurative meanings of idioms are partially motivated by metaphorical mappings of conceptual knowledge from various sources to target domains.

6  I am leaving aside the more technical models or metaphors for language developed by linguists, such as the Chomskyan plant metaphor (tree diagrams, nodes, etc.), or Matthiessen's (1992) metaphors of wave, particle and field.

7  Bakhtin privileged dialogic over monologic texts, precisely because he saw in dialogue the clashing of different Subject positions and ideologies. To understand our identity we have to take into account what others think of us, how we appear from their viewpoint, and how they might think we appear to them. See Holquist (1990).

8  Low (1988: 130), with a slightly different emphasis, points out the tendency of Charlotte Brontë to extend conventional metaphors, rather than simply fall back on them.

# 3 METAPHOR AND THE DICTIONARY: WORD-CLASS AND WORD-FORMATION

1  Coming to imagery from the angle of direct experience, it may be the case that movement to the level of imagery is essential for emotional depth in and responses to relationships. As Milan Kundera put it: "I have said before that metaphors are dangerous. Love begins with a metaphor. Which is to say love begins at the point when a woman enters her first word into our poetic memory" (Kundera 1991: 209).

2  A more delicate kind of metaphorical Transfer between fields operates within mental processes. There is a tendency to conceptualize cognitive processes in terms of perceptual processes (e.g. *if you see what I mean*). A significant three-way ambiguity has arisen as a result with the word *feel*. This mental process of sensing has long been furnishing us with a concept for the mental process of affection. But very often, nowadays, as in CEC524 we use the word virtually as a synonym of *think* or *estimate*:

CEC524     I just meant I mean how he **felt** the thing was going.

Somehow affective processes are closer to physical experience than mental ones, and perceptual processes are designed precisely to bridge the gap between our mental activities and the happenings in the outside world, that is, to register the physical environment.

3 Surprisingly Bauer's standard work on word-formation repeats the highly dubious claim of Levi (1978: section 6.1, quoted in Bauer 1983: 185) that *the transformation of adjectivalization influences the form-class of the lexeme but is totally meaning-preserving* (Bauer 1983: 185).

4 Besides the textual evidence given later in the chapter, there is also some evidence from tests of metaphorical awareness carried out by Steen (1994: 56). The denominal adjectives *dictatorial* and *fatherly* appeared as items with a low degree of metaphoricity.

5 See Bauer (1983: 49, 88) for comments on the inverse relationship between Lexicalization and productivity.

6 This phenomenon is not confined to English. The following evidence shows that word-formation and metaphor go hand-in-hand in Cantonese.

*woo* (1): 'dark grey'; *woo* (1) *seuh* (4) *seuh* (4): 'ignorant'
*faan* (1) (*fuk*) (1): 'overturn'; *faan faan* (1) *fuk fuk* (1): 'vacillate'
*poh* (4): 'grandmother'; *poh poh* (4) *ma ma* (1): 'hesitant, indecisive'
(4 = low rise tone, 1 = high rise tone)

## 4 HOW DIFFERENT KINDS OF METAPHORS WORK

1 Several students of mine interpreted this metaphor differently:

Wind        [blowing over] the fields
[Cows/horses]   stampeding

This perfectly valid alternative is based on the possibility of promoting a locative adjunct to an affected direct object, as in the pair *he swam over the river* and *he swam the river*. My interpretation depends on treating *stampede* as an ergative which can be made effective so that the verb means 'initiate a stampede', by analogy with *the glass broke* and *John broke the glass*.

2 Steen (1994: 124–5) gives some evidence that Vehicle-construction and metaphor construction are spontaneously occurring processes, as well as the pedagogic tools recommended by Leech.

3 Reinhart (1976) refers to the distinction between Substitution interpretation and Interactive interpretation as *focus* (my 'Topic') *interpretation* and *vehicle interpretation*, capturing the idea that Substitution gives more attention to the Topic and Interaction more to the Vehicle.

4 Gentner (1989), Gentner and Jesiorski (1993) and Vosniadou and Ortony (1989) frame the difference between Similarity and Analogy in terms of perceptual similarities and relational similarities.

5 Andros Sandor's persuasive article 'Metaphor and belief'(1986) is an extensive discussion of how metaphorical Asymmetry works interculturally. One person's language and culture may be metaphorical in relation to another's, but is best interpreted Asymmetrically, Phenomenalistically (see section 4.5.5).

## 5 RELEVANCE THEORY AND THE FUNCTIONS OF METAPHOR

1 The stages 1–5 in the inferential process suggest that a certain metaphorical awareness is present in competent speakers of a language; cf. Winner and Gardner (1994: 427).

2 See Petrie and Oshlag (1993: 596) on the effects of different explanatory metaphors for electricity on students' understanding. They recommend that the

limits of the analogy be explored through actual activities; and make the strong claim that metaphors are not just decorative but essential for learning (p. 608).

3 It is a debatable point whether there is any possibility of a scientific theory which does not depend on metaphors or models. There are two schools of thought here.

> One can take two views of the activities of scientists like physicists who are seeking things they call the fundamental laws of nature. Either you believe, as they often do, that they are discovering the real thing, and that one day we will hit on the mathematical form of the ultimate laws of nature.
>
> Alternatively one may be more modest and regard the scientific enterprise as an editorial process in which we are constantly refining and updating our picture of reality using images and approximations that seem best fitted to the process.
>
> (Barrow 1993: 15)

In the second view, images and metaphors are indispensable to scientific theory, and are no different in kind from the metaphors or analogies found in popular science, e.g. "The confinement of quarks is like marbles inside a rubber bag": "superstrings are like elastic bands"; "the quantum wave function is like a crime wave"; "a pulsar is like a lighthouse" (*ibid.*: 15).

The assumption in the first view is that mathematics is a non-analogical, non-metaphorical process. Arguments against this assumption can be found in Lakoff (1987: 353–70), Jones (1982) and Johnson (1987: 39–40). It is also the presupposition behind Hofstadter's (1981) article.

4 Note: the "four creatures" are the thumb, two fingers and the pen, a quill which as a feather had once supported the swift bird and is now dipped in ink. The "struggling warrior" is the arm, and the "gold" is the illuminated manuscript (Mitchell and Crossley-Holland 1967: 52).

5 Both Mayer (1983) and Petrie and Oshlag (1993) suggest that when used for educational purposes metaphors should lead to classroom activities.

6 Walter Nash points out this hyperbolic effect of figurative language in popular fiction: "There is a persistent use of metaphoric cliché, a parading of a few figurative devices, with the aim of infusing energy, excitement, interest into almost every line of the narrative" (Nash 1990: 50).

7 Low (1988: 127–9) gives a list of the functions of metaphor which more or less coincide with some of mine: (a) to make it possible to talk about X at all – roughly equivalent to my Lexical Gap-filling; (b) to demonstrate that things in life are related and systematic in ways we can, at least partially, comprehend – equivalent to my Explanation/Modelling; (c) extending thought – my Reconceptualization; (d) to compel attention by dramatizing X – Foregrounding; (e) to prevaricate and deny responsibility for X – covered under Decoration, Disguise and Hyperbole as covert communication; (f) to allow the speaker to discuss emotionally-charged subjects — Expressing Emotional Attitude and Decoration/Disguise. For my other categories he has no equivalents.

# 6 THE SIGNALLING OF METAPHOR

1 Winner and Gardner (1993: 426) agree that full comprehension of non-literal utterances needs the stage of *metalinguistic awareness* which entails hearing the contrast between what is said and what is meant.

2 See Low's discussion of this point and the problems it may cause for non-native learners of English (Low 1988: 133).

# 7 THE SPECIFICATION OF TOPICS

1 See Glucksberg and Keysar (1993: 415–16) for the notion that metaphors assign to categories rather than identify. Their views fit well with the notion of *kind of* as a marker of metaphors. However, as is the wont of many writers on metaphor, they overgeneralize in claiming that all metaphors in Copula form are class-inclusion statements and so cannot be reversed.

2 Apposition is the classic form of expressing metaphor in another related sense: it clearly demonstrates Jakobson's dictum that "the poetic function projects the principle of equivalence from the axis of selection to the axis of combination" (Jakobson 1960: 348).

3 The research of Just and Carpenter (1984) suggests that ordering is important, and that the claim that readers process in chunks might have been exaggerated: "A reader tries to interpret a word as he encounters it, rather than waiting to make an interpretation until a number of words have been encountered . . . *Interpret* refers to several levels of cognitive processing, such as encoding the word, accessing its meaning, assigning it to its referent, and determining its semantic and syntactic status" (Just and Carpenter 1984: 166).

# 9 THE INTERPLAY OF METAPHORS

1 Compare this with the claims of Lakoff and Johnson (1980: 18) that multivalent orientational metaphors like HEALTHY/LIVING = UP, STATUS = UP are coherent because they are subsumed under, share the Ground GOOD (MORALITY, QUALITY) = UP (see Figure 2.1).

# 10 METAPHOR IN ITS SOCIAL CONTEXT

1 It is the entirely constitutive nature of poetry and novels which allows for polyvalence of meanings (see Schmidt 1980). As Ohmann (1971) pointed out: "Since the quasi-speech-acts of literature are not carrying on the world's business – describing, urging, contracting etc., the reader may well attend to them in a non-pragmatic way and thus allow them to realize their emotive potential."

2 Other examples of obsession as a motivation for metaphor in literature would be Ezra Pound's persona in 'The river merchant's wife: a letter' (*Selected Poems*, p. 52) describing butterflies as *yellow with autumn* because of her preoccupation with the passing of time. In psychoanalytic theory, of course, there are many transferences which are interpreted obsessionally.

3 Wilson and Sperber (1992: 76), in an article later than their book *Relevance*, go some way to acknowledging how important the criticisms are. Assuming the way of computing relevance corresponds to this third way they admit: "It is tempting, in interpreting a literary text from an author one respects, to look further and further for hidden implications. Having found an interpretation consistent with the principle of Relevance (an interpretation which may in itself be very rich and very vague) which the writer might have thought of as an adequate repayment for the reader's effort – why not go on and look for even richer implications and reverberations? If we are right, and considerations of relevance lie at the heart of verbal communication, such searches go beyond the domain of communication proper. Though the writer might have *wished* to

communicate more than the first interpretation tested and found consistent with the principle of Relevance, she cannot rationally have *intended* to."

4 It also correlates with different kinds of comprehension, what Gibbs and Gerrig call *time-limited comprehension* as opposed to *leisurely comprehension* (1989: 238). See Steen (1994: 99–101).

5 The texts used for analysis are listed at the end of the book in the References section, p. 345.

6 This project might be seen as fulfilling part of the agenda set by Steen (1994: 179): "the inclusion of other dimensions such as linguistic form and communicative function and the metaphor properties related to them is essential for a full view of metaphor quality and its relation to different domains of discourse".

7 Though there is some evidence from Steen's studies that quite independent of time available, readers are more likely to look for metaphoric interplay (*refunctionalization*) in literature than they are in journalism (Steen 1994: 137–40).

# REFERENCES

Adams, V. (1973) *An Introduction to Modern English Word-Formation*, Harlow: Longman.

Ballantyne, R.M. (1915) *A Coral Island*, London: Nisbet.

Barrow, J. (1993) 'In the world's image', *Times Higher Education Supplement*, 16 April.

Barthes, R. (1970) *S/Z*, Paris: Seuil.

Bateson, G. (1991) 'Men are grass: metaphor and the world of mental process', in R.E. Donaldson (ed.), *A Sacred Unity: Further Steps to an Ecology of Mind*, New York: Cornelia and Michael, pp. 237–42.

Bauer, L. (1983) *English Word-Formation*, Cambridge: Cambridge University Press.

Beardsley, M.P. (1967) 'Metaphor', in P. Edwards (ed.), *Encyclopedia of Philosophy*, vol. 5, New York: Macmillan.

Berggren, D. (1962) 'The use and abuse of metaphor', *Review of Metaphysics* 16 (2): 237–58.

Bickerton, D. (1969) 'Prolegomena to a linguistic theory of metaphor', *Foundations of Language* 5: 34–53.

Black, M. (1962) 'Metaphor', in J. Margolis (ed.), *Philosophy Looks at the Arts*, New York: Temple University Press, pp. 218–35.

—— (1979) 'More about metaphors', in A. Ortony (ed.), *Metaphor and Thought*, Cambridge: Cambridge University Press, pp. 19–43.

Boyd, R. (1979) 'Metaphor and theory change: what is "metaphor" a metaphor for?', in A. Ortony (ed.), *Metaphor and Thought*, Cambridge: Cambridge University Press, pp. 356–408.

Brooke-Rose, C. (1958) *A Grammar of Metaphor*, London: Secker and Warburg.

Byatt, A.S. (1990) *Possession*, London: Chatto and Windus.

Carter, R. (1987) *Vocabulary*, London: Allen and Unwin.

Chafe, W. (1982) 'Integration and involvement in speaking, writing and oral literature', in D. Tannen (ed.), *Spoken and Written Language*, Norwood, NJ: Ablex, pp. 35–53.

Clark, H. (1987) 'Relevance to what?', *Behavioural and Brain Sciences* 10 (4): 714–15.

Cohen, J. (1979) 'Metaphor and the cultivation of intimacy', in S. Sacks (ed.), *On Metaphor*, Chicago: Chicago University Press, pp. 1–10.

*Collins Cobuild English Language Dictionary* (1987), ed. J. Sinclair, London: Collins.

Crossley-Holland, K. and Mitchell, B. (eds) (1965) *The Battle of Maldon and other Old English Poems*, London: Macmillan.

Crystal, D. and Davy, D. (1969) *Investigating English Style*, Harlow: Longman.
—— (1975) *Advanced Conversational English*, Harlow: Longman.
De Man, Paul (1979) 'The epistemology of metaphor', in S. Sacks (ed.), *On Metaphor*, Chicago: Chicago University Press, pp. 11–28.
Deleuze, G. and Guatarri, F. (1980) *Mille Plateaux*, Paris: Minuit.
Derrida, Jacques (1982) 'White mythology', in *Margins of Philosophy*, trans. Alan Bass, Chicago: University of Chicago Press, pp. 207–71.
Dyer, G. (1984) *Advertising as Communication*, London: Methuen.
Elam, K. (1980) *The Semiotics of Theatre and Drama*, London: Methuen.
Eliot, T.S. (1919) 'Hamlet and his problems', *The Athenaeum*, September: 46–65.
—— (1932) 'The metaphysical poets', *Selected Essays*, London: Faber, pp. 281–91.
—— (1936) 'The Love Song of J. Alfred Prufrock', in *Collected Poems*, London: Faber, pp. 13–17.
—— (1944) *The Four Quartets*, London: Faber.
Empson, W. (1953) *Seven Types of Ambiguity*, London: Chatto and Windus.
Fairclough, N. (1989) *Language and Power*, Harlow: Longman.
Fernandez, J.W. (1977) 'The performance of ritual metaphors', in J.D. Sapir and C.C. Crocker (eds), *The Social Use of Metaphor*, Philadelphia: University of Pennsylvania Press, pp. 100–31.
Ferris, C. (1993) *The Meaning of Syntax: A Study in the Adjectives of English*, Harlow: Longman.
Fowler, R. (1977) *Linguistics and the Novel*, London: Methuen.
—— (1986) *Linguistic Criticism*, Oxford: Oxford University Press.
—— (1991) *Language in the News: Discourse and Ideology in the Press*, London: Routledge.
Fowles, J. (1969) *The French Lieutenant's Woman*, London: Cape.
Freud, S. (1963) *Jokes and their Relation to the Unconscious*, trans. J. Strachey, New York: Norton.
Frye, N. (1957) *Anatomy of Criticism: Four Essays*, Princeton, NJ: Princeton University Press.
Gasparov, Boris (1985) 'Introduction' in A.D. Nakhimovsky and A.S. Nakhimovsky (eds), *The Semiotics of Russian Cultural History*, Ithaca, NY: Cornell University Press, pp. 13–29.
Genette, G. (1970) 'La rhétorique restreinte', *Communication* 16: 158–71.
Gentner, D. (1982) 'Are scientific analogies metaphors?', in D.S. Miall (ed.), *Metaphor: Problems and Perspectives*, Brighton: Harvester, pp. 106–32.
—— (1989) 'The mechanisms of analogical learning', in S. Vosniadou and A. Ortony (eds), *Similarity and Analogical Reasoning*, Cambridge: Cambridge University Press, pp. 199–241.
Gentner, D. and Jesiorski, M. (1993) 'The shift from metaphor to analogy in western science', in A. Ortony (ed.), *Metaphor and Thought*, 2nd edn, Cambridge: Cambridge University Press, pp. 447–80.
Gibbs, R.W. (1984) 'Literal meaning and psychological theory', *Cognitive Science* 8: 275–304.
—— (1992) 'What do idioms really mean?', *Journal of Memory and Language* 31: 485–506.
Gibbs, R.W. and Gerrig, R.J. (1989) 'How context makes metaphor comprehension seem "special"', *Metaphor and Symbolic Activity* 4: 154–8.
Glucksberg, S. and Keysar, B. (1993) 'How metaphors work', in A. Ortony (ed.), *Metaphor and Thought*, 2nd edn, Cambridge: Cambridge University Press, pp. 401–24.

Goatly, A.P. (1983) 'Metaphor in the novels of William Golding', unpublished Ph.D. thesis, University College, London University.

—— (1987) 'Interrelations of metaphors in Golding's novels: a framework for the study of metaphoric interplay', *Language and Style* 20 (2): 125–44.

—— (1990) 'A stylistic analysis of A.E. Housman's "On Wenlock Edge"', *Language and Style* 23 (4): 383–408.

—— (1993) 'Species of metaphor in varieties of English', in M. Ghadessy (ed.), *Register Analysis: Theory and Practice*, London: Pinter, pp. 110–48.

—— (1994) 'Register and the redemption of relevance theory: the case of metaphor', *Pragmatics* 4 (2): 139–81.

Goodman, N. (1968) *Languages of Art: An Approach to a Theory of Symbols*, Indianapolis: Bobbs-Merrill.

Grice, P. (1975) 'Logic and conversation', in P. Cole and J. Morgan (eds), *Syntax and Semantics 3: Speech Acts*, New York: Academic Press, pp. 41–58.

Halliday, M.A.K. (1994) *An Introduction to Functional Grammar*, 2nd edn, London: Arnold.

Halliday, M.A.K. and Hasan, R. (1985) *Language, Context and Text: Aspects of Language in a Social-Semiotic Perspective*, Geelong, Victoria: Deakin University Press.

Hasan, R. (1989) *Linguistics, Language and Verbal Art*, Geelong, Victoria: Deakin University Press.

Hesse, M. (1983) 'The cognitive claims of metaphor', *Metaphor and Religion–Theolinguistics* 2: 27–50.

Hiraga, M. (1991) 'Metaphors Japanese women live by', *Working Papers on Language, Gender and Sexism*, vol. 1, no. 1, AILA Commission on Language and Gender, pp. 38–57.

Hodge, R., Kress, G. and Jones, G. (1979) 'The ideology of middle management', in R. Fowler, R. Hodge, G. Kress and T. Trew (eds), *Language and Control*, London: Routledge, pp. 81–93.

Hoffman, R.R. and Kemper, S. (1987) 'What could reaction-time studies be telling us about metaphor comprehension?', *Metaphor and Symbolic Activity* 2: 149–86.

Hofstadter, D. (1981) 'Metamagical themas: how might analogy, the core of human thinking, be understood by computers?', *Scientific American*, September: 18–30.

Holquist, M. (1990) *Dialogism: Bakhtin and his World*, London: Routledge.

Honeck, R.P., Reichman, P. and Hoffman, R. (1975) 'Semantic memory for metaphor: the conceptual base hypothesis', *Memory and Cognition* 3: 409–15.

Hudson, R.A. (1980) *Sociolinguistics*, Cambridge: Cambridge University Press.

Jakobson, R. (1960) 'Closing statements: linguistics and poetics', in T.A. Sebeok (ed.), *Style in Language*, Cambridge, Mass.: MIT Press, pp. 350–77.

Johnson, M. (1987) *The Body in the Mind*, London: University of Chicago Press.

Jones, R. S. (1982) *Physics as Metaphor*, New York: New American Library.

Just, M.A. and Carpenter, P.A. (1984) 'Using eye-fixations to study reading comprehension', in D.E. Kieras and M.A. Just (eds), *New Methods in Reading Comprehension Research*, Hillsdale, NJ: Erlbaum, pp. 151–82.

Katz, J. and Fodor, J.A. (1963) 'The structure of a semantic theory', *Language* 39: 170–210.

Kittay, E.F. (1987) *Metaphor: Its Cognitive Force and Linguistic Structure*, Oxford: Oxford University Press.

Kress, G. (1985) *Linguistic Processes in Sociocultural Practice*, Oxford: Oxford University Press.

—— (1989) 'History and language: towards a social account of linguistic change', *Journal of Pragmatics* 13: 445–66.

Kuhn, T. (1979) 'Metaphor in science', in A. Ortony (ed.), *Metaphor and Thought*, Cambridge: Cambridge University Press, pp. 409–19.

Kundera, M. (1991) *The Unbearable Lightness of Being*, trans. M.H. Heim, London: HarperCollins.

Labov, W. (1972) *Language in the Inner City*, Philadelphia: Philadelphia University Press.

Lakoff, G. (1972) 'Hedges: a study in meaning criteria and the logic of fuzzy concepts', *Papers from the Eighth Regional Meeting of the Chicago Linguistics Society*, Department of Linguistics, University of Chicago, pp. 183–217.

—— (1987) *Women, Fire and Dangerous Things*, Chicago: University of Chicago Press.

—— (1993) 'The contemporary theory of metaphor', in A. Ortony (ed.), *Metaphor and Thought*, 2nd edn, Cambridge: Cambridge University Press, pp. 202–52.

Lakoff, G. and Johnson, M. (1980) *Metaphors We Live By*, Chicago: University of Chicago Press.

Lakoff, G. and Turner, M. (1989) *More than Cool Reason: A Field Guide to Poetic Metaphor*, Chicago: University of Chicago Press.

Langland, William (1869) *Piers the Plowman*, ed. Walter Skeat, Oxford: EETS/Oxford University Press.

Lawrence, D.H. (1913) *Sons and Lovers*, Harmondsworth: Penguin, 1979.

Lecercle, J.-J. (1990) *The Violence of Language*, London: Routledge.

Leech, G.N. (1969) *A Linguistic Guide to English Poetry*, Harlow: Longman.

—— (1974) *Semantics*, Harmondsworth: Penguin.

—— (1983) *Principles of Pragmatics*, Harlow: Longman.

Leech, G.N. and Short, M. (1981) *Style in Fiction*, Harlow: Longman.

Lehrer, A. (1974) *Semantic Fields and Lexical Structure*, Amsterdam: North Holland.

Leondar, B. (1975) 'Metaphor and infant cognition', *Poetics* 4: 273–87.

Levi, J.N. (1978) *The Syntax and Semantics of Complex Nominals*, New York: Academic Press.

Levin, S.R. (1977) *The Semantics of Metaphor*, Baltimore: Johns Hopkins University Press.

Levinson, S. (1989) Review of *Relevance: Communication and Cognition*, by D. Sperber and D. Wilson, *Journal of Linguistics* 25 (2): 455–73.

Lim, S.H. (1993) 'The positioning of "grounds" in the interpretation of prose metaphor', unpublished Honours thesis, Department of English, National University of Singapore 1992/3.

Locke, J. (1961) *Essay Concerning Human Understanding*, ed. J.W. Yolton, London: Dent; originally published 1690.

Lodge, D. (1977) *The Modes of Modern Writing: Metaphor, Metonymy and the Typology of Modern Literature*, London: Arnold.

Loewenberg, I. (1975) 'Identifying metaphors', *Foundations of Language* 12: 315–18.

Low, G. (1988) 'On teaching metaphor', *Applied Linguistics* 9 (2): 125–47.

Lyons, J. (1977) *Semantics*, Cambridge: Cambridge University Press.

McCloskey, M. (1964) 'Metaphors', *Mind* 73: 215–33.

MacCormac, E.R. (1990) *A Cognitive Theory of Metaphor*, London: MIT Press.

Mack, D. (1975) 'Metaphoring as speech act: some happiness conditions for implicit similes and simple metaphors', *Poetics* 4: 221–56.

Martin, J.R. (1985) *Factual Writing: Exploring and Changing Social Reality*, Geelong, Victoria: Deakin University Press.

—— (1992) *English Text: System and Structure*, Amsterdam: Benjamins.

Martin, J.R. and Matthiessen, C. (1991) 'Systemic typology and topology', in F. Christie (ed.), *Literacy in Social Processes*, Centre for Studies of Language in Education, Northern Territories University, Darwin, pp. 345–83.

Matthiessen, C. (1992) 'Interpreting the textual metafunction', in M. Davies and L. Ravelli (eds), *Advances in Systemic Linguistics*, Pinter: London, pp. 37–81.

—— (1993) 'Register in the round: diversity in a unified theory of register analysis', in M. Ghadessy (ed.), *Register Analysis: Theory and Practice*, London: Pinter, pp. 221–92.

Mayer, R.E. (1983) 'Can you repeat that? Qualitative effects of repetition and advance organizers on learning from scientific prose', *Journal of Educational Psychology* 75: 40–9.

Minsky, M. (1975) 'A framework for representing knowledge', in P. Winston (ed.), *The Psychology of Computer Vision*, New York: McGraw-Hill, pp. 211–77.

Mooij, J.J.A. (1976) *A Study of Metaphor*, Amsterdam: North Holland.

Naess, A (1952) 'Towards a theory of interpretation and preciseness', in L. Linsky (ed.), *Semantics and the Philosophy of Language*, Urbana: University of Illinois Press, pp. 248–69.

Nash, W. (1980) *Designs in Prose*, Harlow: Longman.

—— (1985) *The Language of Humour*, Harlow: Longman.

—— (1990) *Language in Popular Fiction*, London: Routledge.

Ohmann, R. (1971) 'Speech acts and the definition of literature', *Philosophy and Rhetoric* 4: 1–19.

Ortony, A. (1979a) 'The role of similarity in similes and metaphors', in A. Ortony (ed.), *Metaphor and Thought*, Cambridge: Cambridge University Press, pp. 186–201.

—— (ed.) (1979b) *Metaphor and Thought*, Cambridge: Cambridge University Press.

—— (ed.) (1993) *Metaphor and Thought*, 2nd edn, Cambridge: Cambridge University Press.

Ortony, A., Schallert, D.L., Reynolds, R.E. and Arter, J.A. (1978) 'Interpreting metaphors and idioms', *Journal of Verbal Learning and Verbal Behaviour* 17: 465–77.

Palmer, F.R. (1981) *Semantics*, 2nd edn, Cambridge: Cambridge University Press.

Paprotte, W. and Dirven, R. (eds) (1985) *The Ubiquity of Metaphor*, Amsterdam: Benjamins.

Petofi, J.S. (1983) 'Metaphors in everyday communication, in scientific, biblical and literary texts', in J.P. Van Noppen (ed.), *Metaphor and Religion*, special issue of *Theolinguistics*, vol. 2, pp. 149–80.

Petrie, H.G and Oshlag, R.S. (1993) 'Metaphor and learning', in A. Ortony (ed.), *Metaphor and Thought*, 2nd edn, Cambridge: Cambridge University Press, pp. 579–609.

Piaget, J. (1937) 'The construction of reality in the child', in H.E. Gruber and J.J. Voreche (eds), *The Essential Piaget*, New York: Basic Books, 1977.

Potter, S. (ed.) (1962) *Coleridge: Selected Poetry, Prose and Letters*, London: Nonesuch.

Pound, L. (1936) 'American euphemisms for dying, death and burial', *American Speech*, 11(3): 195–202.

Putnam, H. (1975) *Mind, Language and Reality*, Cambridge: Cambridge University Press.

Pylyshyn, Z.W. (1979) 'Metaphorical imprecision and the top-down research strategy', in A. Ortony (ed.), *Metaphor and Thought*, Cambridge: Cambridge University Press, pp. 420–37.

Quirk, R. and Greenbaum, S. (1973) *A University Grammar of English*, Harlow: Longman.

Quirk, R., Greenbaum, S., Leech, G.N. and Svartvik, J. (1985) *A Comprehensive Grammar of the English Language*, Harlow: Longman.

Reddy, M. (1993) 'The conduit metaphor: a case of frame conflict in our language about language', in A. Ortony (ed.), *Metaphor and Thought*, 2nd edn, Cambridge: Cambridge University Press, pp. 164–201.

Reinhart, T. (1976) 'On understanding poetic metaphor', *Poetics* 5: 383–402.

Rhodes, R.A. and Lawler, J.M. (1981) 'Athematic metaphors', *Papers from the Seventeenth Regional Meeting of the Chicago Linguistics Society*, Chicago: Chicago Linguistics Society, pp. 318–42.

Richards, I.A. (1948) 'Science and poetry', in M. Shorer, J. Miles and G. McKenzie (eds), *Criticism: The Foundations of Literary Judgement*, New York: Hart Brace and Co., pp. 505–23.

—— (1965) *The Philosophy of Rhetoric*, Oxford: Oxford University Press.

Roeper, T. and Siegel, M.E.A. (1978) 'A lexical transformation for verbal compounds', *Linguistic Inquiry* 9: 199–260.

Rosch, E. (1975) 'Cognitive representations of semantic categories', *Journal of Experimental Psychology: General* 104: 192–233.

Rumelhart, D.E. (1979) 'Some problems with the notion of literal meanings', in A. Ortony (ed.) *Metaphor and Thought*, Cambridge: Cambridge University Press, pp. 78–91.

Sacchett, C. and Humphreys, G.W. (1992) 'Calling a squirrel a squirrel, but a canoe a wigwam: a category-specific deficit for artefactual objects and body-parts', *Cognitive Neuropsychology* 9: 73–86.

Sacks, S. (ed.) (1979) *On Metaphor*, Chicago: University of Chicago Press.

Sadock, J.M. (1979) 'Figurative speech and linguistics', in A. Ortony (ed.), *Metaphor and Thought*, Cambridge: Cambridge University Press, pp. 46–63.

Sandor, A. (1986) 'Metaphor and belief', *Journal of Anthropological Research* 42 (2): 101–22.

Saville-Troike, M. (1982) *The Ethnography of Communication*, Oxford: Blackwell.

Schank, R., and Abelson, R. (1977) *Scripts, Plans, Goals and Understanding*, Hillsdale, NJ: Erlbaum.

Schmidt, S.J. (1980) *Grundriss der empirischen Literaturwissenschaft [Vol.1] Der gesellschaftlisches Handlungbereich Literatur*, Braunschweig/Wiesbaden: Vieweg.

Searle, J. (1969) *Speech Acts*, Cambridge: Cambridge University Press.

—— (1993) 'Metaphor', in A. Ortony (ed.), *Metaphor and Thought*, 2nd edn, Cambridge: Cambridge University Press, pp. 83–111.

Shaw, P. (1981) *Logic and its Limits*, London: Pan.

Simpson, P. (1994) *Language, Ideology and Point of View*, London: Routledge.

Sinclair, J.M. (1989) 'Uncommonly common words', in M. Tickoo (ed.), *Learners' Dictionaries: The State of the Art*, Singapore: Seameo Regional Language Centre, pp. 135–52.

Sperber, D. (1975) *Rethinking Symbolism*, trans. Alice Morton, Cambridge: Cambridge University Press.

Sperber, D. and Wilson, D. (1986) *Relevance: Communication and Cognition*, Oxford: Blackwell.

Steen, G. (1994) *Understanding Metaphor in Literature*, Harlow: Longman.

Stockwell, P. (1992a) 'The metaphorics of literary reading', *Liverpool Papers in Language and Discourse* 4: 52–80.

## REFERENCES

—— (1992b) 'Do androids dream of electric sheep?: Isomorphic relations in reading science fiction', *Language and Literature* 1 (2): 79–99.

Svartvik, J. and Quirk, R. (eds) (1980) *A Corpus of English Conversation*, Lund: Gleerup.

Swales, J. (1990) *Genre Analysis: English in Academic and Research Settings*, Cambridge: Cambridge University Press.

Sweetser, E. (1990) *From Etymology to Pragmatics: Metaphorical and Cultural Aspects of Semantic Structure*, Cambridge: Cambridge University Press.

Tanaka, K. (1994) *Advertising Language: A Pragmatic Approach to Advertisements in Britain and Japan*, London: Routledge.

Tannen, D. (1989) *Talking Voices: Repetition, Dialogue and Imagery in Conversational Discourse*, Cambridge: Cambridge University Press.

Tillyard, E.M.W. (1963) *An Elizabethan World Picture*, Harmondsworth: Penguin.

Todorov, T. (1970) *La Littérature fantastique*, Paris: Du Seuil.

Tomashevsky, B. (1965) 'Thematics', in L.T. Lemon and M.J. Reis (eds), *Russian Formalist Criticism*, Lincoln, Nebr.: University of Nebraska Press, pp. 61–95.

Tversky, A. (1977) 'Features of similarity', *Psychological Review* 84: 327–52.

Ullmann, S. (1962) *Semantics: An Introduction to the Science of Meaning*, Oxford: Blackwell.

Uspensky, B. (1973) *A Poetics of Composition*, Berkeley and Los Angeles: University of California Press.

Van Peer, W. (1986) *Stylistics and Psychology: Investigations of Foregrounding*, London: Croom Helm.

Vendler, Z. (1968) *Adjectives and Nominalizations*, The Hague: Mouton.

Verbrugge, R.R. and McCarrell, N.S. (1977) 'Metaphoric understanding: studies in reminding and resembling', *Cognitive Psychology* 9: 494–533.

Vosniadou, S. and Ortony, A. (1989) 'Similarity and analogical reasoning: a synthesis', in S. Vosniadou, and A. Ortony, (eds), *Similarity and Analogical Reasoning*, Cambridge: Cambridge University Press, pp. 1–17.

Vosniadou, S. and Ortony, A. (eds) (1989) *Similarity and Analogical Reasoning*, Cambridge: Cambridge University Press.

Waldron, R.A. (1967) *Sense and Sense Development*, London: Deutsch.

Widdowson, H.G. (1975) *Stylistics and the Teaching of Literature*, Harlow: Longman.

Wijsen, L.M.P.T. (1980) *Cognition and Image-Formation in Literature*, Frankfurt: Peter D. Lang.

Wilson, D. and Sperber, D. (1986) 'An outline of Relevance Theory', in H.O. Alves (ed.), *Encontro de Linguistas: Actas*, Minho, Portugal: University of Minho, pp. 19–42.

—— (1992) 'On verbal irony', *Lingua* 87 (1/2): 53–76.

Winner, E. (1988) *The Point of Words: Children's Understanding of Metaphor and Irony*, Cambridge, Mass.: Harvard University Press.

Winner, E. and Gardner, H. (1993) 'Metaphor and irony: two levels of understanding', in A. Ortony (ed.), *Metaphor and Thought*, 2nd edn, Cambridge: Cambridge University Press, pp. 425–46.

Zadeh, L.A. (1965) 'Fuzzy sets' *Information and Control* 8: 338ff.

Zwaan, R.A. (1993) *Aspects of Literary Comprehension: A Cognitive Approach*, Amsterdam: Benjamins.

# TEXTS USED FOR EXAMPLES AND ANALYSIS
# (AND ABBREVIATIONS USED IN REFERENCES)

## Conversation

Crystal, D. and Davy, D. (1975) *Advanced Conversational English*, Harlow: Longman. (**ACE**)

Svartvik, J. and Quirk, R. (eds) (1980) *A Corpus of English Conversation*, Lund: Gleerup. (**CEC**)

## News Reports

*Daily Mirror*, 8 May 1987. (**DM**)
*Daily Telegraph*, 5 May 1987. (**DT**)
*Financial Times*, 16 December 1993.
*Independent*, 29 May 1995.
*International Express*, 1–7 June 1995. (**IE**)

## Popular Science

Attenborough, D. (1979) *Life on Earth*, London: Collins.

Changeux, J.-P. (1993) 'Chemical signalling in the brain', *Scientific American*, November: 30–7.

Gamlin, L. (1988) 'The human immune system', *New Scientist*, 24 March: 1–4. (**NSLG**)

Lovelock, J. (1986) 'Gaia: the world as living organism', *New Scientist*, 18 December: 25–8. (**NSLJ**)

MacQuitty. M. (1988) 'Sulphur on the menu: cuisine for the hairy snail', *New Scientist*, 24 March: 4. (**NSMM**)

## Sources of Advertisements

*Good Housekeeping*, May 1987. (**GH**)
*Popular Science*, June 1995.
*Punch*, 6 May 1987. (**P**)
*Woman*, 9 May 1987. (**W**)

## Poetry

Arnold, M. (1950) 'Dover Beach', in *Arnold: Poetical Works*, Oxford: Oxford University Press. (**DB**)

Auden, W.H. (1970) 'The unknown citizen', in *Collected Shorter Poems of W.H. Auden*, London: Faber, p. 146. (**UC**)

Betjeman, John (1958) *John Betjeman's Collected Poems*, compiled with an introduction by the Earl of Birkenhead, London: John Murray.

—— (1958) 'A child ill', in *John Betjeman's Collected Poems*, London: John Murray, 1958, p. 224.

—— (1958) 'Indoor games near Newbury', in *John Betjeman's Collected Poems*, London: John Murray, 1958, pp. 151–3.

## REFERENCES

—— (1973) 'On a portrait of a deaf man', in *John Betjeman's Collected Poems*, London: John Murray, 1958, p. 96.

Causley, C. (n.d.) 'Death of a poet', in Philip Larkin (ed.), *The Oxford Book of Twentieth-century English Verse*, London: Oxford University Press, 1973, p. 495.

Eliot, T.S. (1936) 'The love song of J. Alfred Prufrock', in *Collected Poems*, London: Faber, pp. 13–17. (**LSJAP**)

—— (1944) *The Four Quartets*, London: Faber. (**FQ**)

Heaney, S. (1966) 'An advancement of learning', in *Death of a Naturalist*, London: Faber, pp. 18–19. (**AL**)

—— (1966) 'Death of a naturalist', in *Death of a Naturalist*, London: Faber, pp. 15–16. (**DN**)

Housman, A.E. (1967) 'On Wenlock Edge', in *Collected Poems of A.E. Housman*, London: Cape. (**OWE**)

Hughes, T. (1972) 'Pike', in *Selected Poems 1957–1967*, London: Faber, pp. 55–6. (**THP**)

—— (1972) 'Wind', in *Selected Poems 1957–1967*, London: Faber. (**TH**)

—— (1972) 'Esther's tomcat', in *Selected Poems 1957–1967*, London: Faber, p. 37.

Larkin, Philip (ed.) (1973) *The Oxford Book of Twentieth-century English Verse*, Oxford: Oxford University Press.

—— (1973) 'The Whitsun weddings', in Philip Larkin (ed.), *The Oxford Book of Twentieth-century English Verse*, Oxford: Oxford University Press, 1973, pp. 540–2.

—— (1973) 'Toads', in Philip Larkin (ed.), *The Oxford Book of Twentieth-century English Verse*, Oxford: Oxford University Press, 1973, p. 527.

Lyttleton, Lord (1948) 'To the memory of a lady' (1747), in J. Sutherland, *A Preface to Eighteenth Century Poetry*, Oxford: Oxford University Press, p. 72. (**LL**)

Milton, John (1952) *Paradise Lost*, Book One; first published in 1667; in *The Poetical Works of John Milton*, ed. Helen Darbishire; Oxford: Oxford University Press. (**PL**)

Pound, Ezra (1949) *Collected Shorter Poems*, London: Faber.

—— (1949) 'Sennin poem by Kakuhaku', in *Collected Shorter Poems*, London: Faber, p. 139.

—— (1949) 'To-Em-Mei's "The unmoving cloud"', in *Collected Shorter Poems*, London: Faber, p. 142.

—— (1957) 'Alba', in *Selected Poems*, New York: New Directions, p. 36.

—— (1957) 'A ballad of Mulberry Road', in *Selected Poems*, New York: New Directions, p. 60.

—— (1957) 'The beautiful toilet', in *Selected Poems*, New York: New Directions, p. 50.

—— (1957) 'The river merchant's wife – a letter', in *Selected Poems*, New York: New Directions, p. 52.

—— (1957) 'In a station of the Metro', in *Selected Poems*, New York: New Directions, p. 35.

—— (1957) 'Lament of the frontier guard', in *Selected Poems*, New York: New Directions, p. 69. (**LFG**)

Tennyson, A. (1969) *The Poems of Tennyson*, Harlow: Longman; contains the text of 'Morte d'Arthur'. (**MA**)

Thomas, Edward (1936) *Collected Poems of Edward Thomas*, London: Faber.

—— (1936) 'A cat', in *Collected Poems of Edward Thomas*, London: Faber, p. 117.

—— (1936) 'Adlestrop', in *Collected Poems of Edward Thomas*, London: Faber, p. 66.

—— (1936) 'As the team's head-brass', in *Collected Poems of Edward Thomas*, London: Faber, pp. 29–30.

—— (1936) 'Lights out', in *Collected Poems of Edward Thomas*, London: Faber, p. 92.

—— (1936) 'Rain', in *Collected Poems of Edward Thomas*, London: Faber, p. 84.

—— (1936) 'The path', in *Collected Poems of Edward Thomas*, London: Faber, p. 34.

Thomas, R.S. (1969) *Not that he Brought Flowers*, London: Hart-Davis.

—— (1969) 'Commuters', in *Not that he Brought Flowers*, London: Hart-Davis, p. 27.

—— (1969) 'Touching', in *Not that he Brought Flowers*, London: Hart-Davis, p. 28.

—— (1973) 'On the farm', in Philip Larkin (ed.), *The Oxford Book of Twentieth-century English Verse*, Oxford: Oxford University Press, 1973, p. 465. (**OF**)

—— (1973) 'The country clergy', in Philip Larkin (ed.), *The Oxford Book of Twentieth-century English Verse*, Oxford: Oxford University Press, 1973, p. 464.

Wong, May (1973) 'Only the moon', in Edwin Thumboo (ed.), *Seven Poets: Singapore and Malaysia*, Singapore: Singapore University Press.

Yeats, W.B. (1933) *Collected Poems of W.B. Yeats*, London: Macmillan.

—— (1933) 'An Irish airman foresees his death', in his *Collected Poems of W.B. Yeats*, London: Macmillan, p. 152.

—— (1933) 'He dreams of cloths of heaven', in his *Collected Poems of W.B. Yeats*, London: Macmillan, p. 81.

—— (1933) 'Wild swans at Coole', in his *Collected Poems of W.B. Yeats*, London: Macmillan, p. 147.

—— (1973) 'Prayer for my daughter', in Philip Larkin (ed.), *The Oxford Book of Twentieth-century English Verse*, Oxford: Oxford University Press, 1973. (**PMD**)

—— (1973) 'When you are old', in Philip Larkin (ed.), *The Oxford Book of Twentieth-century English Verse*, Oxford: Oxford University Press, 1973, p. 75.

# Novels

Archer, Jeffrey (1984) *First among Equals*, London: Hodder and Stoughton. (**FAE**)

Baldwin, James (1979) *Just Above my Head*, London: Michael Joseph.

Bellow, S. (1961) *Herzog*, Lublijana: Mladinska Knjiga. (**HZ**)

Brontë, C. (1953) *Villette*, London: Collins; first published 1853. (**V**)

Byatt, A.S. (1978) *The Virgin in the Garden*, London: Chatto and Windus. (**VG**)

—— (1985) *Still Life*, London: Chatto. (**SL**)

Eliot, G. (1960) *Silas Marner*, New York: New American Library; first published 1861. (**SM**)

Golding, W. (1954) *Lord of the Flies*, London: Faber. (**LF**)

—— (1956) *Pincher Martin*, London: Faber. (**PM**)

—— (1961a) *Free Fall*, London: Faber. (**FF**)

—— (1961b) *The Inheritors*, London: Faber. (**TI**)

—— (1965) *The Spire*, London: Faber. (**TS**)

—— (1979) *Darkness Visible*, London: Faber. (**DV**)

Greene, G. (1955) *The Quiet American*, London: Heinemann. (**QA**)
—— (1960) *A Burnt-Out Case*, Harmondsworth: Penguin. (**BOC**)
Hardy, T. (1991) *Tess of the D'Urbervilles: A Pure Woman*, New Wessex edition, London: Macmillan. (**TD**)
Hartley, L.P. (1973) *The Go-Between*, Harmondsworth: Penguin. (**GB**)
Hawthorne, N. (1851) *The House of the Seven Gables*, ed. S.L. Gross, New York: Norton, 1967. (**HSG**)
Jung Chang (1992) *Wild Swans*, London: Flamingo. (**WS**)
Lawrence, D.H. (1949) *The Rainbow*, Harmondsworth: Penguin. (**R**)
—— (1983) *St Mawr and Other Stories*, ed. Biran Finney, Cambridge: Cambridge University Press; first published 1925.
Lyly, J. (1916) *Euphues*, New York: Dutton, first published 1578. (**EU**)
Maugham, S. (1951) 'The man with the scar', in *The World Over*, London: Reprint Society (Heinemann). (**MS**)
Melville, H. (1983) *Moby Dick*, New York: Cambridge University Press. (**MD**)
Sillitoe, Alan (1979) *The Storyteller*, London: W.H. Allen.

## Miscellaneous

*8 Days*, 14 October 1994, Singapore: SBC Enterprises.
Cohen, J.M. and Cohen, M.J. (1971) *The Penguin Dictionary of Modern Quotations*, London: Allen Lane. (**PQ**)
Crossley-Holland, K. and Mitchell, B. (eds) (1965) *The Battle of Maldon and other Old English Poems*, London: Macmillan.
*Far Eastern Economic Review*, 19 May 1988. (**FEER**)
Milburn, J.A. (1979) *Waterflow in Plants*, London: Longman. (**ML**)
*Punch*, 7 January 1987.
Shakespeare, William, *Macbeth*, ed. K. Muir, London: Methuen, Arden, 1962. (**M**)
'The stress code' (1992) *Seventeen*, September: 52.
*Wheels*,  April 1994, Sydney: Cable Packpress.

## TEXTS USED FOR STATISTICS IN TABLE 10.2

### Conversation

CEC pp. 248–64, 329–46 (line 1), 686–706;
ACE pp. 19–23, 32–6, 40–2, 46–9, 52–4, 56–9

### News Reports

*The Independent* 29 May 1995 'Major recalls MPS after 33 troops seized' (p. 1), 'T&G chief "used bribe" to win poll' (p. 5), 'Thatcher praise for Blair seen as rebuke for Major' (p. 6);
DM May 1987 'It looks good for Thatcher' (p. 1), 'Drunken Botham battered me' (p. 3), 'Torment of the battered nurses' (p. 4), 'Shun stand-in-mums; GPs told' (p. 4), 'Headmistress guilty of fondling girl' (p. 7), 'Beauty with bigger assets than Sam's' (p. 7), 'Sex attacker sent to live with victim' (p. 11), 'Slap!' (p. 13), 'You are my sunshine' (p. 15), 'City boss shamed' (p. 15), 'Big Ron and Villa' (pp. 30–1), 'You're out Nico' (p. 32);
*Financial Times* 16 December 1993 'Gatt accord wins approval' (p. 1), 'UK and Ireland launch outline peace plan' (pp. 1, 16), 'Metallgesellchaft board to grill

chief on liquidity gap' (p. 1), 'Austerity pledge for Venezuelans' (p. 3), 'Hong-kong bill "destroys co-operation" says Beijing' (p. 16);

IE ' "Superman" may never walk again' (p. 1), 'Ealing Studios saved by Pools' (p. 3), 'My marriage gamble by Imran's Jemma' (p. 5), 'Mob screams at Rikki's mother' (p. 6), 'Ex-PC's stress pay-out' (p. 6), 'Summer rail strike threat looms' (p. 6), 'The truck stops here; bitter boss tells ex-wife' (p. 7).

## Popular Science

Attenborough 1979: 11–20, para. 2;

Changeux 1993: 30–4, col. 1;

NSJL, pp. 25–7, para. 2, 'Ethical dilemmas over fetal transplants';

*New Scientist* March 1988, p. 57;

NSMM, p. 50, 'The lymphatic system';

*New Scientist* March 1988, p. 4.

## Magazine Advertising

**W**, pp. 4, 5, 11, 26, 27;

**P**, pp. 2, 3, 6, 54, 71;

*Punch* January 1987, p. 50;

**GH**, pp. 3, 6–7, 10 , 38, 118–19, 28–9, L2, L10–11, L16, L18, L19, 52–3, 159, 210, 211, 212, 214, 218–19, 230, 231, 232, 237, 238, 253;

*Popular Science*, June 1995, pp. 5, 7, 12–13, 15, 29, 33, 35, 38–9, 47, 48, 51.

## Modern Novels

**VG**, pp. 9–13, last para.;

James Baldwin, *Just above my Head*, pp. 65–73;

**BOC**, pp. 160–72;

Alan Sillitoe, *The Storyteller*, pp. 40–8.

## Modern English Lyric Poetry

W.B. Yeats 'When you are old', 'An Irish airman foresees his death', 'He dreams of the cloths of heaven', 'Wild swans at Coole', 'Prayer for my daughter';

Edward Thomas 'Adlestrop', 'As the team's head-brass', 'Rain', 'The path', 'A cat', 'Lights out';

Ezra Pound 'In a station of the Metro', 'Alba', 'The beautiful toilet', 'The river merchant's wife – a letter', 'Lament of the frontier guard', 'Sennin poem by Kakuhaku', 'The ballad of the Mulberry Road', 'To-Em-Mei's "The unmoving cloud" ';

Philip Larkin 'The Whitsun weddings', 'Toads';

Ted Hughes 'Pike', 'Wind', 'Esther's tomcat';

John Betjeman 'Portrait of a deaf man', 'On a child ill', 'Indoor games near Newbury';

R.S. Thomas 'The country clergy', 'On the farm', 'Commuters', 'Touching'.

# INDEX

- Page references in **bold** indicate the page or passage where the concept receives the most important or extensive treatment.
- Page references <u>underlined</u> indicate where the technical terms capitalized in the main text are first introduced and explained.
- Academic research never takes place in a social vacuum. Name references in which the full first name is given indicate that I have at some time been in communication with the person concerned.